W9-BCU-574

FIGURES OF LIGHT

Actors and Directors Illuminate the Art of Film Acting

FIGURES OF LIGHT

Actors and Directors Illuminate the Art of Film Acting

CAROLE ZUCKER

PLENUM PRESS • NEW YORK AND LONDON

Library of Congress Cataloging-in-Publication Data

Zucker, Carole.
    Figures of light : actors and directors illuminate the art of film
  acting / Carole Zucker.
        p.   cm.
    Includes bibliographical references and index.
    ISBN 0-306-44949-8
    1. Motion picture acting. 2. Motion picture actors and actresses-
  -Interviews. 3. Motion picture producers and directors--Interviews.
  I. Title.
  PN1995.9.A26Z83   1995
  791.43'028--dc20   95-2514
                                                               CIP

ISBN 0-306-44949-8

© 1995 Carole Zucker
Plenum Press is a Division of Plenum Publishing Corporation
233 Spring Street, New York, N.Y. 10013-1578

10 9 8 7 6 5 4 3 2 1

All rights reserved

No part of this book may be reproduced, stored in a retrieval system, or transmitted
in any form or by any means, electronic, mechanical, photocopying, microfilming,
recording, or otherwise, without written permission from the Publisher

Printed in the United States of America

"The constant, the eternal, beneath the accidental."
— Robert Bresson

To Mario, grazie per tutto, per sempre.

Table of Contents

Introduction

Figures of Light grew out of my experience teaching a course in film acting. I quickly learned while developing the bibliography for the course that very little in the way of coherent, cogent, or productive dialogue goes on between this society and its actors. There are few interviews that dwell in a serious, in-depth way with the film actor's creative process. This book endeavors to produce a more meaningful discourse about acting, one that assiduously avoids viewing the actor as a commodity or probing into the actor's private life—the interviews focus solely on acting.

I chose to speak with actors who have achieved a certain stature in their careers; these actors value their achievement as actors over the degree to which they might be considered "stars." They are actors whose performances are particularly challenging, subversive, soulful, witty, intense, and/or profound and who have displayed extraordinary skill, complexity, and significance as performers. As I spoke with actors, it became clear that the film director is instrumental and inextricably linked to all stages of the film actor's performance, from casting to post-production. So my undertaking grew to encompass directors who have demonstrated an empathetic and supportive relationship to actors, including directors—Bill Duke, Henry Jaglom, Sydney Pollack, Bob Rafelson, and John Sayles—who have done some acting themselves.

This volume concentrates exclusively on acting in American mainstream and independent feature filmmaking, in celebration of the vitality and sense of urgency that exemplifies American film acting. It is acting that is heavily influenced by the teachings of Stanislavsky (1863–1938). The famous Russian actor, director, and teacher, whose formative work took place in the early part of this century, rebelled against the artificial codes of stage performance in the last century. Influential nineteenth-century drama and dance teacher François Delsarte (1811–1871) decreed that human emotion could be reduced to a given number of gestures, movements, and vocal intonations, which, if learned and repeated, would represent the full spectrum of behavior. Stanislavsky taught that acting had to arise not from externalized, premeditated behavior, but from the inner world of the character, what he called the "logic of emotions" in a given text. The character is then brought to life through the technical skill, invention, and immediate responsiveness of the actor, who creates a full, vivid, emotionally and physically true portrayal of a character.

Although Stanislavsky developed a style of acting that is often called "realistic" or "naturalistic," the Russian teacher never espoused the strictly accurate replication of human behavior; he emphasized the poetic and imaginative dimensions of that behavior. The truth that Stanislavsky advocated is the probing, honest, deeply felt interpretation of a character's feelings and actions. It is that search for truthfulness that guides and inspires the actors and directors who speak in *Figures of Light*.

Even while acting grows out of abstract concept like inner truth, *Figures of Light* is based on the premise that film acting can be investigated in a pragmatic way, and, indeed, the conversations in this book explore how the instinctive practice of acting melds with training, theory, technique, and process. The actors were asked about their training, preparation for a role, and experiences of rehearsing and shooting a film. The directors were requested to isolate their work with actors from their larger function—overseeing a film from preproduction to post-production. They talked about casting, rehearsal methods, working with the actor to achieve a characterization, and acting problems and solutions they've encountered. Both actors and directors were queried about their formative influences and asked to describe what constitutes a great performance. The interviews attempt to account for the creativity that informs an interpretation and the intimate process whereby performers draw on their personal resources—emotional, mental, physical, and spiritual—to develop and enact an interpretation.

From the inanimate words on the pages of a script or play, an actor's task is to produce a living, breathing creation. The process by which language becomes action is complex. First, actors need to be able to play their instrument—themselves—with skill and precision, an ability that requires training, practice, and discipline. Next, actors must comprehend the meaning of the words they speak, in all their amplitude. The text will most likely communicate the character's background, attitudes, beliefs, and relationships to others. Critical as well are the ideas and feelings that circulate below the surface of the text—the subtext, the implied or possible meanings of the written words that suggest the character's emotional journey. To undertake this journey, actors search inside themselves for the requisite emotional material. Using technique, imagination, and instinct, actors—through the medium of the fictional character—reveal the deepest, most private parts of themselves, because acting is, more than any other art, the art of self-revelation. Actors paint an emotional canvas, and the emotions they access for this creation exist within their own psyches. To find the colors with which to create this living portrait, actors engage in an exploration of the self—their own individuality as artists and human beings. This knowledge and awareness will be filtered through technique and artistry in order to inhabit and illuminate the world of the fictional character. Above all, acting is a shared experience; actors must communicate to an audience. They are engaged in a relay of human feelings—their own, their characters', and those of the audience—feelings that are, at base, universal in their meaning. In that space of universal, shared experience lies the power and beauty of acting. Actors have the privilege of revealing profound truths to us about the human condition and, ultimately, about ourselves.

In speaking with the actors and directors represented in this book, I found no common prescription for acting, but rather an eclectic mix of techniques and strategies. What unites all of the figures I interviewed is some combination of playfulness coupled with seriousness of purpose, intelligence, instinct, and imagination at the service of any given project. No matter how far a role or story is from reality (e.g., John Lithgow in *Buckaroo Banzai* [1984] or Bill Duke's highly stylized *A Rage in Harlem* [1991]), every actor and director was concerned with locating the element of human truth in a portrayal. Universally, I found the subjects in this book to have a unique openness to experience, a quality that is at the core of all creativity. When I conducted these interviews—over a period of 4 years— I established certain parameters. I usually entered into the conversation with a list of performances I thought were key or fruitful for discussion. Sometimes those parameters held, and sometimes they were discarded. I felt it was important to respond to the integrity and spirit of the individual's personality rather than to commandeer the interview process. The responses on the part of both actors and directors were highly individualized, and they all invested the greatest energy in subjects of personal significance to them. Some actors and directors wanted to discuss their process; some wanted to talk extensively about their training. Still others warmed to larger ideas, such as the place of the actor in society or the meaning of stardom. The approaches of the participants in this book range from anecdotal to analytical, and often both within the same person. As much as possible, I tried to talk in specifics, about preparation for a *particular* role, or the evolution and dynamics of a *particular* scene. With several directors (Lawrence Kasdan and Sydney Pollack, for example), I chose a segment of one of their films, and we watched the excerpt together while they talked about how the scene was achieved.

A more speculative and less practical view of film acting—and film watching—takes into account the set of phenomena that make these activities unique, mysterious, and deeply resonant experiences in our lives. Film acting—as opposed to acting in any other medium—demands a special capacity. The film actor is dealing with the photographic process, and herein lies a great enigma—the workings of photogenesis. Referring to the almost mystical quality of photogenesis—the ability of a figure to be photographed attractively—director Howard Hawks said, "Either the camera likes you or it doesn't." From all accounts, the physical beauty of the actor has little to do with the quality of photogenesis. Plain people may photograph spectacularly, and people possessed of great good looks may fare poorly in the eye of the camera. Careful, expert make-up and lighting may compensate to some degree, but the relationship of actor and camera is a privileged affair. However, an actor may look perfectly splendid on film and still not be a good film actor.

The actor's onscreen presence needs to be absorbing both to the camera and to the audience, a factor that goes beyond mere photogenesis. The great film actors—Brando, Cagney, De Niro—are capable of owning the space of the screen, ruling it, as if by divine right. Whether in repose or action, they are eminently watchable; they command our attention. They fill the screen with their intense concentration yet seem, at the same time, completely at ease in the camera's eye. (The dual abilities of concentration and relaxation were first prescribed for the actor in Stanislavsky's teachings.) It is the capacity—often alluded to in these interviews—of "being in the moment," of being fully present in that moment of time when they were filmed. They are emotionally available, spontaneous, and undefended; it is a state of grace in which actors achieve a complete engagement and integration with a moment-to-moment reality.

Yet that fullness of presence is also paradoxical, as the film actor is also, literally, an absence. The actor is captured on a strip of celluloid, which is developed and then threaded onto a projector in your local theater. The image of the actor that we see on the screen is the beam of the projector's light shining through the images on the strip of celluloid. Thus, the film actor is transformed virtually into a *figure of light*, an incorporeal spectre on the screen.

What are the implications of being an (absent) presence suffused by light? They are manifold, but I would draw the reader's attention to several of the broader effects. The very fact that what we see on screen is not a material presence endows that figure with an abstract, not-quite-human quality. This abstract level is enhanced by the large format of the screen (making film quite different from television), where a face can achieve monumental dimensions. Framing may isolate one actor from another, or, in the case of the close-up, the actor's face may be fragmented from his or her body. That filmed figure is frozen in time, as film is composed of still images moving through the projector at 24 frames per second. The special look on the actor's face, that gesture, that movement, will—as long as the film exists—remain the same. Unlike theater, film performances never mutate, even with the death of the actor (perhaps in part accounting for the necromantic relationship we have with figures like Marilyn Monroe or James Dean). The film actor's poetic resonance, and his or her capacity to transcend the mundane, is an extraordinary feat.

What do we see when we see this figure of light, and how does this shape our experience of the actor? The light infiltrates—it *is* the actor's face and body—a shining forcefield that illuminates the screen. We see what is visible, the conscious expressivity of the actor, but also what is not visible—the thought, the feeling, perhaps the very soul of the actor. Imbued with such rich and intense connotations, it is not difficult to see how the film actor can attain an emblematic status in our society. Through the repetition of certain types of roles, through the force of personality, the film actor accrues a ritual identity and meaning that supersedes any specific role. Consider, for example, Richard Dreyfuss. Starting from his first major role in *American Graffiti* (1973) and continuing in films such as *Jaws* (1975) and *Close Encounters of the Third Kind* (1977), his characters fulfill one of the main structures of storytelling in Western civilization, the quest. Whether Dreyfuss is leaving the secure world of his hometown (*American Graffiti*), slaying the monstrous whale (*Jaws*), or searching for the alien spaceship (*Close Encounters*), he is the ordinary guy who speaks to our deep longings for adventure, risk-taking, and heroic fulfillment. Certainly not every film actor is able (or would want) to achieve this kind of universal meaning. But it is significant that the actor has the potential to attain mythic dimensions, to embody a locus of meaning, and to address the needs and yearnings of our society. And every actor who achieves a measure of fame fulfills this capacity to some degree.

At the same time, film acting sets up a strange dichotomy in our society. On the one hand, film actors are revered as icons, as "more-than-human" entities. On the other hand, a number of pejorative attitudes toward acting are also endorsed. Jonas Barish in *The Anti-Theatrical Prejudice** traces these beliefs back to the duality Plato set forth in his philosophy. The philosopher viewed feeling and reason as warring faculties, with little value given to feeling and much to reason. Plato contended that passions distort our perception and weaken self-control and that the instinct for self-expression leads to moral corruption. He believed that theater somehow takes us away from our "essential" self. This basic attitude has persisted for centuries in society's disapproval of actors, who have braved a variety of indignities from the time of the Greek empire. They have, for example, been harassed by police, forbidden the right to vote, and, with the birth of Christianity, refused the sacrament.

This prejudice is not alien to contemporary society, although its manifestation is different. It is a rather common notion that acting is a form of lying, or a symptom of a personality disorder—actors are unstable people who seek escape and solace in alternate identities. This disapproving attitude is reinforced by a national media that fixates on the tragic, troubled film actor. In fact, actors must have a strong sense of identity, not only to withstand the mental and physical rigors of their profession, but

---

*Jonas Barish, *The Anti-Theatrical Prejudice* (Berkeley: University of California Press, 1981).

also simply to survive in a business that can be rather brutal. Moreover, actors—far from seeking escape in illusion—have to have the strength and courage to explore positive and negative aspects of themselves and to tell the truth about it. The light of the projector shines through the actor, and the actor cannot lie in the face of that powerful and penetrating illumination. As Lindsay Crouse says in her interview:

> You are a symbol on film for all people . . . You set an example, you're a symbol, so you had better get behind it. Otherwise I think it shows. You're very translucent when you're on film. You are a figure of light; your soul comes through. You can tell, easily, when someone is really doing it or not . . .
>
> People say to me, 'I don't know how you do what you do; I couldn't lie to save my life.' People think I practice telling lies all day, until I'm so good at it that you can't tell the difference. But that's exactly what acting is not. As any acting teacher knows, the most difficult part of the art is the struggle to bring out the truth of your being, the fullest dimension of yourself.

The truth Lindsay Crouse refers to is the essential truth of the self, which is all that actors can bring to a role. Carl Dreyer, the famous Danish film director and disciple of Stanislavsky, made a distinction in his writings on acting between "being and pretending." To pretend to be a character is, indeed, to lie. But in an enigmatic, glorious way, the actor fuses the flood of feelings and sensations that belong to the character with the truth of their own feelings; that is *being,* not pretending. Because the actor, unlike the musician, the painter, or the sculptor, is the instrument; there is no mediation between the actor and the character. Those feelings and sensations come *through* the actor, just as the light of the projector shines through the film actor. And the film actor must be open, aware, imaginative, and skilled enough to allow and encourage this process to take place. The film actor is, perhaps uniquely, a site of human truth: an image of light, a bearer of enlightenment through which primal feelings, dreams, and desires flow.

In preparation for this book and to better comprehend actor training, I was privileged to attend a number of acting and directing classes. I would like to thank the following institutions for opening their doors to me: The Actors Studio, The Actors Studio West, The Neighborhood Playhouse, The Playhouse West, and HB Studios. I am grateful to Harold Baldridge and Robert Carnegie for their welcoming attitudes. I also attended classes and spoke at length to instructors of private acting classes. I extend my gratitude particularly to Jeff Corey, who graciously allowed me to partake of his very special and edifying actor training.

The process by which these interviews were obtained could easily be the subject of a bizarre picaresque novel. Any outsider who has ever attempted to gain access to the Byzantine Hollywood infrastructure will attest to the challenges involved. For their generous guidance through this labyrinth, I commend the personal assistants and office staffs of each of the actors and directors participating in the interviews. Very special thanks to Blakeney Devlin, Tina Foley, Noah Golden, Martha Griffin, Donna Ostroff, Audrey Sinclair, Anne Ward, and Andy Weinrich. I appreciate the cooperation of Gayle Khait, a publicist for Wolf, Kasteller, and Peter Strain (of Peter Strain Associates), the agent for Lindsay Crouse and Joe Mantegna. It goes without saying that this book would not exist were it not for the largesse of the actors and directors involved. Their patience, cooperation, and openness were laudable; I thank each of them sincerely. I would also like to acknowledge the participation of the following people: Frank Corsaro, Stuart Gordon, Julie Harris, the late Daniel Mann, and Delia Salvi.

The Social Sciences and Humanities Research Council of Canada was munificent in their support of this project. This book was also generously funded by Concordia University's Fund for Research and Development and their Aid to Scholarly Activities. Particular thanks to Kathryn Lipke, Associate Dean of the Faculty of Fine Arts, and Concordia's Office of Research Services (and Dr. Erica M. Besso) for their help with the photographs. I would also like to thank my colleague, John Locke, chair of my university department during the time in which this book was conceived and executed. He was wonderfully understanding and supportive in giving me the time and space to complete this work. My research assistant of many years, Eugenie Shinkle, has always been remarkable in her ingenuity, resourcefulness, and precision. She transcribed these interviews and did copious amounts of drudgework on behalf of this project; I owe her a great deal. To Danielle Carter, who read my manuscript with great care, to Ray Carney, for his warm and spirited support, and to Bart Testa, for his constancy and intellectual sustenance, much gratitude. I especially thank my editor, Linda Greenspan Regan, for pushing me to express myself more fully. I also want to acknowledge the contribution of Lindsay Crouse, who forever changed my way of thinking about acting. I had the good fortune to meet many exceptional people while conducting these interviews. Two extraordinary women in particular—Lily Parker and Sandra Seacat—deserve words of appreciation just for being themselves and also for their enduring belief in me and in this project, as well as for some very special life lessons. The bountiful enthusiasm and unflagging encouragement of my friend and colleague, Johanne Larue, sustained me. Her joy and engagement in film—and in the world around her—has always been an inspiration. Mario Falsetto was truly a partner in this project; he was instrumental in every stage of the book's creation. As I negotiated the antic worlds of film and publishing, Mario's simplicity and reasonableness were a great comfort; he was at my side through all the trials, vicissitudes, mini-crises, and craziness that came with the territory. Mario was an exemplar of devotion, unselfishly giving his time and energy to the fulfilment of this project. For his love and support, I dedicate *Figures of Light* to Mario.

An Interview with Lindsay Crouse

Lindsay Crouse. Courtesy of Peter Strain Associates.

In the midst of a successful stage and film career, Lindsay Crouse asked to be admitted to the beginners' acting class at The Neighborhood Playhouse. She recalls saying to Sanford Meisner: "I'm coming as an acolyte. I want to find out what acting is . . . I'm submitting." At the time, Crouse was an accomplished actor who had explored techniques of actor training at The Stella Adler Conservatory and The Stanislavsky Institute and, for many years, with Uta Hagen at The HB Studios. Crouse's decision to devote herself to her artistic development—at a risky and critical juncture in her professional life—is a tribute to her courage, integrity, and commitment. Crouse uses that impressive conviction to immerse herself in the circumstances of a role. For Sidney Lumet's film *The Verdict* (1982), Crouse studied with a voice coach for hours to perform the small but crucial part of Caitlin, an Irish character. This scrupulous dedication to truthfulness conforms with Crouse's ardent beliefs about the ethics of acting. She says an actor shouldn't "take an average, but . . . get out there and go as far as

[you] can." Crouse fulfills that credo in performances that radiate with the intense light of her passion and intelligence.

Crouse was born in 1948 in New York City, the daughter of prominent playwright Russel Crouse. She attended Radcliffe College before pursuing a career as a modern and jazz dancer. Crouse began training as an actor and made her Broadway debut in *Much Ado About Nothing* in 1972. In 1979, Crouse began her association with the Circle Repertory Company in New York, giving her Obie Award–winning performance in *Reunion* and acting in roles such as Ophelia in *Hamlet* (1979), Viola in *Twelfth Night* (1980), Ada in *Childe Byron* (1981), and the Queen in *Richard II* (1982). Her connection with the Circle Rep continued when she acted in resident playwright Lanford Wilson's *Serenading Louie* (1984) at the New York Shakespeare Festival and again with her appearance in The American Playhouse production of Wilson's *Lemon Sky* (1988) for television. Crouse spent much of her stage career in regional theater, playing in *Holiday* and *The Cherry Orchard* at The Goodman Theater in Chicago, in *Reckless* at The Trinity Repertory in Providence, and in *Uncle Vanya* at The American Repertory Theater in Cambridge. In New York, she received critical acclaim for her performance of *The Shawl* at Lincoln Center, *The Stick Wife* at The Manhattan Theater Club, and the Broadway revival of *The Homecoming* in 1991, for which she received a Theater World Award. In 1993, Crouse joined The Matrix Theater Company in Los Angeles and was featured in the revival of George M. Cohan's *The Tavern.*

Crouse's film work began with *All The President's Men* in 1976, followed by *Slapshot* (1977), *Between the Lines* (1977), *The Verdict* (1982), *Daniel* (1983), *Iceman* (1984), *Places in the Heart* (1984, for which she received an Academy Award nomination as Best Supporting Actress), *House of Games* (1987), *Communion* (1989), *Desperate Hours* (1990), *Being Human* (1992), and *Bye Bye Love* (1993). She has done several made-for-television movies, including, most recently, *Out of Darkness* (1993), *Final Appeal* (1993), *Chantilly Lace* (1993), and *Parallel Lives* (1994). Crouse has guest-starred in series such as *Colombo; Murder, She Wrote; Lifestories; Hill Street Blues; Law and Order; Civil Wars;* and *L.A. Law.*

I interviewed Lindsay Crouse in September 1990 in her Cambridge home, which she shared with her two daughters, Willa and Zosh. She has since relocated to Los Angeles.

CZ: How did you train to be an actor?

LC: I had a very interesting road in my training, because when I first decided to become an actor I was doing something else. I was very busy trying to become a dancer. I was dancing and rehearsing dances—dancers rehearse forever, they perform very little. Dancers are not really directed the way actors are. They learn the dance and go out and perform it. Nobody coaches you on the difference between rehearsing and performing. So when I got on stage I had all these actors' questions. What happens if I don't feel like it? What is my relationship to the people on stage? What is my relationship to the audience? What happens if I forget something?

I began to do showcases in New York—off, off, off Broadway, in the Bowery, in horrible little theaters where there was usually some bum getting warm, or only my mother in the audience and the director. They were wildly melodramatic plays, and they required that I really throw myself in. With these questions—whether or not they were answered—it became clear what I needed to know. At that point I decided to go to acting class.

I went first to The Stella Adler Conservatory. I began to get a sense of what it was to simply put myself in imaginary circumstances and live truthfully in them. And I enjoyed the experience of what I was doing. I thought, well, wait a minute, I want to explore more about this, so I went and studied with Sonia Moore at The Stanislavsky Studio. This was a very different, much more formal approach, and one I didn't always understand. I tried very hard, but it didn't seem to be the school for me. Whereupon I went to the HB Studio. I liked it so much that I thought, now I really want to go to the top here. So I auditioned for Uta Hagen's class and got in. That was really the beginning of my formal training. The others were explorations for me.

In Uta's classes you came on time, you were quiet when you were meant to be quiet, you had your work prepared. You did it in a very professional manner in front of the other students, and you were critiqued by her. The moment I stepped into her class, I felt that was the beginning of my being an actor.

During this time, I had been auditioning at cattle calls and got my first parts. So I was acting in the midst of training as an actor. I had always had a sense of the truth, but at this time I had very little technique. I feel kind of sorry for the folks who hired me in those years, because I'm not sure what they got.

CZ: How long did you study with Uta?

LC: I think I was in and out of Uta's class for seven years. I would take work and then come back and study, and sometimes I took classes while I was working. And then on account of a couple of things, probably work habits that I got into and a certain propensity in myself, I began to have problems technically with acting. I became paralyzed—perhaps it was like an acting midlife crisis. I suddenly began to question things that were being asked of me and began to attempt to produce results. [I started] to wonder whether that was really acting. Often when you are out in the professional world for a while there are exigencies which do not coincide with the freedom that you had when you were studying and the correct approach that you've been attempting with your technique. So I became progressively paralyzed as an actor, until I felt that I was in crisis. I thought, "Something is really wrong. I've got to find out what acting is, and start again."

I had been hearing about the Sanford Meisner technique and The Neighborhood Playhouse, and I decided that I would try to study with Sandy. This was at a time when I was successful as an actress, so when I went to Sandy, I told him, "I realize that I am not a beginner, but I would like to be admitted to your beginner's class. I promise I won't put on airs. I won't try to show off. I'm coming as an acolyte. I want to go back to first principles and find out what acting is. And I explained my crisis to him and he said, "Never try to learn how to act when you are performing." I said, "Well, I'm guilty. I'm submitting to you."

CZ: What were the basic differences between Uta Hagen and Sandy Meisner's teachings?

LC: First of all, both these teachers were two of the greatest teachers that I've ever had in my life. They really explored the art of acting from a very original point of view. Uta at the time was writing her book, *Respect for Acting*,* and you can tell from reading that book how deeply and personally she had delved into her own struggle as an actress and how she had attempted to draw from her own life solutions for others who were struggling with the same things. She did, for instance, studies of how to

---

*Uta Hagen with Haskel Frankel, *Respect for Acting* (New York: Macmillan Press, 1973).

portray cold and heat, how to wake up on stage, how to wait, how to talk on the telephone—very basic technical exercises. She devised an exercise in which you would bring in what was in the pockets of the character you were playing, or what was in her purse. It was always a fun exercise to do, and it was a great revelation. Uta would say, keep a book on your character as you're preparing. What kind of music does the character like best? Where does the character go to school? What would he wear to school? What were his favorite colors? What was his favorite birthday gift? She would say, "This may not appear on stage, but you will carry it in with you as a cloak of authenticity when you walk onto a set. You will have fleshed out the character, you will have painted a three-dimensional picture that will ground you."

For emotional preparation, Uta had her own theory about an actor having an obstacle in a scene. She said you have an objective in a scene, and you have an obstacle. And you define both, the objective as that thing you want and the obstacle as that thing which you are pitted against. Working with the obstacle always brought up strong feelings. One of the things that happened to me when I got out in the "field" is that I began to form a bad habit. I would get so hell-bent on performing the objective that I would often railroad my own impulses or things that were really happening in a scene. I would decide what moments in a play meant, where the big moment came. I was choreographing my performance, which is the way a lot of actors work. I became confused about this.

At that point, I was away from Uta, out on my own as a professional actor and acheiving some success. But there was a nagging thought in the back of my mind that somewhere I had gone off the track. When I came to Sandy, one of the things he taught me was that when you perform a play, you are going into unknown territory and you don't know what you're going to meet. If you place your attention on the other person, you will always know where you're at, you will always be in negotiation with them. That was really the beginning of my saying, "Well, I guess I shouldn't just perform a play like a steamroller. I should show up in the first scene and then permit myself not to know what's going to happen; I'm on a ride." That's what his training was rigorously based on, and he did many beautiful exercises to get your antennae out, to sensitize and fine-tune you.

CZ: Can you give me an example of an exercise you did in Meisner's class that was important for you?

LC: I remember one exercise, the repetition exercise, where you have to repeat a phrase with the other actor; it's magnificent. There's so little stimuli when you perform this exercise; you're free to notice very small things that happen. I remember I was doing this exercise with another actor; I thought I was doing rather well. And the actor sitting in a chair opposite me suddenly tipped his chair back and put his hand behind his head in a gesture of boredom. I just kept going, doing the exercise. Sandy stood up and said, "I am absolutely appalled. A gigantic change just happened in the person sitting opposite you and you didn't acknowledge it." I said, "What do you mean? He's just sitting here." My experience was telling me that there was no change, because I was so little attuned to body language, to the power of the behavior that was happening in front of me. Sandy worked with me very diligently on this and gave me an eye and an ear that were sharp and accurate. This technique allowed me to play with a lot of variety, and, I think, with renewed courage. Just being tuned in to the other person, and knowing that your next action comes from what they do and not out of what you decided, gave me a mission to be honest in the plays and films that I did and brought my acting to a new level.

CZ: At this point in your life, what are your feelings about all of your training?

LC: I've come to discover that there's value in all of it. I'm very grateful for the passion and the clarity of my two great teachers. When I've run into difficulties, at times, I've been able to sort through them by returning to the first principles that I'd been taught. Very often acting is Zen, you have to completely avoid the thing you are trying to do. Just as if someone asks you if you know a joke, suddenly you don't know one. It's exactly the same mechanism in the mind. If someone says, "Well, the script says you have to cry here," if you head right for crying, that's the last thing that's ever going to come out of you. You have to perform a kind of mental acrobatics on yourself. That is what all this teaching is meant to help you with. People have different ways of doing it.

I used to try to be very correct in my technique. A director once said to me when I was very stuck trying to perform a scene, "Nobody is going to know how you got this scene." And that's true. If I have to run around the block, if I have to ask everybody to give me a moment alone, whatever it is I have to do, that's the order of the day. And whatever my technique has brought me to, whatever is working, that is what I will use. Whether it's

Meisner's technique or Uta Hagen's technique or my own gestalt, that's what I have to do. So, I feel that ultimately the technique is there to serve the artist. And just the way Uta did, and Sandy did, I will have to find my own way of working.

CZ: I suppose that's something you arrive at after years of experience.

LC: One of the first things Sandy told me was, "It takes 25 years to make an actor. I'm not surprised you're confused, you've only been at it for 15." He was so right. This culture needs to know that good acting requires real maturity, because character in life is no different from the character on the stage. Actors stand for things, and they have to stand for things in their lives before they can be really good actors. The development of character takes time. Acting techniques are meant to develop the inner life of a person and to help an actor so he reveals that life in imaginary circumstances.

CZ: Where does discipline and control come into all of this?

LC: I believe it's the biggest thing missing in American acting. What we're great at is this kind of organic, shoot-from-the-hip, react-off-the-other-person, casual arena of acting. What we're not so good at is the control—voice work, interpretation, clarity, being able to use the text. Lee Strasberg said, "The text is our enemy." Well, yes, but I'll be God-damned if I'm going to go out there with people paying money to see me and not have worked like crazy on that text—to be able to speak it, to know that my voice has the range to handle it, to know that I have enough breath control for it, to know that I can make it loud enough to be heard. These disciplines are disdained in this country. It's what the English are so good at, and also why we love their theater.

CZ: How did you break into film? Was it a deliberate career move?

LC: I played a reporter, Kay Eddy, in *All the President's Men* [1976]. My scene was with Woodward and Bernstein, Dustin Hoffman and Robert Redford. My life in the movies started by doing that scene with them.

I was doing a play, *Present Laughter,* by Noel Coward, in Washington, D.C. As I walked out of a matinee one day, they were filming *All the Persident's Men* in the street. So I thought, "Maybe I'll go over and see if I can get a walk-on or something. Just to find something else to act, to do." I went over to the office and I put my name down. Then I got a call from the casting person who had seen the play, saying, "Would you come in and meet Alan Pacula? There is a speaking role that has only a couple of lines, but he might be interested." So I went and had a lovely meeting with him. He said, "Would you audition with Bob Redford?" And I said, "Of course I will." I met Bob; I auditioned for him. I remember this so well, it's such a classic actor's scene: I was in this little hotel in Washington, and I was making myself a horrible little lunch on an old stove, just thinking, "I'm never going to get anywhere, this is all a futile effort, and blah, blah, blah." The producer called me and said "We would really like you to be part of our movie." I was so thrilled. I would have died rather than not do a good job for them.

CZ: Did you have any difficulty adjusting to the camera?

LC: The biggest thing about film acting is that the physical restriction is just unbelievable. Let's say I'm talking to you, and in order for the camera to get a good angle, I can't really look at you. You need to see my face at some point, so I have to figure out where in the speech I can turn. Or let's say I'm in a shot where my hand comes up, and I cleared my hair out of my ear in an earlier shot—which is the one we are keeping—we want to make sure I do it again, exactly then. If I hold a paper when I have to read something very important to you, the audience can't see it if it's down here. So I have to hold it at a totally unnatural height, like in advertisements for a product, but not appear unnatural doing it.

Film acting is like being in a tech rehearsal for a theater actor. It's those awful couple of days when they have given you the actual props, the actual coat, your hat. Something is too big, too small, something is not quite right. But on film there is no time to change it, and you receive everything right before you go. In other words, you rehearse with a coffee cup, but there's nothing in it, because you can't spill anything on the tablecloth and your costume while you're rehearsing. So you never have the liquid until you actually go. Suddenly there's coffee in the cup—you're playing the scene and all you can think is, "Shoot! This is hot!"

I remember this affected me a lot in Sidney Lumet's films because Sidney often has people eating, but we wouldn't eat the food until we actually got to the shot. I suddenly found my mouth full of something either too wet or dry or too difficult to chew, or I was afraid something was in my teeth. Sidney only does one or two takes of a scene, so we had to deal with the food fast, and that became part of the scene. Tech rehearsal is film, so there is a lot more improvisatory skill required to be a good film actor. Actors never have it all together until the moment they're ready to shoot. Then they bring in the pencil with the lead in it.

CZ: You've worked with Sidney Lumet on three occasions: *Prince of the City* [1981], *The Verdict* [1982], and *Daniel* [1983]. How does he rehearse with actors?

LC: I'll tell you exactly how he works. It's brilliant, and every film director should sit up and take note. Sidney is an example to us all. He brings his films in on time and under budget. At the end of each day everybody goes home at a decent hour and has a good dinner and a good night's sleep for the next day's work. I took such a cold bath after those three pictures when I went to work for somebody else. I was on the set 19 hours, no sleep, no regular meals. Ugh!

Sidney most of all lets his actors know from the beginning that the whole thing depends on you, which creates an incredible atmosphere to work in because actors are usually treated as second-class citizens. He never refers to us as "talent." He enlists you as a colleague.

Sidney rehearses; he puts three weeks aside, and the first week he lets everybody rip. He encourages it. You can chew the scenery, you can over-act, you can talk loud, you can ask questions, you can emote, you can wallow, you can whatever. Then in the second week, he lets you know how the film is going to be orchestrated and what the tone of the piece is going to be. He'll say, "Now everybody got their rocks off, and you're all loosened up, and you kind of know what you're doing. Now we need to figure out where the performance is going to lie."

One thing he did on *Prince of the City* that was so extraordinary was that he sat everybody around this huge Italian banquet hall. He had the sets masking-taped down to the floor, and he had everybody get up and do their scene. He went from one person to another with the cameraman, as if he was filming the scene, and all the actors involved got to see all the scenes they weren't in. You got to see the scenes that were before and after your own. So you knew why Sidney was saying, "You're going to really have to hold back in your scene. It's got to be very intense, very quiet. Because before you there's this big chase, this shoot-out, it's loud." He brought you into the whole, to seeing what the tapestry was going to look like, and you saw exactly where your piece fit. He wasn't going to waste time on the set with you saying, "But I feel like it this way, I want to do it loud." He had you positioned precisely in the orchestration of that scene, and you understood why. You didn't spend any time fighting about whose interpretation was right because he'd really enlisted you as a colleague and you trusted him. You wanted to give him what the big picture needed.

CZ: What if you disagree with him?

LC: You can talk to Sidney if you disagree with him. Sidney knows how to answer actors' questions. He knows how to keep actors fresh. What he does in rehearsal is he watches; he's a great watcher and a great listener. He says that what he observes is your hottest performance in rehearsal, then he tries to figure out how to tell you to get there, so he's armed with that when you're on the set.

He does a brilliant thing. He often gives you a very small physical thing to do when you arrive on the set the day of your shooting. He'll say, "Oh, there's one thing I haven't mentioned—you've been up all night. Maybe dozed off for an hour." He'll give you one little physical thing, and actors love that. You are so busy thinking, "Oh, this is really fun now," it relaxes your mind, so you aren't so intensely focused on "Will I fulfill this scene?"

CZ: Your role as Caitlin in *The Verdict* was relatively small but very crucial.

LC: Yes, a powerful role. I was doing an Irish accent, and I worked a long time with a voice coach to do that performance. My text was "yes" and "no," until the very last moment of the scene. And my job in that picture was to be open enough to allow all that was going on in me to come out in those brief responses.

Now imagine you have the pivotal moment in the film, and you've got to go from A to Z in that scene. You know you have got to get to a certain pitch at the end of the scene; it's like your whole life is breaking open. That's a hell of a thing to walk in at 5 a.m. and know you have to do and not clutch. That scene is one of the best pieces of acting I ever did. I discovered something which I still try to do with everything in me, with every part I do. Because I believe that great acting happens when what is going on in the scene dovetails exactly with something that you have to do in your life—it *is* your life in that moment. And that girl was making a confession. I worked for months to figure out for myself what confession would be absolutely impossible for me to make, that I absolutely couldn't make in front of anybody. And I confessed that in that scene. And the event was cathartic for me. I made the confession, and I've never had to deal with it again. I did it! Now, you may see the scene and have your interpretation of what I confessed. Another person may have another interpretation. But what came out in that scene, universally, was a woman really confessing.

There's something interesting that happened in the performance of that part. I was very frightened that morning. I'd done one picture for Sidney [*Prince of the City*], and this was my second opportunity with him. I would have died rather than not do a good job. The part was extremely intense. And I wanted to get everything out and not go home with it.

Sidney always calls you by your character's name when you arrive on set, which is very sweet, and he came up to me as I started the first take, and said very softly in my ear, "Caitlin, just talk, just open your mouth and talk." Which is, of course, the nature of a confession. The hardest thing is to open your mouth and talk. So I kept that with me. I didn't have to perform a scene. I didn't have to be a great actor. I just had to open my mouth and talk. The effort to do that was so moving.

CZ: Lumet tends to work with classical editing patterns, which means he breaks the scenes into relatively short shots. How does that affect your emotional arc in a scene?

LC: You have to realize what the shot is for. Your master shot is probably for the opening of the scene and the end of the scene. You are going to have the two-shot or medium shot, then over the shoulder to each person, then the single or the close-up shot, and whatever else they decide to do. And that's going to take all day, maybe two days. And you are going to have to sustain. So you have to know where the emphasis is in the shot. Sidney had designed four different shots for [the confession] scene. He said, "O.K., we're going to do four moves in, closer, closer, closer, closer." So I knew that I had to do the scene four times. And each time he gave me a segment of the scene to do, from the beginning to here, and from the beginning to here, further [along], and then the whole scene. And on the third move-in, we were really cooking, we went over the top. It was a beautiful, beautiful day. Everyone in the courtroom stood up for me. It was a great moment. And, he said, "O.K., let's move in." And I turned to him and said, "Sidney, I'm willing to do anything for you, but I just gave everything that I have, I don't know how I'm going to do it." And he came over to me, and said, "That's O.K., we'll go onto the next scene. New deal." I thought that was very telling of Sidney's knowledge of acting—he realized he could get the closer angle, which was his plan for the scene—but why the hell do it if the actor had given 150 percent? You really weren't going to get the same performance, even though you were going to get your angle. Not a lot of directors would have given up their plan and just gone with what happened.

CZ: Let's move on to *Daniel*. It's based on the Julius and Ethel Rosenberg case, fictionalized in Doctorow's novel *The Book of Daniel*. How much research did you do into the Rosenbergs and the period? Do you think it's necessary to do a lot of research for a role?

LC: That's a good question. I think actors are very different on that score. I feel that to play any part, most of what is required is inside me. Whatever I know about the world that the character inhabits, *I* have to inhabit that world. And I have to bring to that world my experience of my own world. Because I was doing something very specific like *Daniel*—it was fictional but it was based on historical characters, and everybody knew it—I had to know what was up at that time. The person who gave me most of my information was Sidney Lumet. Sidney was called before the House Unamerican Activities Committee, and he knew a lot about the period. I also read a great deal about it.

I felt a great deal for Ethel Rosenberg. She would consistently maintain her innocence and her dignity. She's one of my great, great heroes. I absolutely dedicated my performance to her, because I felt she had no spokesperson. I said to Sidney before I began, "What do you think, was she guilty or innocent?" He said, "It doesn't matter, you're going to play her the same way. You have to step into her shoes, whether she was guilty or not."

But I did do a quite a bit of research on that film. I worked about 40 hours with my voice coach to try to figure out how she talked. I felt it was really important to the credibility of the role that she be placed in the context of her Russian, Orthodox Jewish family. Being cast in that role, I felt a great responsibility to be authentic. And not being Jewish, not being of a Russian background, not coming from that period, I tried very hard to enter it as much as possible, so that nothing would interfere with people hearing her story.

Lindsay Crouse in *Daniel* (1983), directed by Sidney Lumet. Courtesy of Paramount Pictures. Copyright © 1994 by Paramount Pictures. All Rights Reserved. Museum of Modern Art Film Stills Archive.

CZ: The way the script is structured and the film is shot gives absolute sympathy to these people. It's very wrenching to watch the scenes leading up to their execution, and the execution itself.

LC: It's brutal. I found it hard to play for the same reason. And I discovered in doing it that when you play someone who you know is going to die, you're always overcome. You're always overcome by the aura of any script, and you always try to deny it. You play Othello and say, "I can't play Othello because I feel so jealous, jealous of the other actors, jealous of the director." It sounds funny, but it is a phenomenon that happens over and over again. I thought I couldn't play the part in *Daniel* because everything seemed futile. I felt like I couldn't act. I drove Sidney quite crazy, because I kept saying, "I've got to rehearse this again." He'd say, "There's absolutely nothing wrong with this, you are doing beautifully." I'd say, "No, I'm not doing enough; I'm not there yet." And it's what I experienced during the entire piece, this accumulation of "I'm not doing enough," which was coming right out of the script. Ethel couldn't do enough, she was totally helpless, and this thing was snowballing over her. She was a target, there's no doubt about it.

CZ: Can you talk about how you analyze a script and develop a character, relating it to the role of Rochelle Isaacson in *Daniel?*

LC: What I do is, first, look at the overall script and say, "This is a story about . . ." I make one sentence of what the story is about. Then I take the character and I say, "What this character wants in the story is . . ." And I make one sentence, "Rochelle wants . . ." Then I lift the story of Rochelle out of the script. I take Rochelle's scenes and I type them out and staple them together: Rochelle's story. I describe the story as if I were going to tell it to you in one sentence: "This is a story about a woman who . . ." The first job I feel I have as an actor is to say, "You could read the story in a library. What am I going to give you that you couldn't get in a library, reading this script?" So I have to get rid of what you could get in the library. My responsibility is the second thing, which is: What is it that I am really doing? Not what is Rochelle doing, but what am I doing? So, let's say this scene is—just an abstract scene I've made up—a character coming to get money from his father. But what I am really doing, what I feel is the essence of that scene, is that I'm coming to get restitution for a wrong done. OK? It's a little different from coming to get the money. What you get in the library is: "This is a scene about a character coming to get some money." But what you can't get in the library is the coming to get restitution. The third step that I have to do is: What does that mean to me? Why do I have to get restitution? So that it is so important to me that I don't care if a million people see me do it. I'm going to go up there and do it no matter what. That's where the real work of acting lies; I have to think carefully about that. That's what I have to rehearse, getting restitution. So, I do those steps and what I feel happens is that the audience sees me getting the money, but they *feel* me getting restitution.

In life we never do what we say we're doing, that's why drama works so well. There is always something else going on underneath, some people call it subtext. What I say may be the opposite of what I am really doing. I have to be doing that second thing so strongly that you know it, and it's clear, even though I'm saying something entirely different. That's why Lee Strasberg says that text is your enemy. Because you are not there to act out the text. You are there to bring out—with all the force of your being—the action of the play. The through-action of the play, as Aristotle said—there's only one from beginning to end. That's true. It's quite a trick, especially for young actors. It's like patting your head and rubbing your stomach at the same time.

CZ: Can you think of an example from a film you've worked on where the words are different from the internal action?

LC: Sidney is wonderful at directing this way. There's a scene in *The Verdict,* in which James Mason has a black actor on the stand, a doctor who has come to give expert testimony for the other side. James is supposed to really nail him, put him down. So he did the scene, he was unctuous, wonderfully evil; he was fine. I thought we would go onto the next scene. Sidney sat and thought a long time, and he looked up, and said, "James dear"—he always called you dear—"I want to do it again. This time I want you to try something different. I want you to thank this man from the bottom of your heart for coming here today, for taking the time to help everyone in this courtroom get to the truth of this case." Well, Mason became evil personified. You knew why he was the highest-paid lawyer in Boston and why he had a following of 25 young kids who wanted to work in his office. Because this man was a gentleman; he was the model of courtesy, he was magnanimous; you couldn't find a hole in him, he was perfect. The guy on the stand started to squirm, he started to flub his lines. He was being nailed to the ground with such precision and such tact! Sidney's direction released James from the obligation to act out the text and made it a far more powerful scene. That was great directing. Because an actor will always want to act out the text. It's the easy thing to do; it's the obvious thing to do.

CZ: Did you generally watch dailies when you're shooting?

LC: No. I don't go to dailies unless I feel there is something I need to adjust or if the director says to me, "I want you to come and see something." Or if I really want to see whether something I'm doing is coming across. But I don't feel I can be inside something and witness it from without at the same time. Some actors can; I'm too critical, too much of a perfectionist. I don't even like to go see the films I'm in right away. I'll see them in a year or two, when I feel I can really enjoy them. But I'm too close to them when I'm making them. I would tear myself down, and why? If I had a great time doing it and it's done, what can I do? I can't fix it, and I'll want to. You know you did the best you could at that time with the technique you had at hand. Sometimes a film comes out a year later, or, as in the case of *Prince of the City,* almost two years after we did it. I thought I was a much better actor by then. You say, "I wish I had that opportunity again." Why put yourself through that? So I tend not to look at it while I'm doing it; it just hamstrings me.

CZ: Going back to *Daniel,* I remember when I was a kid going to the Smithsonian Institute and seeing the Jello box on display that was supposedly used to transmit material between the Rosenbergs and David Greenglas. I've always remembered that box in connection with the Rosenbergs.

LC: That's exactly the kind of emotional memory Uta Hagen talks about, something small but extremely significant. Something on the floor, or a stain on a tablecloth. She says you remember by some very mundane object, and that memory will trigger the whole emotion. She says when you have to act a very traumatic moment, sometimes the big moment is not when the emotion hits. It's not the moment of death, it's when you have to take the key to the car out of your dead husband's pocket. It's something that surrounds the event that is so mundane yet expresses all the pathos of the situation. I think it's really true.

CZ: The execution scene is very difficult to watch. What was it like to film?

LC: It was like bondage. It was amazing to have it actually happen to me, because in the dress and all the straps, the humiliation of it was far worse than the fear. It was the humiliation, and the sexual nature of it.

Here's something I can add about film acting—people always say, "You have no audience when you're acting for film." But that is not true. There are a lot of people on a set when you work in film, and they are absolutely your audience. How the set is run is so important to how an actor performs, and Lumet's sets are exemplary. Those technicians have read the script, so they know what is going on that day. They know if an actor has serious emotional work to do, and they are respectful. The days that we did the execution scenes and the scenes saying good-bye to the children, you could have heard a pin drop on the set from the moment we arrived. Everybody knew how difficult it was going to be and how horrendous.

A funny story about when Mandy Patinkin gets strapped into the electric chair. He was the first one to do the scene, just as Julius Rosenberg was the first one to be executed. And everyone was trying to do it as quickly as possible, because it was so grim. He got in the chair, they pretended to pull the switch, he started to shake in the chair, and the back of the chair broke. [*Laughing*] Oh Lord, poor Mandy—he had the hood on, it was one of the worst things I ever saw. He didn't know what had happened. You can get pretty paranoid when you get strapped in an electric chair [*laughing*]; it's a game called trust. But it broke the ice, so the rest of the day we were shaking off the tension.

CZ: It's very affecting when he collapses on his way to the chair.

LC: That was incredible. When you act you get an education about a world you might otherwise never know anything about. Now I feel I know something of what it was like to be part of that whole situation in the 1950s. I know where I would have stood if I was this person. That woman's life had a big effect on me. It took three zaps to kill her, not for no reason. She was defying everyone.

CZ: But, what happens if your sympathies are *not* with a character?

LC: Then you don't take the part. And chances are you won't get the part. Because you play roles that have resonance for you, where you can literally say—with every experience of your life leading up to that moment—"If this were happening to me, I would . . ." Otherwise you cannot play with authenticity, you can't play with any kind of commitment to the part.

When I did *Places in the Heart* [1984], I had a long talk with Robert Benton. My marriage vows were based on the fact that if my husband was unfaithful I would leave him. But in *Places* I was being asked to play a part where I take my husband, Ed Harris, back after he's made love to Amy Madigan. I had to really talk that over with Benton, because I felt that I had to truly understand that. Especially because in the moment in which I took Ed back I had no words, no speech, I had no way to get there. I had to be there, I had to communicate that silently and fully. I didn't want to play a part in which I felt I was doing something that was against my own values.

I grew up by doing that part, in the sense that I took a leap in my own life. I took in the fact that there are things that can happen in a marriage, where indeed you would say, "We're going to wipe the slate clean. We're going to step over that and go on." I really possessed that by the end of the movie.

I also nearly lost that part because Benton wanted me to be nude in a scene. I didn't feel that it was warranted, and I said, "No, I can't do this." He said, "Well, I have to think about it then," because it was a very personal script for him. And I waited 24 hours thinking, "Maybe I'm not going to be able to do this film." But I stood by my conviction. I felt I really wouldn't be able to enter into the spirit of it. He called back and he said, "OK, we'll do it your way."

CZ: That was very courageous of you.

LC: It was. It might not be right for every situation, but you have to define what you can really get behind. You are a symbol on film for all people. The great ethic of acting is that you are going to do what you said you were going to do, no matter what. If I had promised that I would get up there and offer forgiveness in that scene, then I had better bloody well do that. That's all we offer to people witnessing the story. So that they can say, "If that woman can get up there and do that when she has all this pain inside her, I can do that." You set an example, you're a symbol, so you had better be able to get behind it. Otherwise I think it shows. You're very translucent when you're on film. You are a figure of light; your soul comes through. You can tell, easily, when someone is really doing it or not.

CZ: In discussing the ethical dimension of acting, the famous example is Falconetti in Carl Dreyer's *The Passion of Joan of Arc* [1928]. Dreyer did torturous things to Falconetti so she could get into the suffering of the character. And she ended up, after that experience, spending most of her life institutionalized. Of course, we don't know what her mental state was before doing the film, but that's the archetypal story of something disastrous that can happen when an actor embraces a role very completely.

LC: Listen, I feel very strongly, and I teach my students this: you're either an actor or you're not. Even beginning actors with no training can put themselves in imaginary circumstances with all the truth of their being.
    For the most part, going to that extreme is bull, that's someone who is not an actor. You don't have to cut your leg off at the hip to play a paraplegic. People say to me constantly, "Did you do a lot of research on psychiatry to play the psychiatrist in *House of Games* [1987]?" I say, "Look, a psychiatrist is someone who listens and who helps." End of sentence! There are 10 people on my block who are psychiatrists, and one couldn't be more different than the other.

Taking on a role is a very tricky thing. And one of the things that technique is based on is protecting the human mind. There are people we know who are locked up in institutions who declare themselves to be Jesus Christ. The point is, as Sandy Meisner very elegantly puts it, it's not that you *are* Jesus Christ, it's "as if" you are Jesus Christ. And there is a world of difference. Technique makes that extremely clear—you train your mind to think in those terms so that you yourself remain intact. That's what personalizing a role means, bringing yourself to that situation, not crowding out your own identity with another one. People say to me, "I don't know how you do what you do; I couldn't lie to save my life." People think I practice telling lies all day until I'm so good at it that you can't tell the difference. But that's exactly what acting is not. As any acting teacher knows, the most difficult part of the art is the struggle to bring out the truth of your being, the fullest dimension of yourself. Sandy constantly said to his students, "I don't want to hear about how the pirates stole your wallet, I want imagination based on truth."

It's amazing how people will avoid using themselves in art, because we instinctively know that everything we do is a self-portrait. Acting is the art of self-revelation. We want to avoid that knowledge like the plague because of all the ambivalence we have about ourselves. We are not good enough, we are not good-looking enough, we're not whatever enough, and if what we are doing is a self-portrait, everybody is going to see us. Oh my God, what will happen then? Technique is there to enable us to step forward and shine and remove all that fear, remove the tension, the self-consciousness, the defenses, all the reasons we say we can't step out. But what a great example we set when we do.

Acting is an art like any other, and art requires practice and control. Artistry requires craftsmanship. But the instrument is not some object removed from us; the instrument is *us,* and that's where the confusion lies. Because when you deal with training an actor, you're training an actor's mind. You're creating thought patterns, you're creating habits—habits of work, of thinking, of behavior. You're dealing with a human being. And that's where it gets tricky; you want to deal correctly with that human being so that you focus solely on training an actor. To me the other is like telling a sculptor he has to mutilate himself in order to learn how to chop away at a block. An actor has to consider himself an instrument. He doesn't have to mutilate himself in order to play a crazy person. I have a wonderful voice coach, Liz Dixon, who says if you're playing someone who's uptight, you can't play her if you're really uptight. You have to be open and give the appearance of uptightness. A magician doesn't really need to disappear, he just needs to direct your attention.

CZ: *House of Games* is very different from the more naturalistic films you've been in. How did you go about developing the character of Margaret? What was the character's "through-action"?

LC: The character of Margaret wanted to serve; that's what I played in that film. She said, "I just want to do good." She wanted to serve, and that was her tragic flaw. She wanted to serve to the point that she couldn't bear not being of service. A kid comes into her office and says, "I'm going to die. What can you do about it? What do you know?" She can't bear the accusation. She has to help him. If she can't help him, her life is a lie; she doesn't know anything, and she's not of service. So, she has to help him, and that's what drives her to the "house of games."

CZ: Why does she have this obsession with being of service?

LC: Well, that's where the work comes in for the actor, what does that mean to me? My imagination had a lot to feed on there, because being of service is the devotion of my life. And on a personal level, I found there was a great deal to think about. That part had tremendous resonance for me, because I understand what it means to just want to do good. I think it is a very human motivation for living.

CZ: But don't you need to know where that need comes from in the character?

LC: All you have to know to play that person is that you are compelled to serve. And the "compelled" part comes from, what does it mean to *me?* How important is it that *I* serve? If you need to up the stakes of a script, a scene, whatever, you just need to find a better reason. If you have to do something and it's a chore, you could do it or not do it. But if you have to do something and it's a mission, you have to find a very good reason to do it. If I have to come back in this house that's burning to rescue Willa [Lindsay's eldest daughter], I don't give a damn how many people are looking at me. If I have to come back to the house in order to get an extra key, that's quite a different thing. So in a script like this where the woman is compulsive, you have to find a driving reason for her to want to serve that badly, to that extreme. That's all that technique would require.

She risks her life to help this kid; she goes to the "house of games" with these thugs. All you really have to know to play her—you don't have to have sat in a psychiatrist's office, you don't have to study psychiatrists— you just have to know what it's like to need to serve so badly. And the effect of doing that is the portrayal of someone who doesn't think enough of herself, a person who feels her life's a lie, a person who searches outside of herself for her own value.

CZ: Margaret is an extremely controlled, repressed character. Was that difficult to play?

LC: People say, "Was that a really fun part to play?" And I say, "No." A woman who wants to dedicate her life to service is a passionate person, but Margaret couldn't show anything. The "obstacle," as Uta would say, was so powerful. It's as if every day you went out to dig a ditch, and someone kept holding the shovel.

David [Mamet's] direction to me constantly was, "Calm down, calm down, just talk in a normal voice, don't show them anything." The essence of that character, and why it appears so stylized, is that she couldn't, she couldn't, she couldn't. My instinct was to let the variety out, let her be . . . something. But the essence of her was that she was restricted. To play her was quite an acting challenge.

CZ: What about the language of the film? It's very ritualized and repetitious, and you're speaking almost in a sing-song voice. You must deal with it differently than you would a naturalistic text.

LC: Well sure, if there's a formal approach to something, there are many ways to justify that internally. If it's a poem, there are many ways to justify that language. Uta gave me a great clue to this; she said, "Poetry is the most specific language that you'll ever speak." In other words, when Shakespeare says, "Make me a willow cabin at your gate, and fall upon my soul in your house," she says, "What Shakespeare's saying is that it's not a log cabin, it's not a concrete block cabin. It's a willow cabin, and only a willow cabin could possibly express the unutterable dedication of that girl. Make me a willow cabin." God! It's so unbelievably delicate and so poignant an image. That was one of the greatest perceptions that Uta gave me, and something I've held with me always, that a poetic text is more specific than anything. And therefore you need to deal with it specifically; you have to give yourself specific reasons.

If you live a life of service, you have to remove yourself. If you're living for something higher than yourself, you are not the point. How you say something, or the baggage you're bringing, is not the point. David kept saying, "Don't show 'em, don't show 'em, you are not the point." In a way you are very self-effacing when you live a life of service. Your existence is not in color; you're in black and white, maybe just gray. Because everybody else is the point, that's what you're in service to.

David's language was terribly appropriate and gave the film a very strange life. David pared down everything to the essentials. That's why the film is so powerful and has such unity. Nothing is extraneous, not even the expression of the actors. It's bizarre, too, but highly poetic. David used to say to me when we first talked about acting, "Everyone thinks my plays are kitchen plays, but they're operas!" And that gave me a great clue to David's work. Joe Mantegna appears to be, "Oh, I'm just shootin' the shit with Margaret here." But really, he's singing a song.

Battleship gray—Margaret. I used to study fine arts with James Ackerman at Harvard; he talked about the Lindesfarne Gospels. Monks that wore hair-shirts and went barefoot, senses deprived, did these incredible illuminations. They'd do the capital letter in gold, and these beautiful, very elaborate pictures. I remembered that image when I was playing Margaret, because I felt that longing was inside her. But the outside was this monk with a rope-belt, cloth that was rough. She was in this life of service, but inside was an explosion, this passion, this life, like an octopus coming out of her. But that was not what the world saw.

CZ: You teach acting classes; what is the most important lesson for future actors to know?

LC: The great example I can talk about as an actor is that most people spend their lives—and I'm including myself—taking an average. In other words, "Well, I'd really like to, but this is all I can do. If only I could save my mother, or, if only I hadn't done that." We're filled with wishes. And actors are meant to get out there and take themselves to the edge of the edge of the edge. To go as far as they can. Not to take an average. I say to my students, "Don't take an average. If you are coming in to cheer someone up, if you're coming in to lay down the law, if you're coming in to get restitution, you get restitution! Let the playwright stop you. But until the last breath that you have, you do that with *all* the strength of your being." Because everybody needs to be told that they can shoot for that dream. That's what all our stories are about. That's what all our myths are for. To take us to the next level, to say life can be better. You can bust through the thing you never thought you could. You can change tomorrow what you thought you couldn't today. That's why actors are leaders, taking people, as Joseph Campbell would say, "into the forest of original experience." They're going in themselves and coming back to recount what it was like, and we can witness them.

That's why when you see great acting, something happens which changes you, which is so overwhelming, you don't have words. When you give a great performance you don't feel it was yours, you feel it came through you. That's the Zen of it. All you can do is prepare correctly so that, hopefully, you have the privilege of delivering a message that came from above.

An Interview with Tommy Lee Jones

Tommy Lee Jones in *Coal Miner's Daughter* (1980), directed by Michael Apted. Copyright © by Universal City Studios, Inc. Courtesy of MCA Publishing Rights, a Division of MCA Inc. Museum of Modern Art Film Stills Archive.

As an actor, Tommy Lee Jones resists easy categorization. His gruff, rugged, *joli laid* appearance references the Clark Gable/Spencer Tracy credo of masculinism. At the same time, his aura of barely suppressed rage and passion situate him as heir to the particular gifts of Marlon Brando and James Dean. Jones is a rare entity in post star-system Hollywood—an actor with a strong persona. And, just as impressive, he is an archetypal figure who can act. In many of his roles, Jones strongly recalls the heroes of the classical western; he often portrays the stoic loner, curt and enigmatic. He is clearly a man of action, rough and ready, with a capacity for hell-raising and violence. He lives—for good or ill—by his own code; he is, in sometimes dark ways, stubbornly principled. Jones has a somber, powerful, and, at times, threatening presence that conceals as much as it exposes. Both complicating and enriching this picture is the fact that Jones is classically educated, a *cum laude* graduate of Harvard (in English) and

35

a great believer in the "life of the mind." Jones' charm and power lie—as with most actors who become stars on film—in his uniqueness, his ability to declare the existence of a strong self while acting someone else.

Jones was born in San Saba, Texas (where he now maintains a large ranch and polo club), in 1946. After graduating from Harvard in 1969, he immediately made his Broadway debut in *A Patriot for Me,* appearing the same year in an off-Broadway production of *Fortune and Men's Eyes.* His first film role came the following year as Ryan O'Neal's roommate in *Love Story* (1970). (Jones' real-life Harvard roommate was current Vice-President, Al Gore.) Jones continued working on the stage and in films and television, doing a four-year stint on *One Life to Live.* His first major work on television was in the title role of the made-for-television movie *The Amazing Howard Hughes* (1977). Two of Jones' most crucial roles came in the early 1980s—as Sissy Spacek's (Loretta Lynn's) husband Doolittle "Mooney" Lynn in *Coal Miner's Daughter* (1980) and on television as Gary Gilmore in an adaptation of Norman Mailer's *Executioner's Song* (1982), for which he was awarded an Emmy. Through the 1980s, Jones continued to do smaller movies, e.g., *Nate and Hayes* (1983), *The River Rat* (1984), *Black Moon Rising* (1986), *Stormy Monday* (1988), and *The Package* (1989), and TV movies (*The Park Is Mine, Stranger on My Land*). Another turning point in his career was his memorable rendering of Woodruff Call in the mini-series *Lonesome Dove* (1989), where he managed to embody the Texas of our collective imagination. This was followed by his surprising turn as the homosexual Clay Shaw in Oliver Stone's *JFK* (1991), for which Jones received a long-overdue Oscar nomination. Jones has consolidated his career by his appearances in two mega-hits, in *Under Seige* (1992) as a rock-and-rolling psycho-terrorist, and as Lt. Gerrard in *The Fugitive* (1993), for which he received the Academy Award for Best Supporting Actor. He was reunited with Stone in *Heaven and Earth* (1993) and *Natural Born Killers* (1994). Jones also acted the part of an Irish bomber in *Blown Away* (1994), a Bible-quoting lawyer in *The Client* (1994), and the eponymous anti-hero baseball player in *Cobb* (1994).

I talked with Jones near his ranch in San Saba, in the hill country of Texas, in August 1992.

CZ: You grew up in a small town in Texas. What was your early experience of watching films?

TJ: I started growing up in extremely small towns. Up until the age of 6 I lived in small towns, and even after that for a certain period of time. The first movie I ever saw was at a movie house in the town of Rotan. It was a double bill of an old Tarzan movie and a movie called *The House of Wax* [1953]. It was a huge experience. It cost 25 cents, I believe: a dime to get into the theater, a dime for popcorn, and a nickel for a Coke. I'd been looking at this building in the town whenever I was in town. I knew that there was something going on, and I thought I had it pretty well figured out until I got in there and a guy's face melted, and Tarzan was surrounded by the pygmies in the tribe, and the big monkey tried to kill him. It was a fantastic experience. I was a little old to be that naïve, probably 5 or 6 years old.

I remember I'd just, that very day, joined a baseball team—what you would call Little League—and we'd all been given orange ball caps. I took mine to the movie theater with me and got so badly scared that I bit the little button off the top and was ashamed when I went to the baseball diamond the next day that I had no button on top of my new ball cap.

CZ: Did you have any idols in the movies that you really wanted to emulate?

TJ: I thought Johnny Mack Brown* was rather special. I didn't really see that anyone could aspire to be like Johnny Mack Brown; there couldn't be but one. I thought he was awesome.

CZ: When did you first think about becoming an actor? Where do you think that came from?

TJ: I don't know. I don't suppose there's a turning point; I wanted to be an actor all my life. I was a very enthusiastic and quite histrionic backyard foot soldier as a child. I enjoyed school plays, in the second and third grade, and thought it was a wonderful experience. It was scary. The world of the imagination appealed to me early on, but when I specifically decided to make my living with my imagination, I don't know.

CZ: Did you see any theater when you were growing up?

*Johnny Mack Brown was a star of 1930s westerns, such as *Riding the Apache Trail* (1936) and *Wells Fargo* (1937).

TJ: I had never really seen any legitimate theater other than little school plays, where you play a mole who's been blinded by the sun and held captive by the god of the corn. Some pseudo–Native American myth, turned into a little school play. Or *Snow White and the Seven Dwarfs,* put on by the entire second grade of Rotan; I played Sneezy.

CZ: Were your parents supportive of your decision to become an actor?

TJ: Yeah, sure, I suppose. Actually, they took me to see Lefty Frizell perform from the back of a flatbed truck, in a little knot of oak trees along the Concho River below San Angelo one time. I'll never forget that as long as I live; it was an amazing thing to see. I was taken to rodeos as a child. Town was always a big deal and a big surprise when I was a child. Speaking of theatrical events, going to town . . . that's probably when it started, when they took me to town [*laughs*]. It's a long way to answer your question, but that's it.

CZ: When you went to Harvard, did you take any theater classes?

TJ: They don't have any; we're not a trade school. They had a legitimate theater company there, several of them. Lots of plays going on in a lot of colleges. Theater was a part of the undergraduate life in the late 1960s in Cambridge.

CZ: After you graduated, did you do repertory theater in the Boston area?

TJ: That was my summer job. After I graduated, I went to work in New York.

CZ: And you worked in the theater?

TJ: Mm-hmm.

CZ: Did you ever have any formal training as an actor?

TJ: Well, I'd say my education as an actor has been entirely practical. Beginning at the age of 16, I started working on plays and did a minimum of three a year until I was 24 or 25 years old and working as a professional. I did a lot of classical plays in repertory and helped run theater companies, was in theater companies, acted and directed in plays, constantly, for a long time, until I was too busy working in movies and television.

CZ: Did you ever regret not going to classes?

TJ: No.

CZ: If you were talking to a young actor just starting out, would you recommend on-the-job training rather than acting classes?

TJ: I'd say do what I did in this sense only: Cultivate your mind at every opportunity, and broaden your education. What do I mean by education? It's the classical concept of a liberal education—learn. The study of history, science, especially the English language, the history of art, the history of aesthetics, no small amount of religion. Study those things because they inform your work. It's the mind that will give your work any kind of breadth or scope or purpose or service.

CZ: Do you make any distinction between the mind and the emotions?

TJ: Oh, yeah—the heart, the mind. Of course you do, it's an old dichotomy. One informs the other in a properly balanced world, of course. The broader they are, the better actor you'll be. Pretty simple outlook. Of course, you do need all the practical experience you can get. Sooner or later, you're going to have to learn your way around a theater, and how light works, and how the process works, and how it can be manipulated to the greater good of the greatest number.

CZ: What kind of adjustment was it to go from theater to film?

TJ: Well, you had to think about a lot of things and make the obvious adjustment, one that for some people is easiest to forget, which is the matter of scale. You'll find that actors who have a sense of scale in the theater will have an equally adept sense of scale before a camera. Those who cannot suit the action to the word and make too broad a gesture onstage are the same ones who are liable to jump out of frame in the middle of a good shot, or wave their hands in front of their face while they're wearing white gloves, or some other mistake.

CZ: What attracts you to a project?

TJ: Well, people really. The person who wrote it, what he's done in the past, what kind of writer he is. The director, the company, and the people that make it up. The question is, "Do you want to make this movie with these people?" You really want to consider the people you're going to be working with; it's very important. Also, is it fun? Very important [*laughter*]. Fun is a highly underestimated thing in this country, especially in the arts.

CZ: Have you ever had a problem with a director because he approached the work differently than you did? How did you resolve that?

TJ: The directors have all been different. So adaptability is important. A director told me one time that I couldn't watch dailies because I'd change my performance and would be out of control. I'd been making movies for a few years and made some really good ones at the time, and dailies were an important work tool. You'll find that people make up their minds ahead of time. Ordinarily, a person would find their intelligence insulted by such a thing. But you get over that and go on, you try to be adaptable. This is twentieth-century America, the audience is huge, these are important matters. You just go right by that kind of thing, just put it by and go on to the next deal. You try to be adaptable—very, very, very important—key.

CZ: Once you're committed to doing a script, how do you get into the characterization?

TJ: Well, you just read it! That's why it's important for actors to be good readers and to have had some kind of academic life where they're required to write a bit, essays and so forth, and organize their thinking. You just respond to the writing.

CZ: What sort of questions do you ask yourself when you read the script?

TJ: How would a director respond to the writing? Will the director see the same thing in this that you do? Are you seeing it correctly? Are you working with people who appreciate what you see in it? Can you all become of a single mind and translate this literature into dramatic art or a commercial action adventure that's interesting in some way? Are these things possible? Those are the questions you ask yourself. I think training in literature is very helpful to an actor; it has been to me.

CZ: What excited you about the role of Gary Gilmore in *The Executioner's Song* [1982]?

TJ: I'm a Norman Mailer fan, and have been all my reading life. He was very important to us in Cambridge, Massachusetts, in the 1960s, and continues to be important to me. His book, translated into his own teleplay, was irresistible—to be part of Norman's mental journey. I came to think of this as his *Crime and Punishment.* Having read the book and been in a play based on the book *Crime and Punishment,* it was a pretty good frame for huge dramatic events. And this was modern American art, with one of our great minds behind it. It was just awfully good company.

CZ: Did you go out on your own and do research into ex-cons and the Mormon community, that kind of thing?

TJ: Yeah, sure. I had all the material available to me that Norman had available to him when he wrote the book. I had a collection of every magazine article and photograph that had ever been published of Gary, and every videotape interview—hours of tapes, interviews with Gary and his family—and every foot of news footage. Everything there was. And I became good friends with his family. His cousin Sterling became a teamster, and I got him on as my driver. I lived in that little community.

CZ: How did you come to feel about Gary once you got into the part?

TJ: They didn't kill him soon enough.

CZ: Both the series and the book seem to suggest that prison had warped him. What was your thinking about that?

TJ: I think prison helped warp him. He wound up with no conscience, essentially. The movie shows how the conscience and crime and punishment are not as simple as we think they are. I'm sure if you go amongst the citizens and ask them if they would like to have a prison system that is rather brutal, offers no chance of rehabilitation, and will make a steady source of ever more highly educated criminals, they'd say, "No, we really don't want that." Most of them would be surprised if you were to say, "Well, that's what you have, and it's the best possible thing you can have." These are not simple questions. We don't have a horrible prison system on purpose; it's very difficult. The strength and beauty and power in organized society is vulnerable; it's fragile. And it requires a lot of work to maintain it, by individual people and by society, even if it means killing somebody.

You could say he's a product of our prisons; it's true. The temptation is to say, "Well, okay, let's don't blame him. Let's don't kill him, let's let him live." The prosecution argued that it would cost a million dollars a year to keep him alive in maximum security—because of his prison record, not simply because of his shooting spree that one wild, drunken, stoned, crazy, idiot night. Because of his record in prison, it would cost a million dollars a year to hold him, to keep him alive, and you still could not guarantee the safety of the other inmates around him, or the prison guards, or his own safety. That was the decisive argument.

CZ: When Gary kills the people, he does it in a very dispassionate way. Would you bring in biographical material as a way of understanding that?

TJ: Yeah. He doesn't have much of a conscience. I think he probably had a delicate conscience to begin with; he didn't have a very happy childhood; he spent a lot of time in detention centers as a child; he rebelled against an unhappy family situation by stealing cars; he went to reform school.

CZ: Norman Mailer's book focuses on the big brouhaha going on with the media and on Gary demanding to be executed.

TJ: Yeah, he enjoyed that, he was a real showboat, this guy. He loved that to death. Atrocious bullshit artist, this guy.
    Hurting people, doing something just horrible gave him a sense of well-being and achievement. Any atrocity did. Kind of a perverted outlook.

CZ: Do you find that you have to achieve some degree of empathy with a character, no matter how despicable he is? I'm thinking, again, of Gary, and also of your character in *Stormy Monday* [1988], who really didn't have many redeeming features. Sometimes actors say, "I had to learn to love that character. Even though she was a person I would have hated in real life, I had to learn to love her in order to get inside of her."

TJ: You can't take a moral attitude toward these characters while you try to build a life for them. It shouldn't be a moral process. You're out there like a mad dog in a meat-house. You're not really thinking about what you like and don't like about certain characters; you're putting them together from your experience. That should be the only thing on your mind.

CZ: Is there anything that you wouldn't consider doing, because you were morally opposed to the character?

TJ: No. How silly. I'm morally opposed to all bad guys, but you can't make a movie without a bad guy, whether you're the good guy or the bad guy. So what are you going to say, "I'm morally opposed to this character because he's evil?" You can say, "Oh, I don't like this movie because it admits of this evil, or it implies that this evil is greater than it really is, or it takes an attitude toward good and evil that I think is mistaken. I don't want to lend my efforts to this point of view of our world." You can take that hifalutin' posture, if you can afford it. Work should speak for itself.

CZ: You tend to play very intense characters; do you ever find that you take it home with you?

TJ: No. A lot of young actors wind up doing that, but eventually you have to quit.

CZ: So you never had that problem, even at the beginning of your career in *Jackson County Jail* [1976]?

TJ: I was a young actor at that time. I wasn't really a young actor; by the time I did that movie I'd been an actor for a good long time. I'd done twenty-five or thirty plays by then. I wasn't taking the character home with me as much as I did when I was a teenager. It's kind of an adolescent thing to do, whether you're an actor or whatever you are.

CZ: When you are in the process of doing a real-life character—and you've played a lot of them—Howard Hughes [*The Amazing Howard Hughes*, 1977], Doolittle [*Coal Miner's Daughter*, 1980], Gary Gilmore, and Clay Shaw [*JFK*, 1991]—how much do you feel you need to be faithful to the real person? How much imagination is involved?

TJ: Your first loyalty is to the man who signs your paycheck, then your loyalty is to the script and to the director and the work at hand. In some of those television shows and movies, it was important to the script that we create a convincing picture of what this person really was and really did, how they acted, even how they used their hands in certain circumstances, how they breathed—when they breathed in, when they breathed out. So you spend hours studying that, and you come up with a piece of film that looks astonishingly like RKO news footage from the 1920s, down to the patterns of speech and breath and details of clothing. So that's part of the style of the script. In other cases, that's not so important. It wasn't so important, for example, to be *the* Gary Gilmore, as it was to be a Gary Gilmore. The theme was crime and punishment, so I didn't look very much like Gary. Sometimes you need to try to look more like a historical figure than others.

CZ: Do you like to rehearse?

TJ: Yeah! I do.

CZ: Have you ever wanted more rehearsal than you were able to get?

TJ: Yes, I do! [*laughter*]

CZ: Some actors say they want to do it once and that's it; they can't stand rehearsing. Some people say it and, apparently, they don't mean it.

TJ: Everybody I've heard say it didn't mean it.

CZ: Do you like to improvise? Have you ever been on a shoot where there's been a lot of improvisation asked of you?

TJ: Look, I hate improvisation. I hate it. I don't mind planned accidents.

CZ: What would they be?

TJ: There's a very subtle difference here, which I'm trying to figure out how to explain [*laughter*]. You can say, "Look, I want something to happen at this particular point in this little piece of literature." Somewhere, you can add a veil of spontaneity. How's that phrase? What I mean is something that seems uncontrolled, but isn't really. I don't like uncontrolled efforts.

I really feel that it's easy to abandon your narrative responsibilities when you are doing what most people would call improvising. I don't think anything unplanned has a significant place in any drama that purports to exist for the improvement of the time of good Americans.

CZ: Did you ever see a film with a lot of improvisation that's been interesting for you?

TJ: *McCabe and Mrs. Miller* [1971] was an interesting film; I liked the way it looked. Improvisation . . . I've made things up and put them on camera very shortly thereafter.

CZ: I notice that all your performances are very intensely physical. Your posture and your gestures are really different in every film. When people discuss acting they talk about working from the outside in or the inside out. Where would you be on that spectrum?

TJ: I've heard this description before: This actor works from the outside in, that one works from the inside out. I've read interviews with actors who describe themselves accordingly to be one way or the other. The influences on my work are wide, very wide. I find that's very important. So I don't care if you go from the inside out or the outside in.

CZ: But physicality is obviously important to you . . .

TJ: Hell, I want to get where I'm going; I don't care which way we go to get the character to seem real, to have the appearance of reality. You select those details of his behavior—mental, physical, emotional presence—that will inform the story and improve the time of the audience.

CZ: Mary Steenburgen said that she always gives an editor a place to cut a shot. Do you do that?

TJ: That's one way an actor can control his performance, by creating cutting points. If you want to be a serviceable actor—which everyone should and has to be, if they're going to last—you do try to create cutting points in good and rightful places. Usually, you want to create about three, so the scene can be as short or as long as you need it to be. You can put cutting points in the middle of scenes; also, it depends on the relationship that you have with the editor. That relationship is something in our industry that's getting closer. Most motion pictures are shot on location, so everybody doesn't go home at the end of the day; nobody has anything to do but work on the movie. These relationships naturally cultivate, and that's an important one to a healthy movie: the relationship between actor and editor. Please don't try these stunts in your own backyard, film students; these people are seasoned professionals.

It's not a socially facile thing; it's not an easy thing. When directors, actors, editors, and cinematographers are all working as a team, with lots of mutual respect, I think those are the ideal conditions. The whole point is that, yes, you do create editing points, good ones, but you don't want to overdo it. Read Hamlet's advice to the players: he tells you how to create a cutting point.*

---

*See Aidan Quinn's remarks on Hamlet's speech to the Players on p. 114.

CZ: I wanted to go on to *Lonesome Dove* [1989]. Is the process any different when you have more screen-time for your character to develop—8 hours as opposed to 1½ in a feature?

TJ: It wasn't much of a consideration. You have these events, the great arc of the story, and your character is here, here, here, and here, and you just play the character. It's a long journey. The fact that it was an 8-hour show really didn't affect any single decision.

CZ: Was it shot chronologically?

TJ: No.

CZ: Did you discuss the relationship among the characters with the other actors and the director? I'm thinking especially about Gus and Call. Did you have discussions with Robert Duvall?

TJ: No, no, not at all.

CZ: I was wondering about the two of you using what seemed to be Indian gestures all through the series. Would that be something that you would decide on together, or would something like that just happen spontaneously?

TJ: I don't talk to Bobby a lot about anything other than football, or the weather, or to ridicule some young actor, or to tell jokes. I've known him a long time and have a close relationship with him; it really doesn't require a lot of talk to get down to work.

CZ: Did you use someone as a basis for the deportment of your character in that series?

TJ: Oh yes, a collection of people. The book is a collection of ideas and jokes and fact and legend. All of it is centered around a place that happens to be my own place [Texas]. I kind of built the character as a composite of several different people: the way one person used his hands, the way one person wore his hat or walked, especially around horses. I knew a man who was always tapping a horse between the eyes. The same thing applies to language and all the elements of character: moral outlook, etc.

CZ: Call is very well-dressed compared to all the other people in the film—he has pressed shirts, he's always well-groomed. Is that something you would bring to the characterization?

TJ: Well, Woodrow's rather formal in his approach to life. Very perceptive on your part, keen observation.

CZ: Call and Gus, Robert Duvall, have a relationship that is very much like a marriage.

TJ: Well, yeah, a close relationship, born of a place. Being out there, on horseback . . . all those years, chasing those bandits.

CZ: In the scene where Gus is dying, which is very moving, would you use the imaginary circumstance, or would you call on emotional memories of your own? You break down during that scene, you're obviously overcome with emotion.

TJ: Actors call on emotional memory, that's what the job is.

CZ: People mean different things by emotional memory; they can be thinking about the death of their own father or brother, or something like that.

TJ: Anything on heaven or earth, anything. The kitchen sink. So the answer is probably yes.

CZ: Whose idea was it to cast you as Clay Shaw in *JFK?*

TJ: Oliver Stone's, I believe.

CZ: You're very elegant, and erudite, and refined. It's very different from any other role that you've played. What kind of research did you do for the role of Clay Shaw? Did you study the gay milieu in New Orleans?

TJ: No. I interviewed Jim Garrison. What I wanted to understand first was Jim Garrison's understanding of Clay Shaw, so I sat with Jim for hours and hours, three 2-hour interviews, and took notes and asked questions steadily, until he got too tired—he's sick.* He explained at the beginning of the first interview that he could tell me more about Clay Shaw than Clay Shaw's mother could have ever told me. By the end of the six hours I was convinced that he was right. I'd read a lot of books about Shaw. I kind of went around town and talked to different art gallery owners, retired attorneys, people on the street, and so forth. Then there were the endless volunteers with Clay Shaw stories.

---

*Jim Garrison died in October 1992.

Tommy Lee Jones in *JFK,* directed by Oliver Stone. © 1991 Warner Brothers, Inc.; Regency Enterprises V.O.F.; and Le Studio Canal +. Museum of Modern Art Film Stills Archive.

One of the most useful sources was an interview 2 hours long with a man who was in the hospital, who worked for Clay Shaw. His son conducted this interview with him to get the old man to talk about Shaw, and what kind of work they did, and what he was like, and what he sounded like. I was told this man had an accent almost identical to Clay Shaw's. It was from this interview that I learned that he had painted himself up like the winged Mercury one Mardi Gras, and I went running, tape in hand, to Oliver and said, "Got to paint myself gold, man," and he said, "What?" I finally sold him on the idea. I would say that tape was the most useful thing, that tape and Jim. The main task at hand was to understand Jim's understanding, rather than to exhume *the* Clay Shaw. Or at least that's what I think Oliver wanted me to do; and I was working for him at the time.

CZ: What do you feel has been your most difficult and challenging role? Has there ever been anything that really stumped you, where you said, "I can't crack this guy, I don't know what he's about, I need help . . ."?

TJ: Yeah. With a terrible screenplay based on a cheap book, with a stressed-out, overly burdened director, movies sometimes will get into a situation where it's one long series of more or less controlled wrecks and accidents. Pretty soon people begin to work not for the movie, but for survival. Their proper job description becomes guilt evasion/credit theft. Everybody, especially if they're young, will get confused at such a time, possibly even be so naïve as to go to a director and ask for help.

CZ: Why do you think that's naïve?

TJ: Well, I'm being facetious. It is a bit naïve; you're not supposed to need help, you're supposed to *be* help.

CZ: A lot of actors say directors are terrified of actors.

TJ: I would think so. As I think back, some are.

CZ: They'd rather be doing anything than talking to an actor.

TJ: I'm sure it's because a goodly number of actors seem to be such doofuses, such dingbats.

CZ: Maybe it's because directors are often people who need to control things, and actors are the one unpredictable element in their job.

TJ: Oh, absolutely. What other kind of person would have that job? At some point, a director will have to turn an actor loose in front of a camera that's actually turned on, the actual lights up there. I'm sure Mike Ditka would rather be on the playing field, having fun. He'd want the same money, the same prestige, the same clothes, the same everything else that he's got now, but he'd still enjoy being out there on the field. He's gone to all the trouble to put that football team together, and he has some 21-year-old kid throw the damn ball? It should be Ditka out there playing quarterback [*laughs*].

CZ: You're living in Texas—in San Antonio and on the ranch—and you're also working on films that are produced in Hollywood. Do you ever find that creates a conflict, or is it a dichotomy you deliberately have built into your life?

TJ: I don't see it as a dichotomy. I don't see anything unusual about my life. Communication and transportation being what they are today, people can live anywhere they want to live, for the most part. I certainly can; my work doesn't require me to go to the same place every day, so I can live at home if I want to. I don't have to live next door to a motion picture or a television studio in Southern California, or next to a soap opera television studio in New York convenient to all those theaters. I did that for 8 years. I can live anywhere I want; so I live at home, and I enjoy the cattle business. That's not an unusual thing. In acting, you travel a great deal, and you use your creativity, your imagination, in very real ways for a very specific job, and you go far and wide to do that. And insofar as you get paid well and have a chance to do the world some good, I'm really grateful for it. I don't see any dichotomies; I see more harmony than anything else.

An Interview with Christine Lahti

Christine Lahti. Courtesy of PMK.

"The more I can enrich the character's life, the more alive I can make her." Christine Lahti speaks in her interview about the meticulous preparation she does for her performances, working out detailed investigations of the character's "physical appearance, background, and psychology." Once this information is processed, Lahti can go into rehearsal or onto a set and "go from [her] gut." It is this subtle, supple balance between reason and instinct that is the quintessence of Lahti's work as an actor and the gift through which she gains privileged access to the hearts and minds of her characters. Lahti has brought that "aliveness" to a wide range of characters, from the tough, straight-shooting Hazel in *Swing Swift* (1984), to the gentle, eccentric Sylvie in *Housekeeping* (1987), to the lost, anguished mother in *Running on Empty* (1989). The depth of Lahti's understanding gives substance to these portraits, which are then brought to life by her extraordinary ability and originality.

Lahti was born in Detroit in 1950 and completed her B.A. in speech at The University of Michigan in 1972. She pursued postgraduate studies at

The University of Florida before moving to New York, where she studied with Uta Hagen at The HB Studios and took professional classes with William Esper, long associated with The Neighborhood Playhouse. Her first major role for the stage was in David Mamet's *The Woods* in 1978, directed by Ulu Grosbard, for which Lahti won The Theater World Award in the role of Ruth. She continued to perform for the stage on Broadway, off-Broadway, and in regional theater, playing in *Division Street* (1980), *Loose Ends* (1981), *Present Laughter* (1983), *Landscape of the Body* (1984), *The Country Girl* (1984), *Cat on a Hot Tin Roof* (1985), *Little Murders* (1987), *The Heidi Chronicles* (1989), and *Three Hotels* (1993). She worked briefly in episodic television in *Dr. Scorpio* and *The Harvey Korman Show,* both in 1978. Lahti's first made-for-television movie was *The Last Tenant,* in 1978, followed by *The Henderson Monster* (1980), *The Executioner's Song* (1982), *Single Bars, Single Women* (1984), *Amerika* (1987), *No Place Like Home* (1989, directed by Lee Grant), *Crazy from the Heart* (1991, directed by Lahti's husband, Thomas Schlamme), and *The Fear Inside* (1992). Lahti began her career in feature films with . . . *And Justice for All* in 1979. She essayed roles in films such as *Whose Life Is It Anyway?* (1981), *Swing Shift* (1984, for which Lahti won the New York Film Critics Circle Award for Best Supporting Actress and Academy Award and Golden Globe nominations), *Just Between Friends* (1986), *Housekeeping* (1987), *Stacking* (1987), *Running on Empty* (1989), *Gross Anatomy* (1989), *Funny About Love* (1990), *The Doctor* (1991), and *Leaving Normal* (1992).

I met with Christine Lahti in her Santa Monica home in January of 1992.

CZ: When you came to New York from The University of Michigan, in the mid-70s, you studied at The HB Studios with Uta Hagen?

CL: I adored Uta; she was a great teacher for me. She was really good, really supportive. I studied with her for 2½ years, and then I went to Bill [William] Esper from The Neighborhood Playhouse, who was really different. Had I to do it over again, I probably would go to Bill Esper first and then Uta, because Uta's so technical. She really helped me learn how to score a scene—with objectives and actions breaking down the scene—whereas Bill helped me learn how to use myself. His was a professional class, twice a week, for 2 years; the whole first year is improvisation. The training I got was really wonderful, and my own acting method is a combination of many different teachers, but primarily Bill Esper and Uta.

CZ: Were you doing anything else in New York besides studying?

CL: Waitressing, waitressing, waitressing, and doing a ton of off-off-Broadway plays, learning my craft. It was a great way to learn, actually having the training and then being able to practice it, low stakes. I was trying to get commercial agents—any kind of agents—it was really a struggle. I pounded the pavement, like everybody else, stuck my picture and resume under doors, knocked on hundreds and hundreds of doors. Finally, I guess, my big break in theater was getting a part in *The Woods* [1978], the David Mamet play that Ulu Grosbard directed.

CZ: Were your parents supportive of your decision to go into acting?

CL: Very, very much. The best gift they ever gave me was the feeling that I could do anything I really set my mind to, which was amazing. So I had the confidence that I could do it, although there were many, many, many times when I felt like giving up, in New York, in the early days. I would be so discouraged and so frustrated, but something in me, some little voice hiding behind my pancreas or some organ in my body would . say, "Keep going, keep going." There was something I needed to say—I need to say—with my work; sometimes it's political, sometimes it's just from my heart, or sometimes it's from my sense of humor. Whatever it is, there's a real need that I feel to act.

I think it's lessened now, since I had my son, who's 4 years old. When I didn't work before, I used to be really crazy. Early on, I would be completely without an identity when I didn't work; I didn't know who I was, I would feel empty. Recently, I went nine months without working; I was fine, because I have a very rich life now, with my son and my marriage. In the old days, if I had gone six months without working, I'd be climbing the walls.

CZ: How did you get your first film role?

CL: Actually, first I got a TV film, *The Last Tenant* [1978], with Lee Strasberg and Tony LoBianco. I got ... *And Justice For All* [1979] because Norman Jewison was watching *The Last Tenant* for Lee Strasberg, and saw me, and asked about me. So it was one of those things.

CZ: When you look at your acting in . . . *And Justice For All,* what do you see?

CL: Now when I look at . . . *And Justice For All,* I see myself working too hard; I see myself trying to be charming, trying to be . . . just trying. And I don't think it was the character who was trying, I don't think there's a scene where the character was trying to charm somebody, or working a little hard, I think it was me just not trusting myself enough. Now, I've become simpler, and I trust myself more. I don't have to work as hard.

CZ: What makes you take a part? It probably isn't always up to you, but are there parts that you won't take or that you've turned down?

CL: It always *has* been up to me. I haven't really listened to anybody else; I've pretty much stuck with my own set of criteria, although I do ask people's advice. Mostly I look for variety, I look for different kinds of characters. I won't do—or I've tried not to do—anything that I find exploitive of women. I'm a feminist, and I'm so grateful to the women's movement and feel so empowered by it. And, being a feminist, to do any kind of part that is exploitive of women is completely objectionable to me. I've turned down many parts because of that; whether it was because the nudity was unnecessary and exploitive or I felt the woman was primarily a two-dimensional sex object, an accessory. I'm not interested.

I have done—especially in my early days—parts that on paper read like two-dimensional sex objects, like my first television pilot. It was called *Dr. Scorpion* [1978], and I was a CIA agent. There were a lot of scenes written: "bikini-clad." I worked really hard with the director, and with my co-star, Nick Mancuso, to try to give this woman three dimensions, a sense of humor, and some vulnerability. I basically think I raised the level of it by a couple of notches, but it was still pretty tacky.

I've had to do certain things that I may not have otherwise done because I needed money. But basically, I feel my integrity is intact. There's lots of different reasons to take jobs. And needs change; sometimes I just need to work because it's been so long. Or the need for money—but my lifestyle's not that extravagant that I need to keep working all the time to support it. I've kept it that way on purpose because I don't want to have to take stuff I don't believe in. It's important for me to feel passionate about what I do, and if I don't really have empathy or a connection with the character, I don't know how to do it.

Other times you take it for the artistic challenge. I've often done parts that I had no idea how to do, but I've thought, "Mmmm, wouldn't it be neat if I could get this." That's happened a lot on stage; one play that comes to mind is *Landscape of the Body* [1984], by John Guare. I had no clue how to do this lady, but it was such a great, exciting, scary experience. In *Housekeeping* [1987], I had no idea how to do the character of Sylvie. But I knew—in the back of my mind—that if I really took the chance, it might be something very exciting. I love parts like that, where I don't know what's going to happen, where they're going to end up.

CZ: You sound like you like a good challenge. Would you categorize yourself as a risktaker, in general?

CL: Yeah. I think so, I'm an Aries. [*laughter*] Actually, that's the most exciting work that I do, when I'm really scared. I remember saying to my shrink, when I used to see one—usually there'd be a dark night just before opening in a play or a dark week during the filming of a movie or rehearsal—and I'd say to her, "I'm so scared, I think I'm going to fail, I don't know how to do this . . ." And she'd say, "You know, you keep insisting on going way out on these limbs and taking these chances, but what you don't get is that there's no safety net. If you take those chances, you may fall. You can't continue to challenge yourself and take these huge risks and expect there to be some safety net underneath—there's not. So if you go out there, that's the risk; you fall and pick yourself back up again, or you fly." That was a really great lesson; I realized that those dark nights, those dark moments are part of it; just as much a part of it as that feeling of exhilaration when you're flying.

CZ: Once you're committed to a project, what kind of research do you do? Do you create a biography and a backstory? How do you work with the directors of your films? The characters that I'm most interested in are Hazel in *Swing Shift* [1984], Sylvie in *Housekeeping* [1987], Annie in *Running on Empty* [1988], and Darly in *Leaving Normal* [1992].

CL: You've picked my four favorites. Well, my homework is the same regardless of the director I work with. First I go through the script, and I write down everything other people say about me and all the clues about her history. Any clues about her parents, or birthplace, or background, or education. Then I fill in all the blanks with my own imagination. I follow an outline in terms of this biography that I got from a book on writing screenplays. It's really for a writer; it's an outline of a character, what you're supposed to cover in terms of background, physical appearance, psychology. The physical appearance is obvious, the background is in terms of parents, education, sisters and brothers, where you were born, place in the community, jobs, income, hobbies, interests, magazines you read, all that biographical stuff. The psychology is chief aspirations, dreams, goals, chief frustrations, obstacles, religion, whether the person is an optimist or a pessimist at the base of themselves. It's very specific, and I try to do it for every part.

Then I personalize everything, make it my own. Before I personalize everything, I try to think about objectives; I really score everything like Uta taught me. I think about what this character really wants in her life, scene by scene, in order to get this super-objective. In the script I draw lines where the beat changes. It's very method; it's very Stanislavsky. Then for every scene I think about actions, in terms of: "What do you do to get what you want?" Sometimes I think about the obstacle, what's in the way. But basically, it's to find behavior which is really interesting to me.

CZ: Do you write all this down?

CL: Yeah, I do. Usually I fill out cards, because I'm shooting out of continuity. I fill out index cards with the scene number on it and what's just happened. What I do is create a literal arc with my cards, because if I'm shooting scene seventy-three on one day, and I want to know where I am emotionally in the arc of this character's growth, I grab scene seventy-three. I just have a general idea, and I look at the card, and I see the specifics.

Of course it all changes in rehearsal; the ideal thing is that I do all this background stuff, break down every scene, personalize everything, and then try to forget everything I've done and go on the set, or into rehearsal, and go from my gut. That was the problem with Uta, for me. Sometimes it remained in my head, it became so intellectual that it didn't really come out of my heart. So I do all that great work, which I find really fascinating. For example, with Hazel in *Swing Shift* I saw a lot of documentaries about women during World War II, and Rosie the Riveter, read a lot of *Life* magazines from the period, and looked at pictures.

This is all work that sounds tedious, but I love it. The more I can enrich the character's life, the more alive I can make her. I create an arc for every character I do, that is really specific. She starts at A and ends up at Z, or D, or however big the arc is, however much the character changes. Usually it's about a journey of the character, it's like layers of an onion being removed. Layers of skin taken off until you get to the core of the person. What defenses does she start out with? What covers does she start out with? How does she lose them? And what does she lose, to reveal— usually by the end, hopefully—a more honest, evolved person?

That was definitely true of Hazel; she was very guarded and used humor a lot as a defense. She was a very lonely and insecure person underneath. So I plotted all that out as to how much I wanted to reveal in every scene and what would make her more courageous about opening up to somebody. Now, Jonathan [Demme] works incredibly collaboratively, and he encouraged me to try anything, which I love. I love being able to, again, take risks and try wild things. So, Hazel wants to prove that she's superior to everybody, especially people she knows are putting her down. At the beginning of the movie, Goldie [Hawn's] husband [Ed Harris] is ridiculing her, yelling at her: "Hey, you slut, turn down the music." What do I do to make myself more superior, and act like I don't care what he says? Again, it's all behavior for me: What do you *do* to get what you want? "Do" is the operative word. If I shimmy at him as I'm walking by, it shows I'm completely impervious to his comments, and couldn't give a shit about him. So I came up with that piece of behavior, the shimmy, as a way of getting what I want. I remember discussing this with Jonathan, and he loved it. Many times, I make a complete fool of myself, and I like that. If I'm in an atmosphere where the director is supportive of me and says pretty much anything goes, then I'm able to take the most risks, and I'm able to either come up with great stuff or make a fool of myself. Both things happen.

The dream thing is to do all that research and all that homework, and then forget it, go on the set, and work off the other actor. That's really it, in a nutshell. That's what I got from Esper: Put all your attention on the other person, which frees you from any self-consciousness. If you can see the experience *they're* having—What's their face doing? What are they feeling?—that's truly listening and responding. That's the give and take, and the aliveness, that I value. I really am dependent on my fellow actors.

CZ: Let's talk more specifically about the character of Sylvie in Bill Forsyth's film, *Housekeeping*.

CL: With Sylvie, I had no idea who this character was. Diane Keaton was supposed to do it; she dropped out to do *Baby Boom* [1987]. I met with Bill and I instantly knew that we would work well together, and he felt the same way. It's very interesting; I read the original book thinking, "I'm gonna really get many clues into this mysterious character that Bill has written." Bill wrote a kind of skeleton, and I had to put flesh and blood and muscles and guts on her. I thought, "I'll read the book and get a lot more." Well, I got some more, but, the truth is, the book and the script were written from a little girl's point of view, and Sylvie was such a mystery to this little girl that a lot of the blanks weren't filled in. So Bill and I had to fill them all in. I remember calling Bill up saying, "What does this character need? I can't play a character who doesn't need anything. It seems like she's above it all; she just floats through life like some kind of eccentric Auntie Mame character." He said, "Oh, no," in this very thick Scottish brogue, which I barely understood, "Oh, no, there's stuff there, you know." Well, I had to find out; I had to create a much more complex character. And he encouraged that and helped me a lot. I had to find out what was wrong with her, what she needed. I decided that she was a drifter, a loner, an eccentric, because she had suffered so much abandonment in her life—she was left by so many people—and that in order to survive, she lived alone, like a hobo. She was fine with that, but that door of vulnerability, of intimacy, had been slammed shut.

CZ: Do you think Sylvie sees herself as lonely?

CL: She doesn't know she's lonely. It's not until she meets these little girls, Lucille and Ruthie, that, especially in Ruthie, she finds a kindred spirit, and the door that had been shut for years starts to open up a little bit, and she allows herself to get attached to these little girls. She finds herself needing them and loving them. But it's a real slow arc, a real slow evolution. It was interesting: Bill chose not to come in close; there were very few close-ups in the first half of the movie because he wanted Sylvie to be mysterious. But I had to do all the work.

CZ: Sylvie has this childlike quality, and a great sense of wonder.

CL: She loves nature; she's incredibly in touch with that and in touch with that childlike wonderment. Annie Dillard wrote this amazing book about nature called *Pilgrim at Tinker Creek**; it so reminded me of the way

---

*Annie Dillard, *Pilgrim at Tinker Creek* (New York: Harper's Magazine Press, 1974).

Sylvie must look at a pond. If you ever want to know about a pond, and the bugs, and the algae, read that book; it's looking at a pond with the most childlike wonderment, but also with a knowledge of what everything is. So Sylvie—who I think is really bright, and has that wonderment—looks at nature this way. I re-read the book, and there was something about Annie Dillard saying that she wanted to feel the curvature of the earth. Remember those long strides that Sylvie would take? That came out of Annie Dillard's book.

Some people—not too many—thought that Sylvie was a terrible influence on Ruthie, and that it was a tragic ending that Ruthie was going off with Sylvie. Did you think that?

CZ: No, I thought Sylvie was liberating her.

CL: Yeah, that's what I thought. But there were people who thought that Sylvie was so dangerous for this little girl, she should have been locked up! It was shocking when I heard this stuff because I'd thought of Sylvie as one of the most incredible people that I'd ever come across, and that she was liberating Ruthie from a life of rigid normalcy that would have killed her spirit.

CZ: Would you make up something about what happened in her marriage that made her husband leave her?

CL: Oh, yeah. Everything I created in the background supported this idea of abandonment being the key issue for Sylvie. I thought maybe Sylvie took a job, and her husband was away in World War II, and when he came back she had changed. She had become independent in a way that he couldn't handle. So there was a kind of feminist value issue going on. He left her, and it was a devastating blow. And she was incredibly close to her father, but he died in a train wreck, so he was gone. We improvised in rehearsal; Bill didn't know much about that, but we did it anyway, and I kind of taught the little girls about improvisation.

CZ: So, I gather you're an actor who likes to rehearse and likes to improvise?

CL: Love it. I love rehearsal. There are some actors who feel that the more they rehearse, the less spontaneous they are. For me, it's the opposite: The more I rehearse, the more spontaneous I can be, the more I can explore and discover and reject certain choices. Then on the day of shooting, I'm much more spontaneous because I've got all this stuff that has secured me, that has planted me on the earth, that has given me a real life. Then, I can forget about it and just play. Often I improvise on a scene that I don't understand in a deep way. If I just don't get it, I'll improvise with the other actor to try to figure out what I'm doing in the scene, what it is I want in the scene. Using your own words and the same circumstances as the scene, you often find out what you're going after.

CZ: Did you ever work with a director who didn't want to rehearse?

CL: That's horrifying to me. I think I've been really lucky—most directors I work with want to make me happy, and if they don't know much about rehearsal, they will rehearse because I want to. With Sidney Lumet on *Running on Empty* it was the most rehearsal I've ever had. He rehearses a film like a play; that was great.

CZ: How much did you relate to your character, Annie, in *Running on Empty?*

CL: In that film, I did a lot of research. Although I was in college during that time and I was not as radical as Annie, I was certainly an activist. So I understood a lot of that period of time, and what that meant. Again, I created a whole biography on her: why she fell for this guy, what was wrong with her marriage. Annie was a person who, at the start of the film, was pretty numb, had pretty much given up, and found her passion again by the end of the movie.

I could relate to her in that what I feel as a feminist often is as passionate. Taking a stand as a woman on certain issues—for abortion, say—I try to substitute those kind of things that I feel really strongly about, for Annie, in terms of protesting the war back then.

CZ: *Running on Empty* is a wonderful character study, and the ensemble work is really beautiful. I was wondering how Lumet talked with you, with the cast, about your various roles, how you felt about your son and your husband. I didn't think that you loved him at all.

CL: I think that the marriage had pretty much run out of gas—running on empty. The thing that united us, at this point, was our flight, our escape, our being underground, and the kids. But yeah, I think you're right; as I recall, we had all kind of decided that the marriage wasn't great. He was

Christine Lahti with River Phoenix and Jonas Abry in Running on Empty (1987), directed by Sidney Lumet. © Lorimar Film Entertainment Company. Museum of Modern Art Film Stills Archive.

older, he was the star radical, an Abbie Hoffman type of character on campus, and I had a more sheltered, wealthy background. He was so passionate and flamboyant and powerful. It was one of those relationships where he was my mentor and took me under his wing. And after 15 years underground it was like, "Please, enough already."

Annie's own potential was squelched because she was so young when she went underground, and became a mom early on, and was trying to do her best, raising kids in these circumstances. So her opportunity to be heroic, in a way, to do something that really mattered to somebody, was a chance that she grabbed. The opportunity to save her son—to release him—was not just about Annie or the kid; it was about her own need to do something, to realize her own potential. Why she married him probably had to do with her low self-esteem. Why do women glom on to these powerful, charismatic guys who probably aren't that good for them? Probably because of their own lack of self-worth.

CZ: He's also someone who's not like Daddy. I mean, he's a Jewish "red-diaper" baby!

CL: Very different from Daddy. So that was part of her own rebellion. The scene that everybody wants to talk about is the scene with my father. It's a wrenching scene, and it was written perfectly. Usually I find that we change a lot of dialogue in scenes, but that scene we didn't touch. We didn't change one word, which is highly unusual in film. We didn't rehearse it too much either; I remember Sidney didn't want to, and I didn't want to. By the time we did it, I knew so much about Annie, and it was such an emotionally painful scene that we didn't want to mess with it too much. Steven Hill was incredible. We all got the beat; we knew what we all wanted, we didn't have to improvise to find it.

We staged it a couple of times, and it was simple: two people in a restaurant. Sidney used two cameras that day, which was very helpful. It was so emotional that we didn't have to do it that many times—I think we did it 5 times. I knew that it was working when the entire crew was crying after the first take. We all looked around, Sidney and Steve and I, and these big burly guys from the union were wiping their eyes. It was really fun.

CZ: There's so many things in that film I really like.

CL: *Running on Empty* is one of my favorite films that I've done.

CZ: Have you noticed any similarities in the characters that you've chosen to play?

CL: Well, I think that Annie was kind of going through the motions of her life, and then she came into focus. It's something that's a recurring theme in my work; I find that even Sylvie was going through the motions. She was fine—certainly Annie's motions were much more anxious and troubled and fearful—but both were disengaged from their lives, from their spirits. Through the course of the film, they come into focus, they become in sync with their truest, most alive, open, and passionate selves, uncensored and unblocked.

I'm just realizing that is a pattern, because in the last film I did—*Leaving Normal*—I think that was also the case. Darly, who was really blocked, by the end of the movie found her truest voice again. She was going through the motions of her life, too, in a different way.

CZ: How do you find these characters in yourself? Do you believe that your life dovetails with your roles and that you are shown things about yourself by the roles that you choose?

CL: With every part, every part. The parts I choose often reflect some change that I'm going through in my own life, that I can identify with. I believe there are facets of almost everybody in us, that we're like prisms, and if you look deeply enough, or hard enough, you can find those people inside of you. I think that all these characters are in me. Sylvie I had to really do some looking for; Darly in *Leaving Normal* is closer to me in a way, but then Darly was the most covered up, the darkest character I've ever played. By darkness I mean "hidden," obscure dark secrets. Darly's not so sad; she's dark in that she's so mysterious and has this kind of self-loathing.

CZ: That performance was so different from anything you've done— it's so bold and brassy and loud and vulgar. It must have been really fun to do.

CL: It was so fun. I got to fly for that part, and I just loved it. She was outrageous, and again, Ed Zwick [the director] loves rehearsal. We did a lot of improvisation. There was one time, I remember, Meg [Tilly] and I were working on this scene where we're having a contest about who's done the worst things in our lives. We were doing it, and it wasn't costing enough. So Ed suggested this great improv where it's Meg and Christine revealing the worst things we've ever done to someone. We did this improv, and it was so personal. We both revealed this horrible stuff, and of course that is exactly what these two characters are doing. So we got to feel how much it cost to do that. It was really successful. It's dangerous stuff to play with, but it was successful because it allowed Meg and I to trust each other in a way that we hadn't. It allowed both of us to feel the kind of closeness these two characters finally do feel.

CZ: I like the script for *Leaving Normal*. I thought it was really good.

CL: Me too. I loved that script, and I loved the making of that movie; I loved everything about it except how it was released and how the critics compared it—very unfairly, I thought—to *Thelma and Louise*.

CZ: Well, it's about two women in a car.

CL: That's where it stops. Mostly male critics dismissed it as a second-rate *Thelma and Louise* [1991]. Had they reviewed it as a film on its own terms and didn't like it, that's fine. But to review it in comparison to this other thing—they were really apples and oranges. On the surface, yeah, there were a lot of similarities, but the journeys of these women were completely different. The focus of our movie was on the friendship. There was no action, and there was no violence.

But anyway, that part was really disappointing to me because I felt like *Thelma and Louise* was the beginning, opening some doors for other movies about women. And instead, it seemed like it closed doors, for some critics. *Thelma and Louise* was popular, it was received well critically and at the box office. That makes it all the better for us, because people will want to see movies about women. The studio will support it because, "Well, this movie made a lot of money, maybe this one . . ." Instead, it was the opposite: "Well, you women, you had your shot at a female buddy movie, and no more." So, basically, the studio dumped it.

CZ: That must be really upsetting.

CL: It was. I think it's some of my best work. It was a wonderful movie for me, and Meg, and such a departure for Ed Zwick, after *Glory* [1989]. It was a small movie that didn't have any action and violence and sex, so it had to be handled in a special way.

CZ: Have you ever worked with actors who you felt weren't doing their homework?

CL: Oh, yeah.

CZ: Does that piss you off?

CL: Yeah, it does. I've been lucky that I've worked with some great, great people, but there have been times where I've felt that people are making choices that were way off circumstances, and don't make any sense, because they want to be charming or sexy in a scene, or they want people to like them; they make completely weird choices that have nothing to do with the character. They're more personality-type actors than character actors, people who just use their own personalities.

CZ: A lot of actors have told me that directors are terrified of actors and don't want to deal with them.

CL: Well, I've only worked with two directors—who shall remain nameless—who were afraid of me. And that fear manifested itself in a kind of indifference, or a kind of condescension. But basically, I think, it was that they were afraid of the intimacy and openness with which I like to work. I demand a lot from a director; I bring a lot of stuff to the table, a lot of ideas. A lot of them suck, and a few of them are really good. The directors who are able to listen and able to say, "I don't know," are my kind of directors. The directors who have a quick yes or no response, I don't want to work with. It's the directors who are the most secure who are able to say "I don't know. You tell me. Let's explore. That sounds good, let's try that." The ones who are insecure will say, "Oh, no, no, that's not going to work. The way this has to be done is . . ." I don't want to work with them.

CZ: Has there ever been a part that you turned down because of a director?

CL: No, I don't think so. I've turned down films for political reasons, or violence. But directors, no. I've taken a couple of chances that I probably shouldn't have taken, in terms of directors, but usually it's the script that makes me take it. I have the audacity to think that I'm kind of director-proof, and for the most part that's been true. But in a couple of instances, I feel like I was not only not helped by a director, I was hindered. For the most part, I feel like I have my own way of working that works for me, and as long as a director doesn't get in the way too much, then I can do my stuff.

CZ: I want to ask you about stage versus film. How do you feel they're different, and how you tone down or bring it up?

CL: Truthfully, I don't make any adjustments between stage and film; they're the same exact thing for me. The only slight thing I might do, depending on the theater, is project a little bit more. That's it. I don't tone anything down, or tone anything up, or change my body. Some people say, "Well, what about for close-ups?" No! I don't change my face, I don't think about what my face is doing. My face is my face, and if I'm telling the truth, it's going to be alive, it's going to be honest. If I think about my face, then I'm not in the scene. I'm not in the scene if I'm thinking, "Well, I have to keep my face kind of calm and expressionless, because the camera's so close, and after a bit I should go [screech]!" If the look on my face is ugly, I don't care, it's not my concern.

Now, before the camera's rolling, I've learned to become aware of lighting and things like that, because it is a very visual medium, and I'm learning that it's an important thing. And makeup is important; how I look is important. But while the cameras are rolling, if I think for a moment about how I'm looking, I'm not there. As Bill Esper used to say, "A mirror is the worst enemy of an actor." Self-consciousness. I'm really just saying the old Jimmy Cagney thing: "Plant both feet on the ground, say your lines, and tell the truth." There's no difference between on stage and in front of the camera. I do like the slowness, the intimacy of film; I like not having to think about projecting my voice. But even in film I find that often the sound man will say, "Project, you gotta project," and I say, "But then I'll be on stage! Why do I have to project? Put a mike right in this leaf so I don't have to." But often you have to project anyway, because of outdoor noises, airplanes, or crickets, or something like that.

CZ: Have you done a lot of overdubbing?

CL: Not a lot, but enough to know that it's horrendous. I don't like it, but there's a few situations where I felt a performance was improved by dubbing.

CZ: How do you feel about fame?

CL: Well, I don't feel that I'm that famous, so it's not that big a problem. The amount of fame I have, frankly, is kind of nice. It's not too intrusive—it's not like every time I go to a restaurant, I'm stared at. Sometimes it makes me uncomfortable, and a lot of times it makes me feel good when people—not when they stare at me or intrude—but if they come up to me on the street or in a store and say, "I love your work," or, "I loved this movie"; that makes me feel good. It's not gotten to the point where I imagine it is for Julia Roberts, who is just inundated, who has no privacy. I have a lot of privacy, and I think if it ever got to the point where I was like a Tom Cruise, or something—I doubt that's ever going to happen to me—if I was that mainstream a success, it would be horrible. I don't know how those people deal with it. But the amount of fame I have in my life now is nice, it's fine.

An Interview with Richard Dreyfuss

Richard Dreyfuss. Courtesy of Richard Grant and Associates.

Richard Dreyfuss says in his interview, "Each person who becomes a film star speaks to something in people's hearts." Dreyfuss speaks to our culture on a basic level; his career is characterized by the structure that—according to literary theorists—underlies the master narratives of western civilization: the quest. Dreyfuss represents the yearning of the little guy for love, adventure, and personal heroism. He has, as well, an extraordinary approachability—he makes dreams accessible to the everyman.

As a film actor, Richard Dreyfuss has had two phases in his career. The first phase saw a precipitous rise to fame, exemplified by appearances in hugely successful films like *American Graffiti* (1972, George Lucas), *Jaws* (1975), and *Close Encounters of the Third Kind* (1976), both for Steven Spielberg. Dreyfuss became an emblem of the "New Hollywood," not only because of his association with directors Lucas and Spielberg, but also by virtue of qualities he shared with his filmmaking contemporaries— ambition, talent, and a brisk intelligence.

The change in Dreyfuss' career can best be examined by considering two films he did with Spielberg. In *Close Encounters*, Dreyfuss portrays Roy Neary—obsessively trying to articulate his otherworldly experience—with an aggressive, manic energy. Thirteen years later, as Joe, the doomed pilot in *Always* (1989), Dreyfuss achieves a simplicity and grace reminiscent of one of his favorite actors, Spencer Tracy (who starred, not coincidentally, in the film *A Guy Named Joe* [1943], of which *Always* is a remake). As Dreyfuss says of his more recent work, "I became more willing to trust myself, and to try other things, and to slow down." While the energy can still be formidable—witness *Once Around* (1991) and *Rosencrantz and Guildenstern Are Dead* (1991)—there is, in the second phase, a control and comfortability to Dreyfuss' work that was absent in his earlier incarnations. Dreyfuss' evolution as an actor mirrors the growing-up process of the baby boom generation; he has evolved from an immensely gifted, anxious, smart-alecky kid into a composed and contemplative adult.

Dreyfuss was born in Brooklyn, New York, in 1947. He moved to L.A. at 8, where he first began acting at the Westside Jewish Community Center (with Rose Jane Landau). Dreyfuss appeared in episodic television during the 1960s in shows such as *Judd for the Defense, The Big Valley, The Mod Squad,* and *The Bold Ones.* After bit parts in films like *Valley of the Dolls* and *The Graduate* (both 1967), Dreyfuss began his career in earnest with *American Graffiti* as the college-bound Curt Henderson. This was followed in the 1970s by *Dillinger* (1973), *The Apprenticeship of Duddy Kravitz* (1974), *Jaws, Close Encounters,* and *The Goodbye Girl,* for which Dreyfuss won the Academy Award for Best Actor in 1977. In the next decade, Dreyfuss was side-lined by personal crises but made a triumphant return after several years' hiatus in *Down and Out in Beverly Hills* (1986). He subsequently appeared in *Tin Men* (1987), *Nuts* (1987), *Stakeout* (1987), *Moon over Parador* (1988), *Let It Ride* (1989), *What about Bob?* (1991), *Lost in Yonkers* (1993), and *A Silent Fall* (1994).

During the two decades in which Dreyfuss has achieved fame as a film actor, he has continued to perform on stage in New York and in regional theaters, acting in works by Shaw, Shakespeare, Strindberg, *et al.* He has also appeared in contemporary dramas such as *Whose Life is it Anyway?* (1979, Williamstown Theater Festival, which he also filmed in 1981), *A Day in the Death of Joe Egg* (1981) and *Requiem for a Heavyweight* (1983, both at the Long Wharf Theater, Connecticut), and *Incident at Vichy*

(1985, Mark Taper Forum, Los Angeles). Dreyfuss began a parallel career as a producer with *The Big Fix* in 1978 (in which he also starred) and continues to produce work through his production company, Dreyfuss-James.

I spoke with Richard Dreyfuss in New York in June of 1992, during the run of *Death and the Maiden,* a play by Ariel Dorfman dealing with the consequences of political imprisonment. He co-starred with Gene Hackman and Glenn Close in the play's Broadway premiere, which was directed by Mike Nichols.

CZ: What first attracted you to acting?

RD: I don't really know. I wanted to be an actor when I was a tiny little child. I just knew I wanted to do it, and I did it. I started when I was 9. I can't remember the why of this. It's the one question I've never been able to answer. There's a lot about acting that I've come to know and to love, but if you're asking me my original impulse, I couldn't answer.

CZ: You never had formal training, is that correct?

RD: Yeah. I actually did apply, and was accepted, to both Yale and the London Academy of Music and Dramatic Arts, but the circumstances of the draft in the late 60s were such that I didn't go. And I didn't take it seriously enough; it's one of the few regrets I have in my life. Because I think that, especially with the ambitions I had to be a certain kind of actor, it would have held me in good stead.

CZ: Have you ever been coached by anyone?

RD: Oh yes. When I was 12 years old, I found out that there was a class in Beverly Hills in acting and improvisational techniques. The teacher was a woman by the name of Rose Jane Landau; she was a very formative influence in my life. It was a powerful thing to take, and I recommend it to all young actors. Because improvisational techniques not only teach you something about acting, they teach you about writing and directing. If you're really improvising smartly, you've got to know when to get on, when to get off, and what to say. It was very important in allowing me to become the actor I am now.

CZ: Did you have an interest in films when you were growing up?

RD: One of the things that is different between the way I grew up and the way people younger than me grew up—which I don't think has been acknowledged yet—is that when I grew up I could see every single American movie ever made between 1929 and 1960 on American television all the time, seven days a week. Now you see one Warner Brothers gangster movie, for instance, on *Nick at Nite,* once. That was my training, other than Rose Jane, watching all these old films at 3:00 in the morning, over and over again. I deeply regret that we've become whoever it is we've become, that we can't make movies like this any more.

CZ: You've done a lot of stage work as well as film. What do you see as the major differences?

RD: In the theater you get a sense of the whole; in film acting, you don't. When you're working on a movie you're working in someone else's milieu, and you work out of sequence, and you work for thirty-second bites. I don't feel a sense of completion [in film], in the sense of carrying a character from beginning to end. When you're working on a stage, you have a concentrated rehearsal of some four weeks, perhaps more, and then you perform every night, from A to Z. So that's one major distinction between the two. The other is that the feedback you get in film is personal; it's intimate. You work with actors in a given scene, and everyone watching you is working; they're not watching you, they're working. Your feedback is from the other actors and from yourself. In theater, you're not only getting feedback from the actors, but you're getting feedback from an audience.

CZ: Do you think the way the house feels each night influences what you're doing on stage?

RD: It doesn't necessarily, but it can. And sometimes you can affect them. In other words, you can start a performance at a certain energy level and bring the whole house up. You can start at another, lower, energy level and the house stays the same, or sometimes their enthusiasm is so high that they goad you on. In film, in a sense, it's kind of self-generated.

CZ: What's the difference between theater and film in terms of movement and voice?

RD: Surely you have to carry the voice more strongly on stage, and you're in constant vision. But I don't really notice a difference. You work in a smaller way on film; the camera is right there, so that your eyes tell a lot of the story. In theater, if you let your eyes tell the story, then 6 people are going to know what the story is.

CZ: Do you feel it's a big adjustment for you to make, or is it very automatic?

RD: I was taking tennis lessons, years ago, and I said, "I also like to play racquetball, and I was told that the wrist movement was different; is this going to screw me up?" The coach said, "All you have to do is remember what court you're on." That's all, you just remember what court you're on.

CZ: Did you always have ambitions to become a film actor?

RD: The idea that I was actually going to make it as a star in America was a laughable idea to everyone but me; I thought it was a given. Everyone else said, "What, are you nuts?" But I knew it was going to happen.

CZ: When you watch your earliest performances, what do you see? And how do you view your evolution since then?

RD: It's hard for me to say. Some of my early work I think is pretty hideous. I did a lot of television, and I look at the television work now, when it comes on, by accident, and it's amazing to me that I ever got another job. What also amazes me is how much I thought I was a great actor at that moment.

I don't really have a sense of my own "arc," as it were. There are individual performances that I like, and I like the later performances more than the earlier ones. I think I slowed down some and was willing to not hurry. I didn't need to be so energetic.

In the middle 80s, I became more willing to trust myself and to try other things, and slow down. I don't think I could have performed *Tin Men* [1987] in 1975 in the same way that I did later on, or *Stakeout* [1987], or *Let It Ride* [1989]. I think in that way my work has improved. I'm not an actor who works well alone; I like to have a strong director, and I like to have rehearsal, and I like to have someone who will tell me, guide me, and say, "This is right, this is wrong." Most often that doesn't happen.

CZ: Why not?

RD: Because directors no longer know anything about acting.

CZ: Why do you think that's happened?

RD: Oh, I don't know why. I think directing in movies is such a complicated, demanding position. He or she has to have a certain grasp of so many different things. They will say to an actor: "You know what you're doing? Good, because I've got to do all these other things."

I was speaking to Steven Spielberg one day—and other directors have mirrored this thought—I said to him, "What's your favorite part of directing?" And he immediately said, "My favorite part of directing is editing. Number one. My second is writing, my third is post-production, my fourth is casting and pre-production, and my last, the one I have to endure, is shooting." I said, "Why?" and he said, "Every other part of it I can control. When I write, it's my fantasy, when I'm editing, it's my project," and so on, "but when I shoot, I've got to hand it over to other people, and it goes away, and it becomes something else." I said, "Steven, never forget that the only time I'm around is when we're shooting."

There are directors, and fine directors, like Barry Levinson and George Lucas, who basically will say that their job with actors is done when they've cast the movie, which is unfortunate. Where a stage director creates a moment of timing, for instance, a film director will do that in editing. Oftentimes, I think my work would be improved if a director said something simple like, "You're talking too fast," or "You're moving too slow," or whatever. And for the most part, they don't.

CZ: Do you think it's true that directors are afraid of actors?

RD: Directors are inadequate about actors. There's a lesson to be learned, it's called "Actors." Directors should take a class not only in acting, but in actors, because the fears, anxieties, thoughts, wishes, or opinions that an actor has are pretty important to how the character is coming out. And the director should know how to do that. An actor, of course, should know also not to inflict his own bullshit on directors. That interaction can be improved; it's not there yet, not at all.

CZ: Who do you think directs actors well?

RD: I don't know. I have an idea in my mind of what a good director-actor relationship is. When Herb Ross and I did *The Goodbye Girl* [1977], that was the relationship I always thought actors and directors would have. He listened, he was funny, he was creative, he was intrusive.

He said, "Get in here and do this and that." And we went back and forth, and it was very relaxed and very happy, and he spoiled the shit out of me, he really did. I thought all directors were going to be like that.

CZ: What happens once you get a script in your hand?

RD: My "technique," as they sometimes say, is very mysterious to me. It's instinctual, it's not thought out. I'll read a script once, and I'll get a picture of the character in my mind, and then I'll try to be that picture. That's basically it. I normally don't do a lot of formal research. In other words, if I'm going to play a doctor, I don't feel it's necessary for me to go and spend two days with a doctor, although I might do it, just because it would be fun. It may be a failing of mine, but I didn't go and sell aluminum siding to play *Tin Men*. Most of it is in my imagination, and I try to achieve my imagination.

CZ: As the character Sam Sharp in *Once Around* [1991], you have a lot of complicated relationships with the family. Would you assess what your relationship is like with each character, or would that also be very instinctual?

RD: I felt I knew him. The story of this movie is real simple: A girl falls in love with a guy who her family thinks is an egregious schmuck, and by the time they find out that he's more than an egregious schmuck, he drops dead. That's the story, and that's what he was. If a person is loudmouthed, overbearing, whatever, it means he's blind. He doesn't see things, he sees what he wants to see. That's Sam; I knew that. It wasn't more intellectual than that.

CZ: What kind of rehearsals did you have for that film?

RD: We had some pretty good rehearsals for that one; we were on the set in North Carolina. We didn't rehearse everything; we rehearsed some complicated scenes. Holly [Hunter] likes to rehearse; she's an actor. Most directors, like Barry [Levinson] or Lasse [Hjalstrom], don't feel it's necessary to go through more than a few minutes of blocking: "You got the blocking down? Great!" Well, wait a minute . . .

CZ: Do you ever demand more?

RD: Oh, yeah, sure. As a matter of fact, I've made sure of that; there were films where I said, "I'm demanding a week of rehearsal." But there are also directors who'll say, "Do it by yourself; I ain't gonna be there."

There are also films that you don't need to rehearse; it's not like it's brain surgery.

Rehearsal, to a great extent, is used to create relaxation. You try to do it enough times so that you can relax and let something happen. You do it a hundred times, or fifty times; the more you do it, the better you're going to get at it. When you don't have rehearsal time, and you're doing it when the money clock is on, forget it. Your first instinct is going to be what's on film.

CZ: Was there ever any role where you said, "I can't get this, I really want someone to help me?"

RD: A lot. Especially once I became a celebrity—when no one helps you, they just think that you know how to do everything, or that whatever you do is OK. A lot of thoughtlessness goes into making films and theater, as opposed to thoughtfulness. There have often been times when I've said, "I'm at sea, here, I don't know what the hell I'm doing. I need some help."

CZ: There was a moment in *Always* [1989] that was particularly moving. It's when you watch Rick Rossovich kissing your former girlfriend, Holly Hunter, and you can't stand seeing it; you're close to tears. What kind of emotional preparation did you do for that? Do you get to that emotion by using the memory of a feeling or by using the given circumstance?

RD: It's mostly circumstance. But you're an idiot if you don't try to remember when it really happened to you so that you can recall that memory, that feeling. For the most part, I'm not an instinctual person, except when it comes to this, where I rely on my instincts more than thinking it through.

CZ: Do you look at dailies?

RD: It depends on the need. For instance, when I did *Stakeout,* I watched dailies every day, because I wanted to see what I was doing in relationship to the girl, and myself, and I'd never done a part like that. Sometimes I'll watch dailies, or sometimes I'll watch a particular scene: "Did I do that right?" I neither stay away from dailies, nor am I attached to them.

CZ: In *Rosencrantz and Guildenstern* [1990], the use of language is non-naturalistic, and that makes it pretty different from your other roles. How did you deal with that kind of speech?

Richard Dreyfuss with Holly Hunter and Brad Johnson in *Always* (1989), directed by Steven Spielberg. Copyright © by Universal City Studios, Inc. Courtesy of MCA Publishing Rights, a Division of MCA Inc. Museum of Modern Art Film Stills Archive.

RD: It was fun to deal with it; it's like Shakespeare. And it was fun to play another person. In my mind, I was simply playing Donald Wolfit, and I love that. There have been times when I played Spencer Tracy, and no one knew it, or I played Jimmy Cagney, and no one knew it; that time, I was playing Donald Wolfit. That's something I'd like to do again.

CZ: Why?

RD: Because I liked doing it, and I'd like to do it better.

CZ: Do you usually feel that way?

RD: No, I don't. I'd like to play some of the character's attributes again. When I see *Rosencrantz,* I'm happy with this thing, but I could do better. I could do it better today; I could have done it better the Tuesday after. But it was a lot of fun.

CZ: What performances have been especially meaningful to you? And what do you think makes a great film actor?

RD: When I was growing up, there was a large group of actors that I loved. Tracy, Laughton, Brando, Stewart, Cagney, Grant, Fonda, all of them, the panoply of American and British actors. I used to watch all their films all of the time. I couldn't tell you how many times I have seen *Captain Blood* [1935], a hundred, at least. Each one of these actors offered me something different, something that I loved; that's why they were movie stars. Stardom is a love affair. It's a friendship and a love affair between the audience and the performer, and you love someone for a reason. There was no one more heroically graceful than Errol Flynn, never. Never was, never will be anyone who could make you believe in that myth as much as he could. He was beautiful and substantive in his beauty, and a far better actor than he or his contemporaries ever knew. Laughton was someone I listened to. I could listen to his voice and what he did with prose for hours. There was something unique about him; he could find a kind of rhythm in prose that no other actor has ever found as far as I know.

There's no one thing that makes a great film actor, because it is a mystery. There are great actors who aren't great film actors or great movie stars. There are great movie stars who are clearly not very good actors, yet somehow they are. I think there's a clear difference between celluloid and video and the stage. Celluloid helps to create a mysterious feeling, a kind of semi-religious experience that you can't articulate. Why is John Wayne great? And he is great. He was magnificent, and he was necessary. But was he a good actor? I don't know any more what that means. I used to say he wasn't, now I say he was. I think that *True Grit* [1969], *She Wore a Yellow Ribbon* [1949], and other performances of his are magnificent.

It's different in each person. Each person who becomes a film star speaks to something in people's hearts. Whether it's Kevin Costner, or Robert De Niro, or Jimmy Cagney, people are fulfilled by something, they recognize something, they want to see it again. Not everyone can do it; a person can look exactly like Jimmy Cagney and not have it. A person can act exactly like Kevin, and not be Kevin. It's a chemical thing that is mysterious. It's not a measurable thing—this person's prose is better than that person's prose, or this person photographs better than that person. It has nothing to do with that; it has to do with a love affair. Why does a man fall in love with whomever he falls in love with? Why does a man leave a beautiful woman for an unattractive one? Why does an attractive woman fall in love with a nerdy little geek? Because it's mysterious, and it should be. Because there's something in his or her heart that is being fulfilled.

Sometimes it's easier to equate; John Wayne fulfilled a massive American mythology. We needed it, and we still need it.

CZ: What do you think you personify?

RD: I don't know. I'm kind of in the eye of the hurricane; there's all this turbulence around me, and I'm in the eye of it. I have been told that I represent something about, like, the 60s, and going to college, and taking drugs, and the urban; that's who I am, somehow. I don't really know the answer to this question. I can't put on a mask and sit in an audience and listen to how people are responding to me; I just do the work. So far, no one has ever done a critique of the work of Richard Dreyfuss that I've ever read. One day, that might very well be done, and I'll learn something about myself.

CZ: Do you think film acting is historically bound?

RD: It can be, but it's not necessary that it be. I mean, why was Jimmy Cagney popular in Iowa and not only on the Lower East Side of New York? Because there was something about Jimmy Cagney that you couldn't take your eyes off. That's what charisma is, it can't be defined. If you can define it, it ain't charismatic. Why has James Dean remained popular? It's a mystery to me, I'll tell you that, but certainly not to three generations of people.

CZ: What about Brando?

RD: The gods came together on Marlon Brando. The gods came together and agreed to give this guy everything, because he not only had the most extraordinary intellectualized acting talent that I've ever run across, he had the courage to fulfill it, and he had the nobility of a lion and the grace of a panther; he had it all. Had he been an English actor, they would have named buildings after this guy. As it was, everything he achieved, he achieved against the opposition of a critical community that was incredibly ignorant, and so they turned him into a clown.

CZ: Don't you think he had a hand in that?

RD: In becoming a clown? Of course he did. We live in a culture that does not support—in the sense of intangible support—the art form that he was supreme in. What they said about him in *Julius Caesar* [1953], Hitler said about Poland. And when you look at it now, you see the most remarkable Shakespearean performance of that generation, and all the English actors knew it. Robert Shaw said it was an uncanny experience to have all these young English actors watching this American play Antony the way they'd always dreamed that it could be played. His imagination, his courage, his talent, his natural physical beauty, and his simple charisma—it's not so simple. You couldn't get any better than Marlon Brando. There was a period of 10 years where everything he did was astonishingly good and courageous. Laurence Olivier, on the other hand, who is a great actor, is a great actor because of his courage, not because of his talent.

CZ: Can you talk more about that? I remember a remark by Peter Hall about the difference between Ralph Richardson and Laurence Olivier. He said that Richardson was an actor of genius and Olivier was a performer of genius. I thought that was an interesting distinction.

RD: I think that Laurence Olivier was the most courageous actor I've ever seen. And he was industrious, and industry is rare. I don't think his talent was great. A lot of his performances are kind of silly, but wow, did he eat them, and did he work, on a minute level, to make every moment of them complete. Some of his performances are magnificent, but he's known because he wasn't afraid.

Brando let it all go. Look at the culture that these two guys lived in. In one culture, Olivier was supported, propped up in his pursuit of his career and his ambitions. In Brando's, he was left on his own. Everyone in America is left on their own.

CZ: There was a comment made not only by Brando but also by Mickey Rourke in a recent interview that acting is "women's work." Do you think that there are masculine and feminine vectors in emotion? Do you think that there are emotional constraints placed on you because of your gender?

RD: Of course; if you're going to show emotion, that's considered feminine. In England, there's less of that, because America is a kind of pioneer, frontier, rough-and-ready society.

But I think that acting can be described as inherently silly. One of the things that actors are always fighting against is the fact that they do in public what other people only do in private. There's something always embarrassing about acting, not only to actors, but to the audience. The essence of acting can be considered puerile: You are standing in front of people who are pretending they're not there, you are pretending that you are someone else, wearing clothes that aren't yours and saying lines that you're not thinking; I mean it's silly. And yet it's not. That's why Spencer Tracy, who I think is a fabulous film actor, also denigrated film acting and acting in general. I don't think acting is anything to be denigrated; to quote, it's not "women's work"; it's man/woman's work, and you find your woman in you, and you find your man in you, and you do your job. I try not to sound like Tracy; Tracy meant a lot to me, and when I read the things that Tracy said, which were later said by Brando and Mickey Rourke, I'm so disappointed. If I feel that coming out of me, I stop, because I don't want to mislead myself or anyone else. I try not to lay at the feet of acting what other disappointments or frustrations I may have.

CZ: You've said in an interview that "Nobody knows how to watch acting." Can you address that?

RD: Because we don't consider acting a serious art form. But it is absolutely necessary, and without acting, people would simply drop dead on the streets. But people categorize actors, and therefore they don't have to critique them. When most people write about the work of Cagney, or Tracy, or whoever, they're just telling gossipy stories about their careers. They don't really watch what they do. Most times, people when they watch movies are so assaulted by other influences—music, and editing, and directing, and camera angle, and all that—that you don't know what you're getting from acting and what you're getting from the rest of it. That's OK, there's nothing wrong with that. But that's why people find it difficult to watch acting, or to discern the difference between what the actor is actually doing, and what they're receiving from the whole.

It's funny; when I was a young man and I used to sit around and bullshit about acting all night long, I had all these opinions about it; I don't have very many opinions about this any more. Acting is a fact as an art, and it will always be a fact. And if people have good or bad attitudes about it, it doesn't really matter. Because sooner or later, someone's going to write something, put it on film or on stage, and hire actors. You've got to do that, or else you die, you wither away. Did you ever read a book called *Magic and the Myth of the Movies*[*]?

---

[*]Parker Tyler, *Magic and the Myth of the Movies* (New York: Simon and Schuster, 1970).

CZ: By Parker Tyler?

RD: Yeah. That is a wonderful book. It's the only book I've read that ever had the courage to say, "You want to know what going to a movie is all about? It's a religious experience, surrender to it, it's great." The first time you say that, people react, and then you carry them through it, and they understand.

Someone who really minimized the power of acting, the most damaging influence to the American theatrical culture—and culture even in a larger sense—was Lee Strasberg. Because Lee Strasberg's personality was so powerful that he influenced not only a generation of actors, and succeeding generations, but succeeding generations of writers and directors. We are just coming out of a time, a good 40 years, where Americans were taught that only a small portion of life was to be celebrated on stage, or in movies. There's an old story about what you had to do in order to be able to get into Shakespeare's Globe Theater—you had to be an actor, a dancer, a mime, a juggler, a singer, and you had to play kings and peasants, princes and angels. None of this is demanded of us. After World War II, Lee Strasberg basically said, "No, you have to play just this narrow spectrum," and Stella Adler said, "No, it's not, it's bigger than that," and she was exiled. All of my generation suffer from this; I suffer from it. Bobby De Niro, who, in my opinion, is the finest actor of my generation and who could do almost anything, would be that much better had we not all been so terribly influenced by the restrictions put on us by Strasberg.

CZ: You mean the concentration on emotional anguish, that kind of thing?

RD: The concentration on the lower middle class and on emotional truth, as opposed to style and the rigors of discipline. I yearn, as a lazy person, for the rigor of discipline in my training, which I never had. In America they say, "Go out, sink or swim!" You can go to Carnegie or Yale, or you can get it on your own, but the culture itself doesn't demand the rigor of you. And that is, to a great extent, the pervasive influence of Strasberg. He didn't do this maliciously, but he did it, and we are suffering from it.

CZ: And yet there's someone like Kazan, who had largely the same way of thinking about acting as Strasberg and who is certainly responsible for some of the greatest film performances. For me, he's a great actor's director.

RD: Oh, and there are great actors from The Studio! But how much better would they have been, and what other movies would Kazan have made, had there been an acknowledgement that physical grace and style was demanded of us. I think that Kazan was a brilliant director and Strasberg was a great teacher, but Strasberg should have taught us about other things. Do you find that actors mostly like what they're doing?

CZ: Oh yes, absolutely.

RD: See, I find most actors say negative things. I would have liked to have known Tracy and asked him, "Do you really not enjoy this? Come on, Spencer." When I was younger, I had no friends who weren't actors. We used to sit around and talk about it, and one day, a girl that I knew said to me that she wished that another muse had chosen her. And I said, "You don't understand what acting is. Every art form exists for a reason. Every art form does something to the human soul in a different way—dance, music, whatever it is. And acting is the only art form that does that [*snaps fingers*]." Music can affect you powerfully, and prose, and art, but no art form can make you burst into tears, or make you laugh by the immediate reflection of human behavior like acting can. And that's the nobility of acting, and that's why acting is feared, and that's why people are cautious about actors, and scared of them, and why they also want to elect them for president.

CZ: To me that's why actors should be valued so much, because they're willing to go—as an acting coach said—into the depths of their soul, and come out again, and show people things about themselves.

RD: That's right. What actors can do without lecturing is show that in each of us there is Hitler and Jesus, and if you are a truly gifted actor, you can find that in you, and bring it out, and say, "See, we share this." For instance, a guy like Henry Fonda couldn't find Hitler in him; he was so lovable. There was this movie that he did once where he shot the whole family, and then ended up shooting this 9-year-old girl in the head, and you still didn't want to dislike him. One of the great things about certain actors is their ability to find that. De Niro can do that, he can be loved and hated. To find that is like going to church, except you don't have to stand and listen to the minister just say it to you. You can experience it, look at it, and say, "That's what I do. That's what I wish I could do. That's what I'm afraid of doing."

CZ: You've been acting in films for over 25 years. What's been the biggest surpise in your career?

RD: Life surprises you in a lot of ways. One of them is that I have this friend, this little nuclear pellet right here [*touches chest*], which engined my acting, my career, my ambition, my enthusiasm. Then one day, I realized that it had turned off, and I was filled with a kind of loneliness or despair about that, because it was so constant and had been with me my entire life. I didn't know what to do; I was at sixes and sevens. I realize I just have to adjust to what I am, and who I am now. In many ways, it'll make me a better actor in that I think *Tin Man* is a very good performance, and *Tin Man* is a performance that lacked that nuclear pellet; it was done in the absence of that. So was *Let It Ride*, so was *Stakeout*.

CZ: But you've gained a lot.

RD: At life, in the absence of that. But at the same time, there is an intimate relationship between me and it that isn't there any more. It's like if a marriage changes from love to friendship, or a relationship changes. You have to make that adjustment, that's what the last few years have been about. I'm now 44 years old, I have 3 children, and their welfare is infinitely more important to me than my acting is. My acting career is still important, but before, I was a single person who had nothing but this pursuit to interest him, and that's what I did, and that's what I loved. One day you wake up and you find there are all these other things you love now, and all these other interests.

The compulsion I worked under as a kid no longer exists, and I think my work will suffer from it, because I don't have the interest that I had. I have interest and affection, but I don't have the lust that I had.

John Lithgow. Courtesy of Wolf, Kasteller Public Relations.

An Interview with John Lithgow

John Lithgow differs from other actors interviewed for *Figures of Light* in that he received his primary actor training in London, England, at the London Academy of Music and Dramatic Arts. Lithgow's heroes are the "three sirs"—John Gielgud, Laurence Olivier, and above all, Alec Guinness. He comes, therefore, from the dominant British tradition, in which more externalized manifestations of emotion, or theatricalized behavior, are valorized, rather than the more internalized, anguished, poetic naturalism that prevails among American actors. The British are often admired for a combination of theatrical imagination and technical brilliance instead of for performances that plumb the depths of internal states; this probably accounts for the reason Lithgow never mentions the "truth" in his interview. The performances that exemplify Lithgow's film career are outsized and extravagant—as he says, "There are very few roles that I've done quietly and modestly." What Lithgow brings to these roles—which include a long list of psychotic villains in films such as *Blow Out* (1981),

Buckaroo Banzai (1984), *Ricochet* (1991), and *Cliffhanger* (1993)—are the bold strokes of caricature, transformed by Lithgow's skill, dexterity, and zest, into thoroughly original and vivid creations. His trademark as an actor is his use of the "bigness" of theater performance in the medium of film, a refusal to scale down his work that is never less than exciting, and always fun. Lithgow's performances are sometimes wild—as in "Nightmare at 20,000 Feet," an episode of *Twilight Zone–The Movie* (1983), where he plays the terrified—and sometimes hyper-real—plane passenger, and in his portrayal of the transsexual Roberta Muldoon in *The World According to Garp* (1982, for which he received his first Academy Award nomination as Best Supporting Actor). That being said, Lithgow is also capable of delicate understatement, as displayed in his performance of Sam, Debra Winger's lover in *Terms of Endearment* (1983), which won him a second Academy Award nomination.

Lithgow's roots in the theater go deep. His father was founder of the Antioch Shakespeare Festival, where the actor first performed as Mustardseed in *A Midsummer Night's Dream* in 1953. Lithgow accumulated a long list of theater credits in summer stock and regional theater even before attending Harvard University, where he graduated *magna cum laude* in 1967. Lithgow was awarded a Fulbright Study Grant to attend the London Academy, where he studied for 2 years. While in England, he acted and assistant directed for the Royal Shakespeare Company. Upon his return to the United States, Lithgow began a diverse, busy career in the theater, appearing both in regional companies and on Broadway. Some of his principal roles have been in *The Changing Room* (1973, for which he was awarded both the Antoinette Perry and Drama Desk Award for Best Supporting Actor), *The Comedians* (1976), *Anna Christie* (1977), *Once in a Lifetime* (1978), *Spokesong* (1979), *Bedroom Farce* (1979), *Division Street* (1980), *Beyond Therapy* (1982), *Requiem for a Heavyweight* (1984, winning a second Drama Desk Award), *M. Butterfly* (1988), and *Who's Afraid of Virginia Woolf?* (1990, for which Lithgow won the L.A. Drama Critics Award for Best Actor). The actor also wrote, directed, and starred in a one-man show based on the writings of George S. Kaufman called *Kaufman at Large,* which was produced on Broadway in 1981.

Lithgow's first film appearance was in 1972 in *Dealing,* directed by Paul Williams. He next played his first villanous role in *Obsession* (1976), directed by Brian de Palma, with whom he would make two subsequent films, *Blow-Out* (1981) and *Raising Cain* (1992). In addition to the films listed above, Lithgow has been in *All That Jazz* (1979), *Rich Kids* (1979), *Footloose* (1984), *2010* (1984), *The Manhattan Project* (1986), *Harry and the Hendersons* (1987), *Out Cold* (1989), *Memphis Belle* (1990), *The Boys* (1991), *At Play in The Fields of the Lord* (1991), *A Silent Fall* (1994), and *A Good Man in Africa* (1994). Lithgow has appeared in numerous made-for-television movies, including *The Day After* (1983), *The Glitter Dome* (1984), *The Resting Place* (1986), *When the Lions Roar* (as F.D.R.), and as twins in *My Brother's Keeper* (1995). The actor won an Emmy Award in 1989 for his performance in an episode of *Amazing Stories.*

I spoke with John Lithgow by phone at his Los Angeles home in May 1994.

CZ: When did you first know that you wanted to be an actor? You seem to have started acting at a very young age.

JL: Well, I'll give you my little capsule biography, because it sort of answers that question. I grew up in a theater family—my Dad began as an academic, although he always acted and directed. In Yellow Springs, Ohio, when he was teaching at Antioch, he devised a summer Shakespeare festival back in 1951, which became the model for his own work for the next 30 years. He was a producer of regional theater repertory. So I grew up with it; I was only 6 years old the first summer of this festival.

CZ: Did you grow up in Yellow Springs?

JL: Yeah. Until I was about 10, and then we started a very gypsy-like life, because my father went from place to place, always doing theater work. So I grew up very much in the theater, did a lot of acting for the fun of it as an extra or a bit-part player in my Dad's Shakespeare festivals, and did not really intend to be an actor. In a way, being that close to it, I wanted to avoid it. I was much more interested in painting—that was always the thing. If anybody ever asked me, "What are you going to be when you grow up?" I would say, "An artist."

CZ: Do you still do artwork?

JL: Well, I do it, but it's purely a hobby now, and it's not even a hobby I have much time for. It's one of many regrets.

By the time I graduated high school, I was still very serious about art, studying at the Art Student's League on Saturday mornings, commuting from Princeton, New Jersey, where we had ended up, and working very seriously in charcoal and watercolor, and doing printmaking pretty seriously. Then I went off to Harvard. If anybody asks me, "Why did you go to Harvard if you wanted to be an artist?" I always say, "Because I got in." If Harvard beckons, you follow. It seemed like a very exciting place to go; I was very pleased to have gotten in, and also they had this brand new and beautiful visual arts center [The Carpenter Center], so I thought, "Oh, good, I'll be able to do art."

CZ: What year did you start at Harvard?

JL: I arrived in 1963. Once at Harvard, first of all I discovered that there wasn't much of a program for painting, nor for any of the other creative arts, academically, at Harvard. Naïvely, I didn't really bother to discover that before I went.

CZ: There was no theater program at Harvard, right? What did you study?

JL: English history and literature. But the extracurricular theater was so vibrant and exciting, and I fell into it so quickly and was so good at it, that I was immediately hailed as the big new actor on campus. Even as a freshman, I got the lead in one of the main stage shows. I would say that by the end of my sophomore year, I had decided pretty much to be an actor. By that time I had done seven or eight different roles. I had even started directing at Harvard. So I just felt like I was destined to be a man of the theater. I always thought of it as repertory theater, very much in my father's mold.

CZ: I gather that your parents were supportive of your decision.

JL: They were worried. I find myself, right now, exactly where my parents were at when I was graduating from Harvard. My son is going to be an actor, and I'm quite nervous about it because I know what's involved. The good news is he knows too!

CZ: You then went to London to study; why did you want to be in England?

JL: I wanted to go overseas. I got a Fulbright in my senior year to go to London and study acting in earnest at the London Academy of Music and Dramatic Arts. Back in those days, and I think still, the Fulbright Committee places 2 acting students at LAMDA in their one-year program.

I was infatuated with British theater, and that was a very good time for it. Peter Brook and Peter Hall and Trevor Nunn were all at the height of their powers, doing great things, and there were a lot of great actors at work, and, as I say, I had grown up very much a repertory and Shakespearean actor. So I was very drawn to England.

CZ: Can you describe what the training was like at LAMDA?

JL: It was very, very rigorous and academic. We arrived at 9 in the morning, and we were there until 5 or 6 every day. The morning was devoted to various technical aspects of acting: voice, diction, movement, historic dance, fight arranging, tumbling, all sorts of things, a very detailed schedule. The afternoons were devoted to rehearsals for two-month-long projects. Over the course of the year, we did about four or five plays.

CZ: It says in your credits that you acted with the Royal Shakespeare Company.

JL: That's a mistake in so many bios—I didn't really act with the RSC. I extended my Fulbright a second year and worked as an assistant director and basically a kind of production assistant and intern at the RSC.

CZ: That must have been exciting.

JL: It was great. I was also trying to stay out of the U.S. Army by prolonging my graduate studies abroad. That was certainly an element.

CZ: It's time for the classic question—do you see a big difference between British and American actors?

JL: Yes, I think there is a difference. It's a very complicated relationship between the British actor and the American actor. There's a kind of mutual envy, curiously enough, and a mutual inferiority complex. American actors tend to think the Brits are the great stage actors, and the Brits tend to think the Americans are the ones who act truly from the guts. A lot of them don't like to feel that way, but they do. I myself am such a hybrid, because of having grown up in the tiny little American repertory theater system and having studied in England. I really can move back and forth between two different schools.

CZ: How would you characterize those two schools? You have British training—do you see a difference between yourself and people who trained at The Actors Studio, and The Neighborhood Playhouse, and places like that?

JL: I do think there's a difference. It's very much a difference in approach, and there's nothing preventing us from acting very well together. At its most rudimentary, it's the difference between acting from the outside in and acting from the inside out, the outside in being the British system. I do it both ways: I act from the inside and the outside simultaneously, my own hybrid. Also, every actor has to act according to the project and the material and the director. Every job is so different and the demands made on you are so different, you have to be able to work according to many people's methods.

CZ: Do you ever find it a problem for you to get in sync with people who have different training than you?

JL: Sometimes, but quite rarely. I've acted with a few actors who take acting far more seriously, if not grimly, than I do. I mean, I take it plenty seriously, but I'm also very playful about acting.

CZ: How does it manifest itself when people take it grimly?

JL: Just a different rhythm of working, a different tone. You really run up against tough problems with actors who are very insecure and think that they have to totally be whatever they need to be that day. As a result, you can't enter their world, they close you out, they exclude you.

CZ: That sounds like the standard complaint about actors from The Actors Studio, that they can be self-centered.

JL: Yeah. Certainly it works great for some people, but . . . I would say it's only been a problem with me maybe twice in a hundred jobs. All actors are insecure, and insecurity manifests itself in many ways.

CZ: Let's move on to your career in films. How did you get your first part? Was it in *Dealing* [*The Berkeley-to-Boston Forty-Brick Lost-Bag Blues,* 1972]?

JL: Yes, exactly. It was about dope-dealing at Harvard. Somebody recommended me to Paul Williams, who said "Oh yeah, John Lithgow, he used to act at the Loeb [Theater Center at Harvard]," so I got myself a great big movie part in a Warner Brothers picture. I never thought I would be in movies, and here I was acting in a movie.

CZ: What was the transition to film like for a stage actor? How did you feel when you saw yourself for the first time on the screen?

JL: I hated the sight of myself; it absolutely made me cringe. I think the main challenge was restraint. When you grow up in the theater, especially in the rep theater, you tend to think you're not doing your job if you're not acting your head off. Many directors early on told me, "Keep it more contained; you don't have to do so much, just think it." I worked with a lovely man named Robert M. Young in a film called *Rich Kids* [1979]. There was a very key day when I was confronted by my daughter in the midst of a divorce; it's a harrowing scene, and I was all ready to tear a passion to tatters, and he said to me, "Just do nothing." The nice scenes in that film are those scenes, where there's huge emotion going on, and we make a deliberate choice to play against it. There's a lovely scene where I'm moving out of the apartment, and there's small talk with my wife about what I've left and what I've taken; it's a very prosaic scene, but it's very touching. Bruce Beresford has been like that with me, just containing my work a little bit. It's always an issue, because I will always come on strong and then let the director take it down. I will even tell them I'm going to do it; I'll say, "Let me do it big, and you tell me how you want me to modulate it or moderate it." Unless they see the full extent of it, they're not going to know what they have here.

CZ: So you think it's the directors who have to take it down for you?

JL: Oh, yeah. I encourage them, I say, "You have to watch me, because I'll overdo this given half a chance, so you make sure you keep an eye on me." There's no reason not to put that right on the table. There have been very few roles that I've done quietly and modestly. I'm always looking for them, and very often I start out intending to play something quietly and it just gets bigger and bigger as we go along!

CZ: Were you a film buff in college?

JL: Oh, sure. I loved films. My Harvard roommate was consumed with films—David Ansen, who's now a *Newsweek* film critic. We used to go to films all the time; he was like my film education. You know, Harvard Square was such a great place for movies, back in those days, in Boston.

CZ: Did you ever study film performances in order to act in a film yourself?

JL: No, I never have.

CZ: The reason I ask is because I was watching *Buckaroo Banzai* [1984], and your performance of Emilio Lizardo seems very influenced by German Expressionist film.

JL: Yes, I know, I remember it being compared to *The Cabinet of Dr. Caligari* [1919]. I did see *Caligari* as an undergraduate at Harvard—with Ansen, in fact. I don't know, I have a sort of huge backlog of disorganized memories and impressions that I draw from. I remember quite consciously, in the case of *Buckaroo Banzai,* working from an image of Mussolini.

CZ: I was thinking of Brecht's play *Arturo Ui* also, as I was watching you.

JL: Yeah. That speech to the crowd is very much Arturo Ui. A blend of Leonard Rossiter [the British actor] as Arturo Ui and Mussolini, but not very consciously.

CZ: I'd like you to take me through a specific role you've done and tell me how you work on the character from its inception.

JL: In the case of Roberta Muldoon [*The World According to Garp,* 1982], which is certainly one of my more "noted" performances, the most "out there," we had endless costume fittings, which were necessary anyway, but the costume fittings and the hair and makeup tests were in themselves a wonderful way of building the character. I began to see the character visually take shape before my eyes, standing for 2 hours having basically a body fitted on me and experimenting with the size of the breasts and hips and different pieces of clothing. Ann Roth is a brilliant costumer. We would summon up pictures for each other, you know, who Roberta would look like. We hit on a young Julia Child, which is what she ended up looking like.

I realized that I had done a lot of unwitting research on Roberta Muldoon years before when, purely out of curiosity, I had read a book by Jan Morris, called *Conundrum,* which was her memoir of the transition from being a male to a female. I remembered watching her on Dick Cavett and one or two other talk shows and being fascinated by her just as a person, never knowing that I would play a transsexual. She seemed captivating, and what she'd been through seemed like a fascinating transformation. You know, a sort of Tiresias person, who has seen life as both a male and a female. There was something magical about her, which just captured my fantasy, and there I was, about 5 or 6 years later, playing a transsexual, and remembering her, and summoning up the memory of her extraordinary self-possession and sense of irony about herself and peoples' response to what she'd done. It was a piece of unwitting research, and in a way, it makes me think that I'm doing research all the time, just by being curious about people, and about life. Getting into that character was a very long and elaborate process. We worked with the director George Roy Hill, who rehearsed that movie very much as you would rehearse a play, for two solid weeks.

CZ: That's unusual.

JL: Very unusual for a film, but very necessary for me. The interesting thing was I rehearsed it as a man; I didn't even wear a skirt, or anything.

John Lithgow, Glenn Close, and Robin Williams in *The World According to Garp,* directed by George Roy Hill. © 1982 Warner Bros., Inc. Museum of Modern Art Film Stills Archive.

It was very important to me that everybody got accustomed to me physically, acting that character, that I get very comfortable with Robin Williams, for example. Hugging and being very physical with him, selecting very carefully the moments when I would actually kiss him. There are three kisses, just affectionate kisses between a male and a female friend. Getting to the point where we were so easy with it that it was no longer a joke.

That's a very extreme example of something that you always have to go through—you have to get people accustomed to you in character. There's always a fascinating tension between the person and the character he's playing, sort of a hybrid that's invented, in between, and people get accustomed to that hybrid, and respond to it. Very often that process has to happen very quickly, because often you're doing a movie with no rehearsal at all. So you have to be at peace with yourself and banish your own insecurities as fast as you can, to, in a way, disarm the people you're working with.

CZ: You're an actor who likes rehearsal, right?

JL: Yeah, I do like rehearsal, and if we're not getting any rehearsal at all, I will tend to say, "Well, can we just run this once? Can we just run it in front of the camera? Can I do it one more time before we shoot?"

CZ: Do you find directors are responsive to those requests?

JL: Oh yeah, because it's a very exciting process. You will work with many people in the movies who have never rehearsed; it's not part of their process. They just turn up and turn in what they're hired for, what people are familiar with.

CZ: It's become a theme in this book: people who like rehearsal versus people who don't like rehearsal. Sydney Pollack talked a lot about that, because he doesn't believe in it. He thinks that film actors lose their spontaneity when they rehearse.

JL: There's a degree of that, but I've worked with some actors who I think take it to an extreme. I'm sure Sydney Pollack wants his actors to know exactly what they're doing in the course of a shot. He'll want them to know where to hit the mark, and which way they're going to turn, and how they're going to deal with a prop, and how to keep everything in continuity, from angle to angle.

I'll tell you what's fascinating—in theater, you spend four weeks getting a moment exactly right. In shooting a film, you're shooting the process of discovering that moment, and you want to capture the process. Very often in rehearsing a play, you'll find a moment which is absolutely magic after only ten days. If it's supposed to be funny, it'll be hilarious; if it's supposed to be moving, everybody will be sobbing. But that moment will be gone in three weeks of rehearsal, and then you go into the very difficult process of getting it back to the point where you can do it every night, make it fresh for a new audience every night, and recall the fact that it may be the hundredth time for you, but it's the first time for the audience. In movies, what the director is after is that magical moment ten days into rehearsal—that moment of first discovery.

Of course I see Sydney's point, because I've been through it as an actor before—getting the moment perfect and then losing it, losing the life of it. On movies, you try to carefully monitor the progress of a scene in the course of a day, so that you're reaching the right moment just when you need it most, in a close-up or in the vital two-shot. My own philosophy is, "Get it great in every angle," so that the directors can do whatever they want with the shots. But at heart, you are constantly recalling, "Keep this fresh, remember you'll still be doing the same moment 3 hours from now, make sure you have it right."

CZ: Do you find that you are given the latitude to improvise when you're working on films?

JL: Sometimes. Again, it depends. There are some control freaks and some people who love the freshness of improvisation. It's very rare that you improvise on film, because, as I say, you've got to match everything. But it's a pretty good tool for discovering the essence of the scene. There's an awful lot of talk on a film set, usually, just analyzing what's going on.

CZ: Have you found directors to be very helpful in that analysis?

JL: Some. Theater directors are much more helpful than film directors are because film directors have much more on their minds than just the interplay of the actors. Some film directors don't even think about that. I've worked with directors who say, "I don't even know how to rehearse. I never know what to do in rehearsal." You'd be surprised at how often that's the case. They say, "Well, what'll we do? Shall we read the script? What do you think? What would you like to do?" "You call it, you're the coach . . ."

CZ: A few people I've interviewed have said that there's a war going on between directors and actors, and that directors are often terrified of actors and actors' questions. Have you found that to be true?

JL: I don't think it's a war, but it's probably another theme you've hit on; actors are very insecure, they're worried about a hundred things, and directors don't have time for all those worries. They can get very impatient, and I don't blame them. I know what I put some directors through. You know, the good ones are forebearing and patient, or if they think an actor needs a little pushing, they'll go ahead and give a push, and they'll have the correct manners when doing it. They will have done it often enough to know what works and what doesn't, what shuts an actor down and what opens him up. Believe me, there are all varieties of experience in this relationship.

CZ: I was watching *At Play in The Fields of the Lord* [1991] and wondering what happens when an actor you work with is less experienced than you? It struck me, as I was watching your scenes with Daryl Hannah, that you were very unevenly matched in terms of your talent. I found it very disconcerting.

JL: Well, Daryl and I are very different actors, of course. Daryl is accustomed to being a "movie star," and a very girlish one. That's her great strength; her wonderful performances are in movies like *Splash* [1984], where she is kind of an innocent who has stumbled into someone else's world. Perhaps Daryl and I were mismatched in all sorts of ways. I tend to fault the director when that happens. I think that *At Play in The Fields of the Lord* had all sorts of problems. We were not brought into an ensemble. I think it happened in the casting, but I think it also happened in the making of the movie, and ultimately it happened in the cutting of the movie. The movie was 6 hours long when it was cut together, and they had to cut it in half, and they took all the mortar out of it. It was a very disjointed film in terms of the relationship of those 5 or 6 principal characters.

CZ: Aidan Quinn in that film gives an archetypal example of an "inside-out" performance.

JL: It's funny, because Aidan is a very good friend of mine, and we actually had a wonderful time working together, but he and I are from completely different schools. When people ask me, "Have you worked with actors who don't like to rehearse?" Aidan is always the one I think of first. He really does believe that a performance is ruined by overrehearsing it. It was an enormous explosion on the set of *At Play in The Fields of the Lord,* because the director [Hector Babenco] was making us do a scene too often, because he couldn't figure out how to shoot it. Aidan said, "I'm losing it, I will not be able to play this scene if I do it any more." I never have that problem. On the other hand, I think Aidan really is capable of finding the freshness of a moment better than I am. He is less technical. It's very interesting, because Aidan and I admired each other in many ways for exactly what we felt we were incapable of doing. He and I are polar opposites in many ways, but we really learned a lot from each other. I think from me, Aidan learned to enjoy himself a little bit more. From him, I learned an awful lot about concentration and restraint. He thought I was overdoing certain moments, and then I saw the movie and I saw that he was right. I mean, I come not only from the theater, but from classic theater, and from rep theater, in which an awful lot of wretched excesses and bad habits can grow up.

CZ: Do you find that you watch dailies a lot?

JL: I've started to a little bit more. There was a long period when I didn't watch dailies at all. I never watched them during *At Play in The Fields of the Lord,* and off went Aidan every single night and studied them in great detail. Mainly I'm not very comfortable looking at myself acting. I like seeing the movies, but watching dailies is sort of a no-win situation. If you hate what you're doing, you can't get them to reshoot it, and if you love what you're doing, chances are they'll cut it out! So you end up frustrated anyway. I used to have this kind of theoretical rationale that looking at yourself acting, scrutinizing yourself, only constrains you. I don't really think that's true any more. I basically thought it was boring, and at the end of the day I didn't want to go through it. I'd rather go to supper than go to dailies! I'm a little ill at ease; it's an odd situation where everybody's sitting around watching you, and you hope they'll laugh and they don't laugh, or they make no comment whatever, in which case your immediate reaction is, "Oh, I was terrible," when in fact all they were looking at was the focus and the light and the sound.

CZ: You've mentioned the word excess a few times; do you see it as a postitive quality to your acting?

JL: Yeah, sure. I do believe that you get a sense of what you're good at and what people like about your work, and I think in my case people like to see the exuberance of my acting. It's not to everybody's taste, and sometimes I overdo it and people can't stand it. I think my performances in *The Twilight Zone* [1983], and *Buckaroo Banzai,* and a couple of other things, are so extravagant that people kind of dig that, they'll sort of wait for what [I'm] going to do next. On the other hand, I think it's probably a relief for those people who are paying attention when I do something like *Terms of Endearment* [1983], which is very quiet.

CZ: That's one of the few roles you've had where you get to have a romance. Do you feel like you missed out at all in not getting romantic leads?

JL: Oh, no. I have a pretty good sense of who I am as an actor, and I think I'm sort of appealing without being the stuff of romance. I'm a little bit uncomfortable playing romance, myself.

CZ: Why?

JL: I don't know. Probably because I haven't been in that role very often. It could be because it's too close to home. I feel liberated by playing a role very unlike myself, and romance really is unleashing your own personality and feelings and putting it into play. And I think I'm a little odd for a romantic lead; I'm a little subversive as an actor. And, you know, because nobody's ever thought of me in that vein, I've never acted in that vein, or very, very little, and one thing leads to another—you get hired for what you're known for.

CZ: Do you have a sense of an arc in your performance style from your early performances to the present?

JL: I don't really watch myself that much. *Twilight Zone* was on TV the other day and I watched it through, and that's an unusual experience. I think it's one of my best movie performances, but I hadn't seen it in years.

CZ: It's like a complete little film.

JL: Yeah, a little short story. Very, very high powered. George Miller is a director I learned a lot from. The experience of *Twilight Zone* taught me how far I could go. It was a very liberating experience, because here was a case where at last I had a director saying, "Use everything you've got and then reach for even more." So it was the first time that I used all my theater equipment on film, and George Miller used it so brilliantly, I realized it's not always a bad thing to be big on film.

CZ: Do you find yourself interested in the technology of filmmaking? I was thinking about that as I was watching *Twilight Zone* because there are so many wild camera movements. Does that inhibit you as an actor?

JL: No, you know what they're doing, and it tends to be very exciting. You love it when they pull off a great shot. Brian De Palma is very exciting to work with in that way. He'll spend an entire day just planning a shot, and the next day shooting it.

CZ: Has De Palma been really helpful to you as an actor? You've worked with him three times, in *Obsession* [1976], *Blow Out* [1981], and *Raising Cain* [1992].

JL: Brian is an old friend; he was the one that recommended me to the director of my very first movie, *Dealing*. He saw me in a theater workshop in the summer of 1966; I was doing a Moliere one-act farce, and I remember him sitting in the audience squealing with laughter. That was our first experience of each other. You talk about an arc: I've worked with him on an average of once every 8 years. He's real fun to work with.

CZ: In *Raising Cain,* you're playing five roles. It's like a mini-repertory. Did De Palma write it for you?

JL: Yeah, I believe he did. Certainly he called me the minute it was a go project: "I've got your role." Brian is the maker of all sorts of brilliantly imperfect films. I enjoy the work with him very much, he really does bring me into the process.

CZ: How does he do that?

JL: Well, in *Raising Cain,* we rehearsed for a week. Not since *Garp* had I rehearsed so much for a movie. Loads and loads of things were thrown in and left out, we rewrote moments of the script, I was full of suggestions. It was my idea to make the Dad a Norweigan, it was my idea to incorporate the little nursery rhyme. I had a lot of ideas that he just rejected out of hand, too, but it was an atmosphere where anything goes.

CZ: How did you get into doing mega-action films like *Cliffhanger* [1993] and *Ricochet* [1991]? You really raise the level of those films!

JL: Well, thank you. It was sort of a conscious decision between myself and my agent to try and upgrade my commercial status. You know, look what *Lethal Weapon* [1987] did for Danny Glover, or *In the Line of Fire* [1993] did for John Malkovich, or Tommy Lee Jones in *The Fugitive* [1993]. Those are all top pieces; all of them are a little classier than *Ricochet,* in various ways. *Cliffhanger* certainly outgrossed them all, except *The Fugitive.* It was purely a matter of making a strategic commercial movie. I was very uneasy about it in both cases, really.

CZ: Because of the nature of the roles?

JL: Because of the nature of the movie, and the writing. In neither case was it deathless prose. You hurl yourself into it, and you think, "Well, do it for what it is. This is a big, over-the-top action adventure." They were both fun jobs; *Cliffhanger* was incredible fun.

CZ: Where were you filming?

JL: In the Dolomites, and in Rome. God, it was great. But it's also a different kettle of fish being in a Stallone film. Stallone is a nice guy, he's perfectly easy to work with, but on a Stallone film, in a way, he's in one film, and everybody else is in another. It's not exactly an ensemble, and that can lead to some problems. Sometimes you just feel the indignity of it; it becomes a very heirarchic experience.

CZ: Do you mean that he gets special treatment?

JL: Well, yeah. Basically, you never feel more like a supporting player than you do in a big-star vehicle, and sometimes that's an indignity, you know. You begin to feel like you're lending a touch of class to what is basically a big commercial project.

CZ: Do you have any feelings about this current controversy over violence in film and TV—the issues Michael Moriarty raised about censoring the content of television programs?

JL: I think it'll all shake down. I don't have many strong opinions about it; I don't think things should be censored, because who are the arbiters? It's one thing I just can't get all that worked up about. I don't think there's too much violence, and I don't think there's too much censorship. I don't think there should be more violence, and I don't think there should be more censorship. I think, in a way, it's what the market allows. I don't think violent films turn society more violent.

CZ: So you don't have any compunction about performing the very violent actions you do in either one of those films?

JL: Sometimes I feel a little icky about it, but basically, I don't mind. I think they're great, big, garish morality tales. The kind of thing that Moriarty would say, I agree with: Nobody writes more violent material than William Shakespeare. Read *Titus Andronicus,* where there are rapes, and a mother is made to eat meat pies made out of her two sons, and a woman's tongue is cut out and her hands are chopped off at the wrists so she won't tell on her rapists. I mean, this is all Shakespeare we're talking about! There are definitely uses of violence in dramas that are spun out of the fight between good and evil.

CZ: Who are your great heroes, or people who've really influenced you as an actor?

JL: I'm sure the biggest influence by far is my father, because it's a genetic influence as well as the work. From my father comes both the good and bad habits of sort of stock stage acting, yeoman stage acting. I would say the other big influences on me have been the best directors I've worked with. They range from Mike Nichols to Jerry Zaks . . . Oh, God, there's so many others . . . Jose Quintero . . .

CZ: What did you do with him?

JL: *Anna Christie* [1977] with Liv Ullmann. Not a successful production, but, God, it was amazing to tap into that extraordinary energy flow! John Dexter, even, who was a monster, but a very exhilarating man to work with in many ways, on *Butterfly* [1988].

CZ: What do you think is the best-written piece that you've ever been in?

JL: *Terms of Endearment,* and certain plays, of course: *M. Butterfly* on Broadway was a huge high-water mark for me.

CZ: Did you get offered the part in the film of *M. Butterfly* [1993, directed by David Cronenberg]?

JL: No. Never even discussed.

CZ: Was that disappointing for you?

JL: Oh, of course.

CZ: What did you think of it?

JL: I never saw it; it came and went so fast. Did you see it?

CZ: Yes.

JL: I heard it was awful.

CZ: It wasn't one of Cronenberg's better efforts.

JL: I would be dishonest if I said that wasn't a little bit of a relief to me. I don't feel good for those outstanding people, but if it had been a huge success, it really would have hurt.

CZ: Are there any film actors that you held up as icons as you were growing up?

JL: Well, I would say when I was younger, my icons were the knights in England: Gielgud and Olivier and Guinness. Those three are very different, but they're the three paradigms, in a way. I became a little sceptical, first of Gielgud and then of Olivier. Their British technique overwhelmed me after a while. I used to think they were completely magic. I will always revere Guinness; he's a wonderful combination of a great character actor and a master of restraint. You think of the extravagance of some of his early performances: Gully Jimson in *Horse's Mouth* [1958], Fagin in *Oliver Twist* [1948], *Tunes of Glory* [1960], and *Bridge on the River Kwai* [1957]. That's the career that I wish I had! I do in a sense, but he did so many fine, fine films. The one disappointment is that I haven't been in enough really good films.

CZ: What do you think is the biggest challenge of film acting?

JL: The biggest challenge is making bad material good, elevating bad writing. So much comes from the writing, and the hardest acting is in the worst material. If the material is good, you could be hanging upside down underwater and struggling with an octopus, and, if it's well-written, you're having a wonderful time!

An Interview with Aidan Quinn

Aidan Quinn. Courtesy of Baker–Winokur–Ryder and Bill Unger. Photographed by Bob Frame.

When Aidan Quinn appeared in his first movie, *Reckless,* in 1984, he was widely extolled as the latest incarnation of either James Dean or Montgomery Clift. With his troubled, brooding sensitivity, slender good looks, and soulful eyes, Quinn rode through high school corridors on a motorcycle, wearing a black leather jacket and defying authority figures; the comparisons with Dean and Clift were fitting, if obvious. But there is a scene in *Reckless* when Quinn, at a high school prom, breaks into a wild dance, springing with abandon around the floor of the gym. It is that ability to release physical tension, to be comfortable with himself, that makes Quinn a very different performer from either Dean or Clift. He is able to act an anguished character like Johnny Rourke in *Reckless* without being in agony himself. Quinn's trump card is his ability to play the down-to-earth, ordinary Joe, with the suggestion of subterranean depths of passion.

It affords him the opportunity to avoid being typecast as a rebellious outsider and to play a variety of roles, from the AIDS-afflicted gay lawyer in *Early Frost* (1985) to the family man in *Avalon* (1990), to the sympathetic mechanic-brother in *Benny and Joon* (1993). There is a piercing clarity about Quinn's work; he posseses the gift of penetrating directly to the heart of the material, eliminating the unnecessary. It's precisely this "simplicity" and "subtlety" that Aidan Quinn values in the work of actors he most admires.

Quinn was born in Chicago in March 1959 and moved between Ireland and the "windy" city several times during his youth. He studied acting in Chicago with Byrne Piven and made his debut in *The Man in 605* (1979) in that city. Moving to New York, he performed lead roles in two off-Broadway productions of Sam Shepard plays, *Fool for Love* (1983) and *A Lie of the Mind* (1985). Quinn has also appeared as Stanley Kowalski in the 1988 revival of *A Streetcar Named Desire*, for which he won The Theater World Award as Best Actor. In a departure from his more naturalistic roles, Quinn won widespread praise for his modernized *Hamlet* for Chicago's Wisdom Bridge Theater in 1985.

The actor was nominated for an Emmy Award for his television debut in the ground-breaking TV movie about AIDS, *An Early Frost*. Subsequently, he has appeared in *Perfect Witness* (1989), *Lies of the Twins* (1991), and *A Private Matter* (1992), all made-for-cable movies. Quinn also starred in a production of Arthur Miller's *All My Sons* for PBS' *American Playhouse* in 1987.

Quinn had the lead role in his first film, *Reckless*. It was followed by *Desperately Seeking Susan* (1985), *The Mission* (1986), *Stakeout* (1987), *Crusoe* (1989), *The Handmaid's Tale* (1990), *The Lemon Sisters* (1990), *Avalon* (1990), *At Play in the Fields of the Lord* (1991), *The Playboys* (1992, filmed in Ireland), and *Benny and Joon*. 1994 was a prolific year for the actor; he had roles in *Blink, Legends of the Fall, Mary Shelley's Frankenstein,* and *The Stars Fell on Henrietta* (released in 1995).

I spoke with Aidan Quinn in New York City in July 1994.

CZ: What were the influences in your childhood that might have made you want to become an actor?

AQ: Boy, that goes back. Wow. My parents are Irish, that's a big influence.

CZ:　What does that mean?

AQ:　That means you're part of a rich storytelling tradition, and that's what being an actor is about: being a participant in telling a story. My mother used to love to tell us stories about her father and growing up on the farm. My dad teaches literature, so that was an influence. My mother used to tell great stories and my father would too. Also, we went back and forth between the United States and Ireland several times. Because I had to adjust to living in such radically different environments, I was kind of a class clown. I enjoyed cracking people up, I imitated voices or accents.

CZ:　Where did you live?

AQ:　We lived in Dublin and in Birr, County Offaly—it's in the Midlands. We had lots of relatives throughout the countryside, so we used to spend a lot of time with them.

CZ:　What's your first memory of acting?

AQ:　My earliest memory of anything to do with acting was playing Peter Cottontail or something in kindergarten or first grade and getting a real kick out of it. When I was about 8, my father was friends with the theater teacher at his college, and one of the boys who was supposed to play the little boy in *Waiting for Godot* dropped out suddenly. My father was talking to him, and the theater professor said, "Oh my God, it's a week before rehearsal; what am I going to do?" And my father said, "I have a son, Aidan, he's about that age. He'll do it." He came home and he told me, and I was like, "Do what? Not go to baseball?" So I ended up doing the play, and it was an incredible journey. I was around all these college kids, in rehearsal, with a very intense director. The actors in the play were so good to me, and they were so cool. So that stayed with me.

Then I went to live in Ireland when I was 18 and had finished high school, and I started to see a lot of theater. I would get these cheap seats for fifty pence—lunchtime theater.

When I came back from Dublin, I worked as a hot-tar roofer in Chicago for about six or seven months. I was sitting on a roof—getting passed a joint on one end and a bottle of whisky on the other end by my 2 co-workers, at 7:30 in the morning. Hot-tar roofers have got to have the highest ratio of alcoholics of any job. After having done this for six months, and partying, and trying to be one of the guys, I just wanted to get out of there; it was too much. I looked out across the lake—we were on a huge Lakeshore Drive building—and I said, "Man, I gotta do something else with my life." I thought, "I'm gonna take an acting class."

CZ: Where did you take acting classes?

AQ: I took acting classes with a man named Byrne Piven. I saw an ad in the *Chicago Reader*, and I called him. I got him on the phone, and we spent 45 minutes talking on the phone about Irish literature and stuff, and he asked me to come to his class. He very quickly gave me a scholarship, because I had no money. He was really great. He and his wife, Joyce, ran a theater workshop and acting classes. A lot of good actors started with him: John Cusack, and Joanie Cusack. [Byrne Piven] asked me to help him do this play, where I would be the narrator and one of the lead roles, and he was going to direct it and play the lead. We worked on that for several months, and that was how I got started.

CZ: What was the play called?

AQ: *The Man in 605*. I learned a very quick lesson about the ups and downs of this business. Everyone was congratulating me—here I was with no experience onstage, and I was going to be offered an Equity contract in a regular theater. And then the producers decided that they wanted a name Chicago actor, not me.

CZ: What year was this?

AQ: 1979. So I was unceremoniously replaced. It was very heart-breaking, because we had worked on the role and rehearsed for months. They put it on, and it was a big hit. Two months later I replaced [the lead actor], so I did get to do it onstage for a couple of months. I was getting paid Equity wages—a hundred and fifty a week—and I thought, "This is easy. Acting is not that hard. Really, all you have to do is say the words as if you were in that situation." Then I didn't work for 2 years, and that's when I got really serious about acting. I took more classes and really got disciplined about it, because I saw how much real work it entailed.

CZ: Were you doing things like voice, diction, and movement?

AQ: At that time, I didn't. I did some of those classes as I went along, when I needed them for certain roles. I played Hamlet, so I had to take fencing and voice very intensively for months before rehearsal started. I had to catch up, too, because I never went to college for acting.

CZ: Do you regret not having gone to college?

AQ: No. Not at all. Good Lord. I did take a few courses in literature, but I was out there living, while so many people that I knew were doing college as an obligation. I also think the majority of acting students that are getting trained are learning bad things.

CZ: What do you think is so bad about what they're learning?

AQ: They're not learning practical things. There is a sacrosanct, indulgent, hopped-up kind of attitude toward it. Acting at its best, as big and wild as can be, is simple.

CZ: If you set up your own acting school, what would you teach people? How would you teach people to be simple?

AQ: How do you do it? You just point out when they're not. You have exercises that are absolutely related to connectedness with the other person, connectedness to the space. From a practical standpoint, for film acting—which is where 99 percent of all actors will have to make their living—there are almost no exercises that replicate the chaos of a film experience, the mayhem that goes on on a film set. It is mostly that. It is not a quiet, controlled environment, where the actors get respect, and this and that. In few instances you get that, very few. You have to demand it continuously.

CZ: What's been the most exemplary situation that you've been in on a film set, in terms of quiet and control?

AQ: Well, I'm not looking for corncob-up-the-ass, everyone walking on their fingertips. There have been several situations that I've been in that have been really good. It depends on the film. Sometimes it can work for the film if it's all chaos, everyone going, "Whoops, Oh Jesus Christ, we're losing the light, we've gotta roll now!" That's your line, and you just go "boom!" I mean, you've got to have done your homework, know what's important, and let it all go, and just go with what's happening.

People go to acting school and have no idea. They get their first job or their first little commercial, and they cannot control their breathing, they get dry mouth, they have heart palpitations, they can't stop shaking, because there has been absolutely no preparation. They think it's all about the sacredness of the art of acting, and of your character work. Then it's all out the friggin' door.

CZ: What was it like for you when you did your first film? I was watching *Reckless* [1984] the other day; it's a real star-making film. The first shot of you in that film is a tight close-up.

AQ: Is it? I've never seen the movie since it came out. I sat through the premiere and was dying watching it. Those technical things like hitting marks, and this and that, were not exactly in my repertoire at that time. I had difficulty with some of the technical aspects of it.

CZ: And it was the director, James Foley's, first film, right?

AQ: Yeah.

CZ: Did you find he was helpful to you in figuring things out?

Aidan Quinn in *Reckless,* directed by James Foley. © 1984 Turner Entertainment Co. All Rights Reserved. Museum of Modern Art Film Stills Archive.

AQ: He was very supportive.

CZ: Do you like to rehearse? In my interview with John Lithgow, he talked about *At Play in the Fields of the Lord* [1991], and he said you and he had different ideas about rehearsal—he wanted to rehearse, and you didn't.

AQ: A lot of times I don't want to. I can rehearse; I'm not an actor that's gonna totally lose it if he rehearses. But a lot of times with film, it's best not to rehearse. Rehearse in the beginning, rehearse before the film starts.

CZ: What films have you been in where you had a real rehearsal period?

AQ: Quite a few of them. We had rehearsal in *Reckless,* we had a rehearsal period in *Avalon* [1991], but we never rehearsed, because Barry hates rehearsal. We at least got to hang out together and get to know each other for two weeks. We had a two-week period of doing dance lessons, and all that kind of stuff. We had a rehearsal in *At Play,* we had a rehearsal in *An Early Frost* [1985], which was really important, because in TV you have to work so fast, so it's really good to rehearse before shooting. You're always rehearsing in film; there's no getting around it. I don't like to overdo it, because you can lose real gold by over-rehearsing.

CZ: Why do you think that is?

AQ: Well, there's a lot of reasons. Film is about the immediate, about what's happening now, what's real. For instance, you might want to play something a certain way that's going to make an actor go "My God!"— and that's a great reaction. They do that in the first rehearsal, and then they go, "Oh, that's not dignified, let me think of a better way." There are certain things that happen that you can never get back. They happen once. You can approximate them, you can technically do it again.

I don't mind rehearsing. It's a good idea to mark out where you want to go with a scene so you're all together and all basically agree what the scene's about. But it's not good to solve a scene.

CZ: Do you think it should be left a bit ragged?

AQ: A little bit. Or, if it's beautifully written, don't rehearse it at all. If the actor feels good, the director feels good, and you know this is a gem of writing, don't rehearse, just mark it. For me, as an actor, the other thing is—I don't know how to hold back, off camera. That's something you have to learn in the film world, to hold back a lot of times.

CZ: Can you explain what that means?

AQ: Let's say you're in a hugely emotional scene, and the camera is on the other actor. There are two actors, that's often the case. You're off-screen, giving all you've got. You're crying, you're trying to be completely generous to the other actor. Sometimes you can burn yourself out to the point where you've done thirty takes, more perhaps, yelling, screaming, crying, whatever. When the camera gets around to you, you're nothing.

CZ: Is there ever a conflict between an actor who needs ten takes to get it, where you need only one?

AQ: Sure, there's always little conflicts going on. Me, if I get a great one in take one, I just want to make sure they print it. If you're in a two-shot, and it's great for you and horrible for the other person, they're not gonna print it. Then you go to take two, and it's great for you and horrible for the other person, they're not going to print it. In take three, you're horrible, the other actor is good, they're gonna print it, because they're worried about this other person. They're saying, "Oh, you're great every time." "No, that one was not good. We need to go again."

CZ: Do you often find yourself asking for another take?

AQ: I ask all the time. If someone does ten takes, then I figure I have nine other chances to play, to try something. Unless it's something real simple, then you don't want to belabor it. Some directors belabor something because of their own insecurities. We experienced actors know a lot more about film than some directors, and that can be really frustrating. We've done twenty films. We work with a director and sometimes this is their first film. They're so nervous, and they want to cover this, and cover that, and you know they're not going to use it. Sometimes it's like "Let me just clue you in here, OK? They're never gonna cut to that shot; here's why." The cinematographer wants to stop, the continuity person wants to stop, but the director feels they have to assert their authority, because they're the director.

We actors get very canny about working with directors that aren't good, and just being very nice to them. They say, "Know what? Just yell it, OK?" "Yeah, alright," and you do the next take exactly the way you feel like, which may be talking like this. [*Whispers*] The director comes up again: "Yeah, that was it, that was it." A lot of times they're working in a panic zone, so we have to stay calm and just keep on working on what the scene is about, what we want to accomplish here, and just put all this chaos, and insanity, and yelling and screaming away. That's one of the true arts of film acting: putting all that insanity away.

CZ: A lot of people say that directors don't want to answer actors' questions, or deal with actors' insecurities. Do you find that to be true?

AQ: I've recently worked with a lot of really good directors and good actors who just wouldn't put up with that shit anyway. In general, directors know next to nothing about acting. There are very good directors, great directors, that know next to nothing about acting, but you know what's good about them? They admit it. They are totally straight: "Look, I don't know how to help you here, but can you maybe . . . I feel like it's a little too . . . ?" And then you just give them what they need. Actors love that.

CZ: You mean being given the opportunity to play around?

AQ: No, being given the honesty rather than the bullshit. You know, that horseshit from someone who's inexperienced, is not a particularly good storyteller to begin with, and is trying to tell you how this relates to that, and you don't agree! "When you were seven, you had this dog . . ." That can be very frustrating.

Directing a film is one of the hardest jobs in the world. To deal with a big company of actors is not easy. The amount of pressure, and stress, and money problems, and producer hassles, and diplomacy—to be a good director is not an easy thing.

CZ: You just finished working with Kenneth Brannagh on *Mary Shelley's Frankenstein* [1994]. Did you feel that because he's an actor, he had a better understanding of what to do with the actors?

AQ: Working with Kenneth was really good because he's an actor, but he's not heavy on the psychological stuff. It's more like, "What do we need to make this work? Let's try this, let's try that." Because you like his work, and you like working with him, you're much more apt to just say, "OK, let's go for it." The greatest thing is, if you were unhappy, he would always say, "OK, do it whatever way you want. Here's one for you. I'm happy, I need to move on, but if you're not, let's do another one."

CZ: John Lithgow said that you watched dailies every night when you were making *At Play in the Fields of the Lord.* Do you find that you often use dailies as a tool?

AQ: Yeah. I didn't go every night. I would go twice a week, three times, to check in, particularly on scenes I needed to watch. Yeah, I use that a lot, it's a very useful tool. That's part of my job of constructing a performance. I put that in my contract now.

CZ: That you have to have access to dailies?

AQ: Yeah, unless I'm working with Martin Scorsese and he doesn't want me to, I say "OK." But Barry Levinson and a lot of the best directors I've worked with are very open about it; they want you to see the dailies.

CZ: Can you ever ask for reshoots if you don't like something?

AQ: You can ask. It's a very difficult thing to get accomplished, because usually there's such a strict budget. The money's coming from somewhere else, and it has to be approved by the studio. Sometimes you can sneak in a little shot here or there because you're in the same location and they have another camera, or something like that. I never demand it, but that's partly because I have this worker's mentality that it's not really my right, even though it is and should be the right of a leading actor to go to pivotal scenes and say, "We gotta do this again." I've seen actors ask for it, and get it, but it's usually difficult. Agents are involved, and studios are involved.

CZ: You said that you do whatever work you need to do, and then go with what's happening. What exactly is the work you do? Can you take me through one role and tell me what kind of research and preparation you did?

AQ: Well, it depends. On one role it might be very little in terms of preparation, and in another role it might be pretty extensive. When I played the young lawyer that had AIDS in *Early Frost,* I went to group therapy sessions, I answered the phone at The Gay Mens' Health Crisis

Center, hung out there a little bit. I got together with the Ashanti Group, which is a group of men based in San Franciso that were counselors for other men. They all had AIDS, or they're men just getting AIDS, and they had assisted suicide for people who were really bad off. I went to the hospital and met some friends of friends that had AIDS, and then I would go back and visit them every week, on my day off.

For *At Play in the Fields of the Lord,* I went to an Indian reservation. I looked up some born-again Christians that were doing missionary work in South Dakota, where my character was from. I also went undercover into a missionary place in Brazil, as a prospective missionary from the Midwest, saying I wanted to do God's work. That was scary, because that was like being an undercover cop, and I was actually lying. These people opened their hearts to me and were very nice. I learned a tremendous amount in the day I spent with them that I used in the character.

CZ: *Legends of the Fall* [1994], which you just completed, is a period Western. What kind of work do you do to make that period and that environment more real for yourself? You're also part of a family in which Anthony Hopkins is your father and Brad Pitt and Henry Thomas are your brothers. Did you do anything special to develop that relationship?

AQ: Well, Anthony Hopkins says, "Just say the words." That's all it is. Just say the words, and hopefully what sparked your imagination when you were reading it, and the little scribbled notes you made—will give you a concept of what you are going to do with a role. It's something that keeps you up late at night when you're working on it. Or you may wake up at 2:00 in the morning and jot something down: "I'm gonna do this, I should wear this." That's the honeymoon period, where you're really in love with the idea of playing this character. It doesn't always happen that intensely, but sometimes it does.

CZ: For *Benny and Joon* [1993], did you investigate schizophrenia?

AQ: Yeah, as much as I could. I was hired 10 days before shooting. Woody Harrelson was offered the role originally, and decided not to do it. It was just a whirlwind, I was packing my bags, getting on a plane, going into rehearsal, doing fittings, and getting ready to shoot. Doing rewrites—we were rewriting it the whole time, every day.

CZ: That must be disconcerting.

AQ: No.

CZ: You like it?

AQ: It can be disconcerting. It's not necessarily the ideal way to work, but it is the most prevalent way of working, so it would be silly for me to not like it. I like the process of fixing things, and making it better. I went over and watched my friends drop an engine in a car right after I got the job in *Benny and Joon.* They're 2 mechanics, and I listened to the way they were talking to each other because I didn't know the first thing about being a mechanic. I gave the script to a mechanic and said, "Is this feasible, this mechanic dialogue?" He said it was a joke, the person who wrote it had no idea what he was talking about. Then I said, "Well, tell me, how would you say what the writer intended here?" He wrote it down, and then I'd take that into rehearsal. Most films are rewritten, at least partly, as you go. It's not a writer's medium.

CZ: What's the best-written thing you've ever been in, where you didn't touch the dialogue at all?

AQ: *All My Sons* [by Arthur Miller]. It's a play, you couldn't touch it even if you wanted to. *Early Frost,* we adjusted a little bit, but not much. Even the really well-written ones get tinkered with, and usually directors are nervous about it. After the first couple of days, if they have any brains at all, they see that the little fluctuations that are coming up are working better than what's there, and they're more apropos to the situation.

One of the reasons why you have to stay fluid with film is because a writer is writing for a specific set, with a specific actor in mind, and he never gets that set, and he almost never gets that actor. So you have to use what you get, and not deny it.

CZ: It sounds like you're an actor who likes to improvise.

AQ: When you say "improvise," people get this scary thing like, "They're just making it up." It's not made up, it's rehearsed, and scripted. It's only certain little scenes—the ends of things—that might be improvised just because you're there and they keep the camera rolling. Barry Levinson's fantastic at that. Ninety-five percent of what he wrote for *Avalon* is what we did, but there are a couple of entire scenes that are improvised. There's a big scene with me and Elizabeth Perkins in the bedroom, where she's complaining about my parents, and I'm saying,

"What do you want me to do? Do you want me to tell them to get out?" It's back and forth, entirely improvised. More so than most. Barry Levinson's Baltimore films are what he wrote. Because what he wrote is so good, you don't want to touch it. But in this case, he had written this little scene, and it was too on-the-nose, it was by the numbers. It was 3:00 in the morning, a 16-hour day, it was Friday night, the crew wanted the weekend off. And Barry comes in—he's in the next room with the monitors—"You know, the scene stinks, and it's not you guys, it's the writing"—he wrote it—"So here's what we're gonna do. We're gonna keep the camera wide, so it's a two-shot. Don't worry about continuity, you can overlap or whatever. We're just gonna try a couple of takes before we wrap. Same situation, but just say whatever you want. OK? All right, ready?" We're like, sweating. I remember a sweat drop instantly formed— I had on one of those Italian T-shirts—and rolled down my arm. The crew was mumbling, "Oh, God, no, they're improvising . . ."

We did two takes, and the second take is the one he used, and he used the entire scene. It's a 3-minute scene, and I think it's one of the best scenes that Elizabeth and I have in the movie. So there's a writer and a director who's secure enough to be insecure about some of his own stuff and go, "You know what? Throw it out. We gotta make up something else, because this ain't working."

Barry always leaves the camera rolling at the end of the take. The take is over, you've said your words, there's nothing else you can do, and the camera's still rolling, because he doesn't know what's gonna happen. You always go on, you make up something else, and a lot of those little gold nuggets are in there.

CZ: What do you think makes a great film performance?

AQ: There's a lot of different types of great performances, but for me, the best performances are somewhat seamless. *Tender Mercies* [1983] has an incredible performance by Robert Duvall. It was so simple, and so evocative. I watch that film every 4 or 5 years for his performance. I watch some of these old guys, like Cary Grant, and Spencer Tracy, and Gary Cooper, some of their work is so fantastic. It's so hard to do what they did on film when you work so fast. Talking fast, hitting all these marks, yet getting such sculpted performances. I think filmmaking was more controlled back then because a lot of it was on the set, not on location. On location shooting, it becomes very crazy. So I admire some of the old guys. I don't generally like the "over-the-top" acting style; that school doesn't do anything for me.

CZ: What do you think is the difference between a Burt Lancaster and a Gary Cooper?

AQ: Subtlety.

CZ: I gather you don't like "big" performances?

AQ: It depends; some people do it really well. It tends to get dated quicker. There are "out there" performances that are just bold-faced, I'm-tearing-it-up that I love. There are great performances that aren't seamless, where an actor is just acting, and they're admitting it. Like [Jack] Nicholson, we go with it because he's having so much fun, and he's so good at it. But in general I don't like catching actors acting. Pushed, forced work tends to turn me off.

CZ: Would you like to have the opportunity to be bigger in some of your roles?

AQ: Oh, absolutely. What happens in film is you get typed, so I've had very little opportunity to do that kind of thing. In theater, I've done wildly physical, comic stuff. One of my favorite things to do as an actor is to fall down and hit my head, that kind of stuff. *Hamlet* is the richest comic role I've ever seen, read, or played.

CZ: You were a funny Hamlet?

AQ: You cannot do *Hamlet* and not be funny. There are hysterical passages in *Hamlet*, I mean, just out-and-out gut laughing. If you don't get some gut laughing from an audience when you're playing Hamlet, you're missing the boat a little bit. It's black comedy. It's bitter, it's dark, but it's funny.

CZ: When I interviewed Tommy Lee Jones, I asked him if he gave the editor cutting points in his film performances. He said, "Read the speech that Hamlet has to the players if you want to know how to give somebody cutting points."

AQ: That's the best speech about acting there is. In that speech, he gives you the encapsulation of what good acting is. It can be big, it can be huge—if it's earned, and if it has power. You are giving an editor cutting points, because a good editor's eye will always go to a good performance and say, "We need more of that, that's gotta be in." That's probably what he means. And very little of Tommy Lee Jones' work is left on the cutting room floor when he's working with other actors. I can tell you from watching his movies and from how good he is. Your eye goes to him.

CZ: Did you ever have any idols? Did you have an actor who made you say, "Wow, I really want to be like that?"

AQ: I have a few idols; I don't think there's a male actor on this planet that didn't at one point idolize Brando. He was the only one that I could say that I actually had a "thing" about when I was a young actor.

CZ: What was it about Brando that you really liked?

AQ: I thought he was so funny. And all the passion underneath, and the strength. You know he's just making up stuff as he goes along; he's so incredibly creative. His battling with authority figures is obviously a big thing.

CZ: Does it bother you or do you find it flattering when people compare you to James Dean or Montgomery Clift?

AQ: Well, you know, it's funny. I didn't see—ever—a Montgomery Clift movie, until after I started getting a lot of reviews. It turned out that Montgomery Clift was my mother's favorite actor. My wife took me to a big-screen revival of *From Here to Eternity* [1953]. I must have been 26 before I ever saw a Montgomery Clift movie. And then I said, "Oh, I see what people are talking about. I see how good he was as an actor." The James Dean thing—every young actor that has a strong sense of themselves, that has a bit of rebellion in them, gets that at one point or another. It's just boring . . . .

CZ: Have you watched James Dean's performances?

AQ: Yes.

CZ: Do you like him as an actor?

AQ: Yeah, he's a terrific actor. Very charismatic.

CZ: You've worked with so many people who are great actors. *An Early Frost* was one of the first things that you did, and that was with Gena

Rowlands and Ben Gazzara, and you've worked with Joan Plowright, and Robert DeNiro twice . . .

AQ: Robert Duvall, Anthony Hopkins, Kathy Bates. I've worked with the best, in the last 5 or 6 years especially. Even in the beginning I worked with some very good actors. I've been very lucky.

CZ: Do you feel like you learn a lot from those experiences?

AQ: Yes. I think you're always learning when you work with really good actors. Sometimes it's not just the learning, it's a reconfirming that your process, that your way of working is different, but valid. Everyone has certain talents, God-given. Other talents you can develop and work on. You quickly find out, if you have a good ear or good self-awareness, what's working and what's not, what's real, what has gold in it, and what doesn't.

Lee Grant. Courtesy of Camden, ITG.

An Interview with Lee Grant

I met Lee Grant while auditing a session at The Actors Studio, where she was a guest moderator. Grant has a strong, sharp presence; she is direct and tough, almost intimidating. She was one of the few members of The Actors Studio willing to go on the record for this book; I appreciated the candor with which she described her complicated and still vivid feelings about Lee Strasberg's tenure at The Studio.

Grant has brought a sense of emotional intensity and commitment to an extensive and eclectic career. One of the defining moments in Grant's life occurred in the early 1950s. Following the phenomenal success of her first film role, in *The Detective Story* (1951)—for which she won a Best Actress Award at Cannes and was nominated for a Best Supporting Actress Academy Award—Grant delivered an anti–House Unamerican Activities Committee eulogy at the funeral of blacklisted actor J. Edward Bromberg. She was called before the committee to testify, refused, and was essentially (with a few exceptions) absent from the screen until she performed in *The Balcony* in 1963. She did, however, continue to work on stage during this period, cultivating her gifts in roles such as Eliza in *Pygmalion*, the title role in *Gigi*, Sally Bowles in *I Am a Camera*, Lizzie in *The Rainmaker*, and Gittel Mosca in *Two for the Seesaw*, as well as performing in countless live television dramas of the 50s.

In the 60s and 70s, Grant seemed to redouble her efforts in film and TV. The films she worked on during this period include *In the Heat of the Night* (1967), *The Landlord* (1970), *Shampoo* (1975), and *Voyage of the Damned* (1976). Grant was nominated for a Best Supporting Actress Academy Award for the latter three films and won for *Shampoo*. On television, Grant worked in various series, including *The Defenders, East Side/West Side, The Fugitive, Ben Casey, Ironside, Mission Impossible, The Mod Squad,* and *Name of the Game.* She won an Emmy for her portrayal of Stella Chernak on *Peyton Place* (1965–66) as well as for a performance in a made-for-TV movie, *The Neon Ceiling*, in 1971. Grant also had a short-lived television series of her own, *Fay*, from 1975–1976.

The forcefulness of Grant's personality derives in part from her abundant energy. That vigor finds its way not only into performances, but also into a relentless quest for new arenas for her talents. To that end, in 1976, Grant directed her first short film, *The Stronger,* based on Strindberg's play, for the American Film Institute. She continued directing with *Tell Me a Riddle* (1980), her first feature film, for which she won a Congressional Arts Caucus Award for Outstanding Achievement in Acting and Independent Filmmaking. The same year, Grant directed her first documentary, *The Wilmar 8,* a story about the unionization of women bank employees. Her abiding interest in issues of social importance is evident from the list of films she directed: *When Women Kill* (1983), *Down and Out in America* (1985, winner that year of the Academy Award for Best Documentary Short Subject), *Homeless* (1989, documentary), *No Place Like Home* (a 1989 TV movie on homelessness starring Christine Lahti), and *Battered* (1989, documentary). Grant received the Directors Guild Award for Best Dramatic Television Special in 1987 for *Nobody's Child*, with Marlo Thomas, a film dealing with the politics of mental illness. In 1988, Grant was awarded a Lifetime Achievement Award from Women in Film. Since that time, she has directed one more feature, *Staying Together* (1989). Grant has continued acting in feature films (e.g., *Teachers* [1984], *Big Town* [1987], and *Defending Your Life* [1991]) and TV movies, most notably,

Will There Really Be a Morning? (1983), *The Hijacking of the Achille Lauro* (1989), and *Citizen Cohn* (1991).

Grant, born in 1931 in New York, began her career on the stage of the Metropolitan Opera House, in *L'Oracolo*, at the age of 2. Grant went on to study at the Art Students League, the High School of Music and Art, the Julliard School of Music (where she studied voice, violin, and dance), the Metropolitan Opera Ballet School, and with Sanford Meisner at The Neighborhood Playhouse. The fierce devotion to artistic fulfillment and excellence that characterizes Grant's early training is emblematic of her long and varied career.

Lee Grant was in her New York apartment when I spoke with her by phone in March 1992.

CZ: You studied at The Neighborhood Playhouse, and you're also a member of The Actors Studio. Can you talk about the thrust of the training at each place? How was Sandy Meisner's approach different from Lee Strasberg's?

LG: The Neighborhood Playhouse was my training. I never went to any of the exercise classes at The Studio. I was never a part of that with Lee. The exercises I did see, the private moments, and the work that I saw him do when I went there during the late 50s and 60s really disturbed me a lot.

CZ: What exactly bothered you?

LG: First let me tell you about The Neighborhood Playhouse with Sandy, and then I can tell you in a better way what disturbed me at The Studio, with Lee. Sandy had a very specific, coherent, logical approach. If acting is left alone, you really are swimming in very frightening and uncharted waters, because you're swimming in your own emotion. Your instinct takes you someplace, and you don't know why you got there, and you have no way of knowing how to get there again. It's a very exhilarating, but very misleading, place to be, because you can't be inside yourself and outside yourself at the same time. In acting, you can't be your own critic, or your own director. So whoever gives you the tools to use the inside of yourself to get where you want to go is the one who gives you your lifeline.

And that's what Sandy did for me at The Playhouse. I was 15 or 16 when I went into The Playhouse, and before that I had never absorbed from school a *raison d'être*, a focus, an understanding. He took a very rebellious, spoiled, unconcentrated, moment-to-moment child, and through those two years that I spent with him—in teaching me the use of objectives and the actions that one uses to obtain those objectives—gave me not just an acting lesson, but a life lesson. Because I really understood through that logic that that's what I was doing in life. That I had certain objectives, even when I went to the market; if I wanted to buy a loaf of bread, I took certain actions in order to do it. I walked up to the place, I walked down the aisles, I looked for things. Once I knew what my objective was, I could let go of wondering and worrying *how* I was doing anything. What it released you from—which was the most enormous release in your life, as an actor—was *how* you were doing anything. You want to know why you're doing it, you want to know how to accomplish what you're doing, but you never need to know how. That's up to somebody else. That's up to your director, or your teacher, or whatever.

The other thing that Sandy taught me was how to break down a play. That was crucial for me. To understand that a play has its own logic and that a play or a film is made up of conflict, that every scene is made up of conflict. That it consists of a person having an objective and the other person having the opposite objective. And each scene broke down into the carrying out of those objectives, so it reduced the world that I entered to a world I could handle. It was demystified for me, because I understood the technique and the emotion involved. And as I would go through and break down the beats of my character, I could see exactly where the actions were that fell into the objective. I don't need to do that anymore, because it's now become—not a student's tool—but something that happens instinctively.

You have an inner tool, and there are little lifelines going through your work which say, "What do I want?" That also gave me pages and pages to fill up—which I have always done—on the why. Why I want to do it. So that if I'm working on a character, I want to know the character's overall objectives, what I *want*. In *Born Yesterday*, for instance, as the character, I want to learn. But the "why I want to learn" gives me my whole life and fills in my whole background, and says, "I come from here, I've never known anything but this," so that as you're writing, you're limiting your own knowledge to the knowledge of your character.

CZ: Did Sandy encourage you to do a biography of your character?

LG: I didn't get that from Sandy. That's something that came from me, and that's something I suggest; it was crucial for me. In order for me to limit my own knowledge to my character's and to know the circumference of the world of the play or film that I was entering, I wrote out everything, just a stream of consciousness. By the time it was finished, I created a life for myself. So no matter what situation I hit, in film or on stage, I hit a reality. I knew who my parents were, I knew where I went to school, I knew what my room looked like, I knew who my friends were. I never hit a place where I'd go, "Uh-oh, I don't know that."

CZ: Where does the element of surprise come in when you break down the text so carefully?

LG: Well, surprise is certainly something that is very important in my experience as an actor. I find that the way you leave yourself open for surprise is to concentrate on something else. Everything is concentration, and need: "I need something, I want something." After all, that's what an objective is; it's not an intellectual thing. An objective is "I need," or "I want," or "I've got to have." So that if you have to have something, and that's where your concentration is, you're always surprised by what anybody else does.

CZ: After being at The Neighborhood Playhouse, you went to The Actors Studio and had some kind of disturbing experience.

LG: What I saw there was a kind of hushed, talmudic atmosphere. Sandy was acerbic, very acid, but very approachable. Everything had a reality, no mysticism, no spiritualism. The whole atmosphere around Lee . . . there were tape recorders going so that not a word was missed. I saw a scene done there where the actress did a lovely piece of work, and instead of hearing, "This is what is good about it, this is what is not good about it, this is what you need to work on," he said, "Too conventional." Too conventional! Instead of being given a specific thing to work on, I saw people being pushed adrift. They formed a kind of mysterious spiritual bond, waiting to hear what the Rabbi would say next. And the Rabbi would never say it in terms you could apply immediately to your work, and come back, and say, "Is this what you mean?" He would put it in very general, rabbinical terms.

CZ: Did you feel that people were doing things to please Lee?

LG: Totally. Not to please themselves. I couldn't stand being in those classes. Every year or so I would drop in, and when I came back, Lee was in this period of private moments. I think there's a great value to private moments; it pushes people into exposing themselves on stage in front of other people in a way they wouldn't do otherwise. But what I mostly saw was all those nubile girls, buying new lacy bras and panties, and always setting up situations in their bedrooms, which were sexual. It sometimes went into toilet and masturbatory kind of stuff, where I felt it was totally voyeuristic. And that they were doing it totally for him. The whole concept that I'd been trained on, where anything you did had to apply back to the part, was thrown out the window. It had no application that I could see. When it was applied to a play, it blew the play out of the water, because sometimes the play couldn't contain that kind of exercise.

Everybody looks for God, and I feel a good teacher refuses to be God. A good teacher says, "I'm not God. You're not going to find it through me, you're going to find it through yourself. Stop leaning on me, go back to yourself. This is where you're weak, this is where you're strong, you didn't do this, you need more of this," and to be as specific as they can. Because when you're acting, you're lost, and you should be lost. I mean, it's one of the great lostnesses of our lives, and one of the great insanities of our lives. We're allowed to be involved so deeply that we can't see what's going on, and we're totally dependent on our teacher or our director. So that the great teacher says: "I am not God; I don't accept being God. You have to solve these things for yourself, because you're going to have to go out alone on that stage, in front of those people, and you're not going to have me to rely on. So become better at this, take those weak parts and work on them." This is not what I saw happen.

But on the other hand, I know that it did happen for a lot of people who swear by it and who are extraordinary actors. I didn't see the remarkable work that I understood took place. With Gerry Page, with Al Pacino, where there was a real connection and movement and a remarkable pattern. And Ellen Burstyn, of course, swears by it. Now a lot of them, when they came to him, had very, very solid training before. So that it may be that the actor who had very solid training, you know, the Marlon Brando who came from Stella Adler and the Gerry Page who had gone to The Goodman School of Drama, were able to incorporate the things that Lee gave them without being so thrown.

CZ: You sound very negative about your experience at the Studio, yet you're obviously very involved now. What happened?

LG: First of all, Lee and I became very, very close friends, on the basis of my total disagreement with him. And when he started acting, later in life, his whole approach changed. Because by then he was teaching out in California, where I could see the work. And all the things that he said nobody should mention in the sessions—objectives and actions—all of a sudden were being talked about again, because he was a working actor. And by the way, a remarkable working actor, just remarkable. The work that he did in *Boardwalk* [1979] and in *The Godfather, Part II* [1974] was extraordinary. And with that kind of pressure on him—because after all, when it's somebody who has raised and educated thousands of students, they're going to say, "OK, you're on, Pop, how are *you* going to do?"— he was a remarkable actor. The more that he was involved in acting, the more he was really able to give actors in later life. I saw a profound change in him.

Not that he still didn't choose people to come into The Studio on the basis of how sexy he thought they were or how commercial he thought they were. Because he had a whole split concept on eligibility for The Studio.

CZ: The audition process at The Studio seems very strange.

LG: Well, I was there when he turned down Jack Nicholson because he wasn't commercial enough. And didn't know whether Diane Ladd should be let in.

CZ: When did you become involved with The Actors Studio West?

LG: I went out there in 1964. We started our Actors Studio West with Bruce Dern, Jack Garfein, and Mark Rydell; our group was doing the moderating. It was a carrying out of that sense of not needing to have a father figure. We were very strong; we were very talented and very capable, and we wanted to do our own thing. And so, in those years, Lee only came out during the summer. We ran The Studio, and it was a really golden time out there. Ellen [Burstyn] entered there at that time; Jack Nicholson and Henry Jaglom were there, and countless remarkable talents were working all the time. What happened was that, as each of us started to get more work than we could handle in film, we could give less time to The Studio.

By that time Lee had become a person I could really relate to on many levels, and we asked him to take over. We didn't want The Studio to become mediocre. And that's what it was starting to become.

CZ: So your relationship to Lee changed toward the end of his life?

LG: With all the fighting we had done . . . I think when you fight with people, and they're not afraid of you, there is a sense of relief. And so we had become very close. Lee had dinner at my house the week before he died. He said such interesting things; he said Clifford Odets had told him that listening to music was like having a conversation. That if you got into the music, you could hear the conversation that was going on between the instruments. I loved him for that stuff.

Music was everything to him. He could sit in the middle of the room with his children, when they were little, screaming and carrying on, and completely use a fourth wall to envelop himself and listen to the music; he had great concentration.

CZ: Can you talk about what happened to The Studio when Lee was no longer in the picture?

LG: When he died, there was Ellen [Burstyn], who was like a pretender to the throne. There was Anna [Strasberg], who felt that it was an inherited throne, and the very fact that she was married to Lee meant that she should inherit The Studio. And there were 100 children between 40 and 50, Studio members, who were not the ones who went out in the world and who were allowed to stay children in a certain way, because of their acceptance of Lee as the guru. And there was Susan [Strasberg], who had a leg in a cast up on a chair, being pre-empted by all these middle-age children—who were talking about the loss of their father. I said to her, "It's your father, you talk," but she'd always been shunted aside in a certain sense. It was a very strange vision.

Ellen took over The Studio after that enormous battle between the Anna Strasberg camp—with Al [Pacino] on one side, because he had been so close to Lee, they loved each other like father and son—and the Ellen/Paul Newman and the-rest-of-us camp, which did not feel that Anna knew enough to run The Studio. As an actor, she wasn't well-equipped enough. Although I loved her as a person and I thought she was a really charming lady, the presumption of power was just foolish. I had suggested Clyde [Ventura, the late director of The Actors Studio West] to Ellen, and I think that he did a wonderful job there.

CZ: What are your feelings about The Studio now?

LG: Well, I had also suggested Frank Corsaro on the East Coast. I knew he'd worked in opera and that he had a kind of breadth to him artistically. It wasn't focused just on the theater. He'd produced, he'd been outside, he'd had a career outside, and he could bring a lot of that richness into The Studio. Now, I'm very pleased with what Frank has done. I don't have a problem with it.

I think that when somebody takes over The Studio, it has to be theirs for a while. And since all of us have moderated there for 20 years, I think everybody feels like they own a piece of it. And that's the reason why it's important to them—because they love it, because The Studio is our artistic home. There's a tendency to be overcritical, to pick apart, and that's counterproductive. The story of Frank and The Studio has yet to be told. He invited 100 very young people in, which was a relief to see; I thought his instinct was absolutely right. But I think that what happens is that the war goes on.

CZ: I understand The Studio is constantly in financial crisis.

LG: Well, how is The Studio supposed to support itself? Paul Newman, like an angel, turned his popcorn and salad dressing into money to support it, and so that's who's been supporting The Studio. And we have to find another means of support. All these years, nobody has ever paid to go to The Studio; they've given donations, but on a sporadic level.

CZ: It seems unconscionable that one of the great cultural institutions in the United States has constant money and space problems.

LG: It is, it's stupid, and it's stupid for people to say, "Well, I don't think we should give money because that's the way it's always been." This is a real world that we live in, and bills have to be paid. Every place else where you get what we give, people expect to pay for it.

CZ: Turning to your work as an actor, what experiences do you feel have been the most formative for you?

LG: Many directors who I've worked with have had a very encouraging and opening effect. Hal Ashby opened me up a lot; he encouraged me to take steps in *The Landlord* [1970] and *Shampoo* [1975] that were very fertile for me. Sidney Lumet during the early years when I worked with him, Norman Jewison, all wonderful directors. But what they wanted was for me to come in with a character, to come in with a part, and by that time, it was not a formative effect. Sandy had the formative effect. Herbert Berghof had a formative effect.

I learned in facing the parts that were really difficult for me, like doing *Electra* [1964] in the [Delacorte Theater in Central] Park for Joe Papp, with Gerry Freedman. If ever I used my craft . . . and that means there was not a line I said that did not have a written subtext underneath that I had to use, because it was a whole new language for me. Joe Papp sent me to a speech teacher, because to do that kind of work out in the park is like learning opera. It's using your instrument in a way that you've never had to use it before. It's not like the stage; it's singing opera. So I was tested in a way, both emotionally and physically, breaking into a new, classical form. And in those days, when you worked in the park, it was 7 days a week, there was no day off. It was a tremendous test of endurance, and Gerry Freedman was a great guide for me. But the *Electra* emotional area that I had to draw on was very deep within me. Very deep within me in terms of the longing for the father, the hatred for the mother, all of those things were very available to me. It was the form in which I was now doing it that was very new, and of course Joe Papp was taking a terrific chance in handing *Electra* over to a person who had never worked in the classics before. It was a very big experience for me, and it was a very good *Electra*.

CZ: You did Genet's *The Balcony* [1963] on film. How was that experience?

LG: It was indescribable. It was Shelley Winters and me hating each other, and poor Joe Strick trying to keep this impossible company together. Peter Falk was in it. He [Strick] came up with a great concept and managed somehow to bring it off.

CZ: That's a pretty juicy role.

LG: Yeah, it was, it was a big step for me to take, and he [Strick] pushed me as far as I could go.

CZ: What are the roles that you're especially fond of in films? Can you talk about one role, specifically?

LG: I think *The Landlord* was some of my best work, with a really wonderful, fresh character. It's one of the few times that I look at myself on film and I really love what I did; I love the creation of that lady. It was a part I had to fight for, because the part was older than I was. I had done *In the Heat of the Night* [1967] for Norman, and that was very important for me because it dealt emotionally in an area that was a catharsis for me. I had lost a husband, and the film was dealing with a husband who was murdered. So the attraction to that emotional catharsis was very strong for me, and I really needed to get that out of my system. The next thing that they were doing was *The Landlord,* in which Norman was giving Hal his first chance to direct. I was doing *Plaza Suite* at the time, in Los Angeles, which was also a wonderful challenge for me. In *Plaza Suite*, you play the middle-aged lady, and then the young woman. They felt that even though I was doing those characters, I couldn't possibly do the woman in *The Landlord.* I wanted the part desperately, and I said, "Well, just give me a chance, because I have a point of view on it which I think works, because I think this is a very funny woman."

It was very close to certain colors in my mother, which I was dying to play. A certain kind of elegance, a certain kind of affectedness, a certain kind of unconsciousness, and a person who acts on impulse. I felt when I read it, even to myself, I could feel physical characteristics come out of it. I could feel the kind of things that she would do and say. A great unconsciousness of mind, and a limitedness in a way of thinking, that I felt I knew and could really explore.

I had just seen Vanessa Redgrave in *Isadora* [1968], which I thought was one of the most remarkable performances. She went from being a child, like 15, to 50. And they did it with very, very little makeup, just changes in lighting. So I showed up at Norman's and Hal's office, with this kind of beige makeup, and a beige fur hat, and I put myself under their top light, and I said, "Look at me. With the right lighting, I can do this. And if we get Dick Smith—who is a great, great, character makeup artist—to give me the colors that are right, I can get away with this, and I will look old enough on film." And I did, without having age lines or anything. It was a question of putting together those kind of blonde and tan colors. In a sense, I brought them the character. I said, "Listen, this is how I see it," and they bought it.

CZ: You've worked as an actor in a lot of different mediums—theater, film, series TV, and made-for-TV movies—can you articulate the major differences in the mediums from an acting perspective?

Lee Grant with Pearl Bailey in *The Landlord* (1970), directed by Hal Ashby. © 1970 Mirisch
Productions, Inc., and Cartier Productions, Inc. All Rights Reserved. Museum of Modern Art
Film Stills Archive.

LG: First there's the theater, and there's nothing that's more demanding than the theater. And I think for those of us who were raised when the
theater was at its apex, when *Death of a Salesman* and *Streetcar* were
being done, I mean, it was astonishing to go to the theater. Olivier came
over and did *The Entertainer*, he did *Beckett*. There were extraordinary
experiences, miracles to be had in the theater. I think the most demanding
thing is the theater, if your expectations are as high as mine, in terms of the
kind of performance you expect to give. And can never achieve, of course.

And film . . . film is part of a business. So there are some films that you
get that are just schlock. And because you're in the business, you take it.
It may even be a hit, but it's schlock. And other films you do are not just
commercial successes, but artistic successes also. Those are few and far

between. And then there are the films you do for yourself that are independent and that you know you're not going to make anything off of, that you do to do.

In movies for television, every once in a while, a really, really fine piece of work will get on television that can't make it as a feature because it deals with social issues that features aren't tackling. So you can get an extraordinary piece of work on television every once in a while, particularly with cable opening up.

CZ: What's rehearsal time like on features you've done?

LG: You know, I came from a period where I went into multi-multi-million dollar movies, where there was just absolutely no rehearsal. There was a reading around the table, and then you jumped in, and you went to bed with somebody [in the film]—you didn't even know who they were—they were some big star. And it showed. There was a kind of gloss and impersonality about it that was just pure movie and had nothing to do with how people really acted. And it was a very kind of dopey, self-conscious feeling.

CZ: Was it fun on some level?

LG: Well, it's a heightened something, on some level. But on the other hand, I think that when you rehearse, and when you know the person, and you know what you're doing, you relax and find things. It's just an entirely different thing. I'm sure that rehearsals are going to become a part of films. It doesn't make any sense to have people just show up on the set, unless they're action and adventure things, where there's no way of rehearsing that anyway. But I know there's nothing that I do as a director that doesn't have a week to 10 days rehearsal before it, and sometimes that's not enough. I do it because I think it's an absolute necessity for people to solve those problems before they go in to film, because there are budgets that have to be made, and you have to do a certain amount of work every single day when you make a film. If actors are taking the time on the set to find things that they should have found in rehearsal, you fall behind and you don't get another film to direct. So it's very important for me to finish my film on time.

CZ: Do you feel that someone who is a good actor can be equally adept at theater or film interchangeably?

LG: There's no question about it; it's the same preparation, it's exactly the same thing. Although I do think that the demands in theater are much tougher.

CZ: So you don't think film is a director's medium, and theater is an actor's medium?

LG: It's true that after you put your performance on film, it's shaped by the director and the editor, in terms of making the film work, putting it all together. But film is only what happens in front of the camera. The camera only records what goes on in front of it, and that's either schlock or it's wonderful. And what's wonderful is what the actor is doing. All the stuff Bergman gets out of his actors are great, great performances. And while it is his concept, he has those same concepts on stage, so they're very interchangeable for him.

CZ: How did you get into directing? When you were acting, did you ever feel thwarted by directorial decisions that were being made about your acting? Was that an impetus for getting into directing?

LG: No, not a bit. I've really loved every director I've worked with. And I think the whole essence between director and actor, whether it's in theater or in film, really, is that you place your trust in the man or woman who's out there saying, "Wherever you're going to, Lee, it's a place that I love. Maybe you could go to this place more." The joy of acting is to lose yourself in it, and there's only one person out there who says, "You're lost in the right way," and that's the director. So I've always trusted and been very dependent on the taste and the gifts of the director, and I've loved them. And I've felt that they loved me; I've had wonderful, strong relationships there. And outside of maybe one or two really incredibly crappy movies, where there were one or two incredibly crappy directors . . . but everybody's been through that. You're not an actor unless you get your skirts full of mud, because that's part of it.

The directing really came out of a purely accidental thing. I was asked to join the American Film Institute Woman's Directing Workshop. I'd never even thought about directing at all. I'm a born and raised actor from childhood, so if it occurred to me, I never wanted it. But more and more ideas started to come to me that couldn't be satisfied by just acting; the canvas was too small. Where the canvas of my thinking started to get wider, I needed to express it in a wider way.

CZ: How was your experience directing your first feature? How difficult was it to put together the project?

LG: It was very, very difficult. Fortunately, I didn't have to do it. Three young women in San Francisco, The Godmothers, put it together. It may be the best film I ever made, *Tell Me a Riddle* [1980], with Lila Kedrova and Melvyn Douglas. It dealt with things that were very important to me and close to me. And it was a wonderful, rich experience in which I felt extraordinary things happen on the screen.

CZ: Were you attracted to the Tillie Olsen novella?

LG: Yeah, the women sent me the novella. I remember just lying in bed reading it, crying and feeling, "God, I feel like I've come home to something." I called them and said, "Whenever, however you do this, I'm yours." And out of that Joyce Eliason [the writer] and I started working on the screenplay. It took many, many months, maybe a year, to do the screenplay, while they raised the money from relatives, and God knows what. But at that time, I was facing the loss of my mother, Melvyn was facing the loss of his wife, Brooke [Adams] was facing the loss of her mother. We never discussed it; I didn't even know it until later, but we all needed that film very, very much, as a way of exploring through art the pain of what we were going through, the separation that we were facing. And also, all those things that were so close to me in terms of the revolutionary kind of spirit which I'd believed in. So that it was an investment of a great deal of heart and love.

CZ: What kind of explorations would you encourage during rehearsal? Did you use improvisation?

LG: I used everything. First of all, Melvyn was using an accent for the first time, he was worried about that. The second thing he was very concerned about was that he would be a heavy in the film and that nobody would understand his character. I knew, and he knew, that from the time he tried to climb that ladder and couldn't, everybody would understand him. And the third thing was, he was worried about the love scene. He was worried that he'd be making a fool of himself. That problem was never solved in rehearsal, but by the time we got to it, there was no problem. We had lived out such a life of love and loss and feeling that all I had to do was turn the camera on.

CZ: The actors are so natural at doing everyday things, like preparing food and handling objects. Did you work a lot on that during rehearsal?

LG: Yeah, that was really important to me. Food was very important to me because that's such a part of people's lives. And Patrizia von Brandenstein—who was the production designer and the clothes designer too, and the cook—took over all of that. She made the things that were taken out of the oven herself.

CZ: I was wondering if we see improvised moments in the film? Would you have things that weren't in the script that you would develop in rehearsal, or during the actual filming, that ended up in the film?

LG: You know, everything comes from a different set of realities. The story gets translated into a film script. Then, everything had to be built in the script that wasn't in the novella, because the novella was really a haiku; we had to open it up. Then you go from the script to rehearsal, which goes to your third new reality. It's no longer a script anymore; it's people finding a certain kind of life and using the script to create that life. Anything that happens there, anything that's fresh, anything that's new, is incorporated. And then when you're filming, something different may happen. The element of surprise is the thing to be held onto; you create a framework so that surprise isn't anarchy, but surprise is allowed to happen.

CZ: When you moderated at The Actors Studio, when you were talking to the actors you used terms like, "What do you want from yourself?" "moment-to-moment," "obstacles," etc. Would you use that kind of language on a set?

LG: It's not language that I would use at all in working. That is stuff that you use on the most basic level, when people are working on scenes. By the time I'm finished casting a film—if I cast it properly, just as if I'm cast properly—I have a person, an entity, who brings with them all the baggage that I need to draw on.

CZ: How much control would you have over casting?

LG: The control is so total that, for me, that's all the time I take. I mean, it's like marriage—casting is everything. And I promise you, I lose a lot of friends. Because there are friends who are right for something that I do, but they're not as right in terms of chemistry as somebody else. And that's what I have to go for.

I, as a director, don't want to be bored; I want to be surprised. They have to surprise me, and they have to bring things that I could not possibly know about. And so I explore with them. With Melvyn Douglas, he had such a sense of reality that everything in the film made sense because his reality went beyond anything that I could even talk about; anything he picked up, anything he put down, anything he reached for. The work that he did was beyond anything I could ever expect.

CZ: There are scenes in *Tell Me a Riddle* that are incredibly strong, almost harrowing.

LG: I know. I was behind the camera, crying, hoping that I wouldn't be crying aloud and spoiling a take, because it overwhelmed me. The actors just overwhelmed me.

I felt that the first feature I made was a privilege. Maybe it's all downhill from here on. It may be interesting, it may be other things, but in terms of the heart, I don't think I could do any better than that.

An Interview with Diane Ladd

Diane Ladd and Kris Kristofferson in *Alice Doesn't Live Here Anymore*, directed by Martin Scorsese. © 1974 Warner Bros., Inc. Museum of Modern Art Film Stills Archive.

Diane Ladd counts as her favorite women actors Bette Davis, Simone Signoret, and a trio of actors who epitomize American Method acting at its best: Geraldine Page, Joanne Woodward, and Kim Stanley. She shares with these women a strong, soulful, and gutsy presence. Ladd brings her own distinctive qualities to acting, among them a spirited playfulness with more than a *soupçon* of flamboyance. Her three most well-known characterizations, Flo in *Alice Doesn't Live Here Anymore* (1974), Marietta in *Wild at Heart* (1990), and Mother in *Rambling Rose* (1992), are roles that have strong elements of caricature. On paper, Flo, the foul-mouthed, brassy waitress with a heart of gold; Marietta, the crazily possessive, lascivious, southern ex-beauty queen; and her antithesis, Mother, the genteel, spiritual, progressive southerner, tend toward stereotype. But Ladd endows each of these portrayals with a *largesse d'esprit*—a generosity toward the character, an out-sized gusto, and an intense commitment to bringing the character to her fullest, most vivid dimension. Like the actors she admires, she is willing to go to the edge of the edge with her characters, as in her performance of Marietta, which is truly "wild at heart."

Ladd is a character, as we say of colorful people, and has character, as we say of those with a high-minded system of values. She is very close in essence to Mother in *Rambling Rose*, a role she says she "fell in love with." Like Mother, Ladd is possessed of ethereal concerns: She has a

135

Master's in esoteric psychology, teaches metaphysics, studies kaballah, and is a certified nutritional counselor. Her spiritual inclinations profoundly color her views on acting; she says:

> Even if you don't believe in a God . . . your talent is your soul . . . you have to give it the truth; truth is sunlight, truth is nourishment. Truth sets you free, it sets your talent free to flow like a river of purity, and that's what makes a great performance.

The visceral and the spiritual merge in Ladd's luminous, all-embracing passion for life and performance.

Diane Ladd was born in Meridian, Mississipi, in 1943. After attending high school, she left for New York and trained for the stage with Curt Conway and Frank Corsaro. Her first stage appearance was as Carol Cutrere in (her cousin) Tennessee Williams' *Orpheus Descending*, in 1959. It was during the run of *Orpheus* that she met her future husband, Bruce Dern, by whom she would have a daughter, Laura. In the New York theater, Ladd also appeared in *Carry Me Back to Morningside Heights* (1968), *One Night Stands of a Noisy Passenger* (1970), and, perhaps most famously, as the eponymous heroine in "Lu Ann Hampton Laverty Oberlander," part of *A Texas Trilogy* (1976). With the latter play she toured extensively and won the Broadway Tour Award, the UCLA Favorite Actress Award, and the Eleanore Duse Mask Award.

Ladd has appeared often in both episodic and series TV and in made-for-television films. She had roles in the series *Alice, The Secret Storm, Search for Tomorrow, Love Boat, Father Dowling Mysteries*, and, recently, as Grace's imperturbable mother in *Grace Under Fire*. Among her TV movies are: *Black Beauty* (1978), *Willa* (1979), *Guyana Tragedy: The Story of Jim Jones* (1980), *Desperate Lives* (1982), *Grace Kelly* (1983), *Crime of Innocence* (1985), and *Celebration Family* (1987).

Ladd's film career began in 1966 with Roger Corman's *Wild Angels*. That same year, she became a member of The Actors Studio. Ladd's subsequent film performances include *The Reivers* (1969), *Macho Callahan* (1970), *White Lightning* (1973), *Chinatown* (1974), *Alice Doesn't Live Here Anymore* (for which she received her first Academy Award nomination as Best Supporting Actress), *All Night Long* (1981), *Something Wicked This Way Comes* (1983), *Black Widow* (1987), *Wild at Heart, A Kiss Before Dying* (1991), *Rambling Rose,* and *The Cemetery Club* (1993).

She received her second Academy Award nomination for *Rambling Rose;* it was the first time in the history of the Academy Awards that a mother and daughter (Laura Dern, also for *Rambling Rose*) were nominated in the same year. Ladd directed her first feature film in 1994, titled *Mrs. Munck,* starring former husband Dern, Shelley Winters, and herself.

I spoke with Diane Ladd by phone in her Los Angeles production office in July 1994.

CZ: Where did it all start? Did you have any exposure to film or theater when you were growing up in Mississippi?

DL: Just movies. We usually didn't get the big movies until after everybody else did. Also, they had censorship in those days. In 1957 there was some big movie that came out, and I remember I was in high school, and I went to see it, and the nuns got very, very angry at me. I really couldn't understand why they got angry about the depiction of life. That moment just came to me while I was talking to you.

CZ: Did you do any acting as a child?

DL: I was 13 years old when I did my first play, a little English play. I remember being onstage, and I could feel that the people in the audience had their masks lifted.

CZ: By your performance?

DL: By being in the theater with the dark around them. They weren't frightened about their own lives because they were watching somebody else's. I think theater—and communication is theater—is as important to people as breath. We go back to the caves that were found in France from eons ago, before they had a language. The cavemen had to go out and get the buffalo or whatever, to eat, and they would act out tomorrow's death. They knew that some of them would die, and by acting out the deaths the night before, they could release their fears. So the awe of acting, of watching other people act, is as old as this planet, and as important, because I think that culture is as powerful a weapon as the bomb, maybe more.

When I did my first play, I felt like I could reach out and touch people's hearts. They were more true, more honest, sitting there in that moment; I felt like I was really one with the whole audience. That was the taste of wine that made me want to be an actor. It's probably a little bit of power, too, because when I cried, they cried; when I laughed, they laughed.

CZ: Who were your biggest heroes in film or in theater?

DL: The first time that I saw Bette Davis in a film, she, of course, was one of my favorite actresses. Paul Muni was one of my favorite actors, and Spencer Tracy, and Laurence Olivier, and Marlon Brando for the men. For the women, after Bette Davis came Simone Signoret . . .

CZ: Do you remember what it was that you liked about her?

DL: Her earthiness. When she was in a film she made me love the fact that I was a woman. And she was a great, magnificent actress.

I remember one time, much later, Yves Montand was at a gathering, and he invited me out for dinner, he was coming on to me. I got so nervous I stepped on his toe, and I called him "Ee-vez," and then I said to him, "I couldn't possibly ever go out with you. First of all, I don't date married men. But if I did date married men, I wouldn't go out with you, because that would be like spitting in a museum, because you're married to Simone Signoret."

CZ: What about any of The Actors Studio actors?

DL: Kim Stanley—one of the greatest actresses of all time. You saw her in *Seance on a Wet Afternoon* [1964], one of the most phenomenal films. And Geraldine Page, and then Joanne Woodward. So I guess it's Bette Davis, Simone Signoret, Geraldine Page, Kim Stanley, and Joanne Woodward. That's about the ball game.

CZ: When you decided that you wanted to be an actor, how did your parents respond?

DL: They encouraged me to be true to myself.

CZ: What about other people around you? After all, you came from a small town of 6,000, and you were going off to become an actor in New York.

DL: I don't know how they thought about it. I was Catholic in a non-Catholic world; my life had always been different, you know what I mean?

I graduated from high school at 16; I took so many credits that I did in 3 years what it usually takes you 4 years to do. So really, the obstacle of being in a small town, in a small school, turned out to be a gift. Most of the problems that you get are gifts, if you look at them. So I graduated from high school, and I had a scholarship to Louisiana State University to become a criminal lawyer; that was what I was going to do. Instead, I totally reversed, so that by the time I was 16½, I was already in New York.

CZ: What happened once you got to New York?

DL: I got my first professional part in a [touring] company of *Hatful of Rain*, directed by Frank Corsaro. I was then in *Orpheus Descending*, off-Broadway. Bruce Dern played Xavier. We met when I was 17 in 1959; I was a baby.

In the meantime, I studied with 2 men: Curt Conway, and then Frank Corsaro. Curt Conway was a great teacher and a great director. Unfortunately, he got caught in that whole McCarthy thing. He refused to testify. He was the fair-haired boy in CBS. This happened long before me; I didn't know about any of this. When I came along, Curt Conway, who'd been put through hell, was now teaching acting to make a living. His hell was my heaven, because if he'd been a great successful director, he wouldn't have been teaching.

When Curt Conway talked to other people, I knew exactly what he was saying, but when Curt talked to me, when it was my work, I didn't know what he was talking about. With Frank it was the opposite. When I worked with Frank Corsaro, when he talked to other people, I didn't always know what he was talking about, but when he talked to me, I knew exactly what he was talking about. Isn't that interesting?

CZ: What do you attribute that to?

DL: Their different methods of communication.

CZ: What do you think it was about Frank that made you understand him?

DL: I don't know, I just understood him. I understood Curt too, but in two different ways. But I adore Frank Corsaro; he's great talent, and a great teacher.

CZ: I'm not clear about what happened with you and The Actors Studio. Lee Grant mentions in her interview that they wouldn't let you in at first . . .

DL: A lot of people audition, and I auditioned, and I think I pissed off
Cheryl Crawford [one of the founders of The Studio]. They already had
Joanne Woodward, they already had Carroll Baker and Kim Stanley,
they'd been in there for over a decade. I was another one similar to their
type, you know what I mean? The Actors Studio takes great actors and
trains them, but they also like to get a variety of types.

Cheryl Crawford said, "Why do you want to be in The Actors Studio?"
What had happened was my father had just gotten very ill. I was from a
middle-class family, an only child, and my father had suddenly been
rushed to the hospital and lost all his money. My mother said, "Come
home, you can't stay there. Your father's lost all his stock and everything;
we're destitute, you must come home." It was an interesting thing that this
happened to me just as I was going off on my own.

Orpheus Descending, come on, paid $35 a week! You can't live off $35
a week, so I was modeling, I was dancing, doing shows for conventions
and things, tap dancing and ballet dancing, singing, trying to do commercials, anything and everything. It was exhausting. I wanted to continue
studying my acting, and I didn't know if I had the money to study. I went
into The Actors Studio and auditioned, and Cheryl Crawford said, "Well,
why do you want to be a member?" and I made a mistake. I'm a
Sagittarius, we're too honest, we shoot off our big mouths; I said,
"Because it's free!" What I meant was that I'd always have a home.
Nobody can take it away because of financial reasons. I'll belong to
somebody, like in a socialist state. If I don't have a dollar, I'll still have
this home. That's what I was trying to say.

CZ: What happened?

DL: She got angry with me. She said, "Oh, thank you very much."
She misunderstood me, but Southerners have always been misunderstood
by Northerners [*laughs*]. She said she voted against me, and her vote kept
me from getting in. I didn't become a member of The Actors Studio—I
mean, I hung around the Studio and I worked with the Studio people, but
Diane Ladd did not become a member of The Actors Studio until 1966.

CZ: This was out on the West Coast?

DL: That's right. I auditioned for Lee Strasberg and became a member
in 1966. They asked me to come back and take another audition [after the
first time]; they didn't turn me down. You know, they did this to Jason

Robards seven times, too. But I didn't come back and do another scene for a long time; maybe I was hurt. I was busy trying to make a living, and life went on. I got married to Bruce, and I came out to California, and in 1966 I did my first movie [*Wild Angels*].

CZ: What was your audition like at The Studio?

DL: I was rehearsing at a hole-in-the-wall theater the day that I was about to audition for [Lee Strasberg]. That day the lights went out on the city. Here I am six months pregnant, up on stage, scared to death, in a totally dark room, crawling on the floor and saying, "God, don't let me go now, I got to do two important things: I got to get into The Actors Studio, and I gotta have a baby!"

CZ: What happened?

DL: I'd waited and waited for years to get to Lee Strasberg, and suddenly, they had a rule that if you were putting on a scene, and if somebody else was a member and you were just an observer, they could go first. So somebody else who was a member got to put their scene ahead of mine. Then the word was that Mr. Strasberg might not stick around—he was tired, he'd been traveling, and he wasn't that young a man—so I went up to him and I said, "Mr. Strasberg?" and he said, "Yeees?" and I said, "If you don't stay for my scene"—he said "Yeees?" "I'll cry!" So he stayed. Lee Strasberg was very kind to me.

I wasn't just in the actors group, I was in the Directors/Playwrights Unit. Once upon a time, I put on one of my one-act plays, and Lee Strasberg said, "My God, who wrote this?" He said, "Whoever wrote this is a genius. This is the most exciting material to come along in 20 years other than Edward Albee. Diane, who wrote this?" You want to know what my answer was? I said "Uh . . . uh . . . uh, a man. A man wrote it, and, and . . . he goes to Harvard . . . and he let me do it." Now, does that tell you about the world I grew up in, honey?

CZ: Sure.

DL: Thank you very much. I finally just sold my first screenplay. It's quite a few years later, let me tell you what. I was a protege of Paddy Chayefsky, then I studied writing with Harold Clurman, and then I was in a class headed by William Inge. It took me all these years to say, "OK, I'm doing it."

CZ: How did you feel about the time you've spent at The Actors Studio?

DL: I thank God for The Actors Studio. In a day and age where art is smothered by commercialism, the young actors today have hardly any place to go where they can work on their craft. Television rapes talent. It makes you do junk, because television is concerned with ratings. They do these shows, and they will change the script because they don't want to offend *anybody*—they want the highest rating. All shows aren't like this, I know; I did a series. And I will tell you that the young actors come up, and it's like, "Do it fast." Not "Do it good," but "Do it fast." It's heartbreaking, and a lot of talent gets ruined. A lot of writers get ruined. Where do the writers try out their writing?

The Actors Studio was like the Group Theater. I wasn't lucky enough to be here then, I didn't get to do that. But thank God that I finally got to The Actors Studio. There's a lot of indulgence, a lot of people who get in there who are not the greatest talents. But by and large, it was, in this century, the single organization that gave the most powerful talents from this country to the world. I mean, you name 'em. And Laura Dern was the first honorary baby made a member of The Actors Studio on the West Coast.

CZ: The honorary baby?

DL: Uh huh. Because she was the first baby born of 2 members on the West Coast—me and Bruce.

CZ: Do you ever moderate at The Studio now?

DL: Not lately. I don't have time. I've paid a lot of common duties to The Studio. I went back and helped The Actors Studio raise a lot of money; when they were in trouble financially, I gave money. I also have done a lot of directing at The Actors Studio, and I have done some monitoring. But in the past couple of years, trying to write and wanting to direct and trying to act, too, and make a living, has been a hard row to hoe. But I also took my time and gave back to all my actors by being on the Board of Directors of the Screen Actors Guild for two years.

CZ: What do you feel were the most important things you learned from being at The Actors Studio?

DL: I can't say that it was from being at The Actors Studio—I would have to say it's from using my craft as an actress; I've learned a great deal.

Before I became a member of the Studio, I worked with some great people, like Eugenie Leontovitch, and Luther Adler, and John Carradine. Now these 3 people were not method actors, and they were 3 of the greatest actors that ever crossed this planet. They befriended me and became teachers of mine in other ways, and they inspired me. I also did a lot of comedy, stand-up comedy. I'm almost glad that I became a performer before I became a method actor. It keeps me aware of my obligation to the play and my obligation to my audience.

CZ: I'd like to move on to your experiences in film acting and concentrate on *Wild at Heart* [1990] and *Rambling Rose* [1992], because you did them both recently, and they're such different roles.

DL: Three hundred and sixty degrees apart.

CZ: What do you feel that you brought to *Wild at Heart* that wasn't in the script?

DL: Part of my soul. Whatever part of my soul could pick up and magnify that part of a woman who wanted her daughter to be better than herself. To take the pain and the fear, and multiply it. What I tried to be in that film is a woman who is desperate. All of us have all these sides inside ourselves; we just have to find them and understand them. So I tried to find whatever areas were desperate in Diane, and bring it to the fore, and create a woman who was desperate and fearful. Desperate to be loved, desperate to be secure.

The one thing I brought that wasn't in the script is that I tried to make a statement. When you see, on TV for example, they tell the men that, if they use a certain cologne the women will break down their door, and they tell you that, if you use a certain lipstick, you will be loved forever. Of course, you know that's a lie. So, in one scene I had [Marietta] look like Dolly Parton, in another scene she looked like Kathleen Turner, in another scene someone else. What she was saying was, "If I look like her, am I good enough? If I look like her, am I good enough?"

Part of that was the inspiration for the lipstick thing. If I take this lipstick and put it on my mouth, I'm supposed to be beautiful. Suppose I put it all over my face? There was the association with blood, but it was more than that. What I was saying is, "Can I ever be good enough? Can anybody ever be good enough, with the way we sell things to ourselves, day in and day out, sell, sell, sell?" You only buy things because you're supposed to need them. If you need things, you need 'em because something's missing, right? So when you're bombarded with things like that, then it's programming you that you aren't good enough. I was trying to use that as part of the statement for this character.

CZ: When you do something that's as stylized as *Wild at Heart,* what's required of you that's different from doing a more naturalistic role? You're doing things that are taboo in film acting—like looking directly at the camera, for example.

DL: I don't think it's taboo. Elia Kazan directed *Baby Doll* [1956]; he had Eli Wallach look right into the camera, one of the most powerful shots ever. It's not taboo, it's director's choice.

CZ: Isn't that usually the first thing that they tell you as a film actor, not to look at the lens?

DL: Yeah, but the first thing they tell you on the stage is, "Don't turn your back to the audience." You have to be creative, you have to listen to your own higher self. All rules are made to be broken a little bit, as long as they don't hurt somebody's space.

CZ: How much input did you have with David Lynch?

DL: David Lynch was incredible; he let me do whatever I wanted to do. He let me dress the way I wanted to, he let me use whatever hair I wanted to.

CZ: It must have been really fun.

DL: It was fun. David's wonderful to work with; he's very harmonious. The reason I wanted to be part of a David Lynch movie is I think David is a novelist who writes with the camera. David is an incredible artist and a magnificent director, and I love him. He never says a dirty word, he's a gentleman on the set, he's soft-spoken, treats his crew and his actors very elegantly and extremely fair. It is important that when David Lynch does a film, if God forbid you were about to take your life or take someone else's, and on the way home you stopped and saw a David Lynch movie—honey, I don't think you would do it. Because he makes the violence so ugly that you don't want to be part of it. Violence is sickening, it's a horrible thing. Many movies make violence so exciting for kids. And the way that women are treated on the screen, all these horrible things that are done to them, I think it's disgusting.

CZ: So you wouldn't lend your name to a film in which you felt the violence was gratuitous?

DL: Never say never.

CZ: You're saying that working with David was really harmonious, but has there ever been a time in your life when you worked with a director you didn't get along with?

DL: I have been an actress since I was 17 years old; OK, that's 33 years. In thirty-three years in this business, I have only worked with 3 directors I didn't like. One was somebody in television, and he did not know how to direct. But worse than that, he was cruel to an animal. He wanted a horse to stand up, and he was tying wires to a horse's hooves, and I was livid with rage. I will not abide somebody hurting an animal. I was very young, and I was furious, and I told him off for hurting the horse. The second time I got mad with a director was a director who was being cruel to a child. Nobody on the set liked him, so to get his ego back, he put down a 10-year-old boy. I thought it was disgusting, and I took up with the child. He went and said that I was a pain in the ass to work with, and he talked about me behind my back. Better he should talk about me than a child has to go to a psychiatrist later. The only other person I didn't get along with was truly somebody who didn't know how to direct; he shouldn't be directing. It was a low-budget film, and the man was no director, that's it.

CZ: What does it mean to not be able to direct?

DL: Well, it means he didn't know a darn thing about good scenes, or how to act, or even good camera shots. He had gone to film school and made a junky violent film; I didn't think he knew how to direct. I thought he ought to be in another business.

CZ: What do you do when that happens? When you really can't get along with a director?

DL: You do your work, and you pray.

CZ: What was it like working with a woman director, Martha Coolidge, on *Rambling Rose*?

DL: The nice thing about a woman director is that if you have cramps, you can tell them. You can talk to them. It's sometimes good to work with a woman director—we need more women directors—but just the gender doesn't necessarily mean that that makes a person a better director or better to work with. I got along as well with David Lynch and Martin Scorsese as I ever did with Martha Coolidge. A woman should not be ostracized from directing because she's a woman. Neither should she be applauded and given a break just because she's a woman. Martha's a director because Martha's a wonderful director.

CZ: Did you feel that she handled the set, or conducted herself on the set differently than a man would?

DL: Not always. I think that she handled the [seduction] scene between Lucas and Laura very delicately, being a woman. I think that was a wonderful thing. We need some more women directors, because I think that a picture like *Rambling Rose* was best served by female energy. I'm

Diane Ladd and Robert Duvall in *Rambling Rose* (1991). Still from *Rambling Rose* provided by Carolco Pictures Inc. Motion Picture © 1991. Carolco Pictures Inc. Museum of Modern Art Film Stills Archive.

sure there are male directors who could have done as good a job, but I think they're few and far between, and I think that the delicacy of the material was better served by a female director.

I did a picture for Martha, *Plain Clothes* [1988], about 5 or 6 years earlier, where it was a lot of fun, because women want to make sure that the food is nice for everybody. And we had a masseuse on the set. We were all running around rubbing each other's shoulders to keep each other from tension, so that was an asset. But I don't think Martha, because she was a female, handled anybody any better than David Lynch or Martin Scorsese, at least while I was working with her. I care about how I'm treated on the set. I care about integrity, honesty, fair play, and understanding at all times, and if I can get that from a man or a woman, then it's great.

CZ: Going back to *Rambling Rose:* How did you prepare for that role? Things like using your hearing aid . . . .

DL: I had studied with the deaf. It was a wonderful insight for me because I found a key to her character—that she was able to love her people more objectively and clearly and not judge them so fast, because she listened with the ear of her heart. I also based it on a real character, which was Calder Willingham's [the writer of *Rambling Rose*] mother. I discovered a lot about his mother; I feel that she was a totally metaphysical creature. She was a friend of Thoreau and all of the people who were theosophists at the time, people who believed that philosophy and theology had not always led people the right way. So they combined the two into theosophy, meaning no matter what your race, creed, or religion is, we are all a human race, and we must help each other evolve on this planet. That was the m.o. for the character that I played.

CZ: Going more into the preparation for this role—you seem so comfortable doing all your character's actions, from making lemonade to being in bed with Robert Duvall. Did you rehearse a lot?

DL: No. We did some rehearsal, but I think that a good director chooses their actors and lets them do what they pay them for: Do their work and create the character. Once the director gets the script, and the d.p. [director of photography] and you get the shots that you want to shoot, a good director has to be careful not to get in the way of the actor. You've hired them because they've got the talent, they're buried in the character.

You're the traffic cop, and that takes genius, to be a good traffic cop with actors. You're not doing the acting, they are. What you have to do is guide them, make the street easy for them so that they can do it.

CZ: How much did Martha rehearse with you?

DL: We had a couple of days before we started, and then of course you have to rehearse the blocking so that the cameraman sees what you're going to do. You have to rehearse so that the light man can light you and see what you're gonna do.

I think Martha was very helpful. We talked about the character a lot. I fell in love with this part. She gave me the script to read 6 years before we did it. We were talking about my philosophy, and she said, "My God, you are my mother." I said "I beg your pardon?" and she said, "My mother in that [film]." And then Laura read it and fell in love with it, and Laura said, "Mother, you gotta read this script." I said, "I've gotta do this part."

CZ: Your character is an older women, and someone who has sexuality—that's rare.

DL: Thank you. I love the love scene. That was my idea, that we had to put the love scene in.

CZ: You mean with Robert Duvall?

DL: Yeah. I went to Martha and said, "Martha, we've got a problem. I can see that if we don't have a love scene, it's gonna look like he's just a horny old man trying to catch the housekeeper, but if you show that we really have a deep love, then he's just another human being—welcome to the human race—who's being tempted." That's a big difference, isn't it?

You want to hear an interesting comment? Darling, darling, Lucas Haas, he's a wonderful actor, equal to his peers every step of the way, made a wonderful comment to me. He was 14 years old, and he said, "Diane, you know what my favorite scene in the movie is?" I said, "No, what, Luke?" He said, "You and Bobby Duvall's love scene," and I said, "Why, Luke?" He said, "Well, I can go to a movie any day in the week and see somebody my age getting it on, but I never get to go and see a love story with the married people getting it on, the mature people, and if they do, then they're usually married to somebody else!" Now isn't that a pitiful comment about our times?

CZ: But it's so true.

DL: He said, "Someday I'm going to be married, Diane, and I want people to tell me what my life will be like then."

CZ: That's an incredible thing for a 14-year-old to say. Can you talk about the film that you're directing? Why did you want to get into it?

DL: The past couple of years, different directors have said to me, "Diane, you'd be a wonderful director." I had done a lot of theater, and I said, "Well, films are so involved, you know, the film medium, and this and that." They said, "No, no, you know the best camera angles, you know exactly what you're doing." They just kept saying it, more and more. Then, I optioned a book, and I wrote a screenplay based on this book *Mrs. Munck.* Since that time, I've acted in two other films, and one of the films had trouble with the director. I just felt that his camera shots were wrong, everything he was doing was wrong, and I didn't say it, but I thought, "No, I want to direct my movie." So that's how it happened. It only took me 25 years to do this, that's just a few minutes, right? [*Laughter*]

CZ: What's the name of the film?

DL: *Mrs. Munck.* I'm also acting in it; I play the older Mrs. Munck. Shelley Winters is starring in it with me, and a young, beautiful actress named Kelly Preston. I couldn't use my daughter Laura because this actress has love scenes with Bruce. Bruce plays a sexy 50-year-old, and he also plays an older man of 76 who really has lost his will to live. So Bruce has some very powerful, powerful parts, here.

CZ: How do you feel about directing Bruce?

DL: Well, I've told him he was a terrible husband, but he's a magnificent actor. I'm not marrying him, I'm directing him. So if I can get along with Bruce Dern while I'm directing him, there will be no more excuses on this planet for any wars between anybody [*laughter*].

CZ: I have one final question. What, for you, makes a great film performance?

DL: Truth. An inner truth, whatever that truth is. I think to be a great actor like Marlon Brando or anyone else you have to try to be a great human being. I'm not saying you can't mess up and make mistakes. But you take Marlon Brando, for example: He cared a lot about a whole race of people, the Indians, that he didn't feel were being treated right in this country. He put his money where his mouth was and really tried to help them. That takes a great human being. And you can't be great all the time. The bigger you are, the harder you can fall, you know? But I think that if you don't believe in a God, then your talent is your soul, and you can't beat it over the head day by day and still expect it to work for you. So you have to give it the truth; truth is sunlight, truth is nourishment. Truth sets you free, it sets your talent free to flow like a river of purity, and that's what makes a great performance.

An Interview with Eli Wallach

Eli Wallach. Courtesy of Paradigm.

In the late 1940s and early 1950s, there was an astonishing convergence of talent and originality in the New York theater. Playwrights like Arthur Miller, Tennessee Williams, and William Inge emerged on the scene; directors of the calibre of Elia Kazan, Daniel Mann, and Harold Clurman staged landmark productions; The Actors Studio was established in 1947. Eli Wallach is one of the actors most closely associated with this momentous and dynamic epoch in American theater history. He is a prominent figure in some of the most celebrated productions of the period, notably as Mangiacavallo in the Broadway premiere of Williams' *The Rose Tattoo* (1951), which was directed by Mann. Later, Wallach originated the role of Kilroy in the same playwright's *Camino Real* (1953), directed by Elia Kazan. Wallach remained a durable fixture on the Broadway stage, demonstrating his versatility by moving dextrously across a range of styles, from Shavian comedy to the theater of the absurd. Among the plays he performed in were *Mademoiselle Columbe* (1954), *Teahouse of the*

August Moon (1954), *Major Barbara* (1956), *The Chairs* (1958), *The Rhino-ceros* (1961), *The Typist and the Tiger* (1963), *Luv* (1964), *Staircase* (1968), and *The Waltz of the Toreadors* (1973). He has been the recipient of numerous awards for his stage work: The Donaldson, Theater World, and Antoinette Perry. During the 50s and 60s, Wallach also made appearances in live television dramas such as *Playhouse 90*, *Studio One*, and *Philco Playhouse.*

Wallach's film career started with *Baby Doll* in 1956—for which he won the British Academy Award as Best Actor—and took off in earnest in the 1960s and 1970s, with films like *The Magnificent Seven* (1960); *The Misfits* (1961); *How The West Was Won* (1962); *The Victors* (1963); *Lord Jim* (1965); *How to Steal a Million* (1966); *The Good, the Bad, and the Ugly* (1967); *The Tiger Makes Out* (1967); *Mackenna's Gold* (1968); *Crazy Joe* (1973); *Cinderella Liberty* (1974); *The Deep* (1977); *The Sentinel* (1977); *Girl Friends* (1978); and *Winter Kills* (1979). The next decade saw Wallach appear increasingly in made-for-television movies such as *The Ex-ecutioner's Song* (1982), *Anatomy of an Illness* (1984), *Murder By Reason of Insanity* (1985), and *Our Family Honor* (1985). The actor returned to the big screen in the late 80s and 90s in: *Nuts* (1987), *The Godfather III* (1990), The Two Jakes (1990), *Article 99* (1991), and *Mistress* (1991).

Wallach was born in New York in 1915 and received a B.A. from The University of Texas (1936) and an M.S. in Education from The City College of New York (1938). He then attended The Neighborhood Playhouse, graduating in 1940. Wallach became a founding member of The Actors Studio at its inception; he remains actively involved as a performer and a moderator. After serving in World War II, Wallach began his long acting career. One of his first major roles was in Katharine Cornell's 1947 production of *Antony and Cleopatra*. Wallach consolidated his reputation several years later as a principal in Josh Logan's staging of *Mister Roberts* (1949). He received a Distinguished Alumnus Award from The University of Texas in 1989 and an honorary doctorate from Emerson College in 1991.

Eli Wallach resides in New York, where I spoke to him in January of 1991.

CZ: Let's start with your first film, *Baby Doll* [1956]. Had you ever worked with Elia Kazan before?

EW: Yes, I did a play by Tennessee Williams called *Camino Real* (1953) that he directed. At first, they couldn't raise the money for the production, so I went and did my first screen test for a movie. I was accepted for the movie, and it was agreed that I would play the role. And then the money for the play came through. The play was tailored for me; I had worked on it for a long time with Kazan. So I chose to do the play as opposed to the movie. The movie was *From Here to Eternity* [1953], and Frank Sinatra played Maggio, the part I was offered. And every time he sees me, he says: "Hello, you crazy actor." I don't think I chose unwisely.

CZ: You have a very strong connection with Tennessee Williams.

EW: Basically, the first 7 years of my theatrical life. I met my wife [Anne Jackson] when we were doing a one-act play called *This Property Is Condemned* at The Equity Library Theater. Then she did *Summer and Smoke*, the original; then I did *The Rose Tattoo* (1951) and *Camino Real*. We did a tour of *The Glass Menagerie*, and my first movie was Tennessee Williams. And 2 years ago we did the second annual Tennessee Williams Festival down in New Orleans. He had a big influence on our lives. His sense of language, his sense of situation was just brilliant. The theater had a big loss when he left.

Anyhow, after my screen test, I went back into theater, but *Camino Real* wasn't a success. I went to England and did *Teahouse of the August Moon* (1954) for a year. I came back to America and was doing *Teahouse* when Kazan called and said, "OK, now I got a movie you can do." So my first movie was *Baby Doll*.

CZ: What were your feelings about making your first film?

EW: I came on as a naïve, rather stuffy stage actor thinking movies were like a toy. It's a mechanical medium, and what you see on the screen is what somebody puts up there. They can cut away from an actor in the middle of an emotional scene, and the actor has no control.

CZ: What kind of adjustments did you have to make when you were going from theater to film?

EW: Karl Malden, who had made several movies, said to me: "Listen Eli, when you're up on the screen, your head is about 30 feet high. So don't open your mouth too much because they'll see your tonsils, and your inlays, and your gold teeth." I had to yell to Carroll Baker in one scene . . . She says: "Heigh ho, Silva!" [Wallach's character] I say: "Heigh ho!" And Kazan said, "What's the matter with you?" I said, "Why? I just said

Eli Wallach with Carroll Baker in *Baby Doll* (1956), directed by Elia Kazan. © 1956 Newtown Productions, Inc., through Castle Hill Productions, Inc. Museum of Modern Art Film Stills Archive.

'Heigh ho.' " He said, "I don't want the Japanese version; open your mouth and call." So I came to it.

When we did the scene in the dining room we pleaded with him, "Please let us play the scene. No close-ups, cut-aways, let's play the scene." I mean Karl and Mildred Dunnock and myself were basically stage actors. So he said "OK," and he mapped out a scene lasting 1½ minutes—that's a lifetime on the screen. At one point the cameraman said: "I don't know what's happening, the camera is shaking." And it was Karl, who was so angry . . . it was a dilapidated old floor that shook the camera. I worked very hard on that movie, and Kazan was a marvelous conductor. He wielded his baton very deftly. He has a way of pitting actor against actor.

CZ: Can you give me an example of that?

EW: In the play I did, *Camino*, he'd say to me, "Go on stage and make friends. I can't tell you how, everybody makes friends differently." Then he tells the actors on stage, "Don't have anything to do with this guy, he's got bad breath, he's a bad man." So now he causes conflict, right? And actors love it. It's the kind of game they love to play.

CZ: In *Baby Doll,* you're sometimes playing to the camera when nobody is in the room, gesturing and shrugging your shoulders, using a lot of Italianate gestures. This may be part of Kazan's aesthetic, because he tends to mix theater and film in performance styles. I wonder if you learned any lessons about playing for the camera?

EW: I'll tell you, initially when we used to do live television, there was a little red light at the bottom of the camera, and you knew when the camera was on you because that little red light went on. Wise directors began to cover that little red light with a piece of tape so you couldn't see it. Yes, initially I was aware of this intrusive instrument. But now the camera and lenses are so far away, you don't even know that the camera is on you. I mean, they don't get up close to you. In *The Good, the Bad, and the Ugly* [1967], every time there was a change of lens, we'd do the same scene over. Now they zoom in and zoom out, and the actors are unaware of it.

But once I sneaked in and saw some rushes of *Baby Doll,* and the next day I came on the set and Kazan said, "Why did you turn that way?" And I said, "Well my face, this side . . ." He said, "I don't ever want you to go look at those rushes again. Let me decide." I used to say to him at the end of a shot—we'd do a shot maybe four or five times—he'd say, "OK. Cut." I'd think, "Can I do one more, just one more, I think I found . . ." He said: "Sure, film is cheap. Go ahead, do one more." Every time I asked to do one more, he never printed the one more I asked for, which was his way of saying to me, "Listen Eli, let me be the decider. My objective eye is out here; you're subjective, you're editing as you're shooting. I know which is better, not you." And a lot of times, you know, I stopped asking. The camera is very revealing. That's why I say, if you really think, if you're *really* playing the situation, you don't give a damn about the camera.

CZ: How much rehearsal time did you have on *Baby Doll*?

EW: Not too much. The cameraman, Boris Kaufman, was a brilliant, brilliant cameraman, and he would take hours to set up a shot. While he was doing that, we'd just sit around and talk about the characters, and then we'd do it.

CZ: Going back to *Baby Doll,* there's a lot of physical work going on, like the scene where you and Carroll Baker are running around the house. You get on a hobby horse, and you're rocking back and forth and hitting it with a crop; there's rock and roll playing in the background. That's pretty wild stuff. Did you improvise any of that on the set?

EW: We do make up a lot of things as we see what the set is like. For example, I had seen a movie called *Great Expectations* [1946]. There's a little boy in the cemetery and he turns around, and the camera jumps to a man's face, and everybody in the audience jumped. In *Baby Doll,* I found the head of this deer. We put vaseline on the eyes and I wanted to hold it up when I chase Carroll Baker around, so the audience would jump. Well, we did it. Kazan said: "Oh, that's fine, let's try." It didn't work as well as in *Great Expectations.* But to go back to the actor, for example, there's this scene where she tries to go down the stairs, and I jump over the railing onto the stairs and she falls and I tickle her belly with my foot. Remember? That was done on the set.

CZ: One thing that I really love is your seduction scene with Carroll Baker. You offer her a pecan, and at first she says: "No one would take a pecan from a gentleman when he's just cracked it with his teeth." And then later in the same scene, she takes the pecan without saying a word.

EW: That's like the scene in *On the Waterfront* [1954] where Marlon [Brando] is playing a scene with Eva Marie [Saint]. She drops a glove and walks on. He puts the glove on unconsciously. Now, those things happen in a scene and a director says, "Oh my God, one moment like that is gold on the screen." If you find or discover one little thing like that, it's brilliant. To think on screen is the most difficult thing of all.

CZ: Can you tell me what you mean by that?

EW: For example, an actor learns a line. The line is: "I think I'll go in the front door." The first time I acted with a young actor, he kept saying the line over and over. I said, "Don't think about *how* you're going to say it. Listen to what the other person says. That will color and affect the way you answer." And that's the secret. Really listening to what the other person says. You know? But all these things are arrived at on the set, and we do it.

CZ: How would you go about developing your characterization? Would there be major objectives or actions for your character? *Baby Doll* starts with your cotton gin being burned down, and you go into an old house and see this beautiful young girl, and you also see that Karl Malden, her husband, is an old fool. What is your purpose?

EW: Revenge. I want to get the documents and the papers to prove that this man [Malden] did it. And therefore, he'll gin out my cotton until I rebuild that cotton gin. The means of getting the proof was through this girl. He realizes that here's the answer to what he's looking for: the truth of what really happened that night. He knows the authorities are not going to do it; they cover up everything.

Once this cotton gin's burned down, there's a shot of me standing in the burning ruins. I have to turn and look into the camera; the camera is right there. Now they could have burned all the cotton gins in Mississippi, as far as I was concerned. But I had to find something deeply personal so the audience would feel the meaning for me of the cotton gin burning down. And that's part of Kazan's brilliance. That's the technique that we were bringing to the screen, we actors from The Actors Studio. His movies in the beginning used Marlon, Paul Newman, Geraldine Page and Anne Bancroft, Julie Harris, James Dean, Rod Steiger—all these people came out of his well-stocked acting stream. And we knew we could play the instrument; we knew that when he came out to conduct, we would be able to carry out his desires.

CZ: Carroll Baker is very good in *Baby Doll.*

EW: She's wonderful. I enjoyed kissing her. [*Laughter*] She wrote a book called *Baby Doll* in which she intimated that I had a yen for her. That's not true, I had a wife who just had a baby, as a matter of fact. My second child was born while we were shooting that.

CZ: How did you like seeing yourself on the screen?

EW: I said to Anne when it was over—Karl and I had many confrontational scenes, face to face—and I said to Anne, "How did you like it?" And she said, "Never have two noses so filled the screen!" [*Laughter*]

CZ: What happened after *Baby Doll?*

EW: After I finished *Baby Doll* I thought, now I'll go back to the theater, which is where I want to go. And I didn't go back to films for about a year or so afterwards. The second film, I got a call to go to San Francisco to do a movie. I read the script; it was called *The Line-Up* [1958].

CZ: By Don Siegel?

EW: Yes. My God, I kill 5 people. They said San Francisco is a wonderful city, you'll play a romantic killer, whoever. So I said as a joke, "OK, ten grand a killing!" "OK, you've got a deal!"

CZ: I want to go on to *The Good, the Bad, and the Ugly.* What was it like working with Sergio Leone in Italy? I noticed that even though there's looping in *Baby Doll,* everything seems looped in *The Good, the Bad, and the Ugly.*

EW: At that time, on *The Good, the Bad, and the Ugly,* their system of work was to use a cue track. They would record what was being said, but they didn't give a damn whether an airplane flew over, or my stomach growled because I hadn't eaten for 4 hours, or an ambulance went by. They didn't care. Later I went in a studio and for 7 days, Sergio stood along side me, and we re-did every line I did in that movie. I said, "Sergio, I'm on a horse riding in the desert. Here I am in the studio!" He said, "Do it, do it, make noise, I don't care." So I did it, and it's all done that way.

CZ: What was it like on the set with Leone?

EW: I liked him. He let me alone a lot. When I first met him, he was wearing suspenders and a belt. I thought, gee, he's afraid his pants are gonna fall down. I said, "I want to wear suspenders and a belt." He said, "OK, I don't want you to have a holster." I said, "What do I do?" He said, "You put the gun on with a lanyard around your neck." I said, "It dangles between my legs." He said, "Yeah, and when you want it you shrug your shoulders and I cut and the gun is in your hand." I said, "Show me." He put the lanyard around his neck and pushed at his shoulders; it missed his hand, it hit him in the groin. He said, "Keep it in your pocket." [*Laughter*] So I wore the gun in my pocket.

I knew I'd have to do a lot of shooting in that movie, so I put a fingerless leather glove on one hand and a lot of rings. You never see what the bad people do with the money; I always wanted to show what I did with my wealth. So I put in gold teeth, I wore silk shirts, a silver saddle. I picked out the costume.

And there's a scene where I go to a gun shop and I put a gun together. Now I spent half a morning just taking a gun apart and putting it together. What he was brilliant at was he'd let the actor *do it*. The actor putting a gun together, instead of cutting away. A lot of directors say, "OK, you have the gun, we cut away, we come back, the gun is together." He let me put the gun together. Right? That's his cleverness.

CZ: How was Leone working with you, and Clint Eastwood, and Lee van Cleef as a group? From what I know about Kazan's work, he's a very strong ensemble director. How would someone like Leone differ from Kazan?

EW: Kazan orchestrates and plays one against the other. Leone didn't necessarily do that. Don't forget, I was the virgin in this one. It was Clint's third film for him—*Fistful of Dollars* [1964] and *For a Few Dollars More* [1965]—and this was the third of a trilogy. So Clint had his character down. He used to smoke these small cigars. He knew where that character was going. Lee had the experience of the second film and knew where his character was going. Mine was the newcomer to the scene. And so he let me alone, and they adjusted to what I was doing. I got along very well with Clint, who doesn't talk very much but is very skillful on the screen.

CZ: How were you chosen for the role? Was it because of *The Magnificent Seven* [1960]?

EW: I think Leone had seen me in it. He flew out to California and talked to my agent and said, "I'd like him to do it." I said, "An Italian Western? I never heard of one!" He said, "Well, I'll show you some of my films." I saw 2 minutes of the second film. I said, "I'll go, where do you want me to go?" He said, "Spain." I went to Spain and I did the movie. That was a long movie, over 4 months.

CZ: What were the working conditions like?

EW: Primitive. [*Laughter*] At that time, there were none of these air-conditioned trailers, things like that. We'd go out in the desert at 6:30 in the morning in Almaria, which is on the Mediterranean in southern Spain. And there'd be the camera operator, the director, the guy with the reflector to catch the rays of the sun, and me, and a horse. So when I got out there one day, I said, "I have to go to the bathroom." Leone gestured widely to the whole desert and said, "Go!" [*Laughter*] Clint and I—there were no hotels in this town—stayed at private homes near the ocean, so we always ate fish and swam in the sea.

CZ: Your performance in that film is much more stylized than your performance of Silva in *Baby Doll;* is there any special way that you dealt with that?

EW: Well, it was different. One is a satirical, amusing, cartoon of a Western, and Sergio allowed the humor that you'd bring to it, the fun of it. When I ride away on a horse and Clint *leisurely* reaches over and lights a cannon, that's fairy tale stuff! You can't do that! Whereas in *Baby Doll,* it's a serious situation, it's a true situation. So one is a little fantasy and the other is realistic.

CZ: Was that fun for you, to be big like that?

EW: I love it. I mean, if it gets too much, they cut it down.

CZ: Let's get back to how you work on a character. How analytical are you about your work?

EW: Basically I say, "What if I were this guy, and what am I doing?" Then I leave it alone for a while. I begin to look at the clothing that I might wear and I think what situations I know that are parallel. I'm me, I've never been a Mexican bandit. I once went to Cambodia and did a movie directed by Richard Brooks, called *Lord Jim* [1965]. I was a half-breed and I cut my hair a certain way, and I lifted weights so my muscles would stick out a little bit. That's all my painting. When I gotta go into a studio, I close the door and paint. And come out.

I don't want to sit around and analyze what I did, you know. The painter doesn't do that. He just goes on painting. It's other people who sit down and say, "Now, the inner turmoil of this man, the childhood dream . . ." and it goes on like that.

Well, you know the story of Whistler? Whistler used to sign his name, James McNeill Whistler, and nobody wanted to buy the paintings because, my God, look at the signature, it takes up half the painting. So he said, "I'll never paint again. Never. That's it." Well, a couple of years went by. He got a commission and he said, "Alright, I'll paint. I'll put a butterfly in the corner, that way, you'll know it's mine." That's the way he signed them from then on, with a little butterfly. Well, I studied with Martha Graham for 2 years at The Neighborhood Playhouse, and somewhere in each movie I do this little movement that I put in which is my signature. Nobody knows. It's like E. G. Marshall the actor, no one knows, in the 50 years that I've known him, what E. G. means.

CZ: Tell me how you worked on your character, Guido, in *The Misfits* [1961]. The relationships in that film are fairly complex.

EW: There are some actors who, if they're going to play a coal miner, have to go down a mine and spend 3 months in a mine and get dirty and know what the life is like, right? Some actors don't have to go down in the mine. They put dirt on their face, they come up out of their mineshaft, and you say, "Gee, there's a coal miner." Right? One does it literally, the other imagines, and I fit into the latter group, the imagining-what-it's-like.

I've just been reading about De Niro, who's a wonderful actor, but he's been playing this catatonic [*Awakenings,* 1990], spending 3 months in this hospital and 2 months in that one. And that's where all the hype and the publicity is. And you come and you look at the screen and you say, "Alright, he's doing one of those sickness movies," like *Rain Man* [1988]. And they're the ones who win all the awards. I don't have to analyze it. I played a prison psychiatrist with Barbra Streisand in a movie called *Nuts* [1987]. I didn't go to sit with a psychiatrist. I just put on the glasses that I thought he would wear, and I listened to her, and I memorized the lines, and I did it.

CZ: So with *The Misfits,* you're saying that you put yourself in imaginary circumstances and just got on the set and did it? Did you think about your character's drive or his problem?

EW: Well, they call him Pilot—he used to fly a plane; he lost his wife. People dramatize, make up stories of the past, which are complete fabrications, but they've told the story so many times that they get to believe it. And they use it. That whole story about my wife and the automobile . . . it's self-pity, it's all devised to win this girl who I like, Marilyn. My character was in competition with the other great lovers of the screen, Montgomery Clift and Clark Gable. The first day I worked on the movie, I looked at Clark Gable and kept thinking, this is the "King" of the movies. And he kept looking at me, thinking, this kid comes from New York with this mysterious Method, the gurus. We were both tongue-tied. So [John] Huston said, "Will you two knock it off and just say the lines?"

CZ: How did John Huston work with actors?

EW: Huston was very, very sharp and very smart. There's a scene where Clark Gable and I are sitting, while Marilyn dances with Montgomery Clift, and we're getting drunker and drunker. There are about eight glasses on the table and I was really drunk [*slurs speech*]. And Huston came up to me—they were relighting, we were gonna reshoot the scene. He said, "You know, kid, the drunkest I ever was in my life?" I said, "No." He said, "Yesterday." I said, "Yesterday? But I saw you yesterday! We were in Virginia City, and there was a race between a camel and a horse, and you rode the camel!" He said, "That's the drunkest I ever was in my life." They said, "We're ready to shoot, Mr. Huston." He walked away and I thought, "Oh my God, what he's telling me is that he was so drunk I didn't even know it, and I saw it." That changed my whole drunken approach. A drunk tries to be very sober. He tries to conceal it; he doesn't try to be drunk. That's the way he directed, by indirection. And he rarely said anything. If he liked what you did, he went on; he didn't say, "I want you to play it this way or do it this way."

CZ: What if he didn't like what you were doing?

EW: He'd shoot it again. And he'd say, "Oh, let's try one more."

CZ: Arthur Miller was on location with you, right? Did he ever have discussions with you about what was in the script?

EW: Well, what happened was Arthur had written a valentine to Marilyn. He had gone to Reno to get a divorce and he ran into these cowboys. And in their light, he was this city boy meeting these outdoors men, right? And he was fascinated with this whole life, so he wrote a short story about it. When they were married, Marilyn decided they would do this movie, and he wrote a valentine to her. While we're shooting, the marriage is falling apart, so that the more each man said about what a wonderful creature she was, the sicker she got.

CZ: Do you mean in real life?

EW: Real life. That's why it was so difficult for her to come on the set and face the camera. The camera to her was an X-ray eye. That camera could look through not only the exterior but into the interior, and that drove her up the wall.

I love one sweet story. We were shooting in California and 3 months in Nevada; at the end, we were on overtime. And Marilyn couldn't come on at 8:00 in the morning. She'd come at 10:20, and she rushed in one day and threw her arms around Clark Gable and said, "I'm terribly sorry I'm late." Now, he was on overtime, he was getting $50,000 a week. This is 30 years ago, so that was like $200,000 now. So he said, "There's no hurry honey, no hurry . . ."

CZ:　Your character, Guido, is an outsider; he's more sensitive and intelligent and educated than anyone else in the movie. It seemed to me that there was an obvious parallel with Arthur Miller. What do you think?

EW:　I don't know. You have to insert that. For example, we were told in *Baby Doll,* when I'm sitting on the swing with Carroll, my hand went out of camera shot. They said, "Where was his hand?" They've written treatises about where my hand was. Well it was cold as hell, in November, when we were shooting and we had to suck on ice cubes and spit out the ice cubes before they said "Action" so that our breath wouldn't show all that smoke coming out. And we had long winter underwear on, and they had little radiators at our feet, otherwise we would have frozen. Now I laugh when they write these great treatises about my hand, and what I did, and the seduction of this lady, and so on. I say, let them do that. And the same thing with *Misfits.* They've written all kinds of things about the parallels between Arthur and Marilyn and what was happening.

I stopped giving interviews because one interview, in one book, said that when I was dancing with her, I kept turning her so that my face would be on camera. And I found out who told this story, and I went up to her and said, "How could you do that, you know damn well what Huston would've said, he would've kicked me off the set. He'd say, 'OK, knock that off, kid. I see what you're doing, you can't do that.' " And Marilyn was very wise; Marilyn could read the fine print on a contract. She advised *me* on how to sign a contract. We were very dear friends, and she said, "No, don't sign this, sign this, cut that clause out, do this." She was very wise. So I'm leery of these treatises on what people were doing on the set. When we were doing *The Godfather III* [1990], I read in the paper that we had to have an armed guard take us to the set, which is ludicrous. As though the mafia is gonna waste time screwing up this movie. It's the greatest publicity in the world for them.

CZ:　So it's not true? [*Laughter*] How did you feel about playing an "older" man in *The Godfather*?

EW: Well, I'm in my 80s in that. I said to Francis, I'm not gonna work again. People are gonna look at me and say, "My God, look how old he's gotten." [*Laughter*]

CZ: I know, I was thinking that too, that you have to go right out and make another movie . . .

EW: Francis said, "You're an old, old, old member of the Corleone family." I said, "If I was such an old, old . . . why wasn't I in *The Godfather I* and *II?*" He said, "You were in Sicily . . ."

CZ: You were out of town, right? [*Laughter*] How would Coppola work on scenes? How would he rehearse, and would he use improvisation when he was working?

EW: No, not really. He'd say, "Walk in and show me where you want to sit, how you want to do this. Move over here. Do you think he'd get up and go over there?" Then we'd do it. The first time he directed me, he was in the little trailer. He has a thing called the Silverfish. It has all these computers, and screens, and dials, and everything, and it has a little kitchen and a little jacuzzi and he has this loudspeaker system. So I said, "Where are you? Where's the director?" He said, "I'll come right out, I'll come right out."

CZ: So Coppola's always suggesting little things for you to do?

EW: Yes. It's like tightening a screw. A little tighter or a little looser. He sits there and watches very carefully what the actor is doing. It's like pointillism. The little dots, and you don't see the picture until you step back. It's like a jigsaw puzzle. He knows this piece fits in here, this piece fits in here. When we first got the script, the last 10 pages were missing because none of us were to know our fate. As in life, you go on, you don't know what's going to happen.

CZ: Your character gets to die rather well, eating cannolis and listening to opera!

EW: We did eight or nine takes! You know what was very interesting? On screen, I'm looking at the stage, but the opera had already been shot in a studio in Rome. There was nothing down there in Palermo. Francis was on the loudspeaker saying to me: "Now he's whipping the horse, quick get enthusiastic, wheeeeaaahhh." He was directing me, because they couldn't use the stage in Palermo. That opera house had been closed for 15 years.

CZ: Your Italian is really good. Al Pacino's Italian, well . . .

EW: Al does a very sweet thing. He ad-libs it so it sounds Italian, but he's not really speaking Italian. And then they put the camera far away so you don't see Al. The very first scene I did in *Godfather III* was with the Italian man, where we're plotting, where I'm hiring him to do the killing. Coppola said to me, "I want you to play it Sicilian." I said, "Oh Francis . . ." He said, "Well, get a cassette." And I listened to a cassette with some man saying the lines from the film in Sicilian the day before. And I memorized it, and when I was playing it, I was leery that people were gonna say, "Oh, Italians don't talk this way," but it was Sicilian. Because the patois, the dialect is different from Italian. It's like talking in New Orleans or talking in Brooklyn.

CZ: Maybe you'll win an Oscar nomination for Don Altobello.

EW: I doubt it. It's not a strong enough part. I was gonna be in *Tucker* [1988] at one point, but I was doing a play, so I couldn't do it, and Marty Landau got it. And he won a nomination. He was wonderful. My role in *Godfather* is too small. Andy Garcia could be nominated. And how do you compare my role in the film to Andy Garcia's, which is a much showier part? I don't spend time thinking, gee . . . I won the British Academy Award for *Baby Doll,* which to me shows that the British were very sensitive to a promising young actor. And I never got a nomination for anything in the movies.

CZ: Oh really?

EW: No. *The Good, the Bad, and the Ugly* or *The Magnificent Seven,* those movies were very successful movies, but I never got nominated. So I've memorized my speech and the day'll come.

CZ: We haven't really talked about your training. You mentioned The Actors Studio; can you talk a bit about your work there?

EW: The Studio initially was like a kind of gym, a workout place. You could come and prepare a scene and try it. I did *Hamlet* with Millie Dunnock, playing with a migraine headache. Who has ever played Hamlet with a migraine headache? It colored the whole thing.

Anne and I just went with E. G. Marshall and his wife to China for a month. And we lectured, and we went to all the acting schools we could find in China. And they were all doing Stanislavsky, because the Russians were there before us. So they were doing the same kind of exercises we did. We were at The Comedians Institute and I said, "Do you have any movies here?" One said *San Francisco* [1936]. [Wallach sings "San Francisco," imitating a Chinese person.] So Anne says, "I'll do my imitation of Clark Gable and Jeannette McDonald in a scene from *San Francisco*." And she got up and did it. And I did slow-motion. And the Chinese actor got up and said, "I'll tell you what I'm going to do. I'm going to sing a song for you, three ways, the same song. I'm gonna sing it as though I'm a young boy just graduating from public school who doesn't understand the lyrics. Then I'm gonna sing the same song as though my wife has run away with my best friend. And then I'm gonna sing it normally, just off the top." He sang that song three ways. It was brilliant! It was wonderful! Because what he was saying is: You play a scene, the action is the same, the circumstances change. The action is to sing a song. The circumstances change the way you'll sing that song.

Barbra Streisand made a big hit by taking "Happy Days Are Here Again." Everyone did the cliché, conventional, "Happy days are here." [*Sings up-tempo*] Barbra sang it as though her husband has run away with her girlfriend, and it colored the whole song, right? That's why Frank Sinatra is so brilliant with his phrasing. The way he sings a song, he alters the circumstances.

CZ: You've moderated a lot at The Actors Studio. Do you think it changes the way you perceive acting when you have to deal with other actors' problems?

EW: It helps you as an actor because you can see the pitfalls. You see where actors tend to rely on clichés. They develop their own personal idiosyncrasies, the way they respond to things. Each individual is an individual. They have to bring the luggage of their whole life to it. You say to them: How can we help you achieve what you're seeking in a scene using some of this technique?

I think that basically all acting is making believe—having fun and making believe. It's what children do so well. They play doctor and they play kitchen; they're cooking. It's the adult who says, "That's not a real stove." The kid says, "I know it's not real, I'm making believe." And I think that good actors have great imagination and fun.

Joe Mantegna. Courtesy of Peter Strain Associates.

An Interview with Joe Mantegna

Joe Mantegna is the preeminent interpreter of the work of writer/director David Mamet. He is like a crooner, singing the poetic phrasing of Mamet's stylized language with relaxed composure, endowing the characters with a unique combination of street-smarts and panache. The figures he portrays are Everyman Plus: more aggressive, hip, suave, and savvy than those around him—or so they would like to believe. On stage, he limned the leading roles in Mamet's *A Life in the Theater* (1976–77 at Chicago's Goodman Theater), *Glengarry Glen Ross* (at The Goodman, 1983–84, and on Broadway, 1984), and *Speed-the-Plow* (1988 on Broadway). The actor has starred in three films directed by Mamet: *House of Games* (1987), *Things Change* (1988), and *Homicide* (1991). As Mantegna opines, in a typically cool understatement, "Some people have a flair for Shakespeare . . . maybe I have a flair for David's dialogue . . ."

167

Mantegna's career encompasses more than his collaborations with Mamet. Born in Chicago in 1947, he attended Morton Junior College before enrolling in The Goodman School of Drama. He toured with major roles in *Hair* (1969–70) and *Godspell* (1972–73) before becoming a member of the experimental theater group, The Organic Theater, between 1973 and 1978. With the Organic, Mantegna made appearances in *Huckleberry Finn* and *Bloody Bess*, with which he toured Europe, and *Bleacher Bums*. He was director and co-author of the latter play and won the Joseph Jefferson Award, the New York Dramatists Guild Award, and the Emmy Award when *Bleacher Bums* was aired on PBS. Mantegna also won the Antoinette Perry, Drama Desk, and Joseph Jefferson Awards as Feature Actor in 1984 for his portrayal of Richard Roma in *Glengarry Glen Ross*. He has performed for television as well, in a recurring role on *Soap* (1982) and in series such as *Making a Living, Bosom Buddies, Archie Bunker's Place, Simon and Simon,* and *Magnum, P.I.* The actor's first substantial role in films was in 1985, with *Compromising Positions*. He followed with parts in *The Money Pit* (1986); *Three Amigos!* (1986); *Suspect* (1987); *Weeds (1987); Wait Until Spring, Bandini* (1989); *Alice* (1990); *The Godfather III* (1990); *Bugsy* (1991); *Queen's Logic* (1991); *Family Prayers* (1992); *Body of Evidence* (1992); *Searching for Bobby Fisher* (1993), and *Baby's Day Out* (1994). Mantegna won the Best Actor Award at the Venice Film Festival in 1988 for his portrait of a comically misbegotten mobster in *Things Change*.

I met Joe Mantegna near his home in Toluca Lakes, California, a suburb of Los Angeles, in January 1992.

CZ: What initially attracted you to acting?

JM: My first remembrance of it, which probably got me started, was when I auditioned for a play in high school. I did the audition mainly as a kind of a gag; it was for *West Side Story*. I liked the movie so much; I'd seen it about 11 times, and I thought this would be a kind of a kick. I used to like singing in my house, to myself, to the albums, and all that stuff. So I auditioned for it, and I didn't get in. I think my problem was physical, I sang the songs for the part of Tony, but I was about 98 pounds. But the audition procedure was so exciting, I think that moment—having an audience, singing, and people clapping—did it. The people there, the faculty, were very encouraging and very positive. They really made it clear to me that, "Look, even though you didn't get in this play, we think you've got talent." I think it was the first thing in my life where I had really gotten somebody to come on to me that positively.

CZ: What is it that makes you want to be an actor?

JM: From the first time I started doing it, I felt something in me that said, "I can do this." I feel proficient at what I do; I don't feel intimidated by it. And that, coupled with the actual enjoyment of doing it . . . I mean, I like acting.

CZ: You studied at The Goodman School of Drama, in Chicago. What kind of training did you get there?

JM: Pretty regimented: speech classes, movement classes, scene study, the history of the theater. I started off being much more performance-oriented—in high school and junior college I was doing musicals and plays, and there was not a lot of academics involved. The Goodman was almost like going back and starting over, and it was a little frustrating, actually, the first year, because there was not much performance. It was all studying, and workshops, and no audiences. The second year, all I did was children's theater, and still more classwork. The atmosphere of being at theater school was enjoyable, but it was also kind of frustrating. In retrospect, I think it was valuable. It's just like anything; you have to learn the basics and principles. So the voice training, the movement training, at the time I was doing it, I kept saying to myself, "What the hell am I doing this for? I don't need all this shit." But I think, later on, it held me in good stead.

CZ: Did your family support your decision to go into acting?

JM: They were totally indifferent, which was probably the best possible thing. I think their attitude could be summed up with them saying, "That's nice." I have a brother who's 8 years older than me, and just recently I said, "I never really got any feedback—positive or negative—from them about it. It wasn't a topic of conversation or an issue." And he said there was a time when my parents said to him, "What do you think of your brother who wants to be an actor?" And he said, "Let him be an actor, he's not going to hurt anybody, it's not a dangerous job." He said, "If he's serious about it, he'll do it, and if he's not, he'll give it up." They said, "That sounds alright," and that, basically, was it.

But I could have gone to them on any given day and said, "Look, I'm giving this all up, I've decided to become a forest ranger," and they would have said, "Well, fine." And I think that's the best possible thing, because sticking it out as long as I have in my life is not due to any ulterior motive of either doing it for spite or doing it because I was stage-mothered into it.

CZ: You were with The Organic Theater for 5 years; can you talk about that?

JM: Well, I think I've been lucky enough to have a pretty well-rounded kind of experience and career. I've done everything from classical things, Shakespeare, to things at The Organic, which tended to be more free form. We created our own plays sometimes, from books, or just from ideas. So I think it was very valuable to have all those different forms of input and study. The Organic was really good because it was theater on the cheap; you had to use your imagination a lot to come up with creative ways to do things. We did a production of *Huckleberry Finn*; we couldn't afford elaborate sets, so we invented ways of doing the raft using lights and stuff. Conceptually, it really worked well.

CZ: You also taught at Columbia College in the mid-70s. Did you teach acting?

JM: I taught acting for film, for directors. Only because at that time I felt it was a little presumptuous of me to teach acting. It always used to bother me when I would see other actors who I thought were kind of mediocre teaching acting. When I got this offer to teach directors—so they would get a taste of what it's like to be an actor—I thought that was interesting. I enjoyed doing it.

CZ: What kind of exercises did you do in class?

JM: I started off by doing basic theater games to loosen them up, to get them to understand the fun concept of it. Then once I got their confidence, I would get a little more serious about certain things, like reading a script—how to score a script so it makes some sense—it's almost like reading music, you have to get a handle on it. We worked on all kinds of things, basically a compilation of everything I had learned in school, at The Organic, and in my life.

CZ: What do you feel was your biggest challenge in moving from theater to film?

JM: It's like that old saying, "It's apples and oranges." It takes different muscles; it's almost like two sports, baseball and football. Bo Jackson does both, but you have to make adjustments. I think the biggest thing was just doing those first couple of films. You can't teach anybody that; in other words, you just have to do it. There are certain tricks maybe I could have learned if I'd had some film acting courses, which I hadn't. I might have been able to save a little time. But I think a lot of it is just doing it. If you're aware, and you watch what's going on around you, you start to realize there are certain little things that make acting for film different from acting on stage, and you make those adjustments, accordingly. I think it's easier, probably, to go from theater to film than vice-versa. Because if you already have a sense of performance, it's just a matter of toning it down and centering it, and playing to a camera as opposed to an audience, and learning the glossary of terms—in essence, the tricks of the trade. So basically what I'm saying is you always have to put in your time. It really wasn't until after my fourth, fifth film, especially after I had carried a movie, that I really felt confident.

CZ: The character of Joe in *Alice* [1990] was your first romantic lead. What kind of clues did the script give you for that character?

JM: Well, working with Woody Allen, you have to almost take all your cues from the script, because he's one of those directors who, by his nature, does not direct the actors that much. Obviously he has a lot of input into the script, into how he moves the camera and how he moves the actors, and all that. But he's not a big conversationalist as a director, let's put it that way. He gives you total freedom: "I hired you because I think you have the qualities to play this role. Do it. I'll let you know if it's wrong. If I say nothing, we'll move on."

Basically that film was a long experience, over 6 months. He shoots slow. Very meticulous, very slow, reshoots. You have to take a lot of your cues from the material and trust your instincts. There's a lot of actors I know that don't enjoy working for him for that reason, because they demand a lot of attention, a lot of feedback. But my feeling is my job—especially in film acting, where the director has so much control—is to adapt to what he's doing. I give as much input as I think I have to, I ask the questions I need to ask, and get the information I need to get, but I don't think it's my place to say, "Hey, Woody, lighten up. Talk to me, baby." So once I got comfortable with how he worked, it was OK. And that's fine; it seems to work for him.

CZ: Usually, Woody Allen gives actors only their own scenes. Did you have access to the whole script?

JM: I did. That is unique. He doesn't often give people his whole script, but because of the nature of the role—I was in the movie throughout—it would have been kind of silly if he had just given me my scenes; it would have been like 90 percent of the script in my case. He didn't want to initially, but my agent said, "Look, come on . . ." He talked him into letting me have the whole script.

CZ: How would you go about developing your character?

JM: Obviously, first you read the script and get a feel for it. For me, sometimes, it's: "Is there anything identifiable about this person?" Sometimes I'll read a script, and I'll say, "Oh, God, this reminds me of my grandfather, this reminds me of my Uncle Willy, this reminds me of a combination of three guys that I know," so that helps. Then you start getting a little angle on who this person is. Then, if there's something specific about him that you can research, you do that. In *Homicide* [1991], for example, my character is a homicide detective. Well, it's important to find out what homicide detectives do. That way, I feel comfortable with how I look, how I walk, how I talk, how I handle myself, because I have a specific job. In *Alice,* it's not as important. He's a musician, and I learned enough about it to know, but that wasn't a driving force of the character, where in *Homicide* it is.

CZ: What is the driving force of your character in *Alice?*

JM: I think his job is important to him, but that's really secondary to his quest for happiness. He's a guy caught in a disruptive marriage, as many people are, and I think he's in that limbo world. He's been married for a while, and now he's separated and doesn't know which way to jump. Vulnerable, you know, more driven by emotions than by practical things, like his job. *Homicide* was a combination more of the two—it's a guy who is very obsessed with his work but also has a lot stewing in him personally.

Every role is different that way, but the process is the same. In other words, what you're doing is adding little layers on. The look is very important, because you have to start to picture, "What does this person look like? How does he comb his hair, how does he cut his hair, what kind of clothes does he wear? Does he wear old clothes, new clothes, hip clothes, square clothes, clothes that are too big, too tight? What kind of jewelry does he wear?" All that helps, because clothes are our uniforms, they say so much about a person. Down to little things like jewelry; you're wearing a turquoise ring, what does that mean? Does it have any significance? Was it a gift? Do you just like turquoise? Did you go once to New Mexico? You start thinking about those things, and it becomes important. In one film I did, *Family Prayers* [1992], with Anne Archer, the soul of my character was based on what kind of shoes he wore. At one time they were good Italian shoes, but now he was down on his luck, and he always wore the same pair of shoes. It brought images to me of guys I knew who used to hang out in pool halls; they were sharp, but if you looked up close, they were not really that sharp.

CZ: You played Joey Zasa in *The Godfather, Part III* [1990]. How was Coppola as a director, compared with your other experiences?

JM: I would tend to put him more in the general bag; the only thing that makes him specific is his own personality, which is a bit flamboyant. You know, it's almost like he's directing opera. I love working for writer-directors, because they usually have some imagination, a feel for the material, when they're good, like [David] Mamet, like Woody Allen, like Coppola. There's nothing weirdly quirky about him; he's a big man and he has a big presence.

CZ: For Joey Zasa, there's a lot of information given about you in the script, compared to someone like Joe in *Alice* or Bobby Gold in *Homicide*.

JM: That's true. You take what you can, that's less stuff to have to invent. If somebody says certain things about your character, and you know it's fact, then those are things that you have to adapt into that character.

CZ: You have a big speech, right before the helicopter attack—it's really formal and theatrical. Was it your decision to perform the speech in that way?

JM: That was intentional, because my take on *The Godfather,* when I read the script and made the decision about how I wanted to play this character, I felt that there's something grand, almost Renaissance about him. In essence, if you transposed it to the sixteenth or seventeenth century, Don Corleone becomes the Duke of Milan, and all these other henchmen are barons and dukes. So I felt there should be a certain regalness about it, even though it's 1970s New York. These guys are a little bigger than life: They dress flashy, they drive flashy cars, I even wanted his diction, and the way he talked, to be a little floral.

I think that's what separates the *Godfather* movies from something like *Mobsters* [1991], the little kiddie movies that are just a lot of violence and a lot of bullshit. The words are so important, scripts are so important—dialogue, to an actor, is everything. So, when given stuff that has a little flair to it, I think it was my choice to put a spin on it, yeah. I even had other actors say to me, "Why are you doing it like that?" But I stuck with it, because my feeling was that if Coppola didn't like it, he would have stopped me. Sometimes you've just got to wing it according to what your gut feeling is.

CZ: You've worked with "A" list directors, like Barry Levinson [*Bugsy*, 1991], Woody Allen, and Coppola, as well as lesser-known directors. Is there anything, apart from career moves and economic factors, that determines your decisions?

JM: You can die sitting around waiting to always work with the most experienced and the most talented guy on the block. Filmmaking is very collaborative, and there are so many elements that get involved as to why you make a decision to do something. In other words, in the best of all worlds, let's say ten things, ideally, are in place when you make the decision to do a project. You loved everybody else in the cast; the director is one of the greatest directors in the world; it's the best script you ever read; it's being made by a studio that has all the money in the world; it's shooting in all the locations you want to be in; it's a role you've always wanted to play. You can start ticking off all these different things, but it never happens that you fulfill those ten requirements. So sometimes, you'll read two scripts, and let's say you like them both equally. All right, one's directed by Coppola, and the other one's directed by Mickey Mouse. Well, OK, that's a plus for Coppola. Then the second thing: Who else is in it? Well, the one that's not directed by Coppola has Robert De Niro and Robin Williams, and the one with Coppola has nobody; that's a little plus for the other side. It becomes a balancing act, and you sometimes can't fulfill all your "A" positions in each one. I don't regret any of the decisions I've made.

CZ: I want to move on to *Homicide* because you have a long history with Mamet. He gives you a certain amount of backstory, but not a lot, is that right?

JM: Right. Usually very little.

CZ: What was the most important thing for you in preparing to play Bobby Gold?

JM: Well, the one big hook is he's a homicide detective, and a very good one. He's very obsessed with his job, so it's important to learn everything I can about what that's like. When you're doing a specific job, in a film or a play or anything, you don't want the people in the audience who perhaps really know that job to say, "Wait a minute, this is all wrong." You want to be comfortable in what you're doing so you can forget about it, so then you can concentrate on just doing the script. It was important for me to talk to homicide guys, see how they dress, see how they look. I would ask them: "What are the little things you do that maybe only you guys know?" I would go through the script with them. They said, "Well, one thing homicide guys always do is carry lots of pens," because, at any given moment, they don't know if somebody's going to make a confession. The last thing you want to do is go, "Wait, don't say a word . . ." when the guy's saying, "OK, I did it." So they carry pens all over the place. That was a little thing; I had pens all over my body. And then he said that they use the pens a lot, because if you come on a body, you don't want to touch it, you don't want to get your fingerprints on it, so the pen becomes a tool. You don't want to take your gun out and move shit with the gun barrel. So, when I discovered the woman's body in the grocery store, I pick up the little cross off of her neck with a pen. Those are little touches that I learned from doing the research.

The look of the guy was an important thing: We tried curling my hair, did this and that, and finally just zipped it off. Besides being sort of a psychological thing about Bobby, I was trying to look like David, somebody who has no vanity that way.

CZ: But you dress very well . . .

JM: Pretty well, not as good as my partner. It's a thing of dressing pretty nice but not being self-conscious about it; he wore the same thing almost for the whole movie.

CZ: That's because he never slept!

JM: Exactly. But even if he went home, he probably had the same color shirt, a clean one. His stuff is a little rumpled, as opposed to natty.

You try to get as many clues as you can from the script. And it's true with David, there's not as much as in *Godfather,* so you've got to create it yourself.

CZ: You're the classic self-hating Jew in that film. How did you relate to that?

JM: It's not like this guy hung out at the synagogue on Saturdays or hangs out with his Jewish buddies from college on weekends to go laugh about cops. It's the opposite; this guy has a ham sandwich and a glass of milk on Yom Kippur—that shit doesn't exist for him. This is a guy that's subjugated that part of his life, for whatever reasons. It's something he just chose not to deal with; he wanted to be a cop, probably all his life, and he kind of knew being a Jew on a police force is like being the black guy on a hockey team. He's going to be the odd man in there anyway, so the best defense is negate it, forget about it, play ball with everybody else. So when they say the Yid jokes, it's like a black guy who has to work with the 10 white guys who make black jokes. For his benefit, they'll tell him how much they like Nat King Cole—he's laughing, but behind their backs he's thinking, "These guys . . ."

How do I relate to that? Obviously, I can't relate to it specifically because I'm not Jewish. We've all had experiences where we're the odd man in, of whatever group. For many years, when I first started acting in plays—I did *Hair* [1969–70], I did *Godspell* [1972–73]—I had hair down to my shoulders for 5 years. I was doing it more because that was my line of work, but people treat you differently because to them it's more a statement of what you are. So in a way, I was on the defensive.

I'm probably less method than a lot of other actors. If I'm playing a derelict, I don't feel I have to go dress up like a bum and live in the Bowery for a week. If that affects my performance adversely, then so be it. I do what I feel I've got to do, and as much as I feel I need to do. To do *House of Games* [1987], I didn't necessarily immerse myself in the world of con-men and gambling. I did the script. It's just acting, you know. I'm not putting down the other thing, either; you do whatever it takes. Some of our greatest actors are very heavy on doing that.

CZ: Bobby [Gold, the character] has that very charged scene with the black guy at the end of the film, where he says, "I'm a piece of shit, I'm worthless," but then, it's very interesting, Bobby says, "Your mama turned you over." Almost as if he wants him to feel as betrayed as Bobby feels.

JM: I think so. I think he's taken his last shot. Bobby, in a way, he's surrendered, he's given up. He thinks he's dead. He's burned every bridge behind him—there's nothing to go back to. He's basically saying, "I'm not going to go down alone. You're not innocent. You represent everything that I've been working against all my life as a policeman; I'm not going to give you a pass, here. I have my own demons, and I may die with them, but let me give you this little something to remember me by."

CZ: One of the final images in *Homicide* is an exchange of glances between Bobby and the man who's killed his entire family. What were your ideas about their connection?

JM: Yeah. I don't know. A lot of people try to find the symbolism in that, and I'm really intrigued by it. That's one of those little things about David. We fooled around with the ending a lot, we toyed around with things, back and forth, as in all his movies. For me, that look was almost like a camaraderie. Let me make an analogy: It's Jeffrey Dahmer leaving the courtroom and maybe winking at General Schwartzkopf. One guy's a hero, one guy's a monster, but basically, they both killed a lot of people. Obviously there's a difference, but yet, there's a lot in common. On judgment day, if there is such a thing, will that differentiation be made? "Well, you killed a bunch of guys and you ate 'em, so you're going here, and you killed a bunch of guys and you didn't eat 'em . . ." What does that mean? It was a shared glance of 2 guys who had come to a cataclysmic time in their life. It's something only the 2 of them could understand. It's not typical. It's what makes Mamet different.

CZ: When Mamet is directing you, does he let you look at the rushes?

JM: Yes. Anybody can look at the rushes. David's very open that way.

CZ: I find the positioning of the actors very formal in all three of the films that you did with Mamet. There are scenes in *House of Games* where you share the frame in precise symmetry with another actor, or where you're positioned in full profile. Does that put any constraints on you as an actor?

JM: No, because in film, first of all, what the camera's getting and what you're doing are not necessarily the same thing. In other words, they could be framing a shot a certain way, and it gives the illusion of something a lot more rigid than what is actually happening. On the other

Joe Mantegna and Lindsay Crouse in *House of Games* (1987), directed by David Mamet. Artwork © Orion Pictures.

hand, sometimes you have to do something that's almost like a tap-dance in order to make the shot work, and, watching it, you wouldn't realize that it's choreographed, because of the framing. That's, again, part of the difference between film and stage. On stage, you have to make allowances, too; you find ways to cheat. It's a little unrealistic. It's the same thing in film; you do what you need to do, but sometimes it's done mechanically through the camera lens. I don't find it usually too much of a constraint, no.

CZ: Mamet's use of language is so stylized. How do you work at making that real for you?

JM: I think some of it may be just inherent. I read his stuff, and it makes sense to me. I think some people have a flair for Shakespeare, maybe certain actors can make that come to life better than others. So maybe I have a flair for David's dialogue in that respect. Maybe a lot of it has to do with the fact that we're so alike in our backgrounds; I think so much of his style is rooted in growing up in urban Chicago. It's the language of that town and of those kinds of people. It's not so big a stretch for me; when I read it, I hear what he's talking about. There's no magical trick—either you get it, or you don't get it.

CZ: In thinking about acting for the screen, what do you think makes people interesting to watch?

JM: Obviously it's a quality, and I think a lot of times it's an intangible thing. For me, I think it's a naturalness, a comfortability, I don't know. I've sometimes been surprised to see somebody who I thought was really mediocre do a wonderful performance of something. It's not even cut-and-dried, to be able to say, "Well, so-and-so is good, and so-and-so's not good." Sometimes it can depend—especially in film—on how good the director is, how good the material is, how well it's suited for the person. You can hide a lot of ills in film. It's like recording—you can take a bunch of mediocre singers, and you put them with the right producers in a studio, and you make them sound like Sinatra. Put them on a stage live, then some of the blemishes start appearing—that separates the men from the boys. It's easier to tell in a stage performance who's really got the chops, because they're flying alone. In film, depending how it's orchestrated, a director can certainly help you out a lot. The bottom line is a certain charisma; you meet people who have electric personalities, and people who don't, and if they don't, they don't. You can go until doomsday, you can say, "Now, if you only would do this, or do that, you might be more . . ." but you can't.

CZ: When you were growing up and you watched films, was there anybody who made a big impression on you?

JM: Yeah, I like a lot of the old guys. I like Errol Flynn. He did kind of forgettable movies, but I liked him, because he had that thing. I like Bogart, I like Cagney, I like all the old great actors. I like some of the old character guys, guys that are really obscure or quirky. Guys like Jack Palance or John Davis Chandler. They're guys that are interesting to watch, like Klaus Kinski. They're like, "Hello!" These guys get your attention. De Niro has that, Pacino has that. I have to think a lot of it is intangible. That is why there are movie stars, and there are those that aren't.

CZ: Do you ever look at yourself on screen and not like what you see?

JM: Less and less, because I think, initially, it's like when you first hear yourself on a tape recorder. No matter what anybody tells you, you can't stand it, you just go, "Oh, fuck, that's awful." You hate it. I think people are the worst critics of themselves, but I've done enough now that I think I could be somewhat objective. Sometimes I'm disappointed, sometimes I think I could have been better. But I feel confident enough now, going in, that I can at least get a general idea of how it's going. In other words, if it takes to the final product to see how bad it is, then I screwed up somewhere a lot earlier. If you're doing something shitty while it's being shot, it shouldn't magically change and become great, later. You shouldn't say to yourself, "Gee, I know that's terrible, but maybe they'll fix it." You've got to have enough wherewithal to feel at least comfortable about what you've done. Sometimes it's trust, sometimes what you think is best.

Don Ameche twice in his life asked for an extra take. The director says, "We got it, that's great, let's move on," and he said, "No, no, no, I really can do this better." Twice he did that, and the director, of course, said, "Alright, Don, we'll have another take," and he did it. He said in both those instances, when he saw the rushes, the director was right—the take that Don thought was perfect was not as good as the one the director wanted. He said, "After that I realized that you always got to trust a guy." Because unless you have total control of the movie—unless you're directing it and in it yourself, and have final cut, and you can edit it—they're going to pick what they want. I asked Warren Beatty when we were doing *Bugsy* why it was important for him to let Barry Levinson direct the film as opposed to [James] Toback, the writer, or Warren himself. He felt it was too big a project to trust himself to do it. He needed a third eye. It's hard sometimes, it's like trusting your kid with a babysitter, in a way. Sometimes you gotta do it.

An Interview with Eric Roberts

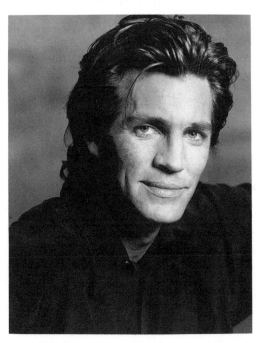

Eric Roberts. Courtesy of Mr. Roberts.

Eric Roberts comments on his performance style as a young actor: "I was really out there, man." Indeed, Roberts possesses an astonishing intensity in his earliest film work—*King of the Gypsies* (1978), *Star 80* (1983), *The Pope of Greenwich Village* (1984), and *Runaway Train* (1985)—each in their own way a spectacle of explosive, unbridled passion. Roberts' hyperkinetic physical presence is counterbalanced by the suggestion of a hidden inner life, an unspoken, supressed text of pain and vulnerability only thinly disguised by motion and chatter. Two of Roberts' favorite performances, adaptations for PBS—Nathaniel West's *Miss Lonelyhearts* (1983) and Willa Cather's *Paul's Case* (1980)—display the actor in a contemplative mode. In both instances, Roberts has little recourse to language, and the performances rely on Roberts' moody, haunting sensitivity to convey his characters' silent suffering. Like most successful film actors, Roberts has a special relationship to the camera—his expressive face is like a screen registering the extraordinarily subtle range of his

181

feelings. *Paul's Case* and *Miss Lonelyhearts* give Roberts an opportunity that has been all too rare in his career: to focus on the internal rather than the external dynamics of emotion.

Roberts was born in 1956 in Biloxi, Mississippi, but was raised near Atlanta, Georgia. His father was the founder of The Actor and Writers Workshop, a community-based theater in which Roberts performed from childhood. He then went to the summer program of the Royal Academy of Dramatic Art in 1973, followed by a year at the American Academy of Dramatic Arts in New York. Roberts appeared in the afternoon soap, *Another World*, during the 1976–77 season, before he was "released" for insubordinate behavior. The actor made his film debut in the lead role in *King of the Gypsies*. He then performed in *Raggedy Man* (1981), *Star 80*, *The Pope of Greenwich Village*, *Runaway Train*, *The Coca-Cola Kid* (1985), *Nobody's Fool* (1986), *The Best of the Best* (1989), *The Ambulance* (1990), *Final Analysis* (1992), *The Specialist* (1994), and *Love Is a Gun* (1994). For television, Roberts appeared in *Miss Lonelyhearts* (American Playhouse, PBS) and *Paul's Case* (American Short Story, PBS) and in numerous made-for-cable movies, including *Slow Burn* (1986), *To Heal a Nation* (1988), *Lonelyhearts* (1990), and *Lie, Cheat and Steal* (1993). On stage, Roberts originated the role of Mark Dolson in *Mass Appeal* at the Manhattan Theater Club in 1976. He has also appeared in *A Streetcar Named Desire* (1976) at the McCarter Theatre Company in Princeton and in *The Glass Menagerie* and *Alms for the Middle Class*, both in 1983 at the Long Wharf Theatre in New Haven. Roberts was awarded The Theater World Award for Best Actor for his performance of Pale in *Burn This* in 1988, after replacing John Malkovich in the lead role.

I interviewed Eric Roberts at his home in upstate New York in April 1994.

CZ: When did you first know that you wanted to act?

ER: I've wanted to be an actor ever since I can remember. One of my earliest memories is being an actor and being scared about stuttering; learning lines was a solution. I was a little bitty kid, I'm talking about 5, 6 years old.

CZ: Your father ran The Actors and Writers Workshop?

ER: In Atlanta, Georgia, yeah. It was funded in part by the Martin Luther King Foundation. My father basically copied Joe Papp's format in

New York. We toured two seasons, summer and fall, and every weekend we'd have theater for an hour in Piedmont Park. We had a permanent stage and a showmobile for touring. I grew up doing anywhere from eight to twelve plays a year.

CZ: You were 17 when you went to the Royal Academy of Dramatic Arts. What was the impetus behind that decision not to study in the United States but to go to England to study?

ER: I grew up with my favorite actor being Robert Donat. When I was a little boy, my father woke me up one night to watch the late show, to watch *Goodbye Mister Chips* [1939]. I was probably 8 or 9 when I saw this. Here was this guy who played a man's whole life in 2 hours, and I said, "That's what I would love to be able to do." He was English, and everybody who was great in my small-minded Atlanta, Georgia, way— Laurence Olivier, John Gielgud—came from London. They were all on the board at the Royal Academy. So I flew to New York and I auditioned, and I got in. It's always stated that I went for the whole course, but I wasn't old enough; I only went to the summer program there.

Anyway, I got back from that, and I said to my father, "OK, where do I go from here?" And Dad says, "Well, you either go to New York or L.A. New York is like what you've done already, so I think that's where you ought to start." So I flew to New York again, and I auditioned for the American Academy of Dramatic Arts, and I got in. I went there for a year, had a great junior year—I thought—but was not asked back for my senior year.

I was lucky enough to be seen by Juliet Taylor [the casting director] in some plays I did there, and they gave me to Bill Treusch, who was a manager. At the time, he handled some great, great talents. He basically discovered all of them—Sissy Spacek down in the Village playing the guitar, Tom Berenger when he was an airline steward. He revitalized Chris Walken's career; the list is endless. So I got on his client list and then proceeded to be in The Reading Company with Joe Papp; we'd go down there every week and play with people like John Heard. He had all the new up-and-coming guns.

CZ: Let's go back to The American Academy. What was it like there?

ER: Well, the American Academy was a bad version of the Royal Academy. The Royal Academy taught you discipline, it taught you really the fundamental work routines that I still use. It also taught you how to research things from language to physicality. At The American Academy, there was one person named Jory Wyler, who was an incredible gold mine; I fell very much in love with her as my teacher. This was in '75 or '76. She was wonderful, she was bright, she was inspirational, she was also educational. But for the most part, the teachers there were out-of-work actors who were lying to us. Of course, I had an upstart attitude as a youngster who'd been in the theater all his life and who thought he knew everything, so I was like, "When are you going to teach us how to act?"

CZ: What do you mean when you say they were lying to you?

ER: They were lying to us—with the exception of Jory—in that their format for us was very lazy. It was all this bullshit about, "If you have the right look and the right attitude, anything can happen." Well, as I've gotten older, I know they're right to some degree, but it's only a little bit of the big picture. As far as developing my craft, they didn't help me at all. I had a bad attitude about the fact that I wasn't being helped, so they didn't ask me back.

CZ: You're saying they didn't teach you certain things; what was missing in the training?

ER: It's a huge list. I knew what I wasn't getting because I had already spent 15 years being taught my craft. I knew I wasn't getting the education when they taught Shakespeare. They didn't teach that he writes to be recited and/or played in iambic pentameter; I never heard that phrase at The American Academy. They would say, "Make sense of the line," but they wouldn't tell the actor that before you make it your own, there's a technical way to approach things.

CZ: You're also a member of The Actors Studio; what was it like when you started in the mid-1970s?

ER: I had a great time there. It was great in that it was the first time since I was a child in my father's school that I saw a group effort to supposedly everybody's benefit. We'd sit there and we'd watch a scene, and then Lee [Strasberg] or the guest speaker would ask, "OK, what do we see here?" Everybody would say what they saw. It gave me the courage in my 19-year-old mind to decide I was going to do a scene from *Equus*, and I was going to do what I felt it was really about and see how it was received. I did a scene with a guy there, of course he was playing the doctor and I was playing the kid—all the stuff about the horses I decided was sexual. So I took off all my clothes and I climbed up on this guy's shoulders, and he was hypnotized. Lee asked for responses, and it was rather embarrassing. You know how brave we are at 19. I was so uninihibited as a kid. I was out there, man, I was game for anything.

CZ: You must have been a big fan of private moments at The Studio.

ER: Well, it's overstated. We have private moments all day, every day, all of us in this room, and they're just flashes in reality, in your work, and in your character study. But they're not a place to live. If we played a part through the approach of a private moment, we'd never get out of brushing our teeth in the bathroom, for Christ's sake.

CZ: Can you talk about an important learning experience you had at The Studio?

ER: The most fun I ever had at The Studio was the last time I was involved in anything there. It was a play I did with Paul Newman and Joanne Woodward; they played my parents. It's a real shame I can't remember the title, but it was quite a wonderful play. It was really funny: In the readings of the play and in rehearsal of the play, you saw Joanne always struggling and always deciding to read a line slightly differently. Paul is always smooth. Then we do the play, and Joanne is kicking ass, she's got all the layers, and she's changing stuff every show, a little bit depending on what she's getting from other actors, and Paul's always the same, smooth as ice. That was probably my biggest learning experience. Watching 2 actors who were both members, who had completely different styles and who were not self-conscious, for totally different reasons.

CZ: You did soap for about a year also, *Another World*?

ER: Yeah, I did soap for 6 months. They canned me.

CZ: What happened?

ER: I'm 19 years old, and I got the world by the balls, I'm making like 200 bucks a show, three shows a week, I think I'm rich, I got this little tiny penthouse apartment on the Upper West Side, I got it made—[the producer] calls me into his office and explains that the writers are a little bothered by my approach to their work. I said, "Why?" He says, "Well, you change your dialogue." I said, "But I don't change anybody's cues."

He says, "But you change your dialogue. We can't have that. These writers have been running the show for whatever it is, 800 years, and so this has to come to an end." I said to him, "Are you firing me?" and he said, "Yes I am." Then, a year later I got my first feature film—*King of the Gypsies* [1978].

CZ: Your first role in a movie was in a major motion picture—you were really young, and you're acting with all these famous people. What was that like for you?

ER: It was spooky. I was real scared, I was real green. Frank Pierson [the director] took great care of me; he was very supportive of me, he let me take chances. He let me do stuff that I look back on and think that he was braver than I was.

CZ: What kind of stuff?

ER: There's a scene in that movie where I haven't seen my mother or my sister in quite a while—I ran away from home when I was a little boy, and I'm a young man now—and they show up at my apartment. They've shown up to explain that our father has sold my sister into a marriage. I have all this, "What has happened, Mom? How can you do this?" I learn my scripts like plays, so I knew what I was going to do predominantly, but I always use last-minute brainstorms. So I'm at home the night before the scene, and I decide, "Well, real anger's called for here." My girlfriend— who is played by Annette O'Toole—serves coffee during the scene. So I call the prop man, and I say, "I may or may not do something tomorrow, I don't know, but on the chance that I do, bring a lot of extra coffee cups." He goes, "OK." I didn't tell anybody except him, that's all I said. Then we're shooting the scene—and I got moved to go that far—I throw the coffee all over, breaking this shit, and I give a whole monologue, and then Frank says "Cut," and the crew's applauding, and everybody's thrilled. And Frank says, "We've got a problem, he broke all the cups," and the prop man says, "He called me last night, it's fine." I was very proud of that. Frank would let me run, bless his heart.

CZ: Here you were in your first film with Sterling Hayden and Shelley Winters. Was it intimidating?

ER: As a matter of fact, Sterling Hayden came on the film after I'd been working for 3 weeks, and he sends for me. The assistant director came and said, "Mister Hayden wants to speak to you." "Ooh, cool," I'm a kid. I knock, and he's all loud and gruff. It smells like hash, and he offers me his pipe, I say "no thank you"; he offers me a drink, I say "no thank you." And he proceeds to talk: [*imitates Hayden*] "Well, what's the scene about?" I said, "Well, it's about you trying to get me to come back home," etcetera. "How you gonna play this thing?" So I tell him . . . "Well, how's your character feel about me?" I basically tell him the story, and we ad lib this whole scene. It was supposed to only take half the evening—it was a night shoot—and it took all night, because Sterling was saying "Let's do something a little different, here. Let's try it." We basically improvised the scene. Dino [de Laurentis, the producer] wanted to fire him after that, and Frank and I had to go to bat for him to keep him in the movie. To go to dailies and watch this guy—right in the middle of a take he'd say, "That's good, Eric! That's so good!" It was funny as can be. I was in heaven, because here was a guy who was showing me that he was human, who had made great movies, had given great performances and was one of my father's heroes, and I'm getting to work with him. It was not intimidating, it was just balls-out fun.

CZ: I'd like you to take me through one of your roles. Why do you take a script? What do you do once you commit to a film? How do you prepare?

ER: An easy one to do that with is *Pope*. I'm up at Hartford Theater doing *The Glass Menagerie*, I'm playing Tom, and I get a script from Gene Kirkwood called *The Pope of Greenwich Village* [1984]. I read the script, and my character was [*speaks in character*] a kind of a tough New York guy, fuck you, a stupid-head. Easy to play, really kind of pointless and thankless and not very rewarding for the actor. So I take a train into Manhattan, and I start spending time down in Little Italy. I've got a week to get an answer on this role. I spend every day down there, I'm looking at these guys, I'm beginning to watch them interact. I'm not having conversations with them about their life, I'm just watching them at different outdoor cafés and stuff. I'm watching guys drinking at night and having coffee in the daytime. I'm beginning to catch on to what they are: they're all a bunch of—this is an old saying that's going to make a lot of people mad—momma's boys. And they talk about stuff like [*in character*] "I don't believe what he said to him! He said dis, and he said dat . . ." They're talking like women. You know what I mean by talking like women: Women have much more interesting conversations in that they talk about [*impersonates a woman*] the personality involved: "Well, let me tell you this about him . . ." I'm beginning to get this guy in my head who's not on the paper. And so, I accept the role.

And when I accept a role, to put it very simply, I always want to be the greatest character actor ever born. I take on roles like science projects, you know. This guy is fascinating in this story, so how do I make him fascinating to watch? Why does he fascinate me? I've got about a month to prep this role, that's a long time—and I finally get an image about how he's going to be physically. So I'm dropping weight, and I have my hair permed, and I'm gonna be a walking spaz attack, I decide. I want to be John Belushi if he were out of Little Italy and if he were skinny. This is what I decided to do. It was so far from what I am as a guy that from the time I really captured him, I basically stayed in character the whole time. He was far away from my life, but I had so much fun doing it.

Eric Roberts and Mickey Rourke in *The Pope of Greenwich Village,* directed by Stuart Rosenberg. © 1984 United Artists Corporation. Museum of Modern Art Film Stills Archive.

CZ: The characters you and Mickey Rourke play are very intense in that film. How did the director, Stuart Rosenberg, work with you on the characterizations?

ER: Aaah! What a miracle that guy is! He comes in, and he goes "OK guys, how do you want to make this movie?" There's script order and there's also shooting order, and script order is in continuity and shooting order is never in continuity—and I said, "I want to shoot it in continuity. Because these guys have to go through such a change, and I can't bounce back and forth with that whole thing." And Stuart says, "You know what? I'll try." And we almost shot it all in continuity, just because he's a nice man.

CZ: One of your great critical successes was in *Star 80* [1983]—what was it like to work on that film?

ER: Bob Fosse was a genius. He'd get right to the core of things, he'd break your heart in understanding things. I give him all the credit, he was the mind behind that performance, I was the instrument. I leaned on him; he told me every innuendo, every nuance. I asked him a question, I'd always get an answer.

Bob Fosse was the hardest-working man I've ever known in my whole life, and I've known some real mothers. He was insane, the amount of energy he'd put into the work. Days would go on forever. We're in our third week of a 6-month shoot—it's an 18-hour day, and I come home, and I don't even bathe; I drop my clothes and I fall face-first into the bed, boom! I'm in this brand-new house, I don't know the house very well. Fall into bed, I'm just about to really get into a good snooze, and somebody's banging on the front door. So I think it's somebody who owns the house doing something stupid. So in my mindless, brazen, exhausted way, I'm walking down the steps—I'm buck naked, by the way—and some work had been done on the house, there's tools lying around, so I pick up a hammer. The guy's banging on the door like he's violent. So I pick up a hammer and I'm buck naked, and I open the door—I'm going to scare whoever it is by being naked with a hammer—and I open the door, and there's Bob Fosse with this portable typewriter. And I said, "What the fuck are you doing?" And he said, "I type. You dance." That was his phrase for "I write and you improvise." So, every night for several weeks in the beginning of the shoot, we rewrote. I would work his hours at work, his hours at home, and I was becoming—unbeknownst at the time to me, I'm 25 years old—Paul Snider. When I work, I wear my character's clothes, and I wear my hair like they wear it all the time. And I'm basically becoming Paul Snider without even really knowing it . . . [Fosse] put me in such an exhausted physical state that I was a nerve-end like Paul.

CZ: Did you base Paul Snider on anyone you knew?

ER: I never knew anybody like Paul Snider up until I'm playing the part. We all know Paul Sniders, but for some reason I've always disregarded them, they don't interest me, so I just don't pay attention to them. I'm having trouble with a scene in *Star 80,* and I break the take, and I get kind of angry, "Oh fuck, shit, goddammit, I can't do it . . ." And Bob goes, "Goddammit, come here!" and walks across this huge sound stage and I'm thinking, "Oh no, he's going to embarrass me, I hate this," and I get up and I follow him across the sound stage, and the crew's watching us. He says, "Look at me!" and I say, "I'm looking at you," and he says, "LOOK AT ME!" and he gets right in my face, and he says, "What you're doing here is you're playing me if I weren't successful. Do you understand?" So I say, "Yes, I do," and I never had to ask another question. That's the most personal direction I ever had.

CZ: I think that you do end up having some sympathy for Paul, because of your performance. He's a detestable character, but by the end of the film, I felt really sorry for him.

ER: Thanks. That's all you can give people through that kind of a portrayal—an understanding of that tragic personality.

CZ: So you feel that you have to have some degree of empathy with the character, now matter how awful he is?

ER: It's not even conscious. You know what it is: If you live in somebody else's shoes long enough, you understand why they do their bullshit. And why they do their bullshit is not always their fault; in fact, it mostly isn't. Like this guy I played in *The Specialist* [1994]. He's kind of a two-dimensional character—well, I got him up to two dimensions, he's a real bore on paper, but it was a Warner Brothers film, and they offered me the part, and this brilliant guy Jerry Weintraub was the producer.

CZ: Who directed?

ER: Lucho Llosa. My character is this typical asshole, and I decide that he can't be a typical asshole, because you don't get anything from that, either from watching it or playing it, so I decided to make him just a brat who is at his father's mercy, because his father was so dominating. I got a lot of help, because Rod Steiger's performance is perfect. The guy, from *On the Waterfront* [1954] to right here, it's the same actor. The guy is so complete. He and I would ad lib stuff, like at the end of a scene he would say, "OK, do you understand?" I wouldn't say anything, and he would say, "I'm talking to you! Do you understand?"—he was Cuban— and I would say, "Yes." "I can't hear you!" I'd say, "Yes." "I can't hear you!" I'd say, "OK, Dad, OK." We'd have these little things we'd ad lib like that, that make the whole relationship, that bump it up to two dimensions. This kid is so domineeringly loved by his father that he's abused by him. With Rod Steiger's help, just because he's so great, that's what I got to bring to this character.

CZ: *Runaway Train* [1985] seems like such a physically hard movie, it must have been claustrophobic to work on that set of the train all that time. The movie is pitched at such a level of intensity, there's no letup in any scene. What was your experience like on that film?

ER: Alan Hume was our director of photography. He shoots all the James Bond films, and if it weren't for him, I think I would have lost my mind. He's got a wonderful sense of humor; he's the one who kept me grounded during that film. I treated Jon [Voight] like he was Manny, and I acted towards Jon like I was Buck, and I treated Rebecca [de Mornay] like she was somebody not very important who I liked to screw. The director of that movie talked a great deal about Stanislavsky, which wasn't much help to my portrayal of Buck. It's such a physical movie, and such a small space, and you lose your mind, being at all human, if you don't have a grounding point, a reference point.

I used to always do my own stunts, you know. I used to be such a "I can do anything." Bob Fosse's the one who got me into the Stuntman's Association, because he asked me one day in a scene in *Star 80* to hang out of a 31-story building by my ankles. So I get into the Stuntman's Association, and I'm like, "Wow, I'm a stuntman now." We're doing *Runaway Train,* this is my sixth or seventh movie, and I'm supposed to walk on the outside of the train while it's moving, on this small little walkway, with a small little railing, behind Jon's stunt double. Okay, I said, "I can do that no problem." I get out there and it's maybe like 20 degrees, but the wind chill factor's probably about zero now because we're doing about 40 miles an hour on the train, and I take about a dozen steps and I look down, and I see the ground moving, and I see the edges of the track, and I look up and the guy's ahead of me way too far, and I'm way too cold, and my hands are frozen, and I completely folded: "I can't do this . . ." I started wailing and crying in a voice I'd never heard come out of my mouth, and I'm just totally wimping out. They take me in, and all of the stuntmen are laughing their heads off: "Hey, havin' a little trouble out there, huh?" and I'm saying, "Get me out of these fucking clothes, I'm never doing this again!" I'm a complete wimp. And I've never done a stunt since.

CZ: You've done some very villainous roles, like *Star 80* and *Final Analysis.* You obviously aren't a villainous person; was that difficult for you?

ER: Villainous roles started being offered to me after *Star 80.* I started first to try and take them and turn them around; I'd try to go the opposite of what's on the paper, but it was a problem, people didn't know what to do with me at all as an actor.

CZ: You've done some pretty violent stuff in films; does that ever bother you?

ER: I have never been in *The Terminator* [1984], that kind of pointless violence. I have never been in a Bruce Willis film, that kind of stupid stuff. So I'm not one to really ask that to, because I haven't been in there.

In *The Specialist,* I had a scene where I beat up Sharon Stone. So I said, "There's no foundation for having me hit her, let James Woods beat her up. I don't want to be known as kind of a psycho in movies, so I'd rather let Jimmy be the psycho who does this to women." I already blew a woman's brains out in *Star 80,* and that had stuck with me. It was hell getting dates for 18 months after that movie came out.

If we had shown that my character's mother abused me, then we could give the audience, "Here's what happens when your mother beats you. You grow up and you have a problem with women and you beat them like she beat you maybe." We can give them that, but we didn't have that to give them. So I said, "Let Jimmy do it;" they did, and he does it great.

CZ: What's the best advice that you can offer to young actors?

ER: OK, it sounds real pat and real bullshit, and it's something like you'd hear from Henry Fonda, but it's true: It's one of the hardest jobs there is, and you have to be willing to work as hard as any construction worker on a 100-degree day. You've got to be willing to get in there and work until you pass out.

CZ: What's the biggest difference between your early days as an actor and now?

ER: Now, with Eliza [Roberts' wife] in my life especially, I've started to enjoy the fruits and the fringe benefits of being a movie star. I never enjoyed them in my 20s. I really enjoy them now. I enjoy nice tables at restaurants. I'm learning to give everybody time because Laurence Olivier gave me time once when I was a student in London. I went up to him and I invited him to one of our junior plays [*imitates Olivier*]: "No, dear man, I can't come, I've got a reading," but he walks me down the sidewalk, and he has his arm on my shoulder. He was so sweet to me, and we go to his Bentley, and he introduces me to Joan Plowright, and I'm like, "How do you do," and he drives away, and I'm like, "That's so cool!" From then on, I've always given time to everybody who approaches me because it was so monumental to me what Olivier did. I've only now begun to enjoy people who say, "I just loved you in so-and-so." I might say, "Why did you like that part?" and talk to them, and give them a little time. I enjoy the fact that I get to make a living having the time of my life and doing what I want to do. I don't have to go to a job that I have to have in order to pay the bills; I get to go to a job where they basically are known for overpaying people, and I rock and roll.

An Interview with Brad Dourif

Brad Dourif. Courtesy of Dourif, Inc.

Brad Dourif has made a career out of investigating the shadowy, unhealthy side of the human psyche. As an actor, he has a singular presence: high-strung, darkly passionate, and unabashedly eccentric, with an underlying quality of suppressed rage. He has parlayed these attributes into an astonishing gallery of over-the-edge characters, beginning with his first film role as the stuttering mental patient Billy Bibbit in *One Flew over the Cuckoo's Nest* (1975). For his first foray into film, Dourif garnered an Academy Award nomination, a British Academy Award, and a Golden Globe Award, all for Best Supporting Actor.

Dourif was born in Huntington, West Virginia, in 1950 and attended Marshall University. A small inheritance from his art-collector grandfather enabled Dourif to go to New York, where he joined the Circle Repertory Theater. Dourif built sets and studied acting with the company's director, Marshall Mason, and took professional classes with Sanford Meisner. In 1973, Dourif performed the title role in *When You Comin' Back, Red*

Ryder?, where he was discovered by the director of *Cuckoo's Nest,* Milos Forman. He has continued to work in film, appearing in *The Eyes of Laura Mars* (1978), *Wise Blood* (1979), *Heaven's Gate* (1980), *Ragtime* (1981, reuniting him with director Forman), *Dune* (1984), *Blue Velvet* (1986), *Fatal Beauty* (1987), *Child's Play* (1987), *Mississippi Burning* (1988), *Grim Prairie Tales, The Exorcist III* (1990), *Common Bonds* (for which he was nominated for a Canadian Genie Award as Best Actor), *Graveyard Shift* (1990), *Scream of Stone, Jungle Fever* (1991), *Amos and Andrew* (1993), *The Color of Night* (1994), and *Murder in the First* (1994).

Dourif has extensive credits in television as well. One of his first featured roles was the lead in *Sergeant Matlovich vs. the U.S. Air Force,* in 1978, a TV movie about a homosexual serviceman's struggle to stay in uniform. Dourif's other TV movies are *Studs Lonigan* (1979), *Guyana Tragedy: The Story of Jim Jones* (1980), *Rage of Angels* (1986), *Vengeance: The Story of Tony Cimo* (1986), *Terror on Highway 91* (1989), *Wild Palms* (1993), and *Class of '61* (1994). Dourif has appeared on episodic television in *Tales of the Unexpected, The Hitchhiker, Moonlighting,* and *The X Files.* In a world much given over to exploring the underbelly of life, Dourif finds himself a busy actor.

I interviewed Brad Dourif in his Beverly Hills apartment, which he shares with his wife and manager, Joni, and two children, Fiona and Kristina. We spoke in January 1992.

CZ: How did you first get involved in acting?

BD: Well, my mother was an actress. She married my father and moved to West Virginia where my grandfather had built a factory, and that was the end of her career. When I was young she used to read to us all— she read *Huckleberry Finn*, *Tom Sawyer*, and *King Arthur*, and a bunch of really good books. She would always become all the characters; I just remember everything was very alive, I really felt I was wherever she said I was; she was very talented. She was in a play, and I went to a rehearsal and I watched her rehearse—she was doing *Anastasia.* She was incredible, and it just made me want to learn how to act.

CZ: About how old were you then?

BD: Thirteen, when I really caught the bug. I think I still wanted to draw and paint; I did a lot of that. I did a lot of different things when I was a teenager, and the arts were just my way of surviving that horrible period that everybody somehow has to get through, and that's how I did it.

CZ: Did you pursue acting at Marshall University?

BD: Yes, but I was never much of a student. I got a lucky draft number, there was no way I was going to be drafted, so I left school and went to New York.

CZ: And you went to New York with the idea of becoming an actor?

BD: Oh yeah, there was no doubt at that point that I was going to become an actor. I just walked right into the Circle Repertory Theater [in 1969]; I knew how to do technical work because I'd done a lot of summer stock up to that point. So I just worked and worked and worked, and slowly I watched, and studied, and started acting.

CZ: At what point did you go to The Neighborhood Playhouse?

BD: I was never at The Neighborhood Playhouse per se, I studied with Sandy Meisner in what he called his professional classes, which were for working actors. But he would not allow me to work. Lanford Wilson wrote a part for me in *Hot L Baltimore*, and Sandy would not let me do it.

CZ: Because he didn't want you to act and learn to act at the same time?

BD: He felt that I had bad habits, and he wanted to break them first. But by the end of the year I was so hot to act, I did the first production of *When You Comin' Back, Red Ryder?* [1973], when I wasn't supposed to be acting. I got rave reviews, and he read them. I thought he was going to throw me out of class, because he had said he was going to, but he just said, "So . . . you're in a play." I said, "Yeah." He said, "Who told you you could be in a play?" I said, "Me." He said "OK."

CZ: Did he ever come to see you in *Red Ryder*?

BD: No, he never saw me.

CZ: Can we talk about him as a teacher?

BD: Very clear, very simple in what he was out to do. He was a teacher who really understood that you had to get it, and that he really didn't have much to do with that. He was not afraid to allow things to be boring for a long time. He allowed people to struggle, and, more than any teacher I've ever seen, he really, really was not trying to make the class interesting. I think that was his great power.

If you failed, or if it wasn't working, or it wasn't going to work for a long time, he let you just sit there and struggle. That's the way people learn, by their own mistakes. He just allowed people to fight their way through things.

All the other acting coaches that I worked with rescued their students. If something wasn't going well, they'd stop it. And so the only things that would happen were things that went well. They would fix things, but that's really directing, or workshopping; that's where people learn by fixing things. That's not what acting class is.

What acting class is—particularly with Sandy's technique—is to teach you a fundamental skill of survival. What do you do when you have egg all over your face and it's really not working? And understanding that you have to be willing to have egg on your face. And that a lot of times, it isn't working, and it doesn't always feel right, and it's not always exciting, and it's not always fun, and sometimes it's a struggle. Yet you go in and you look at rushes, and when you had egg on your face and you were struggling and it seemed like a crock, it's really good work. That's because I was trained by somebody who made me go through that. So no matter what I did, if it wasn't working, I always fought well. That's what an acting class teaches you to do. And that's why he was such a strong teacher and why his people tend to work well.

CZ: You taught directing in the film program at Columbia University from 1981 to 1986. What were some of the main things you taught your students?

BD: First of all, a director needs to watch where people's energy is. Wherever anybody's energy is is where their life is, and it's probably going to be the opposite of what they would like you to think it is. So always: Don't listen, don't be deceived, it's not what people say, it's what they *do*. What you're working on is your power of observation, your ability to see what's really going on in a person, in their behavior. So we talked about behavior, which was something Sandy Meisner didn't teach, and something I had to add.

I got directors involved in the process of acting themselves, getting them to understand on a gut level what acting is. It is pointless to teach a director to remove himself before he's been there—this is the big mistake that people always make. Because no one ever wants to go into the world where they have to self-disclose, and feel pain, and be uncomfortable, and be humiliated, and feel embarrassed. No director can really go into that world until they've done it, and I've noticed that every single director that I've worked with has done some acting.

Also a director needs to know if an actor's being phoney or not. Are you doing it, or are you pretending to do it? What's the difference between showing somebody something—which is indicating—and really doing it? That's what really bad acting is, just indicating. There's no unconscious involvement at that point.

CZ: How did you teach your class—in a practical way—to recognize indicating?

BD: You know how I did it? I encouraged my students to watch soap opera. I said, "I want you to watch your favorite performance on film, and then watch a soap opera, and try to come to terms with what the differences are." Because soap operas are readings. They're doing it really well, they're good at it, but they're indicating. Because they don't even know what they're going to say, you know? It's not that there aren't some wonderful actors that are doing soaps . . .

CZ: Did you feel there was any difference between dealing with students who were interested in going into filmmaking and students who wanted to be theater directors?

BD: Well, in general, theater directors tend to be more interested in the process. They can have terrible egos because they're really not that important in the minds of the audience, unless they become like Peter Brook, where they're writing plays, and that's a whole different kettle of fish. What a theater director really does is disappear. The play is the thing in the theater. But a film director is the storyteller, he's the poet. The camera is the narrator in a film. Film scripts are not literature, plays are.

CZ: You moved from theater to film when Milos Forman saw you in *Red Ryder* and cast you in *One Flew over the Cuckoo's Nest* [1975]. How did you prepare for that part, and how did Forman work with the actors? There's a very strong sense of ensemble in that film.

BD: Ensemble is part work and about 75 percent magic. If you have a great cast, as long as they don't have enormous egos—the concern isn't who has the biggest trailer, or something like that—you're really going to have a great ensemble. You could have an ensemble with a style; Circle Rep had a style, and that was based on a particular way of working. There was an artistic director there who had strong opinions about what kind of acting he liked, and that's what kind of acting everybody did. But that's not what an ensemble is. An ensemble is a group of people who really somehow, in some kind of a magical way, meld together and really work off each other well. It's the most positive kind of competition there is: the better he gets, the better I get, the better I get, the better he gets, and so forth and so on. When people really pay attention to each other, the stakes somehow are raised.

CZ: Did you have that sense when you were working on *Cuckoo's Nest?*

BD: Oh, absolutely. You walked on the set the first day, after we got our haircuts and so forth, and it was very clear that everybody was dead on the money; it was there.

CZ: How did Forman rehearse people for that?

BD: We rehearsed for two weeks, in a standard way. We sat around where we were supposed to sit and said our lines.

CZ: Did he talk with the group about their characters and their relationships, or did he talk with people individually?

BD: He talked individually with people. He really believed in people exploring.

CZ: What was the transition like for you, from theater to film, in terms of dealing with the camera?

BD: Oh, [Jack] Nicholson was the biggest help there. Here's somebody who had directed before, and edited before, and who liked the camera, and was very interested in the whole process, and was very willing to teach it. Nicholson does not defend himself at all from the camera, as an actor; he really uses the camera. He talked about why James Dean was such a good film actor—he called him "The Great Peeper"— because he was always angular, and coming toward the camera. Playing with the camera made him visually very exciting to watch.

CZ: Do you ever work on a backstory for your character? In *Wise Blood* [1979]—your first leading role in a film—there doesn't seem to be much information in the script about your character, Hazel Motes. How did you develop your characterization?

BD: Actually, there's quite a bit about Hazel Motes. I saw that as very rich in terms of suggestions. It isn't what you know that's important, it's how turned on you are about what you *don't know* that's important. If you're going to make a backstory, if you make a solid, good-sounding, investigative-reporting type of story, it's a useless piece of garbage. I mean, I don't know what my backstory means in my life; it's a total mystery to me. All the power that exists is in things that are basically pretty unresolved and things I can't resolve. That's what you look for in a backstory; you try to make inferences, you pick what it is that's important, what your job is, what you need to bring to the scene, and so forth. You say, "I need something here," and so you write that down, you make a note, "I need something for . . . ," then you find something. You find something real or you make something up, but it's got to turn you on. That's the way I do it, but I don't have to have a backstory. I talked a lot about that when I was teaching directing, that to get into the circumstances, the best thing to do is to stir the actor up—not to give him definite and clear ideas about it.

CZ: In *Wise Blood,* I thought that the character was unusual because he starts out very tightly wound. It's not a dramatic arc like you might have in a more classical narrative, where the beginning is slower; there's a lot of exposition, and you build to a crescendo. He starts out very angry, and he gets angrier; he's always on that level of real intensity throughout the film.

BD: Well, the story does not work unless he is, because that's the kind of person he is: too much. That's why we believe that he really is going for something bigger than life—which God is, he's the only thing that's bigger than life. So, structurally, you can't do the story without it; it doesn't make sense. It's supposed to be a comedy, and the humor is supposed to come out of that, that's the idea.

CZ: Did you find that it worked?

BD: No, I don't think that part worked. I think it's an interesting film to look at, because John [Huston] shot it in such an interesting way, but I don't think it worked.

CZ: Some of the scenes you have in that film I assume were done with
real local people, rather than actors. What was that experience like?

BD: People who've never worked before often do quite well. You
need to pay attention to what you're doing. You need to move the scene,
you're responsible for the rhythm of the scene—because they don't know
anything about that, and they don't have a feeling for it. So you need to
take responsibility, and then do what you're doing. And they get it, or they
don't. You try to be there for them, talk to them, get people to relax; you're
doing a lot more taking care.

CZ: And how was it to work with Huston?

BD: It was very good. John is not real interested . . . he doesn't appear
to be interested.

CZ: In the actor?

BD: Mm-hmm.

CZ: You've done quite a bit of work that would be described as
non-naturalistic. *Wise Blood* is an example, and *Exorcist III* [1990] would
certainly be an example. Since you don't have the life experience of being
one of the devil's minions or entering the body of a dead person, how do
you work yourself into that emotional state?

BD: Yeah, but I do have an incredibly violent heart, and in that sense,
I certainly am one of the devil's minions, aren't I? You know, the great
thing about being a villain, particularly in this culture, is that we love our
villains, we're really fascinated by evil. So, I mean, if you find all the evil
inside you and you're willing to express it, you can survive quite well in
this business.

CZ: In *Exorcist III,* you've got very long speeches, with language that
isn't particularly naturalistic. Do you have some special way of dealing
with that?

BD: Oh, you have to become very used to the language. If you know
the dialogue really well, you can forget about it. And then when it comes
up, it comes up in its own way, full of all your stuff. You conjure images
and feelings while you're working on it, and things from your life. So, if
you're lucky, when you're shooting, it's alive.

CZ: They slowed down your voice, right?

BD: Well, yes, they doctored it. And my voice sounded very different than my voice normally sounds anyway, because when I was doing it, I screamed. So part of it is [the doctoring], and part of it isn't. My high registers were shot, and I had, suddenly, these low sounds. Have you ever screamed? Your voice really sounds strange. So it was kind of neat, I liked the way it sounded.

CZ: You've done "A" movies, and you've also worked on a lot of independent features. What are the major differences?

BD: Well, when I'm working well, there's no difference at all, because I don't care. Except, you know, the place you go to after and in between is nicer, a lot of times. Independents can be the best experience of them all, because you know the crew better, you know the cinematographer better; everybody's a lot less pretentious.

CZ: Do you have more time for rehearsal or less?

BD: You have less time, because independents don't have any money, so they shoot very fast. It used to be different, independents used to have nice, long shooting schedules. It was very common; 13 or 14 weeks was a very common shooting schedule. Now 6 weeks is pretty average, and that's very fast to make a movie.

CZ: You've been working recently with a lot of European directors like Werner Herzog [*Scream of Stone,* 1990] and Hanif Kureishi [*London Kills Me,* 1992]. Do you feel there's any difference working in Europe and working in the States?

BD: There is a fundamental thing that we do differently than Europeans do. We do melodrama, and we do it better than anyone in the world does it. No one has ever been able to do melodrama like Americans do it. We can make you forget you're watching a film. Europeans never do that, they're not applauded for it, they don't even believe in it. The European director really sits beside you in the theater, and he touches you, and talks to you, and shows you what he's doing. The great European actors all have this wonderful, natural style, but they don't bring power to their work, they don't raise stakes to this life-and-death extent that American actors do. When an American actor cuts loose, there's guts there, and real passion.

European actors dance; they don't have that passion. None of them do, really.

CZ: You've been in several of David Lynch's films [*Dune,* 1985; *Blue Velvet,* 1986]; do you consider his work melodrama?

BD: No. David Lynch laughs at melodrama. David Lynch laughs at everything. This man has the sickest sense of humor of anyone walking the face of this earth.

CZ: You once called him the purest, most original director that you had ever worked with. Can you talk about that?

BD: Well, who ever made a TV series like *Twin Peaks?* No one had ever seen anything like that on television before. He took this small town, which is what we're all trying to preserve, this whole small-town morality, and so forth, and showed it, and did a TV series about a cesspool lying underneath that. It's sick, and everybody's dirty inside, really. And he made a comedy out of it. His world is so subjective. It's really not American; we're extroverted, and we don't spend very much time in the inner realms. But he's one of the few real, pure American directors who really found himself.

CZ: Would you have a lot of input about your characters in Lynch's films?

BD: Yeah, we got together, but David knows what he likes and what he doesn't, and you don't want to get in his way, either. So I had my input, but I was more than delighted to hear his.

CZ: What would you consider the most favorable circumstances for making a film? What would that mean for you?

BD: I guess working on a small film with a group of people who really liked what they were doing. Playing something that I could do really well. Going to someplace where I've never gone before.

CZ: You've done a lot of television work, from series TV, to movies-of-the-week, to mini-series. I'd like you to talk about the differences you've found in working in film and working in TV.

BD: There's a lot of differences. First of all, the expectations. Television is, by definition, safe. Now, it's becoming not safe, so film is becoming much safer. We're in a very strange period.

When you're doing television, it's much more of a corporation, even, than film, which is badly overcorporatized. What that means is that when you're working in a TV show, people act like they're not really the people who are making the decisions: "It's not up to me." The director really doesn't have power, and you can feel it. He's just kind of doing a job, and everybody's just kind of doing a job; the people who really seem to care the most on television are the actors. They're the only people who seem to be fighting.

CZ: Is there a difference in the time frames?

BD: Well, television's fast. But, like I say, a lot of independent films are very fast.

CZ: So that doesn't bother you?

BD: Sometimes it's a blessing. You don't think about what you're doing. There's not enough time to spend on the shot, so you take care of it, you shoot it, and it's over with. You get a nice rhythm sometimes, working that way. A lot of pressure, but you get a nice rhythm.

CZ: What do you feel is your best work in TV?

BD: I don't know. I don't think anything I've ever done is good in TV, really.

CZ: You have a very high level of dissatisfaction, don't you?

BD: Have you ever heard yourself on tape?

CZ: Yeah.

BD: How does that sound to you?

An Interview with Mary Steenburgen

Mary Steenburgen. Courtesy of Jason Weinberg and Associates.

Since the beginning of her career, Mary Steenburgen has evoked comparisons with one of Hollywood's most distinctive stars of the 30s and 40s, Jean Arthur. Like Jean Arthur, Steenburgen defies characteristics of a traditional female movie star such as glamour, mystery, and erotic allure—qualities that locate a star somehow beyond the plane of ordinary existence. Her charm lies—like Arthur's—in precisely those attributes that refuse that aura of unapproachability. Physically, Steenburgen has what she calls a "funny face," rather than being a classical beauty. That "funny face" is emblematic of a kind of fresh, off-kilter spirit that makes Steenburgen a unique and special film actor. Like Arthur, Steenburgen brings an uncommon integrity to her work in both film and television movies, a radiant honesty born out of inner strength and conviction. From her first role in the Jack Nicholson-directed *Goin' South* (1978), Steenburgen displayed a distinct persona. She is feisty, independent, and single-minded, a no-nonsense woman incapable of pretense. Her forthrightness is

207

tempered by a sunny, even-handed disposition and a sweet, disarming innocence. In her interview, Steenburgen remarks that "actors are . . . asked to play like children." Indeed, it is that open and uncomplicated childlike directness that is a part of Steenburgen's captivating presence. Mary Steenburgen was born in Newport, Arkansas, in 1953. After attending a small local college, she studied acting with Sanford Meisner at the Neighborhood Playhouse in New York, beginning in 1972. Steenburgen supported herself by waitressing and honed her craft working in an improvisational comedy troupe that toured VA hospitals and rehab clinics. After her first role in Nicholson's film, Steenburgen was the lead in *Time after Time* (1979) opposite her future husband, Malcolm MacDowell. (They are now divorced.) Her next role was in *Melvin and Howard* (1980), directed by Jonathan Demme, where her performance as the tap-dancing Linda garnered Steenburgen both the Academy Award and New York Film Critics Award for Best Supporting Actress. Some of Steenburgen's prominent roles in the 80s were as Mother in Milos Forman's *Ragtime* (1981), as Adrian in Woody Allen's *A Midsummer Night's Sex Comedy* (1982), as Marjorie Kinnan Rawlings in Martin Ritt's *Cross Creek* (1983), a dual role in Arthur Penn's *Dead of Winter* (1987), and the mother in *Parenthood* (1989). She also appeared during that decade as Nicole Diver in Dennis Potter's adaptation of F. Scott Fitzgerald's *Tender Is the Night* (1985), produced by the BBC. Recently, Steenburgen played the heroine in *Back to the Future III* (1990), a chanteuse from Brooklyn in *The Butcher's Wife* (1992), a lawyer in *Philadelphia* (1993, reuniting her with Demme), and a lascivious neighbor in *What's Eating Gilbert Grape?* During our conversation, Steenburgen talked about acting for the stage as a "future dream." That dream became a reality when she starred in a Broadway revival of Shaw's *Candida*, in 1993, as the eponymous heroine.

Mary Steenburgen and I met in January 1992 in her home among the orange groves of Ojai, California, where she lives with her children, Lilly and Charlie.

CZ: You studied at The Neighborhood Playhouse. Would you talk about that?

MS: Well, I went there in 1972 and I studied for 2 years. We got to study with Sandy Meisner maybe once or twice a week, and then in the second year you studied with him more frequently. We had acting classes every day. We had ballet and certain modern dances inspired by Martha Graham. We studied voice, and I lost a great deal of my southern accent, which was very, very thick when I came and which I knew would limit me as an actress.

The training begins as a series of improvisational exercises that Sandy Meisner devised. And the goal of the exercises is to cause people to really begin to act without doing all the things that people innately start doing when they hear the word "act," which usually involves posing, and self-consciousness, and trying to be good. Sandy's exercises call you back to an instinct that you have as a child, before you become encumbered with self-consciousness and a judgmental attitude about yourself and others. When a kid is playing cowboys or whatever, and they go "bang-bang," they just drop dead. They don't say, "Gee, what kind of gun is that?" or "I'm not sure I believe that," or "you weren't pointing it directly at me"; they just drop dead; they play. I think that we lose a great deal of this, and we become much more self-conscious and inward-looking as we grow older. For most people, the initial approach to acting immediately turns you in on yourself; you look inward. Sandy's exercises, which are very simple and very uncomplicated, and very—well, excuse me, but—free of bullshit, are designed to cause you to tell the truth under imaginary circumstances and to focus on the person you're with, as opposed to yourself. Most actors trained by Sandy Meisner are really affected by the other actors in the piece with them in a way that is completely spontaneous.

One of the things I loved about Sandy, as opposed to other acting teachers—who I think mess with people's heads too much and potentially kill off really wonderful instincts—is that his training was designed to be a support for all your great instincts. And he loves it if you bring new ideas, or throw things out, and make additions or subtractions from what he's giving you. It's never failed me as a basis for my work, as a place to start from.

CZ: What were your ambitions when you went to The Neighborhood Playhouse?

MS: I lied about my earliest ambition when I went there. I told people at home I was going to study to be a teacher. The reason I said that was, it was too big a dream. It almost sounded like a little girl's fantasy to say,

"I'm going to be an actress," coming from somebody who'd never met an actress in her life. You have to realize that, for me, they were mythical creatures, they weren't people who really earned a living that way. I justified my trip to New York by saying that I was going to go learn to be a great theater teacher, and the truth was I always wanted to be an actress.

CZ: Were your parents supportive of your decision to act?

MS: I just am one of those lucky people that got dream parents. My father was a freight train conductor, and an incredible man. My mother is still alive. She's a wonderful pal, a sweet woman. When I said I wanted to go be an actress, they were totally supportive: "Wow, we can't wait to see what you're going to do." I've tested a lot over the years; I've done a lot of things that maybe some people would have found embarrassing, and also thrown the good and bad parts of being famous into their laps. They've had to deal with all that, and they've been incredible. When I went to The Neighborhood Playhouse, I think I was one of the only kids that went there with total approval, as opposed to parents who said, "You go try this for a couple of years, and then we'll see what happens."

CZ: Did you have any aspirations to be in the movies when you were at The Neighborhood Playhouse?

MS: No more than most young girls do. I had those nights where I had felt belittled by somebody, or I hated the way I looked, or whatever, and I would have fantasies about how "I'll just grow up to be a movie star, and I'll show them." But I don't think there's a little girl or boy who doesn't say that, who dreams about being something that's going to show somebody else. The irony was, when it actually did happen, I didn't feel vindictive toward anybody! I haven't felt like I showed anybody anything! My struggles are still my struggles, and being a so-called movie star doesn't make your pain any less. It's still a real life. So, in that sense, it wasn't what I might have thought it was going to be.

Being at The Playhouse was an amazing time for me, first of all because I had gone from Arkansas to "the Great City of New York" and I was going to standing room–only seats in theaters and seeing amazing performances of actors, and off-off-Broadway theaters, and all kinds of experimental plays. I was really driven and excited, just wildly obsessed with theater. I really didn't study or know anything about film at that point, I didn't ever dream that's what I would end up doing.

CZ: What was it was like to work on your first film, *Goin' South* [1978]?

MS: Well, it's funny, because there are no words big enough to describe that time in my life. By the time this happened, I had been in New York around 6 years, studying and working and waitressing. And it was as though I said, "I want to fly to the moon," and I had been saying that every single day for many years. And then suddenly one night, someone came and tapped me on my shoulder, and before I could put my bathrobe on or grab my toothbrush, they said, "This is the time your dreams come true, you get to fly to the moon." And, yes, I'd always wanted to fly to the moon, but I needed to get my life in order, or say goodbye to somebody, or prepare for what it's going to be like with no gravity. When it came, it came like that [*snaps fingers*]. I don't mean stardom came so much, because *Goin' South* was not a terribly successful movie. But I was the female lead in a movie opposite a huge movie star [Jack Nicholson], and I had never been around a movie star. And I had never been on a film set; and I had never been in front of a film camera; and I didn't know what all the names of the jobs were; and I didn't know what hit your marks meant. When I'd got a little house in Durango, where we were shooting, I didn't know how to have a maid. I didn't know how to deal with my mother when she called me up at 4:00 in the morning because she'd read in the newspaper that Jack and I had run off and gotten married. I didn't know anything. All I had was this incredible training and an amazing 24-year history of love and support, which was a lot.

Every single thing I dealt with was new. And the technical things weren't as hard as the emotional things. Learning how to hit your marks, even though you can't look down at them—which is one of the great incongruities of film—that was easy compared to learning where I belonged in the world now. Who are my friends? Who's jealous of me, and who isn't? Who is going to say, the first time I'm late returning a phone call, "Well, she's gone Hollywood now." All that was much harder to learn. It took years, actually.

And Jack was an incredible teacher; and I'm lucky that if I was going to be so-called "discovered" by somebody, it was somebody who was so immensely gifted himself. He was very generous; he didn't try to hoard his secrets and his experience to himself, he just gave it generously to me. Jack screened films at Paramount for me, and he would come in and ask me questions about them: "Why was that great?" "Why did that actress do

Mary Steenburgen and Jack Nicholson in *Goin' South* (1978), directed by Nicholson. Courtesy of Paramount Pictures. Copyright © 1994 by Paramount Pictures. All Rights Reserved. Museum of Modern Art Film Stills Archive.

that?" "What did she do there with her eyes that she could have done a different way?" He gave me an incredible film acting workshop in those months before we started shooting. After we watched films, Jack took me over to the screening room and showed me my dailies, and taught me something about editing and how to use the camera better. So now, I hope most editors will tell you that I'm conscious of giving them cuts when I work. I'll turn my head in a certain way or do something at the end of the take so they have a place to cut.

This time for me was agony and ecstasy. I was doing all I could do to stay above water. I really wanted to be good and to live up to Jack's belief in me. He had been the first person that really validated what I felt I had inside. So it was intensely important to me not to disappoint him.

CZ: What do you see now when you watch *Goin' South*?

MS: Now, I can barely watch the film, because I see me, Mary, being so incredibly vulnerable that I almost can't watch it without cringing [*laughs*]. I think everybody has in them a first really pure performance. That doesn't mean after that you're just a big sham, but I think the first time you do a performance like that, it's like the first time you make love. You're a virgin one time, and I was a virgin in film one time, and that was *Goin' South*. I can look at that film and see everything about my life in it. I can see how I felt about Jack, that I hero-worshipped him. I can see my excitement, and my pride, and my terror, and my incredible vulnerability. To me, they're all somehow woven into that performance.

CZ: I often find Jack Nicholson's acting very heightened, and that's certainly true in *Goin' South*. Did you feel you were being asked to adjust your performance because of that?

MS: I think that I will always adjust to another actor's style, because I'm hopefully always connected to that actor. It's the way I work; I never determine something before a film and just go in there and, come hell or high water, do it. I try to know who the character is; I try to know things about her. What sort of person she is, what she would like, what her background is, and how she feels about life. I trust in all that when I stand in front of the other person, and the camera. But I trust that all that work has been done, and I don't act upon it. I act upon what I'm given from the other person. I have something called "actor's faith," which is that all the preliminary work has been done and is in there. So I'm never thinking about motivation, or family history, or any of that stuff when I'm working. I'm thinking about, "Why is he looking at me like that? Why is his eyebrow standing up? Is he lying to me?" Whatever it is that I'm going through with that character, with that other actor, that's what my mind's on, not style or background or anything else. Because of that, I think I cannot help but be affected by the style of anybody who works around me. I'm sure it's probably true that I might be more heightened if somebody else is.

CZ: Are you saying you've already internalized your ideas about the character before you shoot?

MS: I put it in the same way you put it into a computer, and then I just trust that it's there. I don't act from notes. If you look at my scripts, there are no suggestions written to myself about what to do at any moment. Because I don't know what I'm going to do. There may be notes about "it's 'as if' so and so." I use "as if" a lot, which is something Sandy uses. "It's as if it's Lilly's [Mary's daughter] tenth birthday and I don't get to make it there," or something like that. If I think of an idea that will help me to personalize something, I might make a note about that. But I won't say, "and that makes me stomp around the room," or "that makes me cry." I don't ever know what I'm going to do, and so far, I've been lucky enough to work with directors who have respected that, who wait and say, "Well, let's see what happens." It would be real hard for me to work with somebody that just talked in result terms, because I don't know what the results are going to be.

CZ: How do you choose projects? Do you have any overall plan in terms of your career goals?

MS: To be really honest with you—and this doesn't sound very artistic, or it sounds like I'm maybe less of an artist than I would like to think I am—now I figure in things like when my children are out of school, and if somebody's offering me something to do on the kids' spring break. I mean, I'm a mother, and it's really important to me. And I'm aware that I have one childhood for each of these kids. The person that I described to you, who went to New York and was so obsessed with learning her craft, I am not that person any more. Do I still care intensely about my work, and do I have a lot of integrity about it? I hope anybody that's worked with me will tell you that I do. But do I think that the most important thing in the world is acting, now? No. It is certainly, besides my children, my greatest joy. I have never been bored for one second on a film set. I love it, but I also recognize that I gave birth to 2 children and I want their lives to be great, and it can't be great if I'm working all the time. So I've really chosen to limit my career.

I don't want to turn around at 70 years old, and realize I have these important credits. I want to look back and say, "Boy, I had a good, fun life." I've always held that very close and never let go of it.

CZ: But what attracts you to one script and not another?

MS: There's one truth that's always remained the same, as far as how I choose scripts, and that is I try to do things that make my heart beat a little faster. When I read them, there's something about it that's fun, or engaging, or I wanted to work with a certain director, or because I found an element in the script challenging or difficult.

CZ: How did you get involved in *Melvin and Howard* [1980]? That has a wonderful script.

MS: That screenplay, which won Bo Goldman the Best Screenplay [Academy Award], is still the best screenplay I've ever read. Jack Nicholson gave it to me as an example of great writing. Nobody sent it to me. I read it, and I was determined to play that part. I went in and I read for Jonathan Demme, and I got it because I did this really great reading. Including at the end of the reading, grabbing Paul Le Mat's [Melvin's] face, and pulling his face down to mine, and giving him the biggest kiss he's ever had in his life, and walking out of the room. By the time I got home, Jonathan called me and said, "There's no point making you wait, I want you to play that part."

CZ: How do you approach your characters, and, specifically, how did you prepare for the role of Linda in *Melvin and Howard?*

MS: The first time I read a script is really an important moment for me, and I actually treat it in a little bit of a precious way. I don't read scripts and watch TV at the same time. In fact, I don't do anything when I read a script except read the script. Not only because I'm respectful of writers, but also because I find that it's the most pure time for me in terms of my approach to the material. Because I don't know what's around the corner. In films, or theater, or literature, once you've read something, you

Mary Steenburgen in *Melvin and Howard* (1980), directed by Jonathan Demme. Copyright © by Universal City Studios, Inc. Courtesy of MCA Publishing Rights, a division of MCA Inc. Museum of Modern Art Film Stills Archive.

know what's going to happen. And actually I'm in a process of trying to forget that I know what's around the corner, because in life we don't. The first time I read something I find I really listen to all my instincts and all my first responses. Because even though in retrospect they may seem naïve, they were true for that moment, with that lack of knowledge about how everything turns out in the end.

All kinds of things happened to me the first time I read *Melvin and Howard,* including falling in love with Linda. I find that I love all my characters, including the ones that nobody else loves, like *Miss Firecracker* [1989], who was despicable [*laughter*]. When I did *Tender Is the Night* [1985, a BBC television production], everybody kept calling me crazy, and I would look at them like they were crazy, because I didn't see Nicole Diver as crazy. Once I saw her as crazy, I would have been distancing myself from her. I understood why she did everything that she did.

What I always do is approach things symphonically; I will figure it out like a piece of music, in the same way you'd take a piece of sheet music and figure out where's the crescendo, decrescendo, pianissimo. Because you can't do it scene by scene. If you do it scene by scene, it's not seamless when it's put together. If you just act your little heart out in every scene, it won't work. A script has to have highs and lows. There are scenes that aren't my scenes, they're somebody else's scenes, and there are scenes that, "Boy, I better get in there and really make a strong moment." You can only do that by starting with the whole piece, and working it out, so that when it gets broken up and split apart—because we rarely do anything in chronological order—you always know where you are.

I also like to work physically, to give myself a physical task for a character if I can. When I did *Melvin and Howard,* I tap-danced and tried to get really good enough to control how bad I was. I hoped that the end product would be fun; not a truly brilliant tap-dancer, but somebody who's really putting her heart and soul into it. In order to control that, I had to be better than that. So I really worked hard at tap-dancing, every single day for a month.

CZ: The way you're working with objects in *Melvin and Howard* is so real-looking. I was thinking of the scene where you make a hero sandwich for your daughter in about 30 seconds.

MS: It was so real I cut my finger in the scene! [*Laughter*] If you really look closely, you can see that it's not all ketchup on the bread.

CZ: Would that be something you would practice?

MS: I don't know how much I practiced, but I know that there's a way of doing everything. Linda is a completely earthbound, organic person who has had to make lots of sandwiches and stuff. Even though she'd rather be dancing, she knows how to do that. Whatever you do tells the truth about her, in the same way that when I made a cup of tea before, you could either tell I've made a lot of cups of tea or I haven't. The same is true of these people, because every action speaks of all their life, not just their 2-hour life that you get a chance to see.

Actually, if you asked me at the time, how did I approach the character, I would have told you it was very simple: the character loved to dance. I try to boil things down to their simplest and their strongest forms. I don't like to act, "Well, it's sorta this, and it's sorta that." I like to have things very distilled and very powerful in my mind when I work. As an actress I don't like to feel confused, I like to feel very clear. Sometimes my characters may be confused, but as far as how I'm approaching them, I like clarity.

I like the idea, "Why is this day different than any other day?" I'm not crazy about naturalistic acting that's about "a day in the life of." I think that you go to films to be taken away. Sometimes that's by enlightenment, and sometimes that's just by laughing your head off at something that's ridiculous and silly. If it effectively transports you, then the actors and directors have done their own little magic. I don't like doing things in a casual, naturalistic way.

There's all kinds of things I do; I remember saying in that scene, "When you get there tell Nell and Morris . . ." That's my parents. I play around with stuff like that, without managing to come out of a scene. I'm aware that I have the privilege of being able to say hello to my unborn descendants. I get to say "Hi" to my children's children's children's children. I have little moments where I'm aware that if film exists, and survives, and if any of my films do, that people who are somehow friendly will watch them. I love thinking about things like that when I work. I love all the different layers you can play with. But that scene was nice.

Actually, my favorite moment in my film career, so far, is in that movie. And I know that Bo Goldman feels the same way, as far as a line reading of his work. It's the scene where I say, "Well, c'est la vie, Melvin." I so love that piece of writing, and I really tried to rise to that moment. I think I could never repeat it. Melvin says, "Well, what's that mean?" and I say, "It's French. I used to dream of being a French interpreter." "You don't speak French." And I say, "I told you, it was a dream." That moment just came out of something that's so deep in me, and also deep in Bo Goldman. It says a lot about who I was and who I am, and it came without any obstruction, and I am very proud of it.

CZ: Did Jonathan Demme talk to you about the tone of your performance? In one scene you're sitting, drinking a brandy in the middle of the afternoon, watching a game show on TV. Melvin asks you what's for dinner, you say, "Bell peppers," and he says, "You know I don't like bell peppers." What's there is a conflict and antagonism, but it's done in a very understated way.

MS: Sometimes, the words may come out in a very simple way, but what's behind them isn't that simple. We may be talking about bell peppers, but we're talking about our lives, and our frustrations, and the marriage, and my big dreams, and how they're not coming true. I don't remember so much that Jonathan—and this is true of most of the directors I've worked with, the good ones—told me how to do anything, so much as gave me an amazing arena in which to do it. The arena is amazing because they choose great production people. You walk into a house and you say, "This is exactly what Linda's house would look like." Or, you can make some small suggestions and they're open and they hear you.

And Jonathan made me feel safe. If the director doesn't make you feel safe—and to a certain degree actors are a little bit like children, and we're asked to play like children—if they don't give you a place that feels supportive of that, where you won't be ridiculed, where you're not worried that they're judging you, if they don't give you that, you can't fly. So I don't think it's so much what they say to you, it's what they give you, it's where they give you to play. It's not really words so much as support, and their artistic choices so far as your backdrop, the painting that you're in. Jonathan's a master at that. There's something to look at in every single shot, some crazy little whimsical funny thing that's really got his stamp on it. He and Bo were brilliant at providing me with things to do.

I am at my best, and I think all actors are, when you're given something great to do. "The seed to the craft of acting is the reality of doing"; that's the first thing Sandy Meisner said to me. And it's the truth. And so when you were asking me about that scene in the bus depot, I really did make about 20 sandwiches, I wasn't just pretending. When I was tap-dancing as though I had gone on a game show, everything about that felt real to me. Partly, you have to give Jonathan credit for things like casting Bob [Robert] Ridgely, who was brilliant as the game show host; he couldn't have been better. He made that real for me, and I worked off of him, and I used him, and I took what he gave me. Most of that was improvisational, all the interviewing, all the "Where are you from?" and "Would you like to put your hands in Uncle Wally's pocket?" All that was just playing together.

CZ: Do you ever make a distinction in your own mind between art and entertainment? Let's take one of your recent films, *Back to the Future III* [1990].

MS: Yes, that's entertainment. But within that, the people I was working with worked as hard as a lot of people that are so-called "artists."

They didn't phone it in, at all; they really thought about it. They made the film essentially for 9-year-old boys; that's their target audience. And they really think about what 9-year-old boys like, and address that. And nothing was cheap. My costumes were totally researched, and the color of the purple in the train was a color that had been introduced from Paris that very year. The quality of the people that worked on that film was as good as anything I've ever done. It didn't feel like I was just doing this commercial movie where nobody really cared; they cared very much.

I think that, essentially, when we get too highbrow about what we're there to do, we've lost something. If you talk to Lauren Bacall, or any of those people, she doesn't want to talk to you about artists. She wants to talk about, "Was it funny, was it good, did people enjoy it?" I respect the down-to-earthness of the people that were ahead of me, and the way they didn't get too pretentious about what they do. There's this little framed print that's in my bedroom, and it says, "Angels fly because they take themselves lightly." The reason it's there is because I tend not to like people who take themselves too seriously, especially in this business. There's a balance between recognizing that what you do should be entertaining, and yes, sometimes thought-provoking, and maybe challenging, and also trying to do it as well as you can. So that if I do *Back to the Future,* I try to make every moment as true as I can.

Listen, I'm in it because I love it, and I'm also in it because I really want to have a great time in this life. And everybody that's ever worked with me will tell you that it's really important to me to have fun on a film. And it shows in the movie. It's 3 months of my life! This thing about suffering for your art, if I ever did think it was true, then I suppose it may have been true for the first, early years of my life. But now I don't believe in it. To me, it's a joyous enterprise. And I'm lucky as hell to get to do it.

CZ: How do you deal with the fame involved in being a film actor?

MS: I realized even before I had children that being famous, or being a successful actor, was not what people thought it was. Is the work wonderful? Is the actual act of taking words and making them live and breathe, is that a privilege? Yes. Is that so fun you can hardly bear it sometimes? Yes. Is that something you'd like to do forever? Yes. Somebody coming up and asking you for your autograph, does that make you feel better about yourself? No. Does that mean when you're having a bad day, you're feeling sad or lonely, or whatever, does the recognition make you feel better? No. Does reading an article or an interview about yourself, or seeing your name all over the papers, does that make you feel more important, more significant? No, it doesn't.

So the whole thing that people go into it for, for me, I quickly saw, was a myth. It didn't exist. It didn't do one thing for me. I saw that the only thing left that was truthful about it, was the work itself. That the work itself just tickled me to death, and it was an incredible mental and emotional and personal challenge. That got better, but all that other stuff doesn't amount to very much. Early on I realized that I didn't want to structure my life in such a way that that was the focus. So I came to live here in Ojai. I don't do a lot of TV, because I find that TV brings more of it toward you. I don't do publicity unless I have a film coming out, and then I do it because I consider it a part of my responsibility to those people I worked with, who financed it. I made my first film in 1978, that's the first time I had any real brush with fame, although I didn't become, and still haven't become, the most wildly famous person in the world. In that time, a lot has gone down in my life that nobody will ever know about, except close friends. A lot. And I feel like I've lived fully. I think it's very easy, in this business, to surrender your life to a career. I don't want to do that. I won't do it.

CZ: Do you ever study performances by the actors who went before you?

MS: That's part of my ongoing education. There is so much to be learned by watching some of the great film performances of this century, as much as anything anybody can tell you in a book, or by anything you can see today. I've never not gotten something from watching the great actors work. Never. Somebody on film like Spencer Tracy, or Jimmy Stewart, or Jean Arthur, or Montgomery Clift—or any of the great people whose performances are preserved—to not take advantage of that is to say, "Well, I'm going to limit what I do." And I would never do that. I'll listen to anybody who's going to offer a suggestion or give me an idea that I can use in my work. It doesn't mean I'll use it, but I would never cut off a supply line of something that can make me a better actress. I just feel like I've put a toe in the water. I'd be very sad if this is as good as I'm going to get.

An Interview with Sydney Pollack

Sydney Pollack. Courtesy of Mr. Pollack.

Sydney Pollack is a good, classical storyteller, an undervalued craft in contemporary American cinema. A well-made narrative has complex, full-bodied characters whose traits and actions move the story forward. In order to transform those characters into living, breathing creations, the director needs actors. And the actor—if he is to fully embody a character—must fulfill the requirements of the written role *and* bring striking, original, and memorable qualities to the part.

Pollack has worked with some of the finest actors in American film, including Al Pacino (*Bobby Deerfield*, 1976); Jane Fonda (*They Shoot Horses, Don't They?*, 1969, and *The Electric Horseman*, 1979); Paul Newman and Sally Field (*Absence of Malice*, 1981); Dustin Hoffman (*Tootsie*, 1982); Meryl Streep (*Out of Africa*, 1985); and Gene Hackman (*The Firm*, 1993). One might contend (wrongly, I think), that it is no great feat to obtain exceptional performances from excellent actors. But not all great actors are good film actors. And Pollack's talent is evident, first, in

223

his understanding of what good *film* acting is, and, second, in his ability to elicit outstanding *film* performances from his actors.

The actor most closely associated with Pollack—and an exemplar of good film acting—is Robert Redford (*This Property Is Condemned,* 1966; *Jeremiah Johnson,* 1972; *The Way We Were,* 1973; *Three Days of the Condor,* 1975; *The Electric Horseman; Out of Africa; and Havana,* 1990). Redford has the ability to absorb and reflect the camera's minute attentions and to render what Pollack calls the "small moments" of the character's "interior life"—the essence of good acting for film. Other stars who are not necessarily great actors but who have done some of their best work with Pollack include Barbra Streisand in *The Way We Were,* Natalie Wood in *This Property Is Condemned,* and Robert Mitchum in *The Yakuza* (1975). Pollack navigates many different genres: thriller, mystery, comedy, biography, Western, and melodrama. But at base, almost every film Pollack has made revolves around romance. Romance is concerned with investigating the parameters of human relationships and feelings, and Sydney Pollack's work with actors is about that exploration.

Pollack was born in Lafayette, Indiana, in 1934 and left after high school to train for the theater in New York at The Neighborhood Playhouse. After assisting his teacher, Sanford Meisner, for several years at The Playhouse, Pollack conducted private acting classes from 1954–60. During the 1950s he had major roles in several New York plays, *The Dark is Light Enough,* and *A Stone for Danny Fisher* and toured U.S. cities in a production of *Stalag 17.* Pollack acted in episodic TV (*Alcoa Presents*, *Playhouse 90,* and *Ben Casey*) and in several films—among them was a film, *War Hunt* (1962), which also marked Robert Redford's film debut. He continues to act occasionally, both in his own films (*Tootsie,* 1982) and in the films of other directors (e.g., Woody Allen's *Husbands and Wives* [1992]). Pollack directed numerous television pilots and series, primarily in the 1960s, winning an Emmy Award in 1966 for Outstanding Directorial Achievement in Drama for "The Game" on *Bob Hope Presents the Chrysler Theater.* His first film as a director was *The Slender Thread* (1966), starring Sidney Poitier and Anne Bancroft. Pollack continued his film work, and, with *They Shoot Horses,* began to produce most of his own films. In the last decade, Pollack has also produced films by other directors, including *Honeysuckle Rose* (1980); *Bright Lights, Big City* (1988); *The Fabulous Baker Boys* (1989); *Presumed Innocent;* and *White Palace* (both 1990). Pollack was nominated for the Best Director Academy

Award for *They Shoot Horses* and *Tootsie* and won for his third nomination for *Out of Africa* in 1986.

I met with Sydney Pollack in the office of his production company, Mirage Enterprises, in Universal City, California, in August 1991.

CZ: You went to The Neighborhood Playhouse, and you're also a member of The Actors Studio. I'd like you to talk about both places.

SP: Well, I began at The Playhouse. That was the first training I had, when I was really quite young—17, and just out of high school. I studied at The Playhouse for 2 years. Then, at the end of that 2-year period, I was asked by Sandy Meisner to come back on a fellowship, to be an assistant and to teach. I was not particularly interested in teaching. But I did think it was a great way to keep on studying with Meisner, so I spent the next 5 years teaching as his assistant and then gradually started my own private classes.

Then, way, way later, I was asked by Lee Strasberg to help administer The Actors Studio, when we started a branch out here. I never did an audition for The Studio, never got in the normal way, as most actors do. I got in on a free pass, I didn't have to go through the horrible agony of the two auditions, which I'd always heard stories about.

There's a big difference—although the result is the same—between the way these 2 men approached the work process. Putting the controversy aside, there's much to be learned from both of them; they were both great teachers. I frankly preferred Meisner, by quite a long shot. It just worked better for me. There was something in Lee's approach, as brilliant as he always was, that made the process the end in itself. There was something about Meisner's approach that was extremely simple. He kept trying to simplify and simplify until you had some sense of a technique, only insofar as (a) it was necessary, and (b) that its objective was to get you to a result. There was no book in which it said you had to go through all of this rigamarole to achieve a result. He felt that there was a result which had to do with, first, the creation of a kind of reality within imaginary circumstances, and secondly—this was the hardest part—making that reality original and interesting.

I always felt truly fascinated in Lee's classes; he was a brilliant man, but he made the technique such a religion in some ways. Unless one was quite a strong individual, one could get preoccupied with the technique and sometimes forget that it is not an end in itself. It's purely a way to get at yourself, to activate yourself in some way. I don't consider myself an expert on Lee's approach to material, but I did get the sense that Sandy's approach had more to do with your obligation to serve the material. There was a task the author had given you, and everything came out of that. An example of the difference [between them] would be Lee's use of emotional memory at a given moment, and Sandy's feeling that it was really taking you right out of the circumstances of the play.

I've seen actors use both techniques. I wouldn't want to have to say that one or the other is wrong, or one or the other is right. The best actors that I've worked with have a tendency to stick within the circumstances of the play and find the emotion through that. But if you see real disciples of Lee—even those words are emblematic—they can just mesmerize you with a performance, using emotional memory. Ellen Burstyn, for example, is a real devotee of Lee's law, and always has been, and is brilliant at it, a great actress. I think it's a question of suiting the technique to your individual psyche. I've seen a lot of people get lost with Lee, go far afield, and waste years being preoccupied with some kind of mumbo-jumbo ritual.

CZ: You moved from teaching theater performance to directing series TV to film. Can you talk about the way your ideas on acting changed because of your work in different media?

SP: Well, this is a controversial subject, and I always feel uncomfortable talking about it, because what I'm about to say often offends actors. I'm probably alone in this point of view among the directors I have spoken to. Contrary to what everybody says, I do believe there is a radical difference in the approach to film acting versus stage acting. It sounds nice to say, "Good acting is good acting." But is good stage acting good film acting? I don't think so, necessarily. Because the film director is searching with a tool that's like a microscope. In film acting you can convey many more small moments, and the interior life of a character, with much greater ease than you can on the stage. A stage actor has 4 weeks of rehearsal, minimum, sometimes 8 weeks, and the scene prior to the one he or she is doing as a springboard, and the scene after the one he's doing to use as a follow-through. The stage actor must repeat moments, and know how to repeat moments over and over again, must understand the road map of the emotional life of the character and the play. Because the only time it really counts, the director is of no use whatsoever. From the time you say the equivalent of "action," which is "curtain," that whole play runs without anybody saying anything to the actors. Rhythms are set, everything is set. It is absolutely the reverse in film. The only time it really counts there is nobody but the director, alone in an editing room. The actors are gone, the cameraman's gone, the writer is gone. Everybody's gone, and you're going to put this together one way or another. And either you were right in the way you held—in your head—the emotional line of both the film and the roles, or you were wrong. So it's really on your shoulders. It's a little bit like putting your finger on a record, slowing it down so much that the melody is unrecognizable, and trying to make a judgment about whether it's a pretty melody or not. A melody absolutely transforms itself when you slow it down that much. It's not recognizable anymore. That slowed-down tempo never happens on stage, because you do run-throughs of the whole play. But you do 2 minutes of film a day, if you're lucky, in 10 or 12 hours of shooting. The process is pulled apart so much that something unnatural happens, and there's another facility required.

In a film, I'm always trying to catch a performance before it examines itself so much that it loses its life. I prefer an actor to be a little more insecure, in a film. You don't have 4 or 5 weeks to rehearse, where a performance can begin to question itself, tear itself completely apart, lose all of its spontaneity, and then find itself again. You don't often have that time in film, so I prefer to work another way.

This is something that's evolved over the years; I've gotten more and more away from the rehearsal process. I don't want the actors so insecure that they're not able to give the best performance. And I don't want to be a Machiavelli, controlling them. But if I can get them to trust me enough, I find that I get more exciting performances from really gifted actors out of the rush of their own intuitive understanding of the part, usually in the first couple of times that they do it. It has a spontaneity and a freshness and a life that I don't know how to get unless I am able to rehearse for 5 or 6 weeks. And I've never been able to get a whole cast together, on a location, for that long prior to filming. The best I've been able to do is a week's reading, here in my office, or something. I don't consider that a real rehearsal.

CZ: It sounds like you're saying that you want the actor to be—at least to some degree—lost and dependent on the director. When you're working on an epic level, as you did in *Out of Africa* [1985], a lot of time elapses during the story. Don't the actors in that kind of film need a construct for their character?

SP: I don't want ignorant actors. There's a difference here. This shouldn't be confused with not doing homework, or not discussing the part, or not being very clear where you are. In *Out of Africa* we had an absolute graph. It was worked out beforehand. The makeup was worked out; there were four different makeups, four different hairstyles, four different stages—that's just from the outside. And then of course there were the degrees in the relationship. It had to be understood. I would never play a critical emotional scene near the end of a story, before we've filmed the necessary early parts. You do film out of continuity, but there are certain things that have to be done, to work the way I'm talking about. You don't want to start with the end scene, and say, "Oh, don't worry, just trust me." That's silliness.

Because of my own background, I'm comfortable with actors, and, for the most part, I think actors are comfortable with me. They don't often feel that I'm asking them to do something they're either not equipped or capable of doing or that I don't understand the process. I still prefer not to rehearse the way you do on the stage. I still prefer only to know as much as necessary to know to free you, to surprise yourself. Eighty percent of this is casting. If you've cast the person whose responses to the material are going to intuitively be close to what you want, then, really, you're trying to create a degree of comfort and relaxation in them. They'll be capable of even surprising themselves. That's what you're going for.

CZ: You've worked with all sorts of actors; is it ever difficult to mix the emotional work of people with such different backgrounds? What happens when you're working with a Hollywood star like Robert Mitchum [*The Yakuza,* 1975], as opposed to someone like Al Pacino [*Bobby Deerfield,* 1977], who's trained at The Studio and believes very strongly in The Studio work?

SP: The answer to the question is that it's my job to find a method of communication that works with that actor. If I'm doing it right, it doesn't matter what the background of the actor is. Obviously, I'd speak to Mitchum in a different way than I would speak to Pacino. And I would speak to Klaus Maria Brandauer in a different way than I would speak to either of them. To Redford, a completely different way. I'm trying for the same result. I hope it won't look like they're all in different films. Sometimes, you do have to do some sandpapering, so to speak.

CZ: When you say "sandpapering," you're talking about smoothing out the differences in the emotional levels during the shoot?

SP: Yes. And sometimes it creates hostility. There have only been two times in my life where I really felt that actors hated me, where they felt I was not permitting them to act. In both cases, they were European theater actors, who, I felt, were playing out of key with the level of reality in the rest of the picture. My job was, in some sense, to pull them down, and that got perceived after a long time as trying to "keep them from acting." Both of these actors, by the way, were nominated for Academy Awards for the films they did with me, so we get along better now. Both of them had big blowups. One of them, a woman, screamed, "You're not letting me act!" The man I refer to became quite sullen with me. But those are two extreme cases. I've worked with lots of other theater actors and have had absolutely no problem whatsoever. For some reason, with these 2 people, there was a level of theatricality, if you will, which might work in one film but not work in another. This is not a reflection of their talent. It was Susannah York in *They Shoot Horses, Don't They?* [1969] and Klaus Brandauer in *Out of Africa.*

Now, Klaus's theatricality in *Mephisto* [1981] was brilliant, but I didn't want that kind of theatricality in this particular role in *Out of Africa.* I think Klaus is a brilliant actor, but here, he had to play a real scoundrel, and I wanted you to love him. He had to do everything wrong; steal her money, buy the wrong kind of farm, give her syphilis, screw around with everybody, and in the end, they're friends. So this is not a performance that could have an odor of narcissism about it; I didn't want anything that had a sense of theater in it. I wanted his attention always to be concentrated on the other person, with no sense of his own drama. We had an honest disagreement about how to come to this. I win those arguments, because I have the ultimate weapon, which is final cut of the film. There's no way an actor can win that argument, and most actors know that. And so, if they get unhappy and really don't agree with you, it can be uncomfortable for a while. We made the best of it; I knew he wasn't happy. But it's honestly not a problem for the most part. When I pick out those two experiences, that's in 15 films.

Sometimes it's hard to time when to roll the camera if you have an actress, let's say, who likes and needs rehearsal—and an actor who doesn't want to rehearse. That happened in *The Way We Were* [1973] a lot. Barbra [Streisand] really wants to talk about the scene and wants to rehearse it, gets better if she does it a few more times. Redford's much more spontaneous. He feels that too much talk starts to stifle the performance. He really wants to get lost in it himself, and he doesn't want to analyze every moment. It's a little tricky with something like that. You have to roll the camera far enough in that he's not going downhill, and not so early that she hasn't found herself. On the other hand, there were certain scenes with her, alone, that we never rehearsed, where she was just ready to go on the first take. She had one long phone conversation with him, where she broke down. It was all in one shot, and that was the first take, the first time, no rehearsal.

CZ: Going back to this question of different acting styles: Al Pacino, for me, is the quintessential method actor. I see that especially in *Bobby Deerfield;* he's very inward, he's isolated, intense, and concentrated. Did he improvise a lot in that film? I thought he might have because of his line readings. There's a lot of repetition and mid-sentence pauses.

SP: It was a psychological tool of the character's so that he didn't have to surprise himself. You ask a question and he repeats it. That gives him more time to think, instead of taking a risk and surprising himself with an answer. So that was part of the character work. But you're quite right, Al is a quintessentially Studio-trained actor. But what that really meant was that he truly did need more rehearsal than I would normally give, so I rehearsed. And he didn't improvise very much. The only times I remember improvising were in some of those driving shots. We would get the scene, and then he would say, "Let's just try improvising."

It's good that you think it's improvisation, that's what you ought to think about everything, really. If everybody's doing their part right, it ought to have that kind of improvisational feeling to it. Al is very good at that. The whole thing you're taught in the beginning is to stay in touch with real impulses, and if you're relaxed enough when you work, and you're really paying attention to the other actor, you get impulses all the time. In the middle of a sentence, in the middle of a moment, in the middle of listening. And he's trained himself to follow those impulses.

The thing about Al that's wonderful is, for all of that, he's very reverential about the text. That comes from doing plays; it comes from doing Brecht, it comes from fooling around with Shakespeare. He's really a believer in the text, and he'll work on it with you from the beginning. He sat with Alvin [Sargent, the screenwriter] and I for a long time, and we worked very hard on the script. And then, once he says "OK, that's it," then it's pretty much like he's doing a play. In something like *Dog Day Afternoon* [1975], where it's so close to him, it's New York, and it's right in his back yard, then maybe he can improvise more. This was a little more structured.

CZ: Pacino seems to enjoy taking risks as an actor.

SP: Absolutely. This was a big stretch for him. As a matter of fact, after *Sea of Love* [1989], which really sort of revived his career, there was a huge story on him in *Vanity Fair*, and he said his favorite role was *Deerfield*. It got such a bad rap at the time of its release. People just didn't know what to make of it. What the hell was this? Here's dynamic Al Pacino like a somnambulist, and this girl [Marthe Keller] with a funny accent. It was one of those odd films. On the other hand, I've gotten some of the nicest, most interesting letters from that film. It's a film I've always liked. But he is a very brave actor, Pacino.

CZ: You've spoken about how damaging it is for an actor to be conscious of his or her image, and especially of the camera. Can you talk about that?

SP: Well, if you say that the object here is to free that part of you which creates behavior—your unconscious—you're really courting disaster if you try to watch yourself when you act. It's a strong temptation, and it's an absolute impossibility. We know, from psychoanalysis, that emotion is a product of the unconscious, and we know it works best when it's left alone. As a matter of fact, psychoanalysis is based on the theory that if you make what's unconscious conscious, it tends to go away. Well, emotion works exactly like that. You have this sort of dangerous situation where you're trying consciously to trigger emotion, which you know works best from your unconscious. So what do you do about that? Well, that's what technique is. Technique really gives you a series of things to focus on; the doing of something, which requires concentration in itself, and the part of doing it that generates emotion. But if you start to say, "Ooh, I'm feeling something now," or if you start to watch what you're doing, it will dry up. That's really what I mean by being conscious of your image.

It's the opposite of what we were talking about with Pacino. Pacino's smart enough to know that he has nothing to offer by trying to outsmart the truth of what he is or who he is. He knows that the richest thing he has is his own unconscious. And so what he does is set up a series of tasks for himself which enable him to immerse himself sufficiently in the situation and to concentrate sufficiently on the other person with whom he has a specific relationship. So that unconscious engine which produces behavior gets turned on and freed.

The other actor, the less talented actor, has tried to decide what it is he or she is going to do, and then tries to do that from the outside in. What you get, depending upon how clever they are, are more or less intelligent choices executed without real spontaneity or real emotion, and often it's oddly unmoving. You watch something happening, and it doesn't affect you, you're not transported by it. You can admire the intelligence; you can admire the choice.

Again, we have two parts to this equation. One is, in simplest form, the ability to live truthfully in imaginary circumstances, that is, just to create realistic, truthful behavior. The other part is "how?", the choice of a "way" of doing it. That's when you say, "My God. Did you see that moment where he suddenly laughed when he found out this tragic thing was happening?" You're taken by the choice, not just because it seems inappropriate, but because it seems, strangely, more true than a more obvious choice. Those kinds of choices are very hard to make, intellectually. Directorially, you're always playing with those kinds of choices, and you're hoping you can lead an actor to them. Sometimes you make a very bizarre choice at a given moment, and you're really hoping that you can explain it in a way that makes emotional sense to the actor. This happens most often in extreme emotional scenes or in love scenes. Those get very personal; the choices are very personal. I'm not talking about sex, necessarily, but just love scenes: the moment of falling in love, the moment of finding out that someone's in love with you. So you stay very preoccupied with them.

CZ: Are there people who work best when you give them "result" pieces of direction?

SP: There are some people who do. It's not supposed to be true, but some of the best people I've worked with, in the interest of speed, have said, "Give me a line reading." It's quite common. That really has to do with security. If the scene requires rage, you're capable of doing it, if a scene requires tears, you're capable of doing it. Sometimes, the actor will just say, "Well, just say it for me." So you just say it—and they say, "Oh, OK, I can do that," and they do it. [On the other hand,] actors do not want to feel that the director sat the night before in front of a mirror, and acted out all the parts, and then came in and tried to get them to do it. That's a real no-no. A good director really does want an actor to feel that they're bringing a real interpretation.

But this waltz goes on, always, and it's like a love affair when it works well, and it's like a war when it doesn't. Because there's no getting around the fact that your job as a director is to get exactly what you want, without necessarily making waves. You're trying to lead and suggest, rather than impose. It can't be perceived as imposing. But usually, you've spent a year working on the script, preparing. You've got specific ideas of what you want. And then you just have to be open enough to know that you can make a lot of mistakes, that the actor can come and teach you things, too. The actor can come at this with a whole new point of view that's wonderful.

This dance that happens, between the actor and the director, is a very delicate thing. I think it's why people tend to work together on many films over and over, like Scorsese and De Niro. There's a trust there, so both of them do great work with each other. You don't waste time proving that you're trustable. That can be very difficult. There's a real looking-over period that goes on. When you have your first meetings with an actor or an actress, you can feel this. Many times, the better the actor or actress, the more there's this tentativeness. They're sort of hanging on everything you say, and wondering, "What kind of a guy is this? Is he going to leave room for me in this, or is he one of those control freaks? Is this guy going to tell me he understands my part better than I do? Am I going to be able to talk to him? Is he going to listen to me? Can we try things, is there a compromise possible? Do we see the same movie?" All of that does go on.

CZ: Jane Fonda in *They Shoot Horses* worked on her part with an acting coach, Jeff Corey. How do you feel about that, since you're so involved with the actors?

SP: If the final result is that it's helping me, I feel fine about it. If I felt what they were doing was 180 degrees off where I thought the part was, then I would have to say, "Hey, look, this isn't going to work because we're going to pull you apart. You're going to be in the middle of a tug of war." I believe that Jessica Lange—I don't know whether she did it on *Tootsie* [1982] or not—but I know that she worked a lot with Sandra Seacat. It was fine with me, because it was good, and whatever Jane was doing was fine with me. Jeff Corey's a very good acting teacher. I never ran into anybody that I thought was listening to somebody where it wasn't helping. If I really thought that was true, I would stop it, or I would stop it if I could, as much as I could.

CZ: In a lot of your films the audience doesn't know very much about the characters; there's not a lot of exposition. Do you encourage actors to do backstories or biographies of their characters?

SP: We talk about it a lot. I spend a lot of time with the writers talking about backstories, because a lot of times that illuminates problems that we're struggling with in the present. I do talk with the actors about it. I think it's a help to understand what the life of a character is without this story. Suppose what was happening in the script didn't happen? Would that character be able to live in a world that had people in it? Who would they be? What would the character be doing, what would they wear, what would they want, what would they spend their days doing, who would their friends be? It's very helpful in that sense. There is a tendency, quite often, to feel that the world begins and ends between the pages of the script. And that the reason the character is in the script is to have this crisis in their life that is in the script. I don't think you can work as fully, or as well, when you're seeing it that way.

CZ: We agreed to talk about your work with actors in a particular scene; I've chosen something from *Havana* [1990]. Lena Olin learns that her husband [Raul Julia] has not been murdered, as she believed. Her lover, Robert Redford, tells her the news; she slaps him. There are so many conflicting things going on, so many unsaid things, and so many moments where there's nothing said. I think it's a really great scene.

SP: I do too. They play it beautifully. It's very hard to talk about this, because not everything gets communicated by words in directing. This scene was shot the very last day of a long, long shooting schedule. In some kind of strange way, everything contributed to it. The picture was over, people were tired, people's nerves were frayed.

There were technical problems with the scene, because there's a fight, and if an actor's worried about getting hurt, that has to be worked out. That's a question of choreography.

For that scene, the hardest part is that you can't shoot it through because of the fight. You have to break it each time at the fight, then you have to pick it up from the fight on. Then, there is a question of how many times you can do each shot. You have to be very clear what the key angles are in the shot, and don't make them do it over and over and over. So, the emotion doesn't happen in the long master two shot, because there Lena's worried about the slap. She's trying to get into position, she hears the first line, "He's alive." But the camera's not on her face, and I don't want her to act her response out then, I want to wait until the camera's on her. Now, when the camera's on her, we can isolate that moment. It's a whole different technique than a stage play, because we're working on the scene in pieces.

Robert Redford and Lena Olin in *Havana* (1990), directed by Sydney Pollack. Copyright © by Universal City Studios, Inc. Courtesy of MCA Publishing Rights, a division of MCA Inc. Museum of Modern Art Film Stills Archive.

Then, there's this terrible challenge: What you do when you find out a truth like this? You're in love with somebody else, and [this] somebody says, "Your husband's alive." Of course you're shocked, but are you upset? He is your husband, you did love him, you do love him. You think he's dead. It's the only reason she's with this guy [Redford]. It was a very tough moment for [Lena] to get, to be that full, that quickly. The first couple of times we did it, it wasn't happening. When it started to happen at first, there was too much pain, in the sense of disappointment. Then we talked about what, in a lesser actress, would be impossible to do, and that is, to combine all of those things. Yes, it's a disappointment, but it's also an elation, and then finally, it is terrific anger at [Redford] for making her go through this, for feeling all of these things. That's a very hard emotional arc to follow. "My husband that I love is alive, and yet I'm not free to be exuberant about it. The greatest news I could have gotten 24 hours ago is now deeply painful, but it's great news." You can't explain that to an actress. It won't make a performance, because it's intellectual. Then it has to lead to the slap. So the only thing I could say was, "Put the words back into his mouth with your hands. Stop what he's saying," because that's something to do. "There's something bad here, you've got something on your mind, I don't want to hear it, I don't want to hear it." That's what she's acting, never mind what the text is. If you give her something like that, then she can embrace it.

You try to stage the scene comfortably so that she knows she won't have to repeat it too often. She knows that's a tough moment to reach, and she's not going to have to do it ten times, she's just going to have to do it once. We only got it once. There was only one take and one angle. And for a long time, we were worried about the focus on the shot, because we were very tight, with a long lens, and she's moving back and forth. I knew that was it, and she knew that was it, when we did it. Now, if she went off and rehearsed for 5 weeks, she could do it for you 20 times, but not like this. It was too hard, it had too many elements in it. She got the pain, or she got the elation, or she got the shock, in various other takes, but she never got all of them together, in this odd way that she got it in this take.

CZ: There's also a very heightened use of language in this scene. Was that difficult to deal with?

SP: [Lena] had a difficult time with one line. I sometimes do that, I like to push a little bit hard with the language: "For a moment, for one moment, I was lost. In a sweet place, but lost." If you read that, that's not how people talk. It's very stylized; this is not normal conversation.

CZ: It's very poetic.

SP: Hard to do. [Lena's] very deceptive, because you think she speaks totally fluent English, and she doesn't. She didn't quite understand the context of "in a sweet place" and "lost"; is lost good or bad? Of course it's all of those things. "I was lost" is full of an ache to be lost again, but the knowledge that it was wrong. This is one of those difficult scenes because it's full of opposites, two things pulling in opposite directions. The text says, "For a moment, for one moment, I was lost. In a sweet place, but lost." You're in mourning, in a sense, for being lost, but you know it's better not to be lost. This is not easy stuff to act.

With Redford, this is the seventh film I've done with him; we really don't have to say a whole hell of a lot to each other. Most of it is shorthand. He knows that in these kinds of scenes, whether it's *The Way We Were* or *Havana,* what I'm always pushing for is his vulnerability. The thing I want the most is for him to allow that to happen. I think it's fair to say that he's comfortable with me after this length of time and that there is a kind of trust. So he will, sometimes, let himself work in a little more vulnerable way. There's one particular cut back to him in this scene, when she's in the middle of that speech, when he's in pain and turns his head away, that I love. But I don't have to tell him to do that.

A lot of this work was, I would say honestly, creating an atmosphere where the actors are comfortable, and feel free to do what they both know is required, with a minimal amount of discussion.

CZ: The editing's great.

SP: Yeah, the rhythms are nice. I see now, it's almost on the verge of being too long. I was thinking as I was watching it, it's too bad . . .

CZ: The very end of it . . .

SP: Yeah, some of those pauses could have been tightened a little bit. But I don't know. I have to see the whole picture now. I'm just seeing this scene out of context, and it's hard to judge. But, it held for me, as I watched it.

CZ: What about the idea of chemistry? That was something that was criticized about *Havana,* that Lena Olin and Robert Redford didn't have any chemistry together. How do you feel about that?

SP: I guess what that means—if that's true—is that I'm not a good judge of chemistry, because I don't know what it is. I think I know what they mean. They mean that either we have suspense about whether these 2 people are going to be together, or we don't care whether these 2 people are going to be together. Something like that. I don't know what chemistry is, exactly. I don't know how to define it, other than that. If somebody said, "How's the chemistry between Bob and Barbra?" in *The Way We Were,* I would have said, "I don't know how the chemistry is, but they're both terrific in the movie." I would have said the same thing in *Havana.* So, on that basis, I'm probably not a good judge.

I had Redford cast first [in *Havana*], and I was looking for a woman. There were certain circumstances that she had to fit within. She had to be of a certain age, she had to be able in some ways to intimidate him, to make him feel that his life was less valuable than hers. You start to drop people pretty quickly from that point of view; it's not an evaluation of whether they're good or not, it's simply trying to imagine Redford sitting across from them, being intimidated. I hadn't seen *Enemies (A Love Story)* [1989], I had only seen *The Unbearable Lightness of Being* [1988]—and I found Lena Olin very exciting, very interesting, and brand new. You don't find exciting new people that often. So, I went to Stockholm and met her. Now again, I don't know how you judge chemistry; I just sat across the table from her and had dinner with her, and I thought she was not only attractive, but original, not like anybody else. There was something slightly withdrawn, very private, about her, and I thought, "Yeah, I'd like to see her with Bob, I'd like to see what that's like."

Now, if people say there's no chemistry—it's not something that you can argue about. I made an educated guess, knowing that I, personally, would like to see them together. You really don't have anybody to go to except yourself in these things. Sometimes you're right and sometimes you're wrong. I've been right often enough to survive, and wrong often enough to know you're never always right. I would have thought that you would be very interested in the 2 of them.

On the other hand, I thought that you could be bored silly with *Out of Africa.* I liked it personally, but if I'd had to make a bet as to whether or not it was going to be a successful film, and my children's lives depended on my bet, I certainly would have bet that it wasn't going to be. It was 3 hours long, it was talky, there were no action scenes in it, it was not about young people. This was at a time, in 1985, when all the young people's movies were such big successes. I don't know how to make these predictions. So the only alternative is, you end up doing stories that you find interesting, and you're wrong a lot of the time. I was wrong with *Havana,* as I was with *Deerfield,* as I was with *The Yakuza.* But that doesn't mean that I don't like the films! When I say "wrong," I mean wrong in terms of doing something that the public wants to see. I like *Havana* very, very much. And I like *Deerfield* very much. I see some things I might do differently, now, perhaps, in *Deerfield.* Maybe with enough time I'll see some things in *Havana,* too. But I'd make them all again. If a script for any one of the three came in now, I'm sure the thing that made me respond to them the first time would make me respond again. I don't know what chemistry is. I suppose chemistry came from the oppositeness of Redford and Streisand in *The Way We Were.* I've never had anybody talk about chemistry, except in the case of *Havana.* Or they talked about chemistry in a positive way, in *The Way We Were.* I figure I'm lucky if they talk about it well, but I don't have any idea how to fix it or solve it.

An Interview
with
Henry Jaglom

Orson Welles and Henry Jaglom in *Someone to Love* (1987), directed by Henry Jaglom. Courtesy of Mr. Jaglom.

"A lot of people who both love and hate my movies say the same thing: They feel it's almost too intimate, they feel like they're almost embarrassed, like they're eavesdropping on some kind of intense private reality. Some people like that, and some feel very discomfited by it." Henry Jaglom offers an accurate description of his films and the reactions they provoke; few viewers respond with indifference. His films portray a world of unabashed self-engagement, often dealing with incidents and issues—as well as lovers, friends, wives, ex-wives, and relatives—from Jaglom's own life. His films present talk as the principal activity of society; talk that is centered on relationships and feelings. The one theme that dominates Jaglom's universe is—in one form or another—the quest for love; one witnesses the continual formation, dissolution, and dissection of friendships, affairs, and marriages. The conversations in Jaglom's films bear a strong resemblance to classical psychoanalysis, the working out of neurotic patterns through talk. But as Jaglom says, "My job is to bring everybody out of the closet, to make everybody tell the truth . . . I think only that will make you feel sane and survive the complexity of the journey we're on." It is this sense of exposure, both dangerous and salutary, that is vital to Jaglom's films. Acting *is* like therapy, since the examination and purging of emotion has always been one of the critical impulses guiding the desire to act.

Although people are the central focus in Jaglom's films, those who populate his films are not the faces of Hollywood glamour and perfection.

241

The use of non-actors or lesser-known performers provides Jaglom's work with an idiosyncratic and uncommon texture. Whether one finds this quality endearing or irritating, one has to admire Jaglom's stubborn determination in presenting his singular vision on film.

Jaglom is the quintessential personal, independent filmmaker. He directs, writes, produces, and frequently acts in his own films, steadily generating his work in spite of commercial or critical opinion. Born in 1941 in London, England, and raised in New York, Jaglom was trained at The Actors Studio. Once he emigrated to the West Coast, Jaglom became part of a hip enclave of Hollywood outsiders whose numbers included Bob Rafelson, Dennis Hopper, and Jack Nicholson; Jaglom worked as an editorial consultant on their famous collaboration, *Easy Rider* (1969). He directed his first feature in 1971—*A Safe Place,* starring Nicholson and Tuesday Weld. His next film was *Tracks* (1976), with Dennis Hopper, one of the first films to deal with returning Vietnam vets. He followed this with *Sitting Ducks* (1980, starring his brother, Michael Emil), *Can She Bake a Cherry Pie?* (1983), *Always (But Not Forever)* (1985), *Someone To Love* (1987, with his friend, Orson Welles, in his last screen appearance), *New Year's Day* (1989), *Eating* (1990), and *Venice/Venice* (1992). Jaglom's oeuvre has been more highly regarded in Europe than in his own country, with frequent invitations to participate in such leading festivals as Cannes, Deauville, and Venice. Jaglom became a father for the first time in 1991, most certainly the inspiration for his 1994 film, *Babyfever,* with his second wife, Victoria Foyt, as the leading actor.

I spoke with Henry Jaglom in January 1992, at his production house—Rainbow Pictures—on Sunset Boulevard.

CZ: You started out as an actor and still act in your own films. What do you think made you become an actor? Why do actors become actors? Do you think anybody can be an actor?

HJ: No, anybody cannot be an actor. Anybody can have one great moment on film, because the aliveness of every being is interesting. If you can trick somebody into revealing that aliveness, it can be worthy of a moment in a film. However, if that's all they can do—they're not interesting, they can't apply it to other parts—they can't be actors. It's an incredibly special, demanding, unbelievably complex and painful profession.

Why I became an actor was a deep combination of an exterior and interior need. The exterior need was for attention, to be the center of other people's focus. It was a way of saying, "Look at me, focus on me." A need for all that love and attention you don't feel you're getting sufficiently, for complex reasons, in your life. That was the negative reason, the feeling of not having certain things. I think that's the first step for many actors.

It seems to be almost inevitable that the person who feels most out of place in school, the person who's a stranger in his or her class or family, who doesn't feel that they fit in in some sense, starts developing an active fantasy life, and one of the things that you do with an active fantasy life is you invent characters, and that starts preparing you for being an actor. The emotional need—to get attention, to be liked, to not be the weird person that you are socially—puts you into a position where you decide one day, "That's what I am; I'm an actor."

The positive thing is what comes next, which is that you learn to use yourself creatively as your own instrument. Actors thrive not on the simple exhibitionism of being an actor, but on the skill and the art of transforming themselves into various things; it is the ultimate creative work. There is nothing more creative than not having anything between you and your creativity. A musician has his or her instrument, a painter has the canvas and the paint; as an actor, you just have your self. But it starts, I think, for most people, out of deep psychological complexity, need, insecurity, and a desire for an untold amount of attention.

CZ: When did you first become interested in performing?

HJ: I was about 10 years old in summer camp: I played a cuckoo clock—my first part on stage—in a play called *Watch on the Rhyme*. And they wrote in the camp newspaper, "Best cast of the show was Henry Jaglom, who did an excellent job as the cuckoo clock." I thought that meant I was the best one in the show. It didn't mean that, the guy who wrote it was being very sarcastic—best cast meant I was really cuckoo— but I didn't know that at 10. All I knew was I got a lot of attention, I was onstage, they were laughing at me, and I liked that. So I started falling off chairs in school to get attention, and I got laughs. And the bigger the chair, and the harder the fall, the bigger the laugh. I'd dribble on a basketball court, and all my insecurity about whether I was going to be able to make the shot—I couldn't do sports like I was supposed to anyway—would be sublimated into running smack into the wall, purposely, because I knew that then I would get a laugh. Instead of failing at being good at basketball, I succeeded at getting attention and laughter; that is addicting. And that's I think what acting comes from, the addiction of turning people on, of getting them to focus on you, of changing their focus. Instead of ridiculing you, you control them laughing at you. It's taking control over the forces all around you that are scaring you as a child. Acting, I think, is that, and it's always such a wonderfully ironic payoff, that all the kids who felt the biggest misfits in life, the most alienated, isolated, and awkward, are later the ones who all the rest of these so-called "normal" people end up paying money to see. I find the history of my friends who are actors is varied, but for 99 percent of them, it's this I'm-going-to-prove-something-to-these-people feeling.

CZ: What about actors who become directors? Do you find there is a difference between directors and actor/directors?

HJ: It's a third kind of species. Falling off chairs leads you to become eventually Jerry Lewis if you don't watch out. You grow up and you want to get the pie in your face, anything to get the laugh you need so much. Then you say, "Well, wait a minute, I really don't want to have these pies hitting me in the face. I want to sophisticate the process so that I'm making the laughs happen." Then you go beyond the laughs—"I'm making the emotion happen"—by determining what they see on screen, not just by being the butt of it. That's the first step away from acting toward directing, which happened to me in college. I always thought I was an actor, all my childhood, until somebody said, "Do you want to direct this?" And then I saw, "My God, I can do both!" It's a great role for an actor, playing the part of a director. Those of us who started as actors never completely believe ourselves as directors; we're always acting the role of director. Actor/directors frequently feel that nobody will protect them except themselves. I feel too vulnerable as an actor. If I want to be real, and open, and exposed, and I do it with somebody else and they misuse it . . . it's like a bad interview, it makes you seem like somebody other than who you are. Most directors from other disciplines don't like actors very much; there's a big war on, usually, between them. Most directors think they're better than actors.

CZ: Was there a critical experience in your life as an actor that made you want to become a director?

HJ: I wanted the role in *The Graduate* [1967] that Dusty Hoffman got; I wanted it desperately. I gave the best reading of my life, I was excited; everybody liked it, the director, the author, the producer. I'd been guest-starring in dumb TV shows, "Gidget," "The Flying Nun," and finally, this was it! I went home—I still remember to this day—and when the phone rang, I got the news that Dustin Hoffman got the part. I can remember the feeling of powerlessness in that phone call. And I thought, "I can't do this, I cannot be out of control like this for the rest of my life. I can't be desperately wanting something that I can't make happen, and I'm not going to act again until I'm in a position to put myself in the parts that I want." That's when I became a director. It's people who need more than just to expose themselves, who need control, who need power, who need to be able to reshape the universe, to reinvent it constantly.

CZ: So you believe actors are essentially powerless in film?

HJ: It's a director's field, because the director makes the movies. So these poor actors are in my hands. I rewrite what they do, I can make them look wonderful or terrible; I mean, it's a terrible power you have. I love it, I think it's a wonderful power, because my goal is to make everybody look as good as possible. But it's a terrible, terrible life, being an actor. An actor has no control over his own destiny, really, except for the very few who become such big stars that they can start producing their own work.

CZ: Can you talk about The Actors Studio?

HJ: The Actors Studio was the greatest single experience in my creative life, and everything that's happened to me since then, and the way I work, I owe entirely to Lee Strasberg and The Actors Studio. [Strasberg] made me aware that acting was not something separate from myself. I came into it, as many actors do, just wanting to be famous, wanting to be a big star, wanting to get a lot of attention. I was a teenager who felt that I needed more than I was getting in life. I had a lot of battles with him, and I was thrown out of class a couple of times, and once he barred me for many months because I was trying to prove to him that I knew something better than he did. I faked an emotion, and then when he congratulated me on my work, I said, "You see? That was fake and you didn't even know about it, you couldn't tell." He got furious and threw me out. But I learned finally, from him—after a lot of stubborn resistance—that what was really important had nothing to do with my ego and my need for attention, but had to do with the process, the work, the art.

The best story he ever told us, the image he gave us, was about Gauguin painting these paintings in the South Seas. After he finished them, he dropped them on the ground, and if somebody found them, fine, they existed, and if they didn't, fine. For him, the work was what was important, not having the painting as an artifact of that work to be appreciated and applauded. That was such an alien concept to kids who were trying just to get famous and successful that it really made you start examining your interior, about what was important in life. You made the transition if you paid attention to Strasberg, if you really let him take you on the journey that The Studio has been about, and the Method is about, from thinking of acting as something outside of yourself, to understanding its deep relevance to every part of your being. It makes you a much more open and full human being.

I was lying before that, lying all the time. I couldn't cry in front of other people because I didn't think you were supposed to. So as an actor, I would fake crying. I remember the time in class when, for the first time— as [Strasberg] was working on the muscles in my back and I was doing the song exercise—I started really crying in front of an audience. It's an incredibly important life experience; it transcends acting. It teaches you how to be an integrated person emotionally and how not to lie. Finally, acting is about not lying. Everybody, at the first stage of acting, thinks it's about being so good at lying that you make it entertaining, and attractive, and fascinating, and fool everybody. But real acting is about not lying. Real acting is about learning how to express emotions from deep within yourself, having a well of openness inside of you that can allow all kinds of experience and feelings to enter, and then you can give them back through a character. And the richer you are as an actor, the more colors you have on your palette, the more areas you can touch to exhibit the infinite complexity of human behavior, which is what acting at its best reveals.

There are only two kinds of acting, really, and they are bad acting and good acting. Good acting is telling the truth; there is no such thing as faking good acting. There are some great theatrical performances that are external and fake, but even as they come from an external place they start touching a reality. An Olivier—who approached acting completely from the outside—would have told you that even though he started from the outside, by the time he was doing it, he was so connected to what he was doing because it started tapping into him, that, without realizing it, he automatically could reveal all kinds of emotional stuff that as a person he could never reveal. Our way of working—The Studio way of working, the Stanislavsky-based way of working, what I do on my films—has to do with starting from the inside, getting to know that inside well, and being conscious of it. If you can find it by putting on a certain kind of hat, and that hat creates an emotion, and you don't know why, but every time you put on that hat you will express that emotion, and you can get that freedom from that hat, OK. The trouble with that is you can't rely on it, it's not dependable. It's good enough for a movie, because you put on the hat just for the scene, and it makes you cry. All people have these emotional triggers that are stimulated by sensory things, but they don't know how to tap into them. If you want to be an actor and you want to be able to really be in control of your instrument, you have to learn how to tap into yourself. That's all. Somebody like an Olivier does it by the exterior, and he has the gift that allows that. Very few people have that; most people have to go the other way around.

CZ: Do you ever do sense memory with the actors in your films?

HJ: Oh, constantly. They don't know they're doing it, but I do it constantly. See, I like to cast people I know very well, because the more deeply I know them emotionally, the more I know what areas of them to trigger. You put a certain kind of music on, you have them apply a certain kind of perfume, you have all kinds of sensory things. For instance, I always try to have my actors name their characters. Mostly women use their mother's names, the first time they do a movie with me. Automatically, if their mother's name was Marie, and somebody addresses them as Marie, it adds another dimension of emotion, because of all that charge that we bring to a relationship with our parents. I constantly am trying to find ways of stimulating and setting up actors to help them open up areas of themselves that they don't even know about. But the better the actor, the more they've trained, the better they understand this work, the more they've spent their life getting ready for it. That means not interfering on camera or on stage between yourself and what you're doing.

Relaxation is the most important thing to know how to do, because if you're tense, you can't act. The emotions can't come up, they get stopped at the neck, or the chest or the belly. Most people live with tension all the time. An actor has to find ways to break down the tension to get through it. And I as a director have to find ways—if the actor has that tension—to circumvent it, or attack it head on, if the person can take it. The more conscious they are as actors—the longer and harder they've studied, the better actors they are — the more I can let them in on the process. That's exciting for me. And still, they surprise themselves, like everybody, and they surprise me constantly. It's a fascinating business.

CZ: What is the difference, in your mind, between acting for the theater and acting for film?

HJ: In theater you have to be able to call up various expressions of feeling in a very precise and technical way. No matter how emotionally true your work is, there's a technical responsibility: Every night of a play, 45 minutes into the second act, you have to cry. So you have to find something which can trigger that emotion so that you can really cry, rather than indicating or faking crying. That's technical, and that's what a lot of the training was about, having availability to your emotions, so that they can fuse with the character's emotions, and you can, for instance, cry when required. In film, you only have to do it once. That's the enormous difference between acting in film and acting in theater. The similarity is the required honesty and truthfulness, the moment.

But the way to achieve it, I feel, is completely different. There are things you can do in film that are absolutely ridiculous and useless if you try to apply it to the stage, because all I have to do in a film is get that one moment. They don't have to know how to do it again, which is why I use a lot of non-actors, who do some of the best acting in my movies. They don't have to know how they achieved it; in the theater, they must know how.

CZ: How do you get them to do that one moment?

HJ: As a starting-off point you try, as much as possible, to cast actors who are in touch with who they are, who don't have imposed ideas of what they're supposed to do as "acting." You have to tap their emotions, you have to know what buttons to push to create certain kinds of emotions. In film, the art of acting has much more to do with giving yourself permission to have the immediacy and the spontaneity to allow yourself to be as empty a vessel as possible, so you can fill up. You still need the same inner thing that you need in theater, but then what you need is on-screen immediacy. So my job with the actors is to create circumstances where they are as full emotionally as possible. To put them in situations with each other that tap most effectively into what I need from the part. So much about film is surprise. It has to look like it's happening the first time. You have to be completely immediate, so a lot of what I do involves tricking actors. I try to keep them really full emotionally, and then throw them off, literally, so that they're not thinking about anything, so that they're not getting what they expect from the other actor, so that they're not prepared with too much. But they must be emotionally prepared, which is what Strasberg and Stanislavsky and The Studio were about. Then you've got people who are ready to be available for whatever happens emotionally to them. So if somebody else suddenly surprises them, they are there, in present time, being surprised. They are not indicating surprise or suggesting surprise in any way. That's why I don't give them scripts, for instance. It's a very different way of working than traditional Hollywood moviemaking, so it only applies to my way of working.

CZ: How much of what you have on film is written beforehand?

HJ: I have no way of telling you. Sometimes nothing, sometimes everything, sometimes 10, 20 percent, it depends. Every scene is different. I sometimes write scenes, and then I tell the actors to continue in their own words, from their own memory, from their own lives. And frequently, when I go to my cutting room, what's realer, and more fresh, and more exciting, has to do with not what I've written, but what they've come up with.

Theater and every other form of writing—plays or books or poems— exist by themselves as words, and then can be interpreted. Film doesn't exist until it's up there. The screenplay is only a guide. A film is about a look, a feeling, the way 2 people emotionally connect with one another, the response to a piece of music, a smile, a tear, and I can't know what those are until I *get* them. I don't want to know, because then I'm trying to squeeze people into the narrow confines of prewritten parts. What I try to do is extract *out* of them their emotional life, to reach into them and find areas in themselves that are exciting and new. So I have somebody completely shock somebody else, do something totally surprising and unexpected. And within the confines of the character and the scene, they have to create spontaneously what serves the character. So you need very gifted actors, *or* completely non-actors. Anything in between is very dangerous for this kind of work.

CZ: What's the biggest difference between working with somebody who's been acting for years and somebody who's never acted?

HJ: It's a totally different thing. An actor knows the language, and you can work with them to collaborate, to create something. A non-actor you have to trick. I trick them into not being self-conscious, into trying to be as available and natural and spontaneous as they are in life. People are very interesting in life, but they start censoring it when they're in front of a camera, when there are lights, makeup, a script, when there are specific things they must say or accomplish. So I try to take away all of those things that inhibit their acting.

But it's much more exciting to work with a well-trained actor because you can say to them, "Look, this is what we're trying to do now," and they come up with, out of their experience, ways of attacking things that I never could dream of. Which is why actors are more exciting to me than anything I could write for them. Because to me, an actor is not just a face, or a voice, or a body; he or she is a mind, a history, a language all its own, a series of incidents and memories and emotions and feelings that I can't possibly know. If I can find a way to tap into that richness and apply all of that to my character, I've got a much fuller character than if I say to them, "No no, you didn't say 'I want to go to the park,' " if I try to force them to stick to specific words, or narrow ideas. When actors are really not prepared for the moment, but they've actually been prepared by their years of training to allow that moment to fully happen, those are the most exciting film moments.

CZ: You spend a lot of time editing your films. Would you say that process is crucial to this moment-by-moment concept?

HJ: It's about moments in film; it's not about continuity, because I create the continuity of the acting in my editing room. I change it. If I get this moment perfect, I don't care how bad they are at getting *to* this moment, because I just cut from this moment to this moment, to somebody else who is looking at them, for instance, and eliminate all the false stuff in between.

CZ: Do you ever come into conflict with actors over the way you work?

HJ: Actors sometimes get mad during the process, or upset, because sometimes I have to really get things emotionally into an intense and scary place to get what I want. I am a bit relentless. There are some people who you can get there by breaking down certain areas of them, and making them cry, and feeling a great deal. Other people, if you do that, will be completely useless, you really have to make them feel wonderful, and be supportive. In *Eating* [1990], we were all sitting around, the 38 women and myself, and I said: "Look, we're going to now play a game, which is, I'm going to try to get everything I can out of you, and you're going to be angry, scared, and furious with me, but understand that I'm doing it with your permission. Now, anybody who doesn't want me to do that, tell me now." That's the exciting thing about film acting; you can go as deep as you and the actor are willing.

For me, the job is to get that person on screen as fully as possible. Jack Nicholson says he is more Jack Nicholson in *A Safe Place* [1971], which is my first film, than he has ever been onscreen. Dennis Hopper, clearly, is more Dennis Hopper in *Tracks* [1976] than he has ever been. Karen Black in *Can She Bake a Cherry Pie?* [1983], Orson Welles in *Someone to Love* [1987]—these people have been making movies all their lives. But in these movies, I give them a freedom which actors love having, to contribute, totally, their own beingness to the interpretation of the part. I'm much more interested in them than in the part. The reason, for me, that I cast them, is to be able to be free to find out what they are.

CZ: Can you give me an example of a film where you used someone's personal experience?

HJ: In *Tracks* it was Dennis' anger, not mine. I wrote him a great, long, final 3-page speech about Vietnam and the war; it was brilliant, articulate. He tore it up. He was so angry with me at that moment, because it was the last scene, and the movie would be over. And as he says, directors don't need actors any more when it's finished. And instead of my speech, he went into this extraordinarily moving, furious, inarticulate, "I love because I hate, because I love, you motherfucker, you motherfucker . . ." I wasn't going to write "You motherfucker, you motherfucker." Who thinks to write that? He was right, I was wrong. That sergeant, at that moment, wouldn't be making an articulate speech. That's why I'm glad I cast Dennis, because he knew that at that moment the anger would be overwhelming, because his anger was overwhelming, and he was able to fuse his anger with the anger of the character and turn it into an inarticulate rage. It is much better than an articulate description of anger, which is what I had done in my limitation as a writer.

So actors show me the way, always. My job, then, is to look clearly, in my editing room, for months, and frequently years afterwards, at what

Dennis Hopper and Taryn Power in *Tracks* (1976). Courtesy of Mr. Jaglom.

they've done. Try to find the best moments, the highest truth that they've given me, to make it cut together to further my story, and make sure not to miss it. Frequently it throws my whole script out the window, because what they've given me is so much more interesting.

CZ: Do you ever have to go back and reshoot?

HJ: Oh, I always go back and reshoot now, which is very exciting. This way of working allows you to do it like a painting: You're sketching, and then you've got the whole rough assemblage, and you think, "I need . . ." In *New Year's Day* [1989], I didn't know what the ending was. I shot the whole movie, and a year later I went back and shot the end. All the bathroom scenes in *Eating* were shot 8 months after I had made the rest of the movie. Something was missing, which was the kind of private anger that can take place in a closed bathroom as opposed to in an open party. The actors lead me to it; I can see in the performances that they're building to some explosion, and if this explosion doesn't happen in the original shoots, I've got to go back and give them the chance to release it.

CZ: It sounds very much like you're talking about filmmaking as therapy.

HJ: A lot of people who both love and hate my movies say the same thing: They feel it's almost too intimate, they feel like they're almost embarrassed, like they're eavesdropping on some kind of intense private reality. Some people like that, and some feel very discomfited by it. I was an actor at first, I am an actor to begin with, my films are actor's films. So for me, they're all driven by actors, and their performances. And revealing as much about your internal self on screen as you possibly can is the goal for me of my movies.

We're always dealing with real emotions. My job in films is to try to make people feel less alone—audiences, myself, the actors—to make us all feel less isolated, less crazy, less like we're the only ones going through whatever the issue of the film is. I've gotten thousands of letters from people who tell me that sitting alone in the dark, watching my films, they feel less crazy. People tend to stay in emotional closets. So my job is to bring everybody out of the closet, to make everybody tell the truth about everything, because I think only that will make you feel sane and survive the complexity of this journey we're all on. So yes, in that sense they're meant to be therapeutic, for us as well as for the audience.

CZ: Are there film performances that represent the height of acting for you?

HJ: Well, for somebody of my age and time, in the late 50s, when I was a teenager, seeing James Dean on screen was mind-boggling. It was just unbelievable, because it was there, it was so immediately and fully there. It was such an incredibly rich kind of behavior that I've never forgotten it. I still can't get over it, and I still can't watch the three Dean movies without getting crazy a little bit. I can't watch *Rebel without a Cause* [1955], or *Giant* [1956], or *East of Eden* [1955] too late at night, it just sets me up. Dean had a power, in terms of truthfulness, that was unbelievable.

And Brando, you can't believe him. I can watch a movie which is basically silly—*Guys and Dolls* [1955]—and I can't stop looking at what

Brando's doing; he does something that owns the screen. I think it has to do tremendously with concentration, and being present within yourself to such an extent that you are the only thing anyone can see.

CZ: What about contemporary actors?

HJ: Among the actors today, Jack Nicholson—he's a friend—I watch Jack, and within 5 minutes, I totally forget it's Jack doing the part. Because he's so incredibly present. I think he and De Niro are the best actors today. I can't believe what De Niro can do. Scorsese is great at getting great performances. He's our Kazan. De Niro's got a scene in *New York, New York* [1977] where he's listening to somebody on the phone, and the camera must be on him for 30 seconds. I make movies, I act, I direct, I know what that means; 30 seconds is an eternity to do nothing on the screen. He sits there listening to a phone in the middle of a nightclub; you don't hear what the other person's saying, you just see his face. He practically does nothing, he's almost not moving. I keep thinking of that moment as some kind of acting epiphany. I recently rented *New York, New York* and looked at it about 25 times, that 30-second scene, just kept going back to it. All he's doing is listening on the phone in a crowded place, but he inhabits that half minute, motionless, with more life . . .

The people that end up really being fascinating to watch are the people who are, for want of a better word, just completely, fully inside every part of themselves, inhabiting every atom of their space. I know that I get moments from actors that are incredible when I look at them on my editing machine. And it's almost invariably when they're not thinking, when they're not talking, often, when they are feeling something, when they are reacting to something, or when they are having something happen to them emotionally, because they're listening, or whatever. It's breathtaking to watch; it's so exciting. And it's constant, which is why going to films is so wonderful. It's never-ending.

An Interview with Bob Rafelson

Bob Rafelson on the set of *Man Trouble* (1992). Courtesy of Mr. Rafelson.

If Bob Rafelson had directed only three films—*Five Easy Pieces* (1970), *The King of Marvin Gardens* (1972), and *The Postman Always Rings Twice* (1981)—he would already have created some of the most emotionally wrenching moments in contemporary American cinema. His films are occupied by restless characters whose lives are lived *in extremis*, trying to eradicate their desperation and emptiness with sex, money, or love. Pain and confusion prevail; there is little redemption, and less hope. People come together in relationships only to be all the more engulfed by loneliness and isolation. Love is a destructive, sometimes lethal, passion. In this bleak landscape, there is a kind of transcendent beauty and power in revelatory moments of painful truth and vulnerability. It is through this deep, moving acknowledgement of human imperfection that Rafelson's films attain a state of grace.

To represent this state of passionate confusion, Rafelson needs actors who have the stature to engender not pity, but the more profound condition of pathos. Jack Nicholson, whom Rafelson has directed on four occasions, personifies modern man in the tragic state—one who is deluded enough to believe he can exert some control over an unreasoning universe. Nicholson's characters in these films clearly belong in the fallen world, where often temptation is not resisted, desire is unfulfilled, and work is unsatisfying. It is a tribute to Nicholson's profound abilities as an actor—and Rafelson's as a director—that he renders his characters' folly poignant rather than piteous.

Rafelson—born in 1933 in New York—shares the peripatetic lifestyle of some of his characters. He attended Dartmouth College, but before and after held jobs as a disc jockey, a rodeo rider and horse breaker, a drummer and bass player in a jazz combo, and a crew member on an ocean liner. Rafelson's first foray into the media was as a program promoter for radio, followed by a stint as a translator for Shochiku Films in Japan. He worked as a reader and story editor for David Susskind's *Play of the Week*, adapting 34 plays for television. Rafelson first came to prominence as the creator/writer/director of the television series *The Monkees* from 1966–68, for which he won an Emmy for Outstanding Comedy Series in 1967. Rafelson both produced and directed his first feature film, a spin-off of his successful TV series, *Head*, in 1968, which he wrote with Jack Nicholson. His next feature was *Five Easy Pieces,* followed by *The King of Marvin Gardens, Stay Hungry* (1976), *The Postman Always Rings Twice, The Black Widow* (1987), *Mountains of the Moon* (1990), and *Man Trouble* (1992). Rafelson also co-produced several landmark American films, *Easy Rider* (1969) and *The Last Picture Show* (1971), with BBS Productions, which he founded with Bert Schneider and Steve Blauner. BBS—an outgrowth of the late 1960s counterculture—also produced Jack Nicholson's first outing as a director in *Drive, He Said,* in 1972. Rafelson co-wrote *Head, Five Easy Pieces, Stay Hungry,* and *Mountains of the Moon.* In 1970 Rafelson won the New York Film Critics Award and Academy Award nominations for Best Director and Best Script for *Five Easy Pieces.*

I spoke with Rafelson in his office at Marmont Productions in Hollywood in June 1992.

CZ: Let's start by talking about casting. I find that even the most minor roles in your films are perfectly cast. I've read that you looked at 170 people for the part of Cora in *The Postman Always Rings Twice* [1981]; that's very unusual. Can you talk about why you place so much emphasis on casting?

BR: Number one, I don't make movies often. And when I'm not making movies, I'm not necessarily going to the theater and seeing lots of upcoming actors. So I'm out of touch. In order to get in touch, I [read] a lot of actors. Number two, I think the casting process is the beginning of the actual making of a movie. You're going to hear the words spoken for the first time, you're going to see a character inhabited. Whether you've written it or worked on the character with a writer, this is the next phase of discovering how foolish you are. The dialogue sounds horrible, or perhaps you've misconstrued the character, and the actor comes in and gives a completely different representation that opens your eyes to another, possibly more interesting, interpretation. In that sense, casting is an incredibly vital experience, and I indulge it on every movie, to the fullest. Even as years have gone by, I've always had a high regard for the casting process and am willing to put out a certain kind of energy to give every actor who gets past the screening process of the casting director an opportunity to see me, to read, to do their best. So it's not uncommon that I will read dozens of people for any given part, on every movie.

CZ: So I gather you've changed your mind about the characters you've written because of an actor's reading of a role?

BR: I've never had a reading for any movie where that didn't take place. That's what I'm hoping for. The task of making a movie, for me, is to discover what it's about—beyond the literary quality, beyond the vision that first inspired me to pick up the project, to conceive it, to write it, to direct it. Therefore, I like to be free to change my mind throughout the making of the movie, from casting, and, most particularly, in the editing. I don't think a script is something written on sacred parchment. I think it is meant to be interpreted, and if actors are really good, you discover not only the truth of the character, but the vagaries of the character. The lack of clarity that you sometimes have on paper mutates into something special and unique and specific.

I don't have very clear and distinct visions of who most people are. I'm constantly surprised by what I learn of people I thought I knew well: "You mean to tell me that guy, after 40 years of marriage, is a homosexual? Who would have thought that? What a mask he kept on all those years. You mean to tell me that this totally amiable person is an embezzler? What prompted that? Was there something in him all the while?" and so on and so forth. The same thing is true for me in work on character; there should be a mystery and a surprise, and an unpredictability. Therefore, after the writing, where you're representing the essence—and the actor is brought in not only to yield an essence, but to yield its contradiction—casting, which is the initial stage of discovery, seems to me to be the single most important aspect of making a movie, and I indulge it.

CZ: The sense of place in your films is extraordinary. How do you work to develop that authenticity for yourself and the cast?

BR: Let me give you an example using that as a prompting, from *Stay Hungry* [1976]. First of all, the way that film was born—I hitchhiked through the South for several months, with no particular idea about making *Stay Hungry*. I felt that I didn't know the South very well, and that I simply wanted to, and that maybe I'd make a movie there sometime. Then the novel came to me, and I agreed to do it. But I required 6 months before I gave a firm answer, during which time I started to inhabit that world and do my own private research. By the time I got around to casting the movie, curiously enough, I knew the counterparts of each and every one of those roles. So that when my cast arrived, they were asked if they would like to meet somebody who in some way overlapped their character. In most cases, the cast responded favorably to that idea. Every member of the cast of *Stay Hungry* lived with somebody that I had already chosen for them and then were completely free, of course, to do their own explorations with anybody else they cared to. There was no obligation. I think that answers your question: I do a certain amount of research on my own, and then I ask the cast to do the same.

CZ: Can you talk about what you do in rehearsal?

BR: I don't do much in rehearsal. It's the second phase of working with the actor; again, you're discovering certain things. I try to keep the actor as flexible as I possibly can for every scene in the movie. I try to shoot all my movies in continuity. With the rehearsal process, my feeling is I would like to see the actor try any number of different ways, and maybe [I] give a slight approval of the direction the character's taking. But not to nail it down.

CZ: I gather that you encourage improvisation.

BR: As much as the actor wants to do it, I am prepared to do that, sure.

CZ: Do you ever find that there's a clash with actors who want to experiment and people who want to nail it down?

BR: Sure. It happens all the time. And there are actors who are just incapable of improvising; Laurence Olivier was one that I admire greatly. I think the essence of this is that I don't believe there is a particular technique for working with actors. I think that each actor is different, a very specific person in and of themselves. I yield as much as I possibly can to trying to understand how they want to work. I don't say, "Well, we're all going to improvise today," or "We're all going to play the scene for laughs today," or do something that's going to throw that actor off their course too much.

Most importantly, I feel you have to have a real understanding of the actor. To a certain degree, I like to share my anxieties and my confidences with the actor. Now, if that's going to shake up somebody, I don't do it. "God, I don't know where the hell we are with this scene, I'm completely lost, I don't know what to do . . ." Some actors feel, "Well, thank God he said that, because I'm sinking, and at least now I know that he's an equal instead of a boss, and we're all going down together." With others, they need to feel that you are the rescue line, and therefore you don't want to admit of your anxieties. So I behave differently—I'm sure I do—with every actor. There is no technique, so to speak.

CZ: How did you work on the scene in *Five Easy Pieces* [1970] where Jack Nicholson is talking to his father? That seems like a particularly difficult scene to do; it's very emotional and very personal.

BR: I turned to Jack and I said, "Jack, if I don't see the desperation of this character, then I'm not interested in making this movie. Then this is just a study of alienation, and I won't be touched by his nomadic emotional life." "What are you saying?" he said to me, "You want me to cry?" I said, "Yeah, that'd be good enough," and he said "No fuckin' way. You know how many directors have asked me to cry before, on screen? It's all a bunch of bullshit." We had written a movie together, we had been friends for a long time; I rather expected this as the answer, I knew it was going to be a long haul. So I cancelled the shoot and kept him up for 40 hours. And he accused me of trading on our personal relationship. I pointed out to him that in times of considerable anxiety and strain we had revealed each other's emotions to one other, in a most maudlin-like fashion. "I'm playing a part now, Curly [Nicholson's nickname for Rafelson], I am not being Jack." "Yes, I know that, but I think it would be interesting if this character showed a quality to a mute father that he shows to nobody else during the course of the film." "Well, I certainly am not gonna do it there." I said, "Well, that's OK by me; here are three other places where we can do it." This went on for 40 straight hours, no sleep.

I asked the crew to disappear, I took the microphone myself, we took the camera out in the middle of the field, I parked the father. Just before we did the scene, Jack said, "Well, if I'm going to do it, I sure can't do it with this dialogue." I said, "Look, I don't care if you read me the phone book. I want the emotion." He said, "Well, here," and he started to write a few lines. He went out there; he was exhausted. I held the microphone, the camera I simply snapped on—it was a fixed shot—and I turned in the opposite direction and said, "Action." I had a set of earphones on, and I heard Jack emoting. There was a long pause, I figured that the scene was over, I turned around, and Jack was palpably moved. To the father I said, "Don't blink. Do nothing. Stay in character." And I said, "OK, let's do it a second time," at which point Jack said, "Are you fuckin' crazy? You didn't even see the first one." So I said, "Well, I'm sure it was good, but just for protection's sake . . ." This time I watched. He did it, and I wasn't very happy with it, but I figured the first one had bagged it. I've never seen the [completed] movie, and I've particularly not seen that scene since I made the film, because it was so difficult. It was an incredibly costly thing for Nicholson. So that's how that one came about.

CZ: Considering his involvement with The Actors Studio—and their emphasis on private moments and intensity—it's interesting that Nicholson didn't want to cry or do a big emotional scene.

BR: I didn't even know he went to The Actors Studio, but that doesn't surprise me. You have to understand, this scene has been talked about a lot as being a breakthrough scene for American actors. It was not normal to do this kind of thing in 1970; the heroes didn't cry, so to speak. At that point, nobody would have done it readily, or somebody would have done it phonily. If Jack was going to do this kind of thing, he feels he's really got to do it.

He doesn't like to fight, which is a secret about Jack Nicholson: He hates to be in physical fight scenes. There was a time when I was making *Postman,* where Jack had to beat up John Ryan. [Jack] bashed him a few times, and then he went off the set. I said, "Where is he?" and nobody could find him. It turned out that he'd gone a considerable way and was feeling very badly. I said, "Why? What's upsetting you?" and he said, "I'm hurting the guy. I know I'm hurting the guy." And I said "Jack, the door is made out of balsa wood, your knee is stopping it." But he had to feel like he was hurting the actor to act the truth of the scene. Truth is painful. I don't give a shit whether you've gone to The Actors Studio all your life, if it's going to be a really truthful moment, it's going to be painful, or it isn't the truth.

CZ: I want to go on to *King of Marvin Gardens* [1972]. It's a "no exit" situation, very intense and claustrophobic. And the relationship between the actors is so complex. What kind of things would you talk to Bruce Dern and Jack Nicholson about?

BR: Bruce Dern had wanted to play the older brother. He had seen *Easy Pieces,* and he and Jack were very friendly, very close, and even competitive. Bruce came into my office—I'll never forget this—and he had a 200-page notebook of questions about [his] character. I think Bruce had studied with Lee Strasberg in New York. In any event, I said, "Put that book away. I wouldn't have any idea how to answer any of these questions." "Why does the character do this, why does the character do that, wouldn't the character do this . . ." I said, "Put it away." He said, "Do you know how many hours and days I've spent studying for the part? And you, this presumed hot, new, sensitive-to-actors director, tell me to put it away?" I said, "Yeah, put the fuckin' thing away, I don't like to answer questions like that, I don't know the answers to questions 'why?' " So he said, "Well, what am I supposed to do?" I said, "Well, there's two things: I'd like you to wear your coat over your shoulders from now on when you come into this office. Never put your arms in the sleeves, and as far as I'm concerned, that's the way you should dress for the rest of this movie. And I want you to know, I don't trust people who point at me when they talk to me." He said, "What do you mean, you don't trust them?" I said "Well, have you noticed that while you were berating me for not responding to your questions, you've been pointing at me, and if I look at any movie you've ever made, you are always pointing at people?" He said, "Yeah . . . so?" I said, "This guy has a rap in the movie where he's always selling us something, his dream, and I want to trust him. And I trust people with open palms." He said, "Yeah, what else, what else, what else?" and I said, "That's it. Bye. See you when we shoot," and that was it.

Now, I was, in a sense, taking away Bruce's safety net. I didn't want him to go through the same process preparing for this role that he had gone through all his life. I wanted him to prepare for it in a completely different way, in a much more confusing way. I wanted him to be able to discover the part and how to play it when he was in a room with the other actors, so that he would be spontaneous and alive to the situation. And that's the way we worked.

CZ: The casting of Nicholson as the repressed younger brother is unusual.

BR: I didn't offer Nicholson the role in the first place. He knew I was writing it with Jake Brackman, and he stole the script from my house. He said, "Why can't I play the older brother?" and I said, "Well, 'cause that'd be too easy for you to do. If anything, I'd like you to play the younger brother. But I don't think that you'd be interested in doing it, because I want a very, very constipated, reticent sense of the personality." "You've got to let me do this," and he did, thank God. I had actually talked to Al Pacino about doing it, before he did *The Godfather* [1972]. But Al, unfortunately for his own career, elected to do *The Godfather* [*laughter*].

CZ: How much formal planning would go into a film like that? Because it's a very beautiful film, with a lot of long-takes. That's a funny tension in all of your work—this spirit of improvisation coupled with compositions, camera movements, costumes, props, that all seems perfectly worked out.

BR: I don't like perfect pictures, and, to me, the imperfections create a sense of awe beyond order, a surprise, a ragged edge. So when you ask me how much do I plan on these things, I plan on everything. But mostly what I plan on is the possibility for accident—in performance, in light, and in location. I have a very definite sense of how I want every scene to be played in the movie, but I'm, if anything, intelligent enough to know how stupid I am.

If you're going to hire the best actors in the world, and you've spent months and months searching for them, their contribution on the set is going to be infinitely more interesting than your preconceived notions. So you'd better be flexible. The notion for me, basically, in directing actors, is to make them feel as if they have been in this room before—this is their room, their arena. They should be comfortable enough with their fellow actors and with me, and with—hopefully—an invisible crew, to fail, to be foolish, to be naked. If I'm lucky, and right, something emerges from that comfortability. And people are constantly trying something foolish from which might emerge one little tiny particle of the truth of the scene. Something I can respond to, something the other actor can respond to, then let's go shooting. And then, after that's done, let's go and really be foolish and shoot another version of the scene.

My dailies are often extremely bewildering to the actor because they don't have any idea how it's possible to be able to play the scene two different ways and still be in the same movie. I believe very strongly in the editing process, and if the actors are with me in the endeavour, they trust that I know what I'm doing in the editing room. I might pull one line from the eighth take of a scene, just one moment, played radically differently from the way it was in the first take. One aspect of it will inflect the original take—by far and away the most superior—with some small, uniquely specific moment that works.

CZ: If you have the perfect take, and the actor says, "No, let me do it again, I can do it better," do you let that happen?

BR: Sometimes. Sometimes there'll be a pompous role, and I have chosen a pompous actor who has an infinite desire to do about 600 takes to show that each and every one is a minor improvement over the other. At which point this is a considerable waste of time, and his or her pomposity is utterly overwhelming. I'll just say, "No, thank you, I've got what I need." Very often, that frustrates that actor, so they're not always happy: "Well, you did it for Nicholson, why can't you do it for me?" "Because you were brilliant the first time out, and he wasn't. Let's go on."

CZ: In *Marvin Gardens,* there's the scene where Ellen Burstyn is talking to her stepdaughter—she's pretty far gone at that point—and she's holding a pair of scissors as she speaks. It's very menacing, and the psychic and physical violence escalate from that point. Is that the kind of thing that would evolve out of your work with the actors on the set?

BR: I can remember that it was terrifying to me that she had those scissors in her hand. I wanted her breakdown and her vulnerability in combination with how frighteningly strong she was, thereby making the point, I suppose, that it is more painful to witness the breaking down of a strong character than it is of a weak character.

It's very emotional for me; that's why I don't like doing interviews. Just thinking about these scenes for the first time in all these years. Nobody's talked to me about *The King of Marvin Gardens.* If I were to tell you what Ellen Burstyn went through about the scissors scene, how she went completely bananas and crazy. And what really happened to those actors during the course of those scenes; they all went nuts. They got so involved in playing these parts that there was murder and mayhem lingering at every moment of every day on that movie. I mean it; I'm not even approximating how horrifying it was. One reason why I don't like to see the movies that I make is that I don't want to review that anguish. It's there for other people to see; I don't want to see it.

CZ: Let's move on to *Postman*. What was it that struck you about Jessica Lange that made her so right for the part of Cora?

BR: This is a movie where, clearly, the female role is the stronger of the two roles. She's the one who motivates everything in the picture; she's the one who has a clear ambition. I wanted a strong actress. Here's a woman who's made a picture—*King Kong* [1976]—who was lambasted for it by everybody, who walked out of her contract, is banned in Hollywood, and, I hear tell, is performing in a play somewhere in North Carolina. I thought she was quite beautiful, and I liked what I had heard about her resolve. Not the protests of another model saying, "I am not just another pretty face," but somebody who had really told [Dino] de Laurentis to shove it. I sent her the book and went down to see her in North Carolina. There was no script; I had just met David Mamet [screenwriter of *Postman*], in fact. She knew about me, she knew about *Postman*. I arrived late, 12:00 or 1:00 in the morning; I couldn't find the damn motel, it was in some very, very strange little town. I went to the desk and I said, "Is Miss Lange in her room?" and he said, "Yes," and I said, "Well, I don't want to disturb her now," and he said, "Well, you wouldn't be disturbing her, she's on the phone." I didn't know what to do, so I just decided to go to her door and knock on it, but I didn't want to interrupt the call. She'd been on the phone for 15 minutes, and I was tired, and I could just as easily leave a message saying, "I'll see you tomorrow morning." But I wanted to apologize for being late, so I knocked on the door. She admitted me, she had the phone in her hand, and the speaker crooked in her neck, and motioned me to sit down. She got back on the bed where she continued to have this conversation without once acknowledging my presence, for over an hour. When I was looking at her, I just said, "Well, if she can act the way she's acting right now, talking some rather intimate dialogue with her then-boyfriend and father of her child [Mikhail Baryshnikov], she'd be great in this picture."

Then we started to work together, and, over a period of four times where we tested her—I videotaped her, with me playing Nicholson's role—I became more and more persuaded that she was the right person to play the part. I can't tell you what persuaded me, because it's so obvious: she's a great actress, period. It's just that I knew that a little ahead of everybody else. And my gift, if there is one lucky thing that I've got—is some technique, instinct, something, that allows me to recognize the talent. I have the patience, perhaps, and maybe an ambition to recognize the talent, that others don't have. But when it's worked, there's something that just moves me, and catches me, and they get the part.

CZ: David Mamet doesn't do backstories for his character in either his plays or his films. We don't know much about Frank and Cora in *Postman*. How did you deal with character as a director?

BR: With regard to backstories: I play around with them a bit, I make them up on the spot for the actor. If the actor wants to know, "Well, how did I get here, I need to know these things," I'll make up a backstory. And if I find it dull, I'll make up a better one. It's just something that the actor

Jessica Lange and Jack Nicholson in *The Postman Always Rings Twice* (1981), directed by Bob Rafelson. © Lorimar Film-Und Fernsehproduktion GmbH.

needs. Each actor is different from the other—there are actors who cannot get out of their dressing rooms without insulting the assistant director, beating up on the driver, throwing the food away and saying it stinks, and creating complete and total disorder and panic every single day of every single film they're on. Or, perhaps more to the point, any actor is capable of being this way on any given day, in any movie. His son got hit by a truck last night, nobody knows it, he doesn't want to talk about it, so he's rude to somebody. Or they're just hopelessly deranged people to start with, but they are magnificent actors. You just have to be able to understand who people are. You don't walk out there like some martinet and just say, "Well, that's enough of that shit, get her out of the trailer." Sometimes you have to be forceful, sometimes you have to be paternal, sometimes you have to be romantic, sometimes you have to be the fool . . . whatever's necessary. And sometimes they need a backstory.

CZ: So you talk about backstories according to individual needs?

BR: Yeah. A lot of people don't want to know, so you don't bring it up. A lot of people think they don't want to know and do want to know. A lot of people need to know and don't think they need to know. So it's put to them in some way that doesn't offend: "I met somebody just the other day, it's really amazing, because she's just like this character. I thought it would amuse you to hear this. It's got nothing to do with what you're doing . . ." You just make up this stuff. It's a little bit like telling a jury to forget what they've just been instructed—you leave something, and perhaps it's contemplated, or perhaps it's neglected and forgotten.

CZ: That leads me to ask more about interpretation. There's a moment in *Postman,* after Cora's gone away to be with her dying mother and Frank has had a liaison with Anjelica Huston's character. Cora comes back, she's very repentant; she says, "I'm giving up drinking . . ." and she says to Jack's character, "Forgive me." Nicholson has this look on his face that says, "I don't have a clue about my life, and I don't know what I'm doing here . . ." There's a whole subtext in that scene that's driven by that look.

BR: Nicholson has been indulging in a romance; she's come back a new, seemingly spiritually cleansed woman. She's asking for forgiveness, when, in fact, perhaps he is the one who should be asking for forgiveness. What's his response going to be? He can be angry, he can be utterly romantic, he can be asking for forgiveness himself, but not knowing how to articulate it in words. He's got about 50 choices for this act of the play. Nicholson probably gave me all of them. If it's a look, I'm sure that he gave me all of them. He and I work in a very odd way, it's usually by finger snaps. We know each other pretty well and only in case there's a major disagreement about how to play a scene—and there are enough of those, too—it's all done like this [*snaps fingers*]: "Look one, look two, look three, look four, look five, give me another one."

CZ: You've been working with Nicholson for 20-odd years; have you seen an evolution in his work?

BR: Yeah, but I would speak to the role of the actor in movies that I have made. The average cost of a movie today—I'll be off by a few million—is $25 million. The average cost. That means a lot of them are costing $80 million. The picture costs $25 million, and if the actor is a major star, $7 to $10 million are going to the actor, so everything is contingent upon, "Can you get the actor?" If you get the actor your picture is a go movie. This is the frame in which the actor is working today, the atmosphere. So if somebody calls up, early on—the names are inter-changeable here: Dustin Hoffman, Steve McQueen, Marlon Brando, Jack Nicholson, Tom Cruise, it doesn't make any difference who we're talking about—and says, "I'd really like you to do this movie," from that point on they are part producers of the picture. Because the terms of their agreement, the gamble on them, is such that they need to have the terms. If they don't need it, their machinery needs it: the lawyer, the agent. Approval of the director, approval of the project, approval of the final script, approval of the co-star, sometimes a coterie of makeup and wardrobe [people], the trailer—that comes with the actor. You're hiring aboard considerably more than you were 20 years ago when you hired an actor, certainly more than 40 years ago when the actor was under contract to the studio. Things have changed; the actor is now starting work the moment he's offered the part. He's now part of the production. To some degree, it is a diminished sense of what the director does.

Now, how in God's name is the actor's ego not going to be affected by this radical change of his importance in the making of the movie? It's impossible not to be affected by it, and Nicholson has been affected by it. Here's an example of how I'm affected by it: when Jack decided to do *Postman,* in '81, I had, prior to that, produced and/or directed maybe 4 or 5 movies, and Jack's fee [for *Postman*], as I recall, was more than the cost of all those movies put together. The way I knocked on the trailer door was a little bit different from the way we roomed together during the making of *Five Easy Pieces.* Now something is affected by that. There's something else you have to deal with that you didn't have to deal with in another era or at another time of your acting life. The pressures are much greater. I know one actor, who is one of the bunch that I named, who charges $50,000 to read the script when you submit it. His thought being, "I'll give you the interview and discuss this with you, and you'll learn at least $50,000 worth of information about what's the matter with the character. Also, this is a way of proving you're earnest."

CZ: This is a question about the director/actor/screenwriter relationship. When David Mamet makes his own films, he lets people play around with the language to some degree, but he's generally very protective of it. If you're working with a writer who uses language in such a considered way, and you—as the director—are into improvisation, does that create conflict?

BR: With David? There was some conflict. He would always say, "Mine's better," and he was usually right. But sometimes better is not important. Sometimes better is getting the performance and letting the actor change the line rather than having them feel discomfited by saying the line the way it is; it's just simple reality. Those who insist on being letter-perfect to the word get those kind of movies.

I can remember asking David on the set to rewrite a six-line critical scene over 100 times. Six lines where he didn't change but a half a sentence here or there, for 2 straight days. Finally, he left it in my trailer, and I said, "Where the hell's Mamet? Now that I've read it, I want to talk to him"—we were shooting all night long—and one of the assistants said, "Oh, he went home, he was tired." He flew not only to another city, but to another country. That was the last rewrite he was going to do on that scene.

Part of my difficult nature, as a director, is that I make extraordinary demands on everybody, and my demands are that there must be a better way that none of us have figured out how to act a scene, how to write a scene, how to cast a scene. So it's a question of staying power more than anything else. When you're casting a part, it may be the 103rd person who comes into the room that you should see before making the movie. So you stay there an extra hour. Now, there are times when there are more important things to be doing, and, as you get older, perhaps you learn where your time is best spent. But I'm always wanting to hang in there for one more thing, one more chance, one more "We could have done it a better way." And then when you have finished, and all your choices are made, to never have a regret about any of them, because you gave it your best shot, the actors gave it their best shot.

Now, maybe you were just short-sighted that day, and you couldn't come up with the inspiration of how to do it better. But I never think about that, and I don't want to think about it. Which is another reason why I don't look at my movies. I don't want to go back there and say, "Christ, I could've done it better." I'd just as soon move on to the next thing.

CZ: There's one piece of dialogue I especially love in *Postman*. Jack Nicholson is drinking milk out of a bottle, and Jessica Lange says, "What are you, an animal? Why don't you use a glass?" The way she says it, the look he gives her back, and then his line, "Do you want me to leave?" says so much about their relationship.

BR: That's pure Mamet, as I recall. There are certain things about David's work that tend to repeat; "What, are you an animal?" is one of them. I wouldn't mind directing it over and over again. But I can remember that scene, and there was another choice besides drinking milk. Jack will always go for the ugliest, least likeable choice, and he'll say, "What's the matter with that?" That's the way his head thinks. It's not that he's trying to be unlikeable, it's that he has a sense of the character that he's playing. And perhaps he'll take it too far with a choice: "Why not weigh 300 pounds?" "Well, because nobody wants to see you fat and ugly, that's an answer." "Who the fuck cares?" and so on and so forth. The arguments go on about every detail in the movie, particularly between friends like us.

Jessica has to stand up in that scene and tell him to go fuck off, and slam the door. I couldn't get her to be as strong as I wanted to. It called for rage, it called for true anger and resolve. Resolved anger, not the anger of a whimpering child, not the anger of a bullied cat, not the anger of a betrayed sensibility, but the anger of somebody who's confronting sloth and a lack of ambition, and a broken promise of a partnership, and of a man versus a woman—a lot of deep-seated anger.

So here's an instance of something that I rarely do, which is tell the actor who's in the opposing shot that "she ain't pissed off enough at you, so you better get her fuckin' pissed off, and I don't care what that takes, as long as I am capable of patching it all together the moment the scene is over. I don't want any enduring insults, because then you can't work." Well, Jack did it, he provoked her, and boy, she stayed provoked, I'll tell you. Jack is extremely generous in his fashion, because that's hard for him to do. "You want me to fire the gun off to make the horse react, Curly?" "Yeah, something like that." "Looks like she's doing a good job to me." "Yeah, well, she's not doing it for me, Jack, so I need some help." And maybe I have to take it one step further with Nicholson: "You want to see the basketball game tonight? We're going to fuckin' stay here and shoot this thing, I don't care, I'll change the whole scene to a nighttime, Jack, so you better do it," and I have to insult him to get him to a state of rage so that he will bring it out in her.

All of that is part of what I do as a director, and I don't like it one single bit, and after 3 or 4 months of actual production on a film, and 3 to 5 months of preproduction and six months of postproduction, I'm gone for 3 years, because I don't like doing that; I don't like that responsibility. That's why I don't like making movies, and that's why I rarely give interviews.

CZ: I'd like to move ahead to *Mountains of the Moon* [1990] and the portrayal in that film of Sir Richard Burton; he's a fascinating character. He has such a strong rationalist side, and yet he was also a great sensualist. Was it a challenge to reconcile those parts of his nature? Was it difficult for Patrick Bergin?

BR: It took me 9 years to get this movie made. The best answer I can give to you is that surely there's no character in my life that I've identified with more than Richard Burton. It's those irreconcilable factors in a man's life that cause his destruction. The world doesn't appreciate—nor should it—the struggles that go on before a decision is being made by its heroes. They like to think that they always take the positive action, they're always brilliant, they're always charmed. The ambivalences that somebody has are rarely articulated in the newspapers. Politicians don't stand before the public saying, "I've been up for the last week taking uppers and speed, and I'm trying to figure out how to satisfy Iraq and our oil interests at the same time. I can't fuckin' make a decision." Richard Burton was a person who exposed that part of himself, and the world didn't like it. To the degree that he is ambivalent and is complex to that degree, his triumphs are transcendently beautiful, and, so, to the same degree, are his failings.

That's what makes a tragic hero. Perhaps I dwell a little bit more than other directors on the down part of the characters, and that makes them a little less easy to identify with. Audiences want to go in and see somebody—a Rambo character or a Terminator character—blow out 100 people at once; it's not even the slightest bit believable, it's entertaining, it's predictable. But they don't want to see a character amputate their own leg or stick a compass in their ear. That's too painful, it's too real.

CZ: But the magnitude of what Burton was doing must be appealing to people.

BR: Well, it's not going to appeal in great numbers, at least not in my lifetime. There'll be a few people who like your work, thank God, but you're [not] box office. I don't sit down and make those kind of movies. But on the other hand, any number of times I've made movies that have proven successful at the box office, where I didn't expect it at all, for the same reasons. In certain kinds of filmmaking, that's the luck of the draw. Who would think that *Easy Rider* [1969, Rafelson co-produced] was going to make a lot of money? There was nothing to tell us that it would; it was just something that we believed in. Or *Five Easy Pieces,* or any of the other pictures that I've made? Also, it's a big world, and audiences around the world respond differently. *Postman* was the picture that was really punished at the box office—and by the critics, I think—in America. But you can't go anywhere in the rest of the world without people thinking it was some kind of weird, gigantic hit—which it was—and a masterpiece of some sort. You look and you say, "Boy, how do you reconcile the different responses?" The French loved this picture. I remember one of the leading critics in America talking about how filthy Jack Nicholson's fingernails were, and how could he touch this beautiful woman? And the same detail being pointed to in France, saying how brilliant Jack's choice was. A garage mechanic always has greasy fingers, you can't get it out.

CZ: Why do you think that you continue to direct? It obviously creates some difficulty for you. You don't really hate it, do you?

BR: Yeah, I do hate it. My pleasure in life is not in directing films; my pleasure in life is when I'm completely gone from Hollywood and making movies. People say to me very often, "Wow, that's so much fun"; I say, "What are you talking about? It ain't much fun." Adventure, thrills, excitement, feeling alive . . . but fun? Boy, I can't think about any damn day I've had fun making a movie—sometimes, shooting a water skiing scene or something like that. It isn't fun. It's rewarding, it pays the bills, it keeps you off the streets, it stops you from doing certain things with your life that might be too dangerous and gives you an arena of safe risk-taking. I'd much rather hang out with the Kurdish revolutionaries in Turkey than make a movie, but there are times when you've just got to pull in the reins.

An Interview with Karel Reisz

Karel Reisz on the set of *Who'll Stop the Rain?* (1978). United Artists. © 1978 United Artists Corporation. All Rights Reserved. Museum of Modern Art Film Stills Archive.

Karel Reisz began his career as a documentary filmmaker (*Momma Don't Allow,* 1956, with Tony Richardson) and producer (*Every Day Except Christmas,* 1957; *We Are the Lambeth Boys,* 1959), directing films vital to the British movement known as "Free Cinema." It was a socially committed cinema focusing on the problems of the working class. The practictioners of "Free Cinema" believed that film should not merely record reality, but should, in equal measure, exploit the aesthetic capacities of the medium. Poetic expression and social obligation could be fused into a dynamic tool for change. These concerns are evident in Reisz' first fiction film—*Saturday Night and Sunday Morning* (1960), part of the "British New Wave" or "angry young man" films that flourished in the late 1950s and early 1960s. Filmed on location in England's north country,

273

it dealt with a factory worker (Albert Finney) rebelling against the oppressive limitations of his environment. Although Reisz has gone on to make films with far-ranging subjects, his work remains rooted in the philosophy that characterized his early career. Each of his films provides a sympathetic documentation of a social milieu, framed by an expressive *mise-en-scene*. Like *Saturday Night and Sunday Morning,* his films are about figures whose social, artistic, or ethical values situate them in an oppositional relationship to their surroundings, leading to a kind of romantic anarchism. As a Czech living in Britain, but working —for the past 20 years—in the United States, Reisz has a natural affinity with the outsider.

Reisz says in his interview, "What is interesting to me is the collision between the actor and the character; acting isn't some kind of act of illustration of what is on the page; it has to do with the collision—the skill and the psyche of the actor, and what is in the part. And that sometimes makes for mysterious conjunctions. When they go 'click' for you, that's the precious moment." Reisz has gleaned an enviable share of those moments in performances by some of our finest film actors, among them, Albert Finney in *Saturday Night and Sunday Morning* (1960), and *Night Must Fall* (1964); Vanessa Redgrave in *Morgan* (1966), and *Isadora* (1968); James Caan in *The Gambler* (1974); Nick Nolte and Michael Moriarty in *Who'll Stop the Rain?* (1978); Jeremy Irons and Meryl Streep in *The French Lieutenant's Woman* (1981); Jessica Lange and Ed Harris in *Sweet Dreams* (1985); and Debra Winger (with Nick Nolte) in *Everybody Wins* (1990). The performances speak—with an impressive amalgamation of imagination and authenticity—to the requirements of character and place.

Reisz was born in 1926 in Czechoslovakia and emigrated to England in 1939, where he attended Emmanuel College. His first film-related job was as a critic for the magazines *Sequence* and *Sight and Sound.* He co-authored, with Gavin Millar, *The Technique of Film Editing* in 1953, a significant text that is still used in classrooms today. Reisz, in addition to directing the films mentioned above, was co-producer of *Night Must Fall* and *The French Lieutenant's Woman* and producer of *This Sporting Life* (1963).

I spoke with Karel Reisz in his home in London, England, in June 1991.

CZ: You're known for taking a lot of time in preproduction. I'd like you to take me through what you do after you commit to a script.

KR: I'm normally involved in generating the project. I spend anywhere between 3 and 12 months, off and on, working on the script with the writer. Not always, but normally, yes. But I've never written a line of dialogue; I'm no good at it. The collaboration is about sorting out the sequence of events, the connections and the cross-references, and working out the pattern through which we will tell the story. And that's a very complicated to-and-fro process with the writer. I have, on two occasions, worked on films that were more or less formed before they got to me and where the collaboration with the writer was really largely technical. But it's not been very satisfactory.

CZ: The first film you did that was not strictly British was *Isadora* [1968]. How did you become involved in the project?

KR: A French producer came and said he wanted to make a film about Isadora Duncan. He'd just seen *Morgan* [1966], a film that I'd made with Vanessa, and he said, "I'd like a film about Isadora Duncan starring Vanessa Redgrave." And I was intrigued by Isadora Duncan.

Vanessa is a very remarkable actress; it's all intuitive with her. Once she gets on the wavelength . . . she doesn't "work out" a walk, or "work out" a manner of speech, or the externals. She plays around with the character until it seems to come through her, and then she just floats away and does it. She's very untheoretical. Or, rather, to put it in other words, she does like to talk a lot about it, but the talk is always around it.

I remember doing *Morgan* [1966]. She'd gone on the floor one day, and she started sort of touching her chest like this, with the tips of her fingers. I said, "What on earth are you doing?" and she said, "Oh, I read something about gorillas, which says that the female gorilla flirts with the male by touching her chest." You may remember Morgan himself had gorilla fantasies. Well, the way it came out was quite arcane; it wasn't that she was "doing" a female gorilla, what she was doing was some kind of secretive, magical flirting. She grabs these things out of the air and then has the ability to absorb them without them standing out as devices or gimmicks. It comes out of homework, but it's the kind of homework which, with a more earnest actor, could prove really embarrassing. With her, because it's generated by emotion, it comes out fine.

CZ: When you were preparing for *Isadora,* did you read the conflicting points of view about Duncan?

KR: Oh, absolutely, yes. It's a very peculiar thing. The basic facts of Isadora's life are available through her autobiography, which is a pack of lies. It was written quite cynically to make money. Then there are some rather flat bits of hagiography from fans. Then we met 3 or 4 people who actually knew her, and that was all completely different, and we worked from that. I think the whole business of doing a biography is very tricky. To make a coherent drama out of a subject where you don't have freedom to invent . . . you can't say the character should do such and such now, if in real life she didn't [*laughs*]. The way the film worked, it had a kind of—only partly successful—musical structure; things worked by association rather than by narrative. By the end of it, people were allowed to marvel at her, without being really given much of a line on her.

CZ: How faithful were you trying to be in terms of recreating the dances?

KR: Absolutely not at all. We were simply wanting an actress to act a dancer. Vanessa is physically totally different from Isadora Duncan; Isadora Duncan was Rubenesque. The dances are really acting scenes, they are scenes in which she's playing a dancer trying to convey ranges of feeling, like music. For instance, none of the music that she dances to in the film is music that Isadora danced to. No, working with the choreographer, we set ourselves the task of using the dances to dramatize her emotional life; how the dancing expressed or contradicted her feelings, and so on. We then found music. The dance scenes are used as a kind of illumination of her character, rather than in any way attempting a history of Isadora Duncan's dancing style. You couldn't do that anyway, certainly not with an actress, a non-dancer.

CZ: There are still contemporary performers who do Isadora's dances. Did any of them contact you about the film?

KR: Most of them disapproved of the film. Not everybody; I had a very good letter from Lincoln Kirstein at the time, for instance, who understood that this was not a matter of some kind of documentary reconstruction. It's a way of using the dance as an element of the life.

CZ: Jason Robards was your first experience of working with an American actor. How did you find that?

KR: I was lucky with Jason. He had been, up to that point, rather disapproving of the movies. He'd made a few movies and sort of reserved the right to patronize them a little bit. But then he changed. I got him just at the beginning of his real interest in movie acting. He was playing a foolish, foppish person, a man of no great sensitivity, a man used to command, a rich man. I thought he did it with great good humor, with no attempt to make the character cuddly. I had a very good time with him.

CZ: For *The Gambler* [1974], I understand you were in New York for over a year before beginning to shoot. Obviously the milieu of the film is not one you're familiar with; the film is filled with quintessential New York types and mobsters. What kind of adjustment was it for you to work with these characters? How much control did you have over the casting?

KR: Oh, complete. It's the only film with a Jewish middle-class setting that I've ever made—and I felt very comfortable with that. The author [James Toback] knew the world very well, as did the actors. If, like me, you don't make films with any autobiographical content, you're presented with the problem every time of bringing to life a world that wasn't alive before you did it. So whether you're making a film about Victorian London or criminal Brooklyn, it's still the same thing. But if the world that the film presents is integral to the themes of the film, then you don't really have a problem.

CZ: How much work did you do with the actors beyond what was in James Toback's script? What were rehearsals like?

KR: What happens is you have a script, and you have actors, and you have a place, and you have a day, and you have certain light, and you do it until you believe it. You rehearse until it convinces you. If you have a sense of the general structure of the film, so that you know roughly what the scene has to say in the completed film, you have a great deal of freedom on the day to surprise yourself and to allow the actors to surprise you.

CZ: How much latitude do you give your actors?

KR: Any amount of room, which doesn't mean that I don't reject a lot of the inventions if they don't work, or aren't appropriate, or whatever. I try and hold the actors with very loose hands. What is interesting to me is the collision between the actor and the character; acting isn't some kind of act of illustration of what is on the page; it has to do with the collision—the skill, and the psyche of the actor, and what is in the part. And that sometimes makes for mysterious conjunctions. When they go "click" for you, that's the precious moment, and you keep that.

CZ: Lauren Hutton had never acted before *The Gambler*. Did you speak to her in a different way than you did to more seasoned actors?

KR: Working with actors is like any other human relationship; you behave with different people in different ways. There are actors who are frozen by too much direction, and there are actors who are desperate without detailed orders. The director's skill is in assessing that, and working with it. Some very good actors are compulsive preparers; others give it to you on take one or two, and after that you've had it. There's no point in hankering for everybody to be the same. So yes, Lauren was inexperienced, but she really worked hard. And mainly, it worked, because she has a quirky sort of individuality that I liked very much. She obviously wasn't a tremendously experienced actress, but you don't need that in the movies, necessarily.

CZ: I want to go on to *Who'll Stop the Rain?* [1978], which is one of my favorite films. At the time the film was made, you said, "Once the shooting starts, it's the relationship with the actor that is the mainspring for me. I never know where to put the camera until I've rehearsed the scene." Can you discuss that?

KR: Well, look, the range of possibilities in staging a scene is endless, isn't it? You can have a storyboard, so that you know precisely where the actors are, and then make the actors find reasons for themselves to walk into pre-set positions. You can be like Hitchcock and have it all in your head beforehand. Or like Antonioni, who rehearses all his scenes with the stand-ins, and then tells the actors, "This is where you're going to do it." Or you can work from the other end, which is take it from the skill and intuition of the actors, that is to say, let them lead you—by the way they move, and where they want to move, and how they relate. Bring it alive first, and then catch it. Of course you have to catch it expressively. Well, I tend to work in that way. And I don't put this forward at all as a virtue; it's just how I do it. It's in balancing these factors that a director defines his style, how he comes to move things around, and time things, and view things, and cut things. In my own case, I find that if I know the night before where to put the camera, it's always wrong; I'm maneuvering the players into positions. Clearly, lots of directors are damn good at that and have achieved remarkable results by doing that.

CZ: How much would you discuss the characterization with the actor?

KR: Well, a lot, with the principals. I do try and talk about the history of the people beforehand, in the rehearsal period and so on, but I've learned not to do it the same way with everybody. Some actors really can't use it. And the most dangerous are the actors who are all "method-trained" and want to do it in that elaborate theoretical way, [*sighs*] but actually learn nothing from it, and it just confuses and stiffens them. With some actors it's best just to do it. Nick [Nolte] is an extremely self-aware craftsman. He's stage-trained; he doesn't feel confident or free until he's done his homework; so you do a lot of talking with him. Tuesday Weld is different. If you don't get it by take two or three, you won't get it. She started as a child actress, and in a sense still works like that. But it's very fine, very subtle, but completely untechnical. It doesn't do you any good talking to Tuesday about how the character relates to her mother.

CZ: All of Nick Nolte's actions in that film have a great sense of reality. The way that he tosses a cigarette butt, or he drinks at a bar. Is that something you would work on with him?

Michael Moriarty and Nick Nolte in *Who'll Stop the Rain?* (1978) © 1978 United Artists Corporation. All Rights Reserved. Museum of Modern Art Film Stills Archive.

KR: He's extraordinarily good at that. This is a character who is a Marine, somebody who believes in soldiering; his credo has to do with self-reliance, efficiency, and preparedness, in being quicker and better-prepared than the next man. So the way he assembles his gun, and the way he dresses, and the way he straps the hand grenades to his thigh, that's all very important. It's not a documentary about how a soldier behaves; it is character-expressive.

I'll tell you a story about Nick: We had a scene in *Who'll Stop the Rain?* where he has a dialogue scene with Tuesday while he's mending a jeep. He's working on the engine of a jeep. And we were rehearsing it on Friday afternoon, and the sound man said to me, "Listen, we'll have to post-synchronize this because the spanners and all are making so much clatter in his tool-box, it's all much louder than the dialogue." And I said to Nick, "Look, I'm sorry, but I'm warning you that this is a post-synch job, because I can't ask you to handle the implements more gingerly, obviously you can't." And he said, "How awful, I hate post-synching." Then the sun went down, and we had to wrap it, and we started shooting again Monday morning. And miraculously, he was doing exactly the same as he had been before, but in absolute silence. I thought, "What have you done?" He'd taken home the tool box, and lined it with this sort of cushiony material, and then painted the material silver, so that you couldn't tell it was there. In fact, when we were dubbing it, we had to dub in some very discreet metal noises.

CZ: Do you encourage your actors to improvise with dialogue?

KR: We improvise during rehearsal, because it's a good way of getting at the character, but, again, it's a matter of style. If you're making a film in which authenticity and spontaneity is a central thing, then of course improvisation is great. If, on the other hand, you have something that has a real literary spine, and a structure, then improvisation obscures things, because it changes the emphasis. It makes the scenes longer in places where they shouldn't be and throws the rhythm of the text. So, no, I don't encourage improvisation with the dialogue.

CZ: But you rehearse a lot with the actors . . .

KR: We usually have about 8 or 10 days, and we talk, and we try the scenes. I don't plot it out visually at all; I mean, I don't do it on the set. I find the business of shooting out of continuity very alarming; when you're shooting something out of reel six before you've shot reel one. So rehearsals are very important, to give you a sense of progression. And it's usually the period where you're doing the clothes, and trying the makeup and the wigs, and so it all comes together at that point. It's a getting-to-know-you period, to put it quite unpretentiously. But if you work like I do, namely, off the actors, it's very important.

CZ: *The French Lieutenant's Woman* [1981] is like *Morgan,* not a naturalistic piece. The actors are very self-conscious and ironic about what they're doing, how they're behaving. For instance, Jeremy Irons has a line, "I'm afraid I've unbearably compromised you," and Meryl Streep rolls her eyes up as if to say she can't believe what a stick this man is.

KR: Well, I mean, what is the story? The story's about a self-contained, rather cold scientist, a man of privilege. One of the strands of the story is the sentimental education of that man. And he *is* a bit of a stick. Certainly he is in the book. Her emotional range is far wider than his, so I suppose that's in the performances. But the narrative style of the book, and the film, is very particular. You are asked to look at a spectacle: an artifact. You are continually being reminded that this is a work of fiction that is being made: "Let's pretend." That's as in the book, [John] Fowles continually takes you out of his story into direct commentary. The book is not only a fiction, it's also a speculation *about* fiction, with a number of different alienating devices. The alienating device in the film—the modern story—is quite different from the novel. But it's there. So of course, it is reflected in the acting. There are moments in the film where I'm trying to tell the audience, "We're acting." There is a moment right at the end, a crucial moment where they're in that white room, when Jeremy's returned, and he knocks Meryl over, and she hits the floor. And just momentarily she gets the giggles, actually steps out of character. It was very important to me to keep the conundrum going. To keep the *game* of "what-would-happen-if?" going all the time.

CZ: What was your experience like on *Sweet Dreams* [1985]? It's another quintessentially American subject—country music.

KR: I had a very good time with Jessica [Lange], and Ed Harris and with Anne Wedgeworth. It was a very happy film. Jessica's tremendously professional. I mean, the whole business of the songs, you know, Jessica's not musical at all, and she can't sing, but she's got a very fine sense of rhythm. We use the songs not just as songs, but as character stuff, you know, to dramatize where she is with her life, rather like the dances in *Isadora.* For that film, I wanted it to be about a woman who assumes that happiness and fulfillment—having it all—is her birthright. A rather uncomplicated person. When we were preparing it, we saw a tape of Patsy Cline herself, in a television interview. Patsy Cline was quite plump, and the interviewer asked her about it: doesn't it worry her. Patsy Cline simply turns round, and shows her big bum to the camera and says, "Yes." Now, Jessica, who'd played some rather serious parts just before, absolutely swam with that simple formulation that Patsy's life offers. "Yes, great, let's do it like that."

And Ed [Harris], of course, is joy for a director, great, great. I have tended to work with actors—and this is by choice—who are not strongly image-conscious. That is to say, leading actors who want to characterize, who don't care whether the audience will like them, or think them sexy, or whatever. And Ed is completely like that. And Nick, of course, is like that in spades.

CZ: I find it interesting that you've worked with really big stars, and yet you say you work with people who don't have an image.

KR: Well, you see, Meryl is a character actress—of course she's a star—but she's not a star who impinges on the audience by self-reference. You know, she's not Judy Holliday, or Marlene Dietrich, or Garbo; she doesn't work like that at all, she works by character acting of a very high order. Jessica's the same. There are two kinds of stars, aren't there? There are the stars who people pay to see because they like Cary Grant, they like how he is. And then there are the actors who get you with their truthfulness, you recognize things in them: Fonda, Spencer Tracy.

CZ: On a more general level, how do you deal with temperamental actors?

KR: Just like you deal with temperamental friends. There's nothing mysterious about film directing; it's a form of human contact. You have to learn to understand when actors are being "difficult" because they're frightened—which of course happens all the time. Acting is an extraordinarily demanding business, particularly for women. There they are at 9:00 in the morning being photographed in closeup for the whole world to see. It's a very invasive, very assaulting kind of experience to submit yourself to. In those circumstances people get frightened and "temperamental"; you have to be sympathetic. Also, you have to learn to judge when temperament is being used for manipulation. In that sense, it's like parents and children.

An Interview with Lawrence Kasdan

Lawrence Kasdan. Courtesy of Mr. Kasdan.

The tragic and comic—often seen from an ironic perspective—circulate and merge in writer/director Lawrence Kasdan's films. The terrain of his work is varied, ranging from *film noir* to Western to melodrama, but the inhabitants of his world face a similar predicament. From *Body Heat* (1981) through *Grand Canyon* (1992), Kasdan's characters live in an unreasoning, threatening, and dangerous world. Untimely and unnatural deaths haunt the narratives, while corruption and duplicity hover menacingly in the landscape. In the face of this imminent peril, Kasdan's characters look for something—relationships, the community, work, or the family—that will grant them meaning and stability, reconciliation and redemption. Kasdan's films achieve articulation in the space between this overarching theme and the delicate nuances of behavior; it is here that some human truth is located.

283

While Kasdan's concerns are, at bottom, elemental, the presentation of the situations in his films is often heightened and his work populated by complex characters in complicated relationships. To give substance and credibility to these elaborate connections, he needs actors of both style and subtlety. Kasdan has an uncanny knack for finding actors who are, as he says, "powerful presences . . . on the cusp of stardom." Their parts in Kasdan's films are often career-changing; actors like Kathleen Turner, Glenn Close, Kevin Costner, Geena Davis, Danny Glover, Jeff Goldblum, William Hurt, and Kevin Kline received critical and commercial acknowledgment for their work with the director.

Kasdan was born in Miami Beach, Florida, in 1949 and acquired both a B.A. (1970) and an M.A. (1972) from The University of Michigan. In the mid-1970s, he worked as an advertising copywriter, winning a Clio Award for excellence. Kasdan initially worked in films as a screenwriter, and continues, with the exception of *I Love You to Death* (1989), to write (or co-author) the screenplays for each film he directs. His first produced screenplays were phenomenally successful—Kasdan wrote *The Empire Strikes Back* in 1980, with Leigh Brackett, and then scripted *Raiders of the Lost Ark* (1981). He went on to write *Continental Divide* (1981), *The Return of the Jedi* (1983, co-author), and *The Bodyguard* (1993).

Kasdan burst on the scene as a director with *Body Heat,* followed by *The Big Chill* (1983), *Silverado* (1985), *The Accidental Tourist* (1988), *I Love You to Death,* and *Grand Canyon* (1993). The screenplay for *The Big Chill* won Kasdan the Writers Guild of America Award and a Directors Guild of America nomination for Best Director. He was nominated for an Academy Award for his screenplay—written with his wife, Meg—for *Grand Canyon.* He won the Golden Bear Prize at the Berlin Film Festival for the same film.

I interviewed Lawrence Kasdan in his Beverly Hills home in January 1992.

CZ: As a first-time director, what was your biggest surprise or challenge in terms of directing actors in *Body Heat* [1981]?

LK: I had been imagining directing for so long, and all the writing had been about becoming a director—it had been my strategy. So I had thought about the process a great deal. I had studied acting in college and had done some acting in high school; I spent a summer at Carnegie Tech. I was always very interested in acting, for myself, and in other people's acting. I was a very receptive sort of newcomer. We did a couple of weeks of rehearsal on *Body Heat,* with Bill [Hurt] and Kathleen [Turner], so that burned away a lot of anxiety about it. We figured out a way to have dialogue about things. One of the surprises to me was that different actors needed different kinds of language. There was not one language which would suit everyone. In other words, I would have to talk about the material in different terms for different people. They were both relatively new to films. Bill had been in two pictures, *Altered States* [1980] and *Eyewitness* [1981]. He was the experienced one of the trio; this was my first job as a director, Kathleen had never done a film. The three of us were all sort of new, making up our methods as we went along. Bill was an extremely intense theater-trained actor, and for him the process was a serious one. It was a difficult picture, very claustrophobic, really just about the 2 of them. It's very sexual, and there was a lot of nudity. A lot of nudity and sexual material is hard for the most experienced director to deal with. So it was a real baptism, and great in that way.

CZ: So you quickly became comfortable in your role as a director?

LK: The overall sensation of directing was that I had come home, that it was the thing I was supposed to do. That I had not wasted my life up to that point, and that this was my calling. There was that feeling of familiarity, and at the same time it was all new material. So it was like being an explorer in territory that offers great potential promise, yet with the possibility of fear and failure.

"How are we going to do this material?" [*Body Heat*] is a very stylized story, so we're not even talking about standard American naturalistic acting; we're talking about a slightly heightened, stylized kind of acting. What we were doing was a modern day *film noir.* I didn't know if I'd ever get to direct again, and I wanted to do something very stylized. I wanted to pull out all the stops with the camera. I wanted to use what I considered to be my writing experience; it has very stylized dialogue, and so people don't even talk together like real people. It's basis is in 1980s America, but it could be the 1940s or the 1950s, and the talk is sometimes very much of that genre. So you have the added problem of having to deliver a line that's not standard, everyday language. There were a lot of very challenging elements to the brand-new task of directing actors.

CZ: Thinking back to the golden era of Hollywood and the star system, were you looking for actors who were going to somehow carry on in that tradition? You're working with modern actors, who don't have the same meaning for us as stars did 40 years ago. What are your ideas about how contemporary actors relate to the star system? And did you have the sense of *Body Heat* being a star-making film?

LK: In *Body Heat,* I was looking for a kind of archetypal femme fatale. She's not a modern gal. The way she's treated visually in the movie is not as a modern gal—she could almost have come from another era. Kathleen, who was perfectly capable of playing someone modern, with the rhythms of modern speech, also has this ability to do the kind of stylized dialogue I was looking for. And her look, and the dress she was wearing, body language, can be very extravagant. She has a great size to her; she's a big personality, and Matty Walker needed that. And as you say, these were not "stars" at the time, but these were 2 people with enormous star power who no one had heard about. They had that thing that people are looking for all the time, and yet they were completely unknown. Was I looking for that? I was looking for very powerful presences. I tested several people for both those roles—screen-tested them, on film, with different match-ups, different pairings. It was just clear that they were the ones. They popped out of the competition. There was an intensity and a kind of ability to hold the screen that was impressive from the start for newcomers. That sense that I had seems to have been borne out by their careers.

CZ: Kevin Kline plays a rather archetypal character in *Silverado* [1985], which, like *Body Heat,* is a genre film. Yet Kevin Kline doesn't have all the associations and baggage of a star with a strong persona, like Jimmy Stewart. How do you think that impacts on making a modern genre film?

LK: When Jimmy Stewart started making Westerns—his first one was *Winchester 73* [1950], I'm a great Jimmy Stewart fan—he had no baggage. It's only in retrospect that we think of Jimmy Stewart as an archetype of the Western hero. In fact, he's from Princeton, from upper-class Eastern gentry. All these people started out unknowns, as blank pages in the public's consciousness. The thing you're talking about, which is, "Can you hire a star who brings with him a certain persona which augments the role?" Well, that happens, but it happens after stardom has happened. I've generally worked with people who are on the cusp of stardom, who are beginning. I have not tended to go with the big stars, who would automatically fill the role.

CZ: But when Jimmy Stewart did *Winchester 73,* he already had years of stardom, and certainly a strong persona, as a romantic, a man of integrity, an ordinary man with extraordinary moral character, but no association with the Western. The Anthony Mann Westerns used that nice-guy persona, so that when Stewart did perverse or immoral things in that cycle of films, his persona was like a subtext that played into the whole picture.

LK: It was a benefit of whatever persona he had at that time. What you're talking about is him being cast in an unexpected role. Now, it turned out to be a very comfortable role for him, one that he played again and again. The same thing could be said of Kevin, except that there aren't enough movies made where you can fall into that kind of rhythm.

CZ: What would you do to help Kevin prepare for the part? What kind of discussions did you have with him?

LK: We rehearsed for 2 weeks and actually trained for a month, riding, shooting, with a lot of rehearsal in that process. The script is full of clues about this guy's history and what his attitudes are toward the world, what his attitudes are about life and death—which are very much on the minds of people in *Silverado*—and what his attitudes are about loyalty and friendship and trust. Those are very much what's going on in the story. All those clues are there, and what you ask him to play is not some standard Western hero, but this particular guy. The Kevin Kline character is a very weathered, experienced guy. It happens that he's an honorable character and that he tries to act honorably in the movie even though he has a real pull toward the corrupt side.

What do we talk about? We talk about a way of being, a way of moving, a way of delivering these lines. What is the level of irony in them? I think he brings enormous irony to the thing, a kind of cynicism, a slightly sardonic tone to it. At what point is he kidding around, and when is he serious? When they're facing life-and-death situations, how do not just

Kevin, but all the characters, respond to that? Do they respond to it with bravado, or with fear? Do they reveal themselves to their comrades? Those are the issues that we face. He responds to [Brian] Dennehy very strongly, in terms of a past life that he's trying to forget, in terms of the temptations that Dennehy offers to him, that he rejects, in terms of doubting Dennehy's word—he's skeptical and sort of sardonic about Dennehy's attitudes. Those are the things where you put very specific moments in the script, where you say: "How do we play this? How do you move at this time? What puts you on edge? What relaxes you? Where is there grace under pressure? Where is there anxiety? What touches your real core?" Where he rises up, finally, and says, "I'm not on this side, I'm on the other side." Those are the issues of the portrayal.

CZ: I find it interesting that you seem to work with actors who are largely stage-trained, and also people who would not be considered method actors.

LK: No, they're not really method actors. I'm not sure what a method actor is. I think that what's true of every one of these actors is that they have their own method, they borrow from different traditions. Someone like Kline has been very much influenced by the British tradition of acting, and yet he would be the first to tell you that he is an American actor. He doesn't build his performance from his haircut in, you know, he builds it from the inside out. And yet he is delighted and interested in the kind of technical proficiency that a British actor can bring to a role, the voice, the mustache. He's drawing from both traditions equally. That's the most interesting kind of actor for me. In fact, most of the people I've been drawn to are like that; they're not very strongly one way or the other.

I've worked with several British actors, and they have variety in their tradition. Joan Plowright was absolutely one of the most wonderful experiences I'd ever had [*I Love You to Death*, 1990]. She has a very free method, and it comes out of 40 years of British theater. Married to Olivier, worked with Olivier constantly. Olivier is an exemplar of a certain kind of acting; she certainly had to be influenced by him. Yet when we did this knock-down farce where she played an immigrant in America, she was very free about the effects, very concentrated about how she achieved them, and very open to behavioral talk, to psychological talk, and to technique. So what I'm drawn to is people who are very skilled, and, within their skills, don't have to worry too much about technique and can concentrate on the character.

CZ: How closely do you guard your words, as a writer?

LK: When I started, I guarded them very closely, because when I was writing and not directing, I felt that my scripts were not always treated that well. I cringed every time I heard a change that some other director had made in my screenplay. So when I started out, with *Body Heat,* one of the things I was going to do with it was to protect the language. From *Body Heat* through *Grand Canyon* [1991], six films, I tried to be more and more relaxed and looser about that, and, in fact, for at least 6 years, I've invited people to change dialogue. What I find is that they have no desire to. The more open you are about having a few changes, the less changes you're going to get. They tend to like the text. They come to me because they like to say these words. They like an atmosphere in which they have enormous freedom to act, not to improvise the writing. They're two very different things. I always think, since I've invited them to change the dialogue, and they tend not to, that it's because they have so much freedom in the acting. People say to me, "How much of your stuff is improvised?" Well, the dialogue is never improvised, or very rarely—a few instances in any picture. But I think the whole performance is improvised, because it has a quality of lifelike immediacy. Within the lines, all these actors have enormous freedom. And that's exactly what I'm wanting from them—is to surprise me, delight me. I don't want it to be something that I knew was going to happen. I want it to be pulsing right at that moment.

CZ: If people feel that something is improvised, I think it's a real tribute to both the actor and the director.

LK: Yeah, because we're trying to approximate life, at every moment. That's the goal of all my work, that it be as true as possible. That's what everything I do is about: trying to find some kind of truth.

CZ: There's a moment I thought was improvised in *The Big Chill* [1983], when Kevin Kline is singing the theme from *Raiders of the Lost Ark* [1981, scripted by Kasdan] as he's running upstairs to capture a bat.

LK: No . . . no, in fact, I'm a little embarrassed, because I wrote it into the script. I'm embarrassed only because it's a little self-reverential, and it's a little indulgent. At that time, I was proud of my involvement with *Raiders; The Big Chill* was a couple of years later. I thought it would be funny that the guy put on a little adventure persona as he went up to fight the bats. But that's not improvised.

CZ: So these musical interludes that seem improvised, like Mickey Rourke lip-synching to Bob Seger in *Body Heat* . . .

LK: It's all in the script. And carefully chosen, too, you know. You can't commit yourself to a song of any kind on the spur of the moment, because you have to have the rights to use that song, and very often they're very expensive. If you go ahead, and on the spur of the moment, put a song into the acting, and then go out to buy that song, you're at the mercy of the people who own the song, because you can't go back and reshoot. Any time you see a song in a movie, when someone's actually singing on camera, it's very likely it's all been prenegotiated, and written, and decided on. That's just business.

CZ: You directed big ensembles in *The Big Chill* and *Grand Canyon,* and I was wondering how you worked with the cast in terms of developing their relationships?

LK: They're all like that, really. Everything except *Body Heat* has really been an ensemble movie. The actual experience of directing [all of my] movies, in terms of numbers of actors, and the orchestrating of the voices, of the tones, was very similar, all of them.

CZ: In the particular cases of *The Big Chill* and *Grand Canyon,* where you're dealing with many characters and their stories, was there any way that you worked with the actors to make them feel comfortable? Do you work with them on charting their histories and their relationships?

LK: We had very different rehearsal processes for the two movies. *The Big Chill* was the second film that I directed, and we rehearsed for a month, just pure rehearsal. Almost unheard of in the movies. I don't know of another case where they've done that, probably a few, but not too many. The last two weeks we did on location. Even though we weren't literally living together, it was very close.

CZ: How did you manage to have so much rehearsal time?

LK: I started doing this when I had very little power. So I think that the reason I have had it is because I have made it a priority. People ask me that all the time: How come I have rehearsal and other people don't? It's because the other people don't really want to rehearse. There's something you should understand about movie directors—and I'm sure you hear this from actors—most film directors are terrified of actors. The last thing they want to do is spend an extended amount of time in a bare room with the actors, dealing with the actors' questions about the roles and the material.

CZ: I've heard variations on that—first, that directors don't like actors very much, and second, that the actors are the ones who are terrified.

LK: The second part—the actor's fear—is an expression of that terror the director feels. He then puts it on the actor and says the actors are terrified. The fact is, the actors are worried about appearing to be fools. They're worried about not getting guidance. They're worried about not having help. They're worried about not understanding how to say their lines and play the part, but they're not terrified of the directors. Directors tend to be terrified of actors, and they will do almost anything to avoid dealing with them, including projecting a lot of their fears onto them. Most directors are very comfortable with cameras, location, blocking if it doesn't involve them especially with the actors. What they really want to concentrate on is lighting and cutting. But to actually talk to actors about material that the director may have doubts about himself, you'll very rarely hear them talk about [that]. It's terrifying; they're afraid they're going to be asked questions that they can't answer.

Now that's not true of every director. Plenty of directors I know really like actors and like the process. Some of them choose not to rehearse. Sydney Pollack and I once had a conversation about it and he just doesn't believe that it works in film. He has a perfectly good argument about it, and Sydney is not afraid of actors. But for the most part, most directors don't really like actors. They resent them, and they're frightened by their demands, and they think they're self-centered, none of which is really true. Obviously there are bad people in every job, but for the most part, actors are very interesting, lively, and intelligent.

CZ: How do you lead a large group through their various relationships? I know that some directors make charts or graphs of the emotional ups and downs of their characters . . .

LK: No. What we do is we talk. But the point I was making is that we rehearsed for a month on *The Big Chill;* we rehearsed for a week on *Grand Canyon.* And that reflects my own curiosity about the process. *Grand Canyon* was the least I've ever rehearsed. It was a purposeful decision, just as the writing of *Grand Canyon* was a purposeful, conscious effort to strike out in new territory. I thought I had gotten very good at certain kinds of writing, and I wanted to challenge myself, to expand my horizons as a writer. [And] I wanted to try something different with the actors, when we came to do *Grand Canyon.* And my initial instinct [was]—and this actually followed the conversation with Sydney Pollack, in which he raised the argument for no rehearsal—"Maybe this time, I won't rehearse at all. Let's see what happens if the actors and I come to the set each day with many more questions, with less idea about what each other wants." The reverse of all that is what you get out of rehearsal, you get some understanding among you, you get some preparation, some questions are answered. What if we didn't do that?

CZ: How did the actors feel about your decision?

LK: The actors were sort of OK with no rehearsal; they were uneasy, because part of the reason people like to work with me is that they want to rehearse. I told them, "Well, this time we're not going to rehearse." At least I floated that trial balloon. They were very uneasy with it, but they were going to do whatever I said. It's not unusual for movies anyway. Steve Martin was playing a very new kind of role for him; he was very nervous about that; he wanted to rehearse. Part of the attraction of doing something new was to work it through with me in a rehearsal period. I said, "All right, let's compromise. We'll do the least amount of rehearsal I've ever done; we'll do one week." The other actors were thrilled that I had changed my mind. They didn't know that they had Steve to thank for that.

So, in *The Big Chill,* we have a large ensemble, a month of rehearsal, getting to know each other intimately, learning to trust each other, playing old friends who know each other very well, whose references are the same, whose jokes are understood by each other, who constantly refer to things that the audience does not see. And we have to believe their intimacy, right? *Grand Canyon* is a movie about strangers, people who've just met. People bumping into each other for the first time and being uneasy with each other. Practically every scene is about that. It's a very different kind of goal, right? And the rehearsal methods turned out to work very well for both. With one, we got very intensely involved with each other. In the second case, we had a kind of weeklong session about the material. We read the script aloud, as I always do, but it was really about the talk that happened between the reading, the talk about your experiences, and how you relate to what your character is doing, how you relate to what the other characters are doing. What references out of life as you know it does it bring out in you? We had a very pleasant, exciting weeklong session about the material and human experience. And in between, we were doing a lot of reading of the script, playing with the tone, seeing where the humor was. I don't write jokes, but I write a funny script, and we were trying to imagine it.

CZ: How much of your work is precast? And how much do you find that you use the personalities of the actors who are working with you?

LK: I try not to precast. It has happened several times, however. Obviously, with *Body Heat,* I did not know who was going to play those parts. With *The Big Chill,* I knew that I wanted to work with Bill again and wrote that part for him, but everyone else was new to me. When I went to *Silverado,* I now knew Kline, and I wanted him, and I wrote that part for him. I also wrote the Kevin Costner part for him, because I cut him out of *The Big Chill;* I felt guilty about it. So I wrote him this one; I thought it was a terrific part, in *Silverado,* which turned out to be a turning point in his career. But I didn't know anyone else. I sort of had Scott Glenn in mind; I admired his work. On *Accidental Tourist,* I didn't know who would play those parts.

I talked to Bill about it very early on, because it seemed, when I read the book, it suggested Bill very strongly to me. But I had not settled on him. I had him strongly in mind in the writing, but not absolutely necessary as Macon Leary. On *I Love You to Death,* I took it on with the idea that Kevin would play that crazy pizza guy. On *Grand Canyon,* the only part that I knew was the Danny Glover part. I had become friendly with Danny on *Silverado,* and really wanted to use that quality that he has in real life, sort of enormous quantities of power and sadness.

CZ: Going back to *The Accidental Tourist,* watching Bill Hurt was a big revelation for me, because I think I undervalued him. Even though I knew he was a good actor, I never realized how subtle he is.

LK: He's wildly undervalued. This performance in *The Accidental Tourist* was not nominated because it's the opposite of what the Academy looks for. The Academy looks for big . . . you know, you're playing some disability, stuttering, or handicapped, you know.

He's very funny, too, which no one understood. People took it as, "Oh, he's so glum, he's so grim." Well, the guy has had a horrible tragedy happen to him, but his attitude is very funny.

CZ: It's very extraordinary also, the way that the actors in this film really seem like a family. [Ed Begley, Bill Hurt, David Ogden Stiers, and Amy Wright play siblings.]

LK: That comes from an intense commitment to making it true. We talked a lot, we had a long rehearsal period on this movie. We speculated on their childhood. The book provides some information, the script does not, about their childhood, and what happened to them, and why are they like this, and why are the other three [in the family] incapable of going out in the world at all?

Geena Davis and William Hurt in *The Accidental Tourist,* directed by Lawrence Kasdan. © 1988 Warner Brothers, Inc. Museum of Modern Art Film Stills Archive.

CZ: Some of the reviewers complained that *The Accidental Tourist* was just a transcription of the novel. Does it irritate you when you read that?

LK: I don't mind that, because I want it to be as faithful to the novel as possible. Sometimes when you do your best work, it hides itself, it doesn't show itself off. The critical establishment doesn't understand movies at all, so what they respond to is the most flamboyant camera movement, the most flamboyant acting. That's what's considered to be "good" in America.

CZ: I'd like to try something with a scene in *The Accidental Tourist*. It's an exercise I do in a course I teach on film acting; I look at the acting in a scene minute by minute.

LK: Second by second. You can't do it in any other way. You have an overall vision that you are trying to achieve, and everything is a part of that—all the production design, and the camera, and the lighting has to be in your head. It's like writing, right? You can't generalize in the writing, you can't say, "Well, she says something about . . ." She has to say something, the actual words. That's the same way it is in the acting; every moment counts. Nothing generalized about it.

CZ: This is the scene where Macon [William Hurt] comes to Muriel's [Geena Davis'] house and slips a letter under the door:

> WH: [*Voice-over*]: Dear Muriel: I am very sorry, but I won't be able to have dinner with you tomorrow after all. Something has come up. Regretfully, Macon . . .
> GD: [*offscreen*]: I've got a double-barreled shotgun, and I'm aiming it exactly where your head is.
> WH: It's Macon.
> GD: What are you doing here?
> WH: Last year, I . . . experienced a loss. I lost my son. He was just . . . he went into a hamburger joint, and someone came, a holdup man, and shot him. I can't go to dinner with people. I can't talk to your little boy. You have to stop asking me. I don't want to hurt your feelings, but I'm just not up to this. Do you hear me?

LK: The letter, as we've just heard in voice-over, is uncommunicative. It's a dodge: "Something has come up." And she just doesn't accept that . . . "OK, now tell me what you really want." It's so amazing, that moment, that scene: Watch her, here, that very second there, she's just total reception. "OK, now tell me what you really want," and he does. This is a long, complicated speech; it goes on and on. You have a lot of choices here. People said to me, after they'd seen this, "Oh, I wish he'd broken down more, I wish he'd sobbed." He says it quietly, and cries at the end of this thing. I am resistant to the obvious thing. This is almost impossible for him to say to her; he's come to say he can't have dinner with her, but he obviously is in deep need of her at this moment, and she understands that, instinctively. He is telling her what, in his conscious mind, he thinks, which is, "I can't stand what you're offering me, I can't deal with it. You must leave me alone, this is too painful." That's how he struggles through the first part of the speech. The second part of the scene, inside, is about his guilt that he's getting over the death of his son. He can't stand it that it's starting to become an accepted part of his life, rather than the agony every moment that it was. He feels guilty that he can go a day without thinking about it. That's a very different thing than this, in which he is trying to extricate himself at the same time that he's come to her for her help. So he's saying one thing and doing another.

CZ: Was it a difficult scene for the actors?

LK: It's a demanding moment for both of them, particularly for Bill. For Geena, she was very much in this groove where she understood Muriel, who cannot usually keep her mouth shut, knows [here] exactly when to keep her mouth shut. She knew how unconditional her comfort had to be. So it wasn't as hard for her. In fact, she went beyond my hopes for it, because she's so perfect, physically.

The trick is to get it, you have a lot of concerns. You're dealing with the central scene in a movie, right, so everything is sort of focused on that, and you think a lot about how it will be acted, how it will be shot, how is it lit, what part of the set are you using? A lot of the suggestion of it is in the book. The action here is very much in the book—it's almost identical. But again, you say, "What are the shots that convey this?" because the book is just in your mind. So you translate what you see in your head when you read the book, into this.

Then you're trying to get the delicacy, all the things that are going on for them at that moment, and cover it in each of the shots that you use. We had a two-shot, I think we used it once; I very much felt that we'd start with the letter and [have the camera] follow up to her, which means that you don't get to see her [face all the time]. This concerned me a lot when I went to cut the movie. The fact is that you cover the thing in such a way that you have some options. And what you hope is that a cutting pattern will suggest itself, that perfectly reinforces what you want from the scene, and in which the performances are up at the level that you want. Ideally, a performance would be great in every piece of coverage, and then you have endless options, but what you hope is that it's good in those moments you most want to use.

And these actors don't try to ingratiate themselves. Neither of them. That's why this is a difficult movie for people. I'm amazed how many people came to see it.

CZ: It's so subtle. I had to watch it twice, because I felt I missed so much the first time.

LK: That's the problem with a lot of my movies, I'm afraid. I'm amazed my movies do as well as they do, because I think they're just really out of time, you know, they're not what's going down.

CZ: *The Accidental Tourist* is, in some ways, like a chamber piece. In *Grand Canyon,* on the other hand, you have a lot of events and characters in very quick succession; in one sequence you have Kevin Kline cutting his finger, then there's an earthquake, and then a neighbor has a heart attack. Were you going for the sense of "too much"?

LK: The purpose of that is that it is too much. Everybody who ever read it said it was too much. That was the whole intention. You see, they go from whining about his business partner, the normal complaints of everyday life, to seeing his blood spill out of him, which reminds him of his delicate mortality, to the larger nature shaking up their lives, in which even their house is a scary matchbox, to actual mortality next door. Directly into the dream, the evening which sets up the dream; they're just agitated. The whole idea is that we can go in 2 minutes, 3 minutes, from piddling concerns to the biggest questions, and it's so hard to keep your head straight, to keep any perspective. Even though we consciously know that. You know, I'm worried about an appointment I have this afternoon, you're worried about has the interview gone all right? You know, what you're really concerned about is your health, your family, the ones you love, that the plane stay up on your way back to Montreal. And yet, we have to become invested in the little trivial matters. So, it's in your face, that sequence. And everybody who read it said, "Well, is this too much?" and I said, "Yes, yes, yes, it's too much." That's the point. It can happen like that and we go the full spectrum. That's what actually does happen; sometimes lives are just telescoped, and all our concerns are just sort of shown to us in a little rainbow.

An Interview
with
Bill Duke

Bill Duke with Robin Givens on the set of *A Rage in Harlem* (1991). Courtesy of Miramax Films. Museum of Modern Art Film Stills Archive.

Bill Duke says in his interview, "I have a great deal of respect for the audience's intelligence," a position that is all too rare in commercial filmmaking. He asks his audience to partake of a fictional world that is highly stylized and moves beyond the limits of convention. Duke's films—*A Rage in Harlem* (1991), *Deep Cover* (1992), *The Cemetery Club* (1993), and *Sister Act II* (1993)—are each, in their own way, indebted to the theater, where Duke began his career. The set design, lighting, costumes, and compositions are often theatrical; they portray a heightened and exaggerated version of reality. Duke, at times, uses sound and editing in an innovative, non-naturalistic way, presenting a visual and aural challenge to his audience. Yet his films, as Duke says, maintain a "delicate balance"; the reverse aspect of the stylization reveals a core of truthfulness on the level of human behavior. Like many resourceful directors working in mainstream cinema, Duke uses popular genre—romance, thriller, melodrama, screwball comedy— as a kind of envelope to contain a wide and deep range of human interaction, as well as a rich subtext flowing beneath the surface of the work. Duke is abetted in his pursuit of emotional authenticity by a host of gifted actors: Forest Whitaker, Danny Glover, Zakes Mokae, Gregory Hines, Jeff Goldblum, Laurence Fishburne, Ellen Burstyn, Olympia Dukakis, Diane Ladd, Danny Aiello, and Whoopi Goldberg, among others.

299

Born in Poughkeepsie, New York, Duke trained for the theater, receiving a B.F.A. from Boston University and an M.F.A. from New York University. He became involved in theater during the efflorescence of African-American playwriting and directing in the late 1960s and early 1970s. He appeared in the prestigious productions of Lee Roi Jones'(a.k.a. Amiri Baraka) *Slaveship* (1969–70) at the Brooklyn Academy of Music, *Day of Absence* (1970) with the Negro Ensemble Company, and *Ain't Supposed to Die a Natural Death* (1971–72) on Broadway. Duke was also writing for the theater, and the Negro Ensemble Company produced his one-act play, *An Adaptation: Dream* in 1971. He directed for the stage, most notably, *The Secret Place* (1972) for Playwrights Horizon and *Unfinished Women* (1977) for the New York Shakespeare Festival. In addition, Duke staged more than 30 off-Broadway plays.

Duke relocated to Los Angeles in 1978 and performed in the television movie *Sergeant Matlovich vs. the U.S. Air Force* in the same year. He was a leading character in a TV series, *Palmerstown, U.S.A.*, for two seasons, from 1980–1981. Concurrently, he was awarded the role of Leon, the heavy in Paul Schraeder's film *American Gigolo* in 1980. Duke stopped performing for several years while he attended the American Film Institute to hone his skills as a director. He then amassed over 70 credits during the 1970s and 1980s directing for prime-time series such as *Knots Landing*, *Falcon Crest, Flamingo Road, Hunter, Cagney and Lacey, Hill Street Blues,* and *Miami Vice.* In 1985, Duke directed *The Killing Floor* (about an interracial labor organization in a Chicago slaughterhouse) and, in 1989, *Raisin in the Sun*, both for *American Playhouse.* In 1986, Duke made *The Johnnie Gibson Story*, a TV movie about the first black woman FBI agent. His film acting career continued during this period; he had roles in *Commando* (1985), *No Man's Land* (1987), *Predator* (1987), *Action Jackson* (1988), and *Bird on a Wire* (1990).

I talked with Bill Duke at his production facility in L.A. in October 1992.

CZ: Tell me how you got interested in theater and in acting.

BD: Well, it's interesting; I come from a very low-income family, and I was the first one to go to college. My mother and father really didn't want me to get into this business, because it wasn't practical. They were hard-working people, and they said, "If you're going to college, you should be a doctor, or something like that." I tried some pre-med classes, and I was totally out of it. I wasn't equipped for science or math; and I failed miserably.

I always wanted to be involved in the arts, and, strangely enough, my parents really are the ones that encouraged me. There was a point in my father's life when he couldn't afford even to go to movies. My father and mother used to take us to downtown Poughkeepsie, Main Street, and park the car on a Saturday afternoon around 4:30. And we would have big bags of popcorn, and we'd sit on the street and look at people. My father was a great observer of life, he'd say, "Now, what do you think that man does for a living? How old do you think that woman is? Doesn't that person look crazy?"—commentary on people passing by. We did that for 3 or 4 hours, until the sun set, almost every Saturday of my youth, for a very long time. My sister and I appreciated it, but we were pissed off because we wanted to go to the movies. Now I look back on those times as some of the dearest, most formative moments of my youth and my life. I became very interested in the study of people and very accurate in the analysis of people at a very early age, from my father's and mother's insight and instinct. It's the foundation of my interest in the theater, in character study, and writing—the study of people. And it's by default, because we couldn't afford to go to the movies.

CZ: What was your training for the theater?

BD: I got my bachelor's at Boston University School of the Arts, and that was very traditional theater training. It was based on The London Academy of Music and Dramatic Arts, really classical training. I was an acting and directing student, and their philosophy was that if you were a director of theater, then you should be able to do the jobs of everyone that you were hiring for that job. So I had to take design, costume, and mask classes; I had to design a show—not design it conceptually, but literally graph it out on paper—and design it to scale. They taught you the fundamental, classical, Aristotelian rules—not only of theater—but of "aesthetics," and also the practical application of those rules. I found it to be extremely useful, because once you know the rules, or at least a Western sense of what the rules are, it gives you a common ground from which to proceed. At the time, I felt it was relatively arduous, because I thought of myself as a very creative person; I just wanted to break all the rules.

CZ: And then you went to graduate school?

BD: I went to the M.F.A. program at NYU School of the Arts. It was the first year of the school; I was there when the school opened its doors. The theater program was totally the most radical difference from BU that you can imagine. It was like Growtowski, and Richard Schechner, and Andre Gregory, it took everything I'd learned and turned it upside down. I was lucky enough, then, to totally question every rule I had learned, and to experiment, and to really begin to become relatively innovative in terms of my own work as a writer and director.

Then I went into the cold, cruel world and learned about all the things I was not taught in the classroom, which is surviving as an actor, director, and writer in New York City. It was a very painful, difficult, but instructive process.

CZ: What were some of the things you did as an actor and director?

BD: I directed, wrote, and produced my own stuff. I was with the Negro Ensemble Company, which was a really great privilege for me. Lloyd Richards, who was a mentor to a certain extent, got me that job. Then I did a show called *Slaveship* [1969–70, written by Lee Roi Jones (a.k.a. Amiri Baraka)], with a friend of mine, Gilbert Moses. We went to Europe with that show. Then I came back and I did another show that was on Broadway for a year, called *Ain't Supposed to Die a Natural Death* [1971–72], by Melvin Van Peebles. I did a lot of things at The Henry Street Settlement Playhouse, Gene Frankel's Workshop, The Manhattan Theater Club.

CZ: So you were pretty successful.

BD: You know what the irony is? I was working my ass off, but guess what? I never made over $3000 a year. I was starving to death, but I was working. That's one of the most frustrating things about being a stage actor, especially in New York: You can work, everybody can know who you are, but it doesn't mean you're making a dime. You do free showcases, or off-off-Broadway, which is a joke. You get paid what? Enough for your carfare? You're happy, because you're working, and you're learning your craft and so on, and people are loving your work. But I was around 33, 34 years old, and I woke up one morning and I said, "Wait a minute. I want a house and a car, and I'm just not going to do it here."

CZ: So you made the move to Los Angeles?

BD: I was totally intimidated by Los Angeles. When I saw the Academy Awards—that was the only time I ever saw Los Angeles—it was like Gotham City. It was so gigantic and overpowering to me that I thought I'd just come out here and get lost. Again, Lloyd Richards saved my butt by saying, "Hey man, I'm directing this thing about the internment of the Japanese during World War II in the concentration camps in the U.S., and it's called *Go Watch*." It was for a PBS program called *Visions*. I went out with Lloyd to be his assistant; I was a gofer, basically. I got a good salary and an apartment, which was not bad. They liked my work and I stayed on and did two more shows. I got an agent out there, and my first gig as an actor was for a movie of the week about a homosexual lieutenant, *Sergeant Matlovitch vs. the U.S. Air Force* [1978], and I made almost twice as much money in that job, which lasted around 5 weeks, than I had ever made in an entire year in New York as a stage actor. I was very impressed by that. And I said, "I'm going to stay out here and try to make some money, so I can save up and go back to New York."

   Well, the intent was to go back to New York, but I'd been smitten by the fact that there was no snow out here. My first Christmas in L.A. was spent with a friend of mine who lived in this building that overlooked a pool. I'll never forget this day, it was December 25th—he invited me over for Christmas dinner. All these people were around the pool, it was 85 degrees, palm trees just blowing in the breeze, and people were sitting in bathing suits, splashing in the pool. I remember this gigantic Santa Claus sled, with these fake presents, next to the pool. I looked at it, and I said, "What's wrong with this picture, man?" It was the most incredible feeling, because Christmas before that, for me, had always been snow, and buses splashing stuff on you. This was so incongruous! But it was wonderful, because the weather was just great. That was one thing, and two, the salary, and three, the opportunity. The volume of possibilities here was substantially increased by the fact that we were in the sun, and we had theater here, plus TV, plus commercials, plus films. I felt there were more chances for me to succeed, so that's why I stayed.

CZ: Didn't you go to the American Film Institute [AFI]?

BD: Yeah; but first, I had a series for two seasons called *Palmerstown, U.S.A.* [1980–81], which was a Norman Lear and Alex Haley collaboration; I co-starred in that. I was making, in a week, an incredible amount of money, more than I ever dreamed I'd be making. I was on for two seasons, and I said, "Man, I made it. I've died and gone to heaven, and things are going to be great forever." I didn't work for 2 years after that. I couldn't get arrested as an actor, and I said, "Shit, man, I realize, I understand." I had to utilize all of my talent in order to survive in this business.

I'd always been intimidated by the equipment of film, although I thought very filmically as a director of stage. So I took some of the money from my series, and I got a fellowship at the AFI and dropped out of the business for 2 full years.

AFI is extremely good if you want to be a filmmaker, because the first month that you're there, after they orient you, they give you a camera, a crew, lights, a script, and 7 days, and they want you to come back with a film. You don't learn academically as much as you learn through practical experience and failure. By failure, they teach you how to make films. You set out with the best of intentions, and you get into the cutting room, and you say, "Oh, shit, I don't have that angle, I don't have this piece," so the next time, you get that piece. You cut your film, you write it, you produce it, you light it, you do everything. I graduated from the AFI in 1980-something.

CZ: You won an award, didn't you?

BD: Yeah, it was called the Lifetime Achievement Award for Best Young Filmmaker. I had a film called *The Hero,* and that film went on to win a number of awards in festivals around the country. It was my first film, so it was a great honor. As a young filmmaker, you're very insecure; your heroes are gigantic, you haven't made your first film yet, and you're comparing yourself always to "them," and, "How in the hell am I ever going to get there?"

CZ: So you can relate to young filmmakers who are now in the same position.

BD: I go to schools and I speak, and I hire people on my staff whenever I'm doing a film who are young filmmakers. I give them a gig as gofers, or first assistant directors, or first production assistants, or whatever, so they can hang around and ask questions, and learn, and look. That's what it's about. If you don't pass it on, then it's about you, and that's not big enough, that's getting too small.

CZ: Who are your heroes?

BD: Frank Capra, Coppola, guys like John Ford, Antonioni, Bergman, Gordon Parks, all the B-movie directors, numerous filmmakers. Frank Capra, in terms of his overall technical ability, his vision as a director, his ability to work with actors, and his ability to take on this industry in a manner that was straightforward and honest. And most importantly, his balls and his courage in terms of the subject matter that he chose. He's a great hero of mine.

CZ: I wanted to talk about your experience acting in other filmmakers' films. Do you feel that you learned a lot by doing that?

BD: I always learn something from working with directors. I just finished working with the Hughes brothers making a film for New Line called *Menace II Society* [1993]. They wanted me to do a cameo in their film, and I went over there and I did it. I had made a film which they really liked—*Deep Cover* [1992]—and I guess they expected me to come over there and direct myself; these are just kids, they're in their 20s. When they're directing, I'm an actor. I want to know what to do; I'm insecure as an actor; every actor I know is insecure.

I've worked with some directors that gave me a great deal of insight in terms of how to get the best out of actors. There are certain directors that love actors, and they understand what actors are made of, and they hook in. With the people who hooked into me as an actor, I learned not only how to give them everything, but how to utilize that in terms of working with my own actors. A lot of directors just don't like actors, which is pretty ironic, to me.

CZ: Who were the directors you've acted for who have given you the most insight into directing actors?

BD: In *Predator* [1987], I thought John McTiernan was excellent. He's a very quiet, unassuming man, shy almost. He's a lovely man, he really knows people, and he only hires you if he feels that you know what you're doing. Once he does that, he leaves you alone, except if you're straying away from his vision of the character. He tells you very thoroughly: "Here's what I think of this person." It's not like you have to guess. It's clear, he's thought it out, he understands in detail who the person is. If you have different ideas, fine, as long as it's within the context of a certain vision. Paul Schrader was great to work with, in terms of *American Gigolo* [1980], because he had written the character. He gave me the seeds with which to take this character and mold it into this sociopathic bisexual pimp, Leon. Some people I was able to work easily with, because they liked actors. I gave them whatever I could to fulfil their vision.

CZ: How much are you involved in casting your own work? Starting with *The Killing Floor* [1984], I was struck by the way every role is so well cast.

BD: I cast the extras, and it drives the extra people crazy, I see every photograph. Any face that you see in my pictures, if there's a guy in the back over there, you can't really see his face—I cast that person personally. Every infinitesimal thing that you see on the screen is the director's responsibility. And the most important element of that, in my opinion, is the drama itself. The drama has an energy; if 2 people are talking and there's a heated exchange, and a person over there is off thinking about their laundry list, then they're not in the scene. And my attention goes to that person, because something more interesting might happen over there. Everybody, psychologically and emotionally, has to be involved in this moment. For me, the most critical part of making a film is the casting. If the cast is not right, there's nothing I can do. Two things: the script and the cast—without the script and without the cast being what they should be, everything else is bullshit.

CZ: So you're very involved in the writing of the film?

BD: Oh, yeah. Henry Bean and I collaborated for months on *Deep Cover.*

CZ: Do you storyboard?

BD: Yes, I do . . . action sequences only.

CZ: The reason I'm asking is because I find your films so stylized. I was really struck by the compositions in *Rage in Harlem* [1991]: When

Gregory Hines finds Zakes Mokae's body, you use the foreground and deep focus very dramatically. Does that affect the way that you work with actors?

BD: It pisses them off [*laughter*]. But you know, when they see it, they don't care, because they know that it's not me going on an ego trip, I'm just getting the best out of the scene. When we were doing that scene you were talking about, with Zakes Mokae, it was 30, 25 degrees in Cincinnati on a wet street, and even though he had this rubber suit on under his suit, the water was coming through and he was freezing. He did that around 20 times. But in the final analysis, the shot was worth it. It was a very difficult shot to do; it was night, we had a problem with the focus and the depth. But when he saw the footage, he said "OK."

See, actors don't mind, I think, if you put them through whatever, as long as it's not nonsensical. When you really have a vision you're trying to obtain, and the actor understands that, that's one thing. But just to put an actor on the ground for several hours because you think it's interesting, or something like that, is not fair. I think a lot of actors, including myself, resent that. But if I believe in you as a director, and I think that you really are committed to this vision, I'll do anything it takes to help you realize it; that's what my job is. I just don't want to be jerked off.

CZ: Do you insist on having a lot of rehearsal time with your actors?

BD: No doubt about it. The problems that you face in terms of the script and development of character—if you're going to be efficient about it—you don't have time to solve on the set, where a crew is waiting for you, because that's very expensive. All of those problems should be solved outside the set, and rehearsal is the perfect place to resolve them.

CZ: What do you do in rehearsal?

BD: Rehearsing lines is something that I don't do; I rehearse reality. What is going on here? And how do I know that what is going on is true? What specifically is it that you're after? Why are you sitting down talking to this person? What do you want, and how are you going to get it? What are your feelings about it? Did they hurt you? They hurt you; what does that mean? Where did they hurt you, and how do you feel about that? How does that sound; how does that look?

CZ: Do you ever improvise with your actors on the set?

BD: Yeah, when you have great actors, like a Jeff Goldblum, or a Larry Fishburne. They're both theater-trained, so we have a common language. There were scenes that did not work up till the last moment before we shot them. I would say, "Guys, this ain't working." I don't know why it's not working, so I say, "OK, we don't shoot it, we'll shoot it tomorrow." So we dump that scene, and then go to the motor home, and Jeff and Larry sit down, and go, "What the hell's going on with this scene? Bang! That's what's missing. Forget it, we're going to shoot it!" And we're back out there. There's a certain point where the actor knows more about the character than you do. You've written the character, but the actor is in that character's skin. Anything else is work, man.

Making great films is a collaborative process, and to work with actors like Ellen Burstyn, or Olympia Dukakis, or Diane Ladd [*The Cemetery Club,* 1993], they're not looking for you to give it to them, all they want to know is that you understand, that you get it. They look in your eyes: "You get it? OK. Tell me when I go to the left or right. I'm flying the plane, I know where I'm going. I'm not on automatic pilot, but I know my destination. I bring all this experience with me, all this talent with me." It's overwhelming, and it is wonderful. That kind of substance and talent is like a high.

You've been working 6 days straight, and you're working all night, and you have sleep deprivation. And you come in the morning, and you have a scene, OK? Then Olympia Dukakis comes on the set, and she's gonna die, and Ellen Burstyn is her friend, and she watches her die. "OK, we gotta do this rehearsal . . ." And the rehearsal wakes you up, the rehearsal turns you on, the rehearsal gets you going for the rest of the day. Not the performance, just the goddamn rehearsal! I'm not saying it's what you live for, but it makes everything else work. To have that happen to you maybe 5 or 10 times in a film, even if you just get that much, then it's worth it. It's magic; I can't describe it. It's an overwhelming feeling of fulfillment. And you're exhausted.

CZ: What about actors who aren't so wonderful; how do you go about dealing with them?

BD: When you have people who aren't great actors, they don't understand the process of acting. You can't improvise, you're just lucky to get through the goddamn day with an actor who doesn't really get it, or is wrapped up in his or her ego and is staying in the dressing room, and all that ignorant, ridiculous stuff that actors do. That's not fun, that's nothing to do with filmmaking; that's ego and Hollywood bullshit. To me, that's masturbative.

I've had real problems with actors sometimes, because they're really skittish, paranoid, or insecure; it's really problematic. Sometimes you don't get the stuff, and it reflects in your performance; you just cringe. It's painful, it's a horrible experience.

I work on these films for a year of my life; I can measure my life from the films that I've made, to a certain extent. The effort that you put into it, you might as well give it your best shot. And so every bit of your theatrical experience, every bit of your writing and acting experience, comes into play when you're a director because you write the script, you structure it, you have to know the camera, you have to be a good manager. And working with actors is the cream of it, because an actor can either make or break the scene. If he or she trusts you, you get a great relationship. If the actor doesn't trust you . . .

CZ: You've been working for major studios, do you ever get any flak about some of the more radical stylistic things that you do?

BD: Yeah, of course, that's what all the fights are about. Hollywood is a very difficult place to make films. If you're a very serious filmmaker, and if you're not just doing it for the money, and you really want to make great films, it's not easy to do. You're constantly trying to serve Caesar and God, you know. You can't serve God, or the god of your vision, or your talent, whatever the hell you want to call it, in Hollywood, without serving Caesar. Caesar will be fed, and that's the delicate balance. You can have a film that's critically acclaimed and that every critic and every filmmaker and every other person in the world thinks is the best thing since sliced bread, the best film of the season. But if it doesn't bring in a certain amount of profit, you're not getting the second film. I don't care who the hell you are, you could be Jesus Christ, you're not getting no second film, because no one's going to invest in you if you lose their money.

I have a great deal of respect for the audience's intelligence. As an artist or a filmmaker, you're involved in a constant process of "How do I—in a most interesting way—explore the subject matter for the audience I'm addressing?" It's a funny thing, because you don't want to direct your film to the lowest common denominator, so you're always a little ahead of them. But you don't want to get too far ahead of them so that you are talking to yourself. See, I'm walking this funny line . . .

CZ: *Deep Cover* is particularly striking in terms of its visual style.

BD: If you examine that film very carefully, Jeff Goldblum's character, for example, from his hair—which started off in the beginning being very light—by the end of that film it was slicked back, black, Satanic, almost. The colors in the beginning were very pastel and light, then totally dark. Jeff starts walking like this [*hunches over*] in the beginning—he's a guy that's too tall, and by the end of the film he's out, he's open like this [*straightens up*]. Those are subtle nuances, but I think that all those elements add power, and they draw the audience subliminally, if they really adhere to those little micro-elements that we work on and put together. I personally think that they're not a waste of time. Everybody in the studio will say, "Who in the hell sees that?" but what's important is that it's there. You've done your work, and that's part of the work of a director. It's not just to cut action, it's about texture.

CZ: There was one moment in *Deep Cover* that I really loved. When Jeff Goldblum is shot, the expression on his face when he looks down at the wound is a look of amazement, and then surprise. It's completely wordless, and so powerful.

BD: With a great actor you can do that. I think he's totally underrated; the business just screws you that way. He is one of the finest actors, one of the most finely tuned instruments. When we first did that scene, Larry shot him, and he fell against the truck. And he died. Then we talked about it, and he said, "This is the culmination of a relationship that we've seen throughout the entire film; it's like 2 lovers saying goodbye. Even in death they would say goodbye properly, they would take the time; it's quality time between them." So we began to explore what quality time would be, and what we found was that all the things they felt, they had never said, and now it was too late to say. That was the exchange between them as Larry's walking toward Jeff when he's dying. Larry, if you notice in that sequence, has no sense of triumph in his face when he kills him; it's a sense of loss, an irrevocable loss, and Jeff feels the same thing. But they don't speak it in words, they speak it through the truth of the moment. Only with great actors can you do that.

Jeff Goldblum and Laurence Fishburne in *Deep Cover,* directed by Bill Duke. Copyright ©
1992, New Line Productions, Inc. All rights reserved. Photo by Joel D. Warren. Photo
appears courtesy of New Line Productions, Inc.

I get in trouble for saying this: It's a craft, it takes years to do this, it's
not something that you get off a goddamn basketball court. I had a big
fight with a friend of mine, he's a football player, a quarterback; I said,
"So what are you going to do, man, when you retire?" He said, "I'm
going to be an actor."

CZ: Sandy Meisner always told his students at the Neighborhood
Playhouse that it takes 20 years to be even a good actor. Actors seem to
feel like they're only beginning, because they're always learning something.

BD: That's so wonderful about what we do; that's why we got into it.
A friend of mine says that the reason he became an actor is because he had
such a difficult time being a human being; that's what you feel, because in
acting, you never end the exploration, you never "learn it." Just when you
think you've got it, you know, you see somebody do something and you

say, "Jesus Christ, that was good. Why didn't I think of that?" You get pissed off, because you didn't think of it. But the thing is that you always learn. It's a very humbling profession. Sometimes you do it better than somebody else, or somebody else is better than you. But that's great, because if you have people who are pushing for excellence, and you're pushing for excellence, they'll inspire you. They inspire you to keep going, because you're not alone. They're also trying to do the same thing you're doing.

CZ: You're always searching for richer, deeper material . . .

BD: I tell my students all the time: "What you go to a shrink every day to forget, actors call upon every day, to create people for you to laugh at, or cry with."

An Interview
with
Ulu Grosbard

Robert De Niro, Meryl Streep, and Ulu Grosbard on the
set of *Falling in Love* (1984). Courtesy of Paramount
Pictures. Copyright © 1994 by Paramount Pictures. All
Rights Reserved. Museum of Modern Art Film Stills Archive.

Ulu Grosbard brings an impeccable precision and delicacy to his work
with some of the America's finest film actors—Robert De Niro, Robert
Duvall, Dustin Hoffman, and Meryl Streep. And although Grosbard's film
career has been confined, thus far, to five films—*The Subject Was Roses*
(1968), *Who Is Harry Kellerman and Why Is He Saying Those Terrible
Things about Me?* (1971), *Straight Time* (1978), *True Confessions* (1981),
and *Falling in Love* (1984)—that circumscribed field is profuse with
radiant moments of acting. The frame within which Grosbard works is
poetic realism, the most celebrated, home-grown school of American
drama. It is deeply character-driven, rich in psychological tensions, and
refulgent with a sense of time and place. Clearly, we are in the territory of
The Actors Studio, where Grosbard has attended sessions since the 1960s.
The Studio is also the native habitat of the directors with whom Grosbard
inaugurated his film career as assistant director: Elia Kazan (*Splendor in
the Grass,* 1961), Arthur Penn (*The Miracle Worker,* 1962), and Sidney
Lumet (*The Pawnbroker,* 1965).

Grosbard's own films are dense examinations of social microcosms,
studies of the pressures and iniquities embedded in a given milieu.
Whether it is marriage, the family, the church, the penal system, or show
business itself, his films astutely observe the impact of transgressive

impulses on a community. Grosbard's sensibility is an amalgam of intellect and instinct that respects and cultivates the complex ambiguities of human behavior.

Grosbard was born in Antwerp, Belgium, in 1929, and moved to the United States in 1948. He received both a bachelor's (1950) and a master's degree (1952) from The University of Chicago and attended the Yale School of Drama from 1952–53. His first major directorial assignment was the off-Broadway production of *The Days and Nights of Bebe Fenstermaker* (1962). He followed with the premiere of Frank Gilroy's *The Subject Was Roses* (1964), for which he received his first Tony nomination. Grosbard won the Obie in 1965 for his production of Arthur Miller's *A View from the Bridge*, starring Jon Voight and Robert Duvall, and worked again with the playwright in 1968, directing the Broadway premiere of *The Price* in 1968. Grosbard's association with David Mamet has also been fruitful; he directed the first Broadway production of *American Buffalo* (with Robert Duvall, 1977), for which he won his second Tony nomination, and *The Woods* in 1980, starring Christine Lahti. He directed a revival, at Lincoln Center, of Paddy Chayefsky's *The Tenth Man* in 1989.

I spoke with Ulu Grosbard in his New York office in April 1991.

CZ: What attracted you to directing?

UG: Well, I sort of thought about it when I was still at The University of Chicago, going for a master's. It was during that time that I became interested in the theater, and decided directing might be something I'd be good at, and I thought I would find out. First of all learn something about it, and then test myself and see if I could do it well. That's when I decided to go to Yale Drama School.

Yale Drama School was very helpful, for the year that I was there. Not so much any of the acting classes or playwrighting analysis, but in all of the technical aspects—stagecraft, staging, set design—I thought they were a very good school. I felt a year was sufficient. I wasn't going there for a degree, and I felt after a couple of semesters that I'd absorbed as much as I usefully could for the amount of time I had spent there; the additional 2 years would have been a waste of time.

CZ: This was during the 1950s?

UG: Yeah.

CZ: What happened next?

UG: I came to New York and tried to get work as a director. Of course, it was hard to do. I had a hard time, but I did find work in summer stock, that's when I first started directing professionally; I'd really only directed a one-act when I was at Yale. Once I started working in stock, I found that I felt comfortable with it. It reaffirmed my decision to continue to pursue directing as a career.

But I couldn't make a living as a stage director in New York. After a couple of odd jobs, I ran into a friend of mine who was working for a movie company that made commercials. He told me that there were companies here that were doing half-hour television films, making features occasionally, and it was something that naturally appealed to me. So I started working, first as a gofer, and then as assistant production manager, and then as production manager. But I didn't want to stay in the office, so I gave that up and went on the floor. My first job was as a second assistant director for Kazan on *Splendor in the Grass* [1961]; I came in the middle of the shoot; that was my first exposure to feature filmmaking. By then I'd spent a couple of years in a production capacity, so I knew my way around sets and budgets, stuff like that.

CZ: You worked with Kazan, Robert Rossen, Arthur Penn, and Sidney Lumet; do you feel you learned a lot from those experiences that was helpful to you later, as a film director?

UG: Yeah, I did learn a fair amount from them. But there's only that much you can learn being on the set watching someone else work. And obviously, when you're working as an assistant director, you have your own problems. But you do absorb a great deal from the style, from the things that you feel the guy you're working for does well, where you feel he's different from you, and how you would do it differently. I would say you learn more in one day of actually being on the set and making decisions than you do in months of being an assistant director; it's a different reality. But it was very useful.

As an assistant director, I would only take features, so I had time off. I directed an off-Broadway play, *The Days and Nights of Bebe Fenster-maker* [1962], and that was really my start in New York as a stage director. Then about a year and a half later, I ended up directing on Broadway for the first time. I directed Frank Gilroy's *The Subject Was Roses* [1964]. That was my big break as a theater director. And it ultimately opened the way for my career as a film director, because it was the first film I ended up doing several years later. I also went back off-Broadway to direct *A View from the Bridge* [1965].

CZ: Who was in that production?

UG: [Robert] Duvall, Jon Voight, Carmine Caridi, Richard Castellano, and Susan Anspach.

CZ: And you directed the original production of *American Buffalo* [1977]?

UG: Yeah, the original production on Broadway with Duvall and Kenny MacMillan.

CZ: Were you also involved with The Actors Studio?

UG: Yeah, I got a great deal out of it. Strasberg was an influence on me. Not so much in terms of specific technical aspects, although those were helpful, but in terms of being able to discern truthful behavior, as compared to conventional behavior. You very often run into both in the theater and in film, where something is accepted as truthful behavior by both the audience and critics, and it's not. Very often they don't know the difference. The work of honing my sense of truthfulness was very helpful. I do feel indebted to The Actors Studio. It was actually through Kazan that I got into The Actors Studio, as an observer. I did some work there as a director, and in the Playwrights/Directors Unit. I think it was a great help.

CZ: Did you come into contact with any of the conflicts at The Studio?

UG: A lot of what went down there, I felt was like everything: You can choose to look at the failings and pick it apart, or you can choose to look at the achievements. If you want to look at it judiciously, you would have to say that The Studio accomplished a great deal that was positive, regardless of its flaws and failures.

CZ: Going on to your transition to film, did you have a particular aesthetic in mind when you began making films? Were there filmmakers whose work you really admired? Was there somebody's work you studied in order to develop a sense of what your films would look like?

UG: The guys I admired were some of the European filmmakers—the usual. I admired Fellini, Bergman, some of the French: Truffaut and Godard, in his own way. In terms of American filmmakers, there was some of Kazan's work. But I was not a film buff. I always thought of film as going back to real life behavior, not so much drawing on other films. Technically, I obviously tended to be realistic.

CZ: Moving into *Straight Time* [1978], how did your involvement with that project come about?

UG: Well, it came to me in an odd way, because originally Dustin [Hoffman] planned to do it himself and in fact started preproduction on the film and was going to star in it and direct it himself. He called me at the point where he felt he was having problems, both with the screenplay and with handling the film; he was stuck. [Dustin] had a shooting crew on salary, so he was under an enormous amount of pressure. He'd already spent a substantial amount of the budget—and it was a small budget. He had stopped preproduction because he was waiting for the latest draft of the script. He'd gone through about 5 different writers; he was on the latest draft by Michael Mann. I felt they were in serious trouble. So I went to L.A. and read the first half of Michael Mann's draft. It didn't have any kind of strong thrust, and it didn't have a point of view on what the story was really about. So I said, "Let me go back and read all the other drafts." I finally read the first draft, by Alvin Sargent. I saw a direction, I saw a point of view, I saw something that interested me. Suddenly I got excited about it. It was something that I wanted to do and could do something with. It clearly needed a lot of cutting and restructuring. We grabbed a few days, a weekend, we cut down the script to a manageable size. There was no time to lose. We had to cast some people that Dustin hadn't finished casting; there were characters cut and dropped. We ended up going ahead and starting to shoot, and really improvising. I did all this in about 2 weeks. We brought in Jeffrey Boam, and we brought in the writer of the novel [*No Beasts So Fierce*], Eddie Bunker, at one point, for some dialogue changes. But really, a lot of it was the actors. Primarily, it was Dustin, because he was so much at the center of it. We had worked out a pattern of improvising over the weekends and nights for the scenes that we were going to shoot the next day. They would be typed up, I would edit them, we'd rehearse them the next morning and shoot them, and it slowly became a steady pattern.

A great percentage of the lines were improvised, which is not to take anything away from Alvin or Jeffrey. Because both of them, I think, made very important contributions to the script, both in terms of structure, and the focus of the scenes. But in the course of having to bridge some logical gaps, we improvised.

Dustin had gotten hold of the character as we started to shoot, and within a week or two, he really had a bead on the character. His lines, the improvisations, were of enormous value, because he brought to them a real sense of the direction of the character. It was just a matter of structuring and making sure that it all made sense, that we were all heading in the same direction. I had a clear idea of what I wanted to convey, and both Dustin and I agreed—as did the writers—on what we wanted the experience to be, what the character meant.

CZ: Did you do any research into police procedure, or ex-convicts, or prison experience?

UG: Well, Dustin had an associate producer, who became my associate producer, and was an enormous help, Gail Mutrux, who's now a producer with Baltimore Pictures. She's a remarkable researcher, and I had to absorb all of her information in 2 weeks, aside from working on the script. I didn't know that world, but she had done a lot of research. I took a weekend to go to Folsom and San Quentin; that was probably one of the most depressing weekends of my life! It was an eye-opener. The writer of the novel, Eddie Bunker, was at my side. He's a terrific guy, an ex-con, he'd just come out of jail 6 months before. For specific things like the bank robbery. I got hold of a real bank robber. I took him with me when I scouted locations. He advised me on what kind of bank he would pick. "This is the kind of exit, the kind of situation, that makes it easy." And so at every step of the way, as we went along, I had expert help [*laughter*].

CZ: Did you have strong ideas about the character, Max?

UG: Yes, I had a strong idea about the arc of the character. I didn't want to do something conventional; what appealed to me about it was the truth about that character. The typical thematic line that tends to run through conventional movies about criminals varies from the criminal turning out to be a good guy to the criminal being an irredeemably vicious guy, and the reasons for it being either his childhood, or society not giving him a break. And the truth of it, I feel, lies in a very complex interaction between the personality of a criminal, the circumstances that he grows up in, and getting behind the eight-ball in a certain way.

CZ: The last line Dustin Hoffman has in the film is after Theresa Russell asks why she can't come with him, and he says, "Because I'm going to get caught." Do you consider him a tragic character?

UG: Well, you find out—not getting into cheap psychologizing, but there's a reality—that often these guys deliberately trip themselves up. Unconsciously they trip themselves up, so they can go back to jail. Because the difficulty of surviving is very anxiety-provoking. A lot of them choose to take a shot for what they look on, unconsciously, as the brass ring. That will get them inevitably back into jail, where they have status, they have recognition, they know who they are, and they have a sense of identity. Like people in the army, they are relieved from all the major life decisions. Those major decisions are made for them; they can concentrate on other day to day things, some of them involving survival.

If you say, "Is it tragic?" I guess, using that word, classically, talking about the Aristotelian definition, it probably lacks the dimension of greatness and grandeur [*laughter*]. It is tragic in the modern sense of the word. In the sense that what you do see—what is heartbreaking, I think—is that a number of those guys are not just thugs. They're intelligent, capable, sometimes talented people, who have the potential of doing all the things that very highly regarded people in society do.

CZ: Dustin Hoffman's character is pretty unsympathetic.

UG: You see, it's a wonderful thing—I was watching the film with an audience—it was wonderful to see where the audience parted company with his character. The mass audience was rooting for him; he was their hero, really. The peak of which came when he ties the parole officer to the fence on the highway. At that point, they're all with him, he's won them over because they've seen he wants to go straight. And they've seen him taking a lot of abuse, and they identify with him. But as he starts to do the holdups, they begin to see there's another side to this guy, he's not just a good guy. There's another side to him, and you get a sense they begin to back off a little. I think Dustin played him—and beautifully so—without any compromise. All of a sudden, he wasn't your standard likeable character, doling out conventional violence that the audience could still go along with. They realize that there was something off-putting, a ruthlessness about this guy. And it's scary, because the real thing is scary. Unlike the con- ventional violence that we see in movies, the violence in *Straight Time* had a brutality to it, and that's certainly what we were aiming for. It is not fun and games.

CZ: The moment where he kills Gary Busey is really shocking.

UG: And after the movie was put together and edited, in preview, there was a big discussion on the producing end, at First Artists, about whether to remove that, because it made him so "unsympathetic." But I fought it very bitterly, because I felt that taking it out would just totally rob the thing of any truth. It was at the heart of what I felt was the truth about that character and that movie.

CZ: Did you discuss the character's biography with Hoffman?

UG: Very much, endlessly. Dustin had hung around the writer, he had done quite a bit of research, and the biography was a very important element of the character. He started with a kind of rap sheet the guy had, and we used the rap sheet of the guy who wrote the book. It started with the typical thing: At the age of twelve or thirteen, he had gotten into some minor trouble, and ended up in a correctional house, and then it was a series of small fuck-ups that slowly add up. That's the amazing thing, when you look at any one of these incidents, they don't seem to be that significant, and then they start adding up. And then you're 18, then you're 22, and you get caught robbing a store, then it's assault, it escalates. That's the pattern.

CZ: You worked with actors like Harry Dean Stanton and Gary Busey, who are not "method" actors? Was there any difficulty in getting them to "match" Hoffman emotionally? Was there a way that you communicated with them differently?

UG: You have to. You have to communicate with each actor in a language that they understand, and that's not the same for every actor. You have to get a sense of who that person is. It will translate into behavior that is consistent with that character and which will enable the actor to work from himself and meet the demands of the characters he's playing. What will trigger that, I think, depends on the person you're dealing with, and each one is different. So you talk differently.

Harry Dean—I absolutely loved Harry Dean; he went about it his own way, you had to be patient with him. He amazed me, for somebody with his experience, and his track record—he had a total lack of concern for basic things, technical things like hitting the mark. But when he locked in, he was wonderful. And when he didn't, you knew it very clearly, and you then did another take. And you knew how to find out what the problem was until it felt right. And if it didn't, there was a reason for it, it was never arbitrary.

CZ: Theresa Russell was pretty inexperienced when she did *Straight Time*. How did you deal with that?

UG: Theresa Russell had done just one part, she had worked for Kazan on *The Last Tycoon* [1976]. She was very well cast for *Straight Time;* she was very right for the part. She had a good rapport with Dustin, which fed into the relationship. And Dustin is very helpful working with other actors; he's very generous. I think that was of considerable value in working with Theresa. She understood that character; she's a valley girl, I mean, she was 17 or 18 years old at that time. She came from that kind of background, she knew exactly what this was all about. So it didn't require a big stretch.

CZ: How do you work with an actor before you shoot a reaction shot? What kind of emotional preparation goes into that? I'm thinking of the scene that Hoffman has with Gary Busey and Kathy Bates, and their child. You cut to a long take of Hoffman just looking at them. That look was very powerful; I felt that it was saying that he had missed out on all of this stuff—family life, relationships . . .

UG: I think that's correct, that's exactly what it was.

CZ: It seems like there are a lot of silent moments similar to that in your work.

UG: I love silent moments. Some of the best ones I've had were cut out of *Straight Time* and *True Confessions* [1981]. Sometimes you have to kill your darlings. There were a couple of moments in *Straight Time* where I thought Dustin was absolutely brilliant, but I had to cut them out.

CZ: That must hurt.

UG: It hurts, but you've gotta do it. You can't fall in love with these individual moments; you've got to keep the whole in mind. That's your job as a director, that's one of the things you have to do. It is painful sometimes, because, literally, some of your favorite things go out the window, or end up on the floor [*laughs*].

CZ: Have you had the final cut in your films?

UG: No, I never got the final cuts. Actually, I did in *Kellerman* [*Who Is Harry Kellerman and Why Is He Saying Those Terrible Things about Me?*, 1971] with Herb Gardner; both of us did the final cut. We did not have final cut in *Straight Time,* Dustin had final cut, and the studio had final cut in *True Confessions.* The only real differences I had about cutting were with Dustin on *Straight Time,* after the movie was shot. Otherwise, I've never had a problem with a studio on cutting. I never felt that I had to cut anything that I did not want to cut for the sake of accommodating the studio.

CZ: And you work very closely on the editing process?

UG: Yeah, very much so.

CZ: How much input have you had in casting your films?

UG: I've been fortunate, I've had full say in the casting of all of my movies.

CZ: *True Confessions* was based on a real case, right?

UG: Well, it's based on John Gregory Dunne's novel, and John based some of it very loosely on the "The Black Dahlia Case," but I think he just used the skeleton of the case as the trigger. The rest of it is all fiction.

CZ: Would you research the social and political and religious dimensions of 1940s L.A.?

UG: Yes, we did research '40s Hollywood, and again, it's one of the great bonuses of being a director. You literally go into areas of life that you wouldn't have been exposed to otherwise. You're like a writer, to some degree. I find that part of it very rewarding. First, I wasn't familiar with the period, and second of all, I knew nothing of the Catholic Church. I had very little knowledge of the actual practical aspects of the Church as it appears in the story, of the reality of the Church as a temporal or political power. I became aware of it when I read the novel. And I knew nothing about the homicide detectives' background, or the reality of whorehouses in L.A. at that time.

     In order to get into it, aside from the period research, I did the next best thing, which was to get an idea of what the contemporary experience was

Robert Duvall and Robert De Niro in *True Confessions,* directed by Ulu Grosbard. © 1981 United Artists Corporation. Private collection.

like. And a lot of it hasn't changed, except for the outer trappings. I interviewed some older madams who had made their living as whores in the late '40s, early '50s, so I got a sense of that. Rose Gregorio, my wife, actually played the madam. We spent some time with some madams, actually spent a day at a whorehouse. That's contemporary, but the behavior, the attitude, all of that translates. I hung out with homicide detectives, so did [Robert] Duvall and Kenny MacMillan. [Robert] De Niro of course hung out with a priest as a technical advisor, for all of the aspects of the mass.

CZ: He seemed very comfortable with the liturgical rituals.

UG: He did, because he'd prepared for months, really, before we ever started shooting. We started shooting without him, we began shooting Duvall and McMillan. And I was lucky, as I started to say, because we had to wait for De Niro. He was coming off *Raging Bull* [1980], and he had to lose that weight, so our shooting schedule got dislodged by an extra 6 or 8 weeks. It gave me a nice long preproduction period, and even then I really didn't feel totally prepared. I always felt like I was catching it on the run, so to speak, because there was so much more to find out. But I think that is true of any movie you make, even when it's a contemporary movie, but more so with a period movie. Unless you're dealing with an area that's very familiar to you, no matter how much you prepare as a director, you feel—at least I do, and I would bet it's not an uncommon feeling among other directors—you're going in half-cocked, as far as having a sense of the truth of the characters you're dealing with. You just do the best you can.

CZ: What kind of work did you do with the actors on their characters?

UG: Well, we rehearsed. Primarily we read through the script, and we got a sense of the scenes and what needed to be done. As far as preparation, I have never done what Sidney Lumet, for example, does, which is to get the actors literally on their feet, and on the floor, and have a run-through of the thing as if it were a play. I would think that in some circumstances, depending on if it was a very play-like screenplay, I would imagine that would be something I would try and go for. But he sets up his camera angles at that time as well, he pre-sets them. I'm sure he changes them when he gets to the set sometimes, but that's the way he works, and he works very well.

I tend to rely on working with the actors when they get on the set in the morning. I prepare, I may anticipate certain setups. When you're choosing a location, you have to consider setups very carefully: where your windows are, what floor you're on, what kind of location you choose, the light, the nature of your location, the location of entrances, exits. The ground plan, so to speak, will determine very much what your setups are. So you're making those choices as you go along. I find myself changing a lot of that when I'm with the actors. Suddenly you rehearse the scene in the morning, and they start changing things, which come out of their sense of the character and behavior. And it's things you can't predict, can't foresee.

Now, it's true with the kind of stories I've done, that's tended to be the pattern. I'm sure that if you do very heavy special effects stories, for example, you have to pin yourself down, you have to pin the actor down. You have to literally sketch where he's going to be, what exactly the shot is going to look like, and you have no flexibility. I have more flexibility, and I love it because I love that surprise that the actors bring to the scene. If you lock them into positions and behavior to that degree, you turn them into puppets. You're not taking advantage of good actors. You're cutting your own nose.

CZ: What kind of discussions would you have with Duvall and De Niro? You had worked with Duvall on stage several times . . .

UG: Yeah. I'd not worked with De Niro before. Both of them are the kind of actors—I find this true of a lot of very good actors—that very quickly are ahead of you, in a sense, because they know the character from the inside. In the beginning, you know the characters better than they do; very quickly, they know the character better than you do. If you're smart, you pick up from them. Sometimes you can help them if they go off, that happens. But it isn't one of the things where you have to chew it over, or you have to do a lot of talking. I believe in talk when it's necessary; I don't believe in talking in order to prove that you're the director, because it's not necessary. If you're dealing with very good actors, they will instinctively make choices that don't need to be explained, don't need to be theorized about. It's like a writer talking about his writing when he's about to write the scene. Something will leak out of it, some spontaneity. It can become self-conscious if you discuss it too much, or even discuss it at all, when it doesn't need discussing. Again, there are no set rules about it, it depends on the scene, it depends on the problems of the scene. Much of that sometimes gets done simply discussing a logic problem, where an actor will say, "This doesn't make sense to me. This doesn't ring true to me."

CZ: There's obviously a great deal of tension between De Niro and Duvall as brothers, right from the beginning.

UG: They understood that immediately; right after the first reading, they had a sense of it. It was self-evident, in terms of the subtleties of the sibling relationship, as well as the history they had, where they came from, and their present position—the whole relationship of the successful younger brother against the failed older brother, the worldly trappings and power and success of the younger brother. All of that stuff didn't need to be spelled out, they just picked it up instantly. So when it came to specifics—it would all vary with the scene—very little talk was needed. When they got on their feet and they started doing it, it was right there.

CZ: Going back to that idea of silent moments: *True Confessions* seems to be structured around moments like that; the actors have long stretches of action where they have no speech.

UG: One of my favorite scenes is late in the movie, when the two brothers are in a luncheonette, which is built around silent moments. It's built on a subtext of what goes on between the 2 guys, because the conversation, basically, is very simple. Again, when you're dealing with actors like that, you can take advantage of it.

CZ: There was also one scene where De Niro goes back to his room, and removes his vestments. There's a very long take of him disrobing. That's all he does, but it's very strong.

UG: Because you get a wonderful sense of his life, looking at that room, it's the first and only time you see his room. In a sense you see the monastic simplicity of how he lives, and the dailyness of that life, in contrast to all the power and wealth of the Church, and the power he has in his capacity as the Monsignor, handling the affairs of the Church. The contrast of that I felt was wonderful. It just says it, without having to spell it out.

CZ: He also has a great moment, after Duvall makes his confession. There's a very long take of De Niro looking. I think he really starts to think about the corruption he's involved in.

UG: Yeah, it catapults to the end, in a sense.

CZ: *True Confessions* is very much about sin and guilt, absolution and redemption, and it's all structured around the confession. How important are themes to you, as a director?

UG: It's not something that I consciously choose. I responded very strongly to the story when I read the book. The theme of that book had a very strong resonance for me. As a director, your job in a sense is to translate that into action, and by action I mean an Aristotelian sense of action. The sense of not necessarily physical action, but the thrust of the various characters, the choices that they make in the course of the story, all add up to the meaning of the story. That part of it fascinates me, and that is partly, I guess, why I chose to be a director. It fascinates me about my own life, my friends, people I know, people in public life. It's the mystery of destiny. It's got its own drama; that's what drama's all about.

An Interview
with
John Sayles

John Sayles. Museum of Modern Art Film Stills Archive.

John Sayles' films explore the ways in which human beings negotiate the hostile or corrupt systems of society, often focusing on the volatile dynamics of relationships in periods of change or stress. In many ways, Sayles is a screenwriter/director in the classical mold, striving for a kind of dramatic clarity in story and characterization that is uncommon in the late twentieth century. His heros are often virtuous people with tragic flaws, while his villains are impenitent rogues. This Manichean view of the universe locates Sayles' films squarely within the world of melodrama. It is a tribute to both Sayles and the actors he works with that they inhabit this highly moral society with a resonant truthfulness.

John Sayles as the preacher in his film *Matewan* (1987) is a Bible-thumping, fire-and-brimstone, right-wing, anti-union agitator in a town polarized by a deadly labor struggle. The point of view the preacher endorses is far from Sayles' passionate advocacy of the working class. Yet, Sayles observes in his interview that his initial attraction to both acting and

327

writing arose out of the opportunity it afforded him to "get into someone else's head." His writing and casting of himself in the role of the preacher is typical of Sayles' curiosity as well as his desire to explore the multiple perspectives offered in a given situation. After making *The Return of the Secaucus Seven* (1980), Sayles went on to investigate an emergent lesbian identity (*Lianna*, 1983), extra-terrestrials in New York City (*Brother from Another Planet*, 1984), union troubles in a West Virginia coal-mining community (*Matewan*, 1987), the White Sox scandal of 1919 (*Eight Men Out*, 1988), corruption in a decaying urban environment (*City of Hope*, 1991); interracial friendship (*Passion Fish*, 1992; Sayles and Mary O'Donnell received Academy Award nominations for Best Original Screenplay and Best Actress, respectively), and magical seals in Ireland (*The Secret of Roan Inish*, 1995).

Sayles was born in Schenectady, New York, in 1950 and received a B.S. in psychology from Williams College. It was during his college career that he began both writing and acting. During the summers and after graduation, Sayles supported himself by working as a nursing home orderly, a day laborer, and a meat packer—blue-collar jobs that have repeatedly found their way into both his films and novels. Sayles began writing screenplays for low-budget genre films, such as *Piranha* (1978) and *The Lady in Red* (a.k.a. *Guns, Sin and Bathtub Gin*, 1979). After his relative success with *The Return of the Secaucus Seven* (made for the ridiculously low budget of $40,000), he continued scripting his own films and writing both teleplays and screenplays for other filmmakers. Some of Sayles' more well-known titles are *Alligator* (1981), *The Howling* (1981), *The Clan of the Cave Bear* (1986), *Unnatural Causes* (1986), and *Wild Thing* (1987). Sayles also wrote the critically praised series *Shannon's Deal*. Sayles makes the occasional appearance in films directed by others, appearing as a motorcyle cop in Jonathan Demme's *Something Wild* (1986) and as a phony evangelist in Joe Dante's *Matinee* (1992). The prolific Sayles has also written, since 1975, three novels—*Pride of the Bimbos*, *Union Dues*, and *Los Gusanos*—and three collections of short stories, two of which— *I-80 Nebraska* and *Golden State*—won the O. Henry Award. Sayles is also the recipient of the MacArthur Foundation "Genius" Award. He remains an independent, a rare director committed to retaining his autonomy from the studio system by writing, directing, and usually acting in his own films.

John Sayles was in the office of his production company, Skerry Movies, when I spoke with him by phone in August 1993.

CZ: I understand you began your career as an actor.

JS: I started acting in my junior year of college. I played the character Candy, the old man, in *Of Mice and Men*, partly because I'd been around so many old men while working in hospitals. I had a lot to draw on. Then, some of the same people I had worked with in college were at a summer theater in New Hampshire. They brought me up to be in *Of Mice and Men* again, to play Lenny, and then to play the Indian in *One Flew Over the Cuckoo's Nest*. Large, brain-damaged people.

CZ: What do you think was behind your original impulse to act?

JS: I think it's somewhat similar to the impulse to write, or to make a story by directing—which is getting into somebody else's head. An example of the way that acting has cross-fertilized my writing and directing, and been helpful, is that I was in *Of Mice and Men* twice; I played different characters. It's the same bunkhouse, people are going to say the same thing. It's the same place, the same universe, but when you walk into that bunkhouse playing Lenny, your eye hits totally different things. You care about different things; you hear different things; you pay attention to different things than you do if you walk in and you're an old man. That point of view, and "How does this person think?" was always the most interesting thing about acting for me.

CZ: Did you ever want to attend acting classes?

JS: Not especially. But I'm always interested in talking to actors about them. I've found that in working with actors, it's been about 60/40: 60 percent of the time I think that recently being in an acting class has gotten in their way, and 40 percent of the time, I feel like it's been helpful.

CZ: Can you talk more about that?

JS: Some of that is the class itself, and some of that is how people take it. For my particular style of moviemaking, which is a kind of naturalism, the people who consistently seem to be on the same wavelength and have gone to classes tend to be people who are connected with Sanford Meisner. He works on inhabiting a character and really listening. Whereas for people who have gone through places like Juilliard, it's much more formal, more voice and stage combat, real theater training the way people in Britain get it. For movies you have to tone that down a little bit.

It's great if you're playing stuff that is not naturalistic, because you have technique. I haven't found it especially useful for what I do. It's always amazing to me that actors who have totally different training can get together and work with each other. And they can, somehow; they find a way. That's one of the things you do as a director: help them find a way.

CZ: You've done some acting for other directors. Have you learned a lot about acting from those experiences? Do you find you can relax and just be an actor when you're in another director's movie?

JS: It's a chance for me to see other people work. I've hired actors I've gotten to act with who I never would have worked with otherwise. I've seen them in the front lines, rather than in an audition situation, which is always a bit artificial. I've seen technicians work on other people's movies when I was an actor, and later worked with them. So there is a part of my brain that's taking notes.

I did a little part in Joe Dante's movie *Matinee* [1992] the day after we wrapped *Passion Fish* [1992]. I flew from Louisiana down to Florida and worked for 2 days. It seemed like, "This is a vacation. What are actors complaining about? All they have to do is learn the lines and play the part. They don't have to worry about 150 things." So yeah, it is relaxing in a way, although there is always that tension—the more you know about the film process, the more you know when you're fucking up. You try to make yourself useful and fit in to what they need. I've never played anything very big, except in my own movies, so it's always been a day player kind of thing. You realize "OK, there's a larger scheme, I'm just one little piece of the puzzle. Let's find out right away what's needed, and then try to do it for them."

CZ: Let's talk about casting for your films. You tend to work with the same people, often. Do you write characters with them in mind?

JS: Very often what happens is, about halfway through, I realize, "Oh, this would be a good part for so-and-so." And then I may not so much tailor it for them, but have them in mind as I'm writing. For instance, David Strathairn, who I've worked with a lot, is an actor who's very, very competent doing physical things. So I wouldn't hesitate to make part of his character be competent at fishing, or cleaning a fish, or all kinds of things. I also have to be very practical when I write a film. I have to figure I'm not going to have 150 stunt men, and I'm not going to shoot every angle in the world. So it would be great if the actor can actually do what they're supposed to do. I had this terrible streak, in each of my first four movies, the only person who had to drive a motor vehicle didn't know how to drive, and these were people over 30. If the actor can sing, if they're athletic, if they're from the South, that might get into it. Definitely, as I'm finishing up writing, and I'm starting to think, "Who's gonna play this?", I sometimes get ideas from the capabilities or the personality of the actor I'm thinking of hiring.

CZ: Do you spend a lot of time searching for faces and reading people you don't know?

JS: Yeah, I'd say for every movie. Because we—meaning me and the producers—have so many characters in our movies, and we really don't know who they are. And it may be a long, tough search. We just made a movie in Ireland [*The Secret of Roan Inish*], where we didn't know any of the actors. So it was a search, especially for a 10-year-old girl, and a 15-year-old boy, neither of whom had been in a movie before. Our casting people went on all the TV shows and radio shows, and pretty much saw every kid in Ireland who was interested in being in the movies, who could either be, or claim to be, 10 years old. So yeah, we actually do quite a bit of that.

What's interesting about it is, I'm exhausted after a day of casting. We put out as much as the actors do. Plus we do it 20 times a day, and they maybe have 2 auditions a day. I always want it to be a decent experience for the actor, even if they don't get the part, because most of them aren't going to get it. But also, I want to see what the actor can do. I have a file in my head of 20, 30, 40 actors who I've never gotten to use in anything, but who I've really liked and been impressed with in auditions.

CZ: Has there ever been an actor who's interpreted a character in a completely different or surprising way than you envisioned when you wrote the script?

JS: Not really. I'm pretty specific about who the person is, in the writing and in the talking we do before we go. The people don't come from outer space—except for *The Brother from Another Planet* [1984]. There, I would say, is where I left the most leeway. I really needed Joe Morton to be a partner in that movie, because we only had 4 weeks to shoot it, and it was very complex. We were shooting in a big city, and we couldn't shoot in sequence. I had to leave a lot up to him, as far as where he was in his progression. "What do you understand about what's going on in the room? What do you understand about this world that you've dropped into?" Those kind of things. I said "Look Joe, you're going to have to orient yourself every day, every scene, because I'm just going to be trying to get this thing done in 4 weeks." So it didn't surprise me as much as it pleased me; it was always fun to watch. Moving that fast, you're generally using the first, second, or third take, and there isn't a fourth take.

CZ: How do you feel about rehearsing with film actors?

JS: I tend to talk to actors when they get the part, and write them a 2- or 3-page character sketch about who they are, who they are to the other characters, answer any questions they have over the phone before they show up, and say "hello" when they get on the set. The only rehearsal they get is, "Don't give me any emotion while we're setting up the lights and the camera and the blocking." I find personally, with most actors, that if you start doing rehearsals before you shoot, by the time you shoot, it seems like they've heard that line before and said that line before. And then you've got to do it 50 more times, like you would in a theater rehearsal, before you start to break through into something new. With most actors, especially in naturalistic stuff, take one, two, or three is their best stuff. The better a movie actor they are, the more efficient a movie actor they are, the more they can do over the long run—takes seven, eight, and nine—and still have something that seems new. A lot of my job as a director is to find ways to talk to the actors or to restage or restate something. So if we've had to do a shot five or six times—because of a technical problem, or whatever—it still seems new, and they start listening again.

I just worked with a 10-year-old girl who is very, very good, but it's her first time really acting. I found that by take two, she would be anticipating the next line, waiting for her turn. She would look at the person who was about to speak, instead of waiting until they started to speak. So, I'd say, "Remember, you don't know these people are going to say this, and you can't react until they say it." She'd say, "Yeah," and if the scene wasn't too long, the next take would be great. There's an awful lot of that you have to do even with experienced actors. But, I think good, experienced film actors find ways to do it for themselves. Some way to make it new, the way they do with each performance if they have a long run in theater. So I don't really like rehearsal.

The only time that I've actually had time budgeted for rehearsal was *Baby It's You* [1983]. And then all I did was take Rosanna Arquette and the 3 girls who were going to play her friends in high school and drive around New Jersey and let them talk about boys and stuff. So at least they would be familiar with each other, since they were supposed to be these bosom buddies who'd hung out together since they were in elementary school. But we didn't do any lines.

CZ: I noticed in your last few movies the narratives have gotten more complex, and there's a lot more choreography with camera movements and long takes. I was wondering how that affected your work with actors, especially because you say you don't like to rehearse?

JS: Well, it's complicated in one way, and it's simpler in some ways, for an actor. The more you can do without breaking it into little pieces—especially if the actor has the training to handle a long scene of dialogue—the more you get to play out the emotion, and stay in your emotional rhythm. You don't get a quarter of the way through it and have somebody say "cut," break for lunch, come back, go through makeup again, start at another angle, and then get to the point you were starting to get at before lunch. I find whenever I have a big emotional scene, I tend not to cut it too much. I ask the cinematographer to light it in a more general way. Lighting really affects actors. In theater, because there's not a moving camera, you get the show to where you want it, and then the lighting guy comes in. He looks up in the grid, and finds a way to light what you've done. Very often in movies, if you have a consistent lighting pattern, it may staple the actors to the floor. If you let them move around outside the cage of beautiful lighting you've made—this little rim light here, and this little hot spot on their cheek there—that may mess up your lighting totally. What you find is that you're always compromising one or the other; you're always telling the cinematographer, "My actors have to be able to move around. Find a way to do it and not have it look too bad." Or else you're saying to the actors, "You don't have much to do here emotionally, and the lighting is going to be telling a lot of the story, so you really have to hit your mark." That's a huge difference I think, between theater acting and movie acting: there is that back-and-forth compromise between the two things.

In the last films I've made, even though the camera moves have been difficult, what I've often done is make the blocking totally rational. I'll try to have the mark make some sense, and not just be a tape mark on the floor. In *City of Hope* [1991], if 2 characters are walking down a street, I'll say, "When you can find a space, step through the cars and onto the sidewalk." Well, if you park the cars so that there's only one space there, they don't have to go looking for a mark on the ground, they just go until there's an opening, and then walk onto the sidewalk. The focus puller knows where they're going to go, because he knows where that space is. You can go out with a video camera and rehearse that scene without the real actors, so the actors don't end up doing an hour of technical work; they can just hook into each other and do emotional work from the first take. Because your camera guy who's backing up with a Steadicam has done it 15 times with production assistants reading from the script, and he's found those places where they're going to need some light, and you've put the light up there.

Angela Bassett and Joe Morton in *City of Hope* (1991), directed by John Sayles. By permission of The Samuel Goldwyn Company. Courtesy of Mr. Sayles.

CZ: It sounds like you have a mix of things that are accidental, or that you work out on the set, and preplanning. How much do you rely on preplanning?

JS: I tend to preplan almost everything but the most emotional scenes. For the most emotional scenes, I go to the technicians and say, "Give me a nice loose cage here. Be ready for anything." And then I go to the actors and say, "OK, you know where you are emotionally. We're going to do this a bunch of times, so don't worry that you can't go over the top, or you can't play it differently." Then I act like I'm the corner man for two different fighters. I go into one corner, and say, "OK, this time, go for the body," and I go into the other corner, and say, "OK, this time, make sure he doesn't go for the body." And each take, I get something slightly different. Then, after we've played the whole scene several times, and I really feel emotionally the people have done all they can, I'll look at what we've got on video. And I may say, "Well, in order to use the best of this take, and the best of that take, I need a couple of smaller cuts inside." Or, I'll have two cameras running, and I'll have some tighter, detail shots inside, so I can mix and match, and use the first half of take one, and the second half of take four, because that was the best of the actors emotionally.

CZ: Can you talk about some other techniques you would use to get actors to work with each other, or to get the actors' best performance?

JS: Well, one is something I call "handicapping." It's one of the reasons it's nice to work with actors you've worked with before—because you know this already—but within the first day or two you find the actor's rhythm. You know if they're an actor who needs two or three takes to warm up, or if they're an actor who's really going to be good on takes one and two and then start to get stale or fade. So, if you're going to do reverse shots of people, and you have one actor who's really good on take one, two, and three, and starts to fade, and the other actor needs some warming up, you make sure that you go over the shoulder of the actor who needs some warming up first. So they get to play the scene, but the camera's not on their face for the first, second, or third takes. The actor who's good on their first takes gets to do their good stuff on camera.

   Ordinarily, with emotional scenes, I try to do the close-ups first. Because you're probably going to go out to the wide shot only at the very beginning, or maybe the very end of that scene, and you don't want to waste all their emotion on the wide shot. So you do the close-ups with the emotional stuff first. Or, with an actor who needs some warming up, you do the wide shots first, and then you come in, and you've handicapped them to the point where now they're ready to do their best emotional stuff, and now you're moving in to the close-up.

Sometimes, if it's a very emotional scene, an actor might have a hard time coming back to square one. For instance, Rosanna Arquette is a great emotional actress, but because she is so emotional, it's really hard for her to go back to the beginning of a scene right away. So sometimes you'll shoot a couple of takes of the emotional scene, and then you'll have something else to do that doesn't even have her in it, so she can get back to square one emotionally. She's not starting a scene as if she just finished a huge fight. You have to learn that stuff about each actor.

CZ: Do you find actors are always aware of their own best way of working?

JS: Sometimes actors know it about themselves and will tell you, "This is the way I like to work." And other times they either don't know it about themselves or figure, "Well, I'm just supposed to do whatever they tell me." So they're not going to let you know except by seeing when they're good and when they're not so good. There are actors who are terrible if they have to act to a piece of tape—and very often for technical reasons, you have to act to a piece of tape—and some prefer it. Some do their best work in front of a mirror, or in front of nobody, and some really need somebody to hook into.

CZ: What are some other differences you've found among actors?

JS: Some actors are much more emotional, and, in order to do emotional stuff, they have a hard time thinking about the technical side of moviemaking. If it's going to be an emotional scene, you make sure that the people who have a hard time with continuity and moving objects don't get much business to do. You make sure that they're done with their dinner, and all they have to do is put the fork down before they start to talk, rather than worry about, "When did I take a smoke on my cigarette, and when did I take a drink?" Other actors can give you that emotion as well, and they'll go up to the script supervisor on their own and say,

"Which hand did I bang that glass down with? Which hand did I punch him with?" They'll incorporate that, and somehow can do the emotion.

CZ: You've worked a lot with children and non-actors. Are there special techniques you use to deal with them?

JS: When I work with kids, or new actors—I've often cast local people without any theater or movie experience—I'll act with them. I'll be the person on the other side of the scene, rather than another actor, because they're used to talking to me. They're not intimidated by me, whereas if you put them in a scene with somebody they consider to be a professional actor, who starts to get very serious or heavy with them in character, it may freeze them up. With kids, they usually do what they do, and then turn and look at you, or whoever's in authority. So often, if there's an adult in a scene with them, I'll pass my direction through the adult. John Cusack had a lot of scenes with these little newsboys in *Eight Men Out* [1988], and he's really good with kids, so I would have him do a lot of my directing for me. When the kids looked to somebody for approval, it was to the guy they were supposed to look at on screen, rather than to me over by the camera.

CZ: Do you ever work with actors who you feel are too prepared, and you want to get them to loosen up?

JS: Yeah. That will happen, sometimes, later in the movie when people come on the set and they've had two months to work on their part. They've read the script and figured out who the person is. And everybody else has had less time—because we often don't know we have the money until the last minute. What you do is put them in the situation, and try to throw them a little off balance. Sometimes I'll change a line slightly, just to make it new. I don't improvise much on a set, but, if I have a cross-cutting scene, and in the script have left out part of a conversation because we keep cutting away from it, sometimes I'll have the actors play the whole scene. Or I'll have the actors play something that I write on the spot, or that I wrote and threw out of the script, that's a lead-in to where the scene starts. And that's just new enough so they realize, "Oh, I see where I'm coming from. I'm hitting a high note when there's no way I could have gotten into that range yet. This has to build a lot slower." Or, it has to build a lot faster.

CZ: Your films have very low budgets. If you had more money, would you do things differently?

JS: I'd pay people more, that's about it. I actually prefer to work fast. It's my theory that the less trailer time the actors have, the better. The more they can be on the floor working on the character, the less they have to go through the strain of staying in touch with the character when they're off doing other things. I know actors who do these mega-budget things that take 21 weeks, and actors may spend 5 days of every week in the hotel. Every morning they get up: "No, I don't think we're going to get to you today." And then all of a sudden, there's this big rush on Friday afternoon: "We want to get your scene in today." Not having the money to do that, the advantage is I get to work as fast as I like. I don't forget the point of the scene, and the actors don't either.

I think that there is something deadening about shooting every angle in the world. Although they try not to, actors have a sense of pacing themselves, and if they feel like, "Oh God, this guy's gonna do 35 takes, and then he's gonna set up another angle, and he's gonna do another 35 takes," they're gonna start to coast now and then. I'd just as soon have it in their head: "This guy's likely to say, 'That's good, let's go on,' and I want to get my best stuff in before he moves on to another scene."

Also, if I decide that I'm going to do something in a master shot, and it seems to be working, I don't shoot any coverage. I'll time it and say, "OK, is this way too long for the page length, for the pace of the movie; are the actors taking enormous pauses?" and I may come back to them and say, "Think about Jimmy Cagney; just talk faster, it's really bogging down." When you shoot coverage, you can fill up actors' holes by cross-cutting to get rid of all their pauses. I've cut scenes that were 2½ minutes long in the master shot down to 45 seconds, without losing a line, by overlapping dialogue and giving the actors a whole new pace that was appropriate for the scene. When I decide I'm going to do a scene in a master shot, both for the sake of the actors and the sake of the crew, I make that commitment. I say "OK, this is a master shot. It's gonna be hard for you to do all of this in one shot, but I'm not gonna crap out on it and cut it into five pieces later by shooting coverage."

With actors who are new to me, or new to film work, I hold off on how to cover a scene till I check them out. We've had actors who we signed to play a part the night before we shot their first scene because other actors pulled out late for bigger films. And you can't expect them to hit their character's rhythm right away. In a case like that I'll do a lot of coverage, partly to give them a chance to warm up to speed on the character without embarrassing them in front of the others. The alternative is doing 25 takes of the same angle, which can seem like keeping the actor after school and hurt their confidence. Partly, it's so I can help the performance in the editing room. Sometimes with a new or non-actor I'll have lots of angles planned so I can piece a performance together, and the person steps up and blows it away in one piece. It's great—people on the crew step away from their equipment and grin at you. The main thing is to keep the actor focused and confident. And if you have to change tack, they should feel it's because the director has a new idea, not because they're fucking up.

CZ: Can you think of a difficult situation where you said, "This is not working"? What was the acting problem, and what was the solution?

JS: In the final scene in *Passion Fish,* we had both artistic difficulty and technical difficulty. The technical difficulty is that it was supposed to look like late day, and no matter how the boat turned, somebody had the sun right in their eyes. So either Mary [McDonnell] or Alfre [Woodard]— it ended up being Alfre—had the sun blasting right in their eyes, and you can't play that scene with sunglasses on. There's technical difficulty number one. It was rice planting season, so we had these flying tractors buzzing overhead all the time. Then the boat was drifting, and it would keep turning around. I realized that if I cut from one person to the other, one would be drifting frame left and the other would be drifting frame right, which is very symbolic, but doesn't make any physical sense. To keep the boat drifting in the same direction, we had to have trawler motors and use a reflector as an air rudder, trying to sail the boat so it stayed on course.

The other difficulty is that I'd written a seemingly simple scene that had a lot of ambiguity and a lot of emotional clout to it. After all that time Mary and Alfre spent together, are their characters really friends or not? How do you say something to someone in your debt that you mean to be helpful, without it sounding condescending? It was a scene where the actresses had all kinds of questions. And sometimes the answers weren't what they thought they were going to be. For instance, Mary asked, "When I say 'Oh, I wouldn't leave you to go back to daytime TV, I'd only leave for primetime?', am I being noble, am I sacrificing myself for

Chantelle, or is this true? Would I go back if it was a better deal?" I said, "Yes, you would go back. You are being helpful, but you're not being noble." We came back and reshot the scene because of the technical things, but mostly because of that slight change of attitude. It totally changed how Mary said the first line, the middle line, and the last line. That in turn changed what Alfre was getting from her, and because they're both good actresses and they listen, it changed Alfre's performance too.

It's often a problem with non-actors, or new actors, to get them to be as loose as they should be, to not have the "beginner shuffle." I often give them something physical to do, and I may overstress the importance of it. I say, "OK, you've got to hang this laundry up, and make sure that all the socks are together, blue-banded socks with blue-banded socks." Because they're diligent, and they've learned their lines, and they take it seriously, you can mix the socks up, and as they're putting them on the line, they're worrying about the socks much more than, "What am I doing with my hands, when should I look at the other character?" Usually, I'll have them in a scene with a real actor who's experienced, and I'll say to the real actor, "You're gonna have to help me get a performance out of this person and help them do a good job. Your character wants information from them, but they're going to be worried about these socks. So you're going to have to grab them at some point. If they're not paying enough attention to you, you've got to get it." Very often you can enlist the other actor in getting a performance that you're having difficulty with. Another thing I'll do that often works, is after I've shot the angle with the actor who's more experienced facing the camera, I'll go to them and say, "OK, we're over your shoulder now, I want you to overact. I need more out of this other actor, so this time, be really evil. I don't care if you spit, I don't care if you bleed, get as much as you can out of him."

CZ: You said that you give your actors character descriptions. Do you encourage them to do research? Did you have Mary McDonnell learn about paraplegia, or Alfre learn about drug addiction, for *Passion Fish?*

JS: Yeah, I do. I don't encourage them to playwright or to do a backstory. It's one of the reasons I send them descriptions, so they don't end up on the set saying, "Oh, you don't understand, my uncle molested me when I was 3 years old." I'll provide the backstory.

If there's any physical thing, if there's any job thing, I encourage them to do that kind of research. When David Strathairn came down to

Louisiana for *Passion Fish,* we hooked him up with some local Cajun guys who did some of the things that he had to do in the movie. So he got to go out on a mudboat, and fish, and harvest crawfish with them, and he could hear their accents. David always does that kind of physical research, as well as, "Who is this guy, what does he sound like?"

Mary found people who were in wheelchairs and talked to them about that. She got a wheelchair that she wheeled around the set of *Sneakers* [1992] while she was waiting for her scenes to come up. Alfre didn't have much time to prepare, but she'd done some of the emotional preparation in other roles that she'd played. She did as much as she could in the time that she had, because she was coming right off one movie and onto the other. The advantage there is her acting muscles were in great shape; she didn't need any loosening up to do deep character work. Even characters who play very small parts will often go out and yak with somebody who's done the same job they're supposed to be doing. All those women who played nurses in *Passion Fish,* even though they had a character to play for only 1 minute, would have some idea of what they were supposed to be doing professionally.

CZ: You've said a few times, "A good film actor will do this or that." What, to you, makes a good film performance?

JS: Well, this really is just my own taste. It is that sense of inhabiting a character, that if the camera kept following that actor, even when they leave the room, they would still be that character. That they could improvise in that character. That there is something going on in the head of that character even when they're not talking. That they're not just waiting for their turn to come up. That they have a complex mind that doesn't have to do with this story, that there's life they've lived outside of just this story.

My favorite acting lesson of all time was in the movie *Enter the Dragon* [1973], the Bruce Lee movie. Bruce Lee is the sensei for this student. The student comes up to him and says "Sensei" and bows, and Lee stands up and says, "It's time for your lesson." The student tries to slap him, and Lee catches his hand, and says, "Now, what was that? What have I told you? Emotional content." So the student collects himself, and then he gets very, very angry and tries to slap him, and Bruce Lee catches his hand and smacks him in the head and says, "I said emotional content, not anger." Finally, the student collects himself again, and all of a sudden, you see in this student some kind of force, and this time, when he tries to hit Bruce

Lee, he gets millimeters from his face before Bruce Lee can catch his hand, and he says, "Good. Emotional content." That's so much of what I go for, which is that emotional content to your acting doesn't mean that you're having the same emotion that the character is having. It doesn't mean that if you're angry, you're out of control, or if your character is suicidal, you have to have caretakers follow you around because you may kill yourself when you walk off the set. There's always a superego and an ego present, so that you hit your marks, you help the other actors, you don't just say, "Hey, I'm the star here, I'm having an emotional moment. Everybody else has to fall in line with me. They're just character actors and extras." You play the scene with the other people who are in it, and you react to them and what they're doing, but you have emotional content; you're not just a technician. That, to me, is good movie acting. It has something to do with listening, it has something to do with believing yourself as the character.

If you're talking about movie star acting, that's something totally different. There are movie stars who are good actors, and there are movie stars who are indifferent actors, but whatever they're doing, people want to watch them while they're doing it, at least for a while. That is something very different from being able to act, but it is part of good movie acting.

CZ: Do you think that has to do with some personal quality the actors have?

JS: When you're casting, if you're casting very well-known actors, or stars, you're dealing not only with the character they're going to play, you're dealing with a persona they've played tens, or dozens, or hundreds of times before. So, if there's a knock on the door and some guy is there who you've never seen before, the audience says, "Well, what's gonna happen next?" If there's a knock on the door, and a housewife answers, and it's Peter Lorre or Freddy Kreuger, they say "Uh-oh."

So you have a performance like Clint Eastwood's in *Unforgiven* [1992] that's very reflective on all the other movies he's made. The performance doesn't make as much sense if you haven't seen any of his other movies. When he falls off a horse, it's clumsy and awful, but because he's Clint Eastwood, it's funny. What you're dealing with in his case is 20 years of movies that he's carrying with him when he's on the screen, because he stayed very much within a single persona. Woody Allen, the same thing. If you have Woody Allen walk into a bar, and there's a bunch of tough hombres there, you say, "This is a comedy." Not just because of the way he looks, but also because you've had 20 years of Woody Allen movies. To people who are less known, or play a wider range of characters, that's true to a lesser degree. But you're always dealing not only with the physiognomy of the actor—it's going to be tough for James Earl Jones to play a meek little guy, he's a very big man—but with the screen persona they've built up with an audience. Sometimes it's great because it saves you 20 minutes of character-building, you can just cut to the guy, and they say, "Oh, I know, the bad guys are in big trouble now, it's Clint Eastwood." Or, you may have to say, "Oh God, people think that Sally Field is so nice, and she's playing a bitch in this. We're going to have to establish that she's a bitch in the first 20 minutes." Most of the first 20 minutes of the movie is going to be spent in overcoming this nice-girl image. I tend to work with people who aren't that familiar, or who, if they're familiar, are character actors, and they play somebody different every time out. So I don't have either the mountain to climb or the advantage of that character weight that a better-known actor carries with them.

CZ: When you were growing up, was there anybody who you really hero-worshipped on film?

JS: No. I just didn't pay that much attention to it. I didn't even know people made movies until I was in college. I just went to them, and it was not a John Ford movie, it was a John Wayne movie. There weren't that many actors who played a different person every time out; there were movie stars. If there were actors who played a different kind of person every time out, I wasn't aware of them. I didn't see a foreign movie with subtitles until I was about 19 years old. I saw whatever was going on in the '50s and '60s, and not much of it was naturalistic.

The idea of acting came to me fairly late—that you could take a different person and become that person, instead of just take who you were, fit it to a certain genre, and make a nice comfortable living. Not that there isn't a lot of skill to that, but the acting I ask for in my movies isn't that kind of acting.

CZ: If you look at the arc of your work, has their been a real evolution in your ideas about working with actors over nine features?

JS: No, actually, I would say that that's the thing that's been the most consistent, because that doesn't cost money, or take much time. For my first movie, we had no money and no time. In *Return of the Secaucus Seven* [1980], I wrote an acting-intensive movie where the scenes, even the cutting, were dictated by what the people said. We had a 7-person crew, and 5 weeks, and $40,000 to make it. The one thing I figured was, "Well, I know some pretty good actors, some people who can get by playing these parts because they're familiar to them." Nobody's going to have to do a big stretch, we're not doing Elizabethan England here. As the movies evolved, I've had the money and time and, finally, experience, and getting to work with experienced people, to make the other parts of movie-making part of the storytelling as well. In *Secaucus Seven*, I only had the acting and the cutting and the writing. Now I can do stuff with the acting, and the cutting, and the writing, and the lighting, and the camera movement, and the music, and costume design. I'm also better at running a movie set; I'm more efficient. The actors don't have to sit around even as much as they used to on those 5-week movies, now that we're making 6-week movies! You know, the acting stuff hasn't changed that much.

Afterword

Is the work wonderful? Is the actual act of taking words and making them live and breathe, is that a privilege? Yes. Is that so fun you can hardly bear it sometimes? Yes. Is that something you'd like to do forever? Yes. I'm in it because I love it, and . . . because I really want to have a great time in this life.

—Mary Steenburgen

From the earliest times, drama has been a necessary part of the social landscape. In many tribal societies, shamans performed stories for their people in an ecstatic ritual of communication, in which catharsis—the purging of emotion—was the desired outcome. This ritual performance forged a passionate bond between the shaman and his audience. Film is the twentieth-century manifestion of that story-telling rite, and film actors are the shamans of our culture.

The interviews in *Figures of Light* seek to reveal the process by which actors, and the directors who guide them, partake of this communal ritual. A common theme that runs through the interviews is the notion of risk-taking as an integral part of performance. Mary Steenburgen says actors are asked "to play like children," with the attendant connotations of vulnerability, openness to experience, and lack of inhibition and self-conciousness. Actors must get in touch with, and be able to express, very basic, primal feelings—feelings that are surpressed, ignored, or denied as one achieves maturity. To strip away that socially condoned patina of repression is to allow oneself, as Bob Rafelson puts it, "to fail, to be foolish, to be naked." Christine Lahti talks about the risk in acting:

> . . . usually there'd be a dark night just before opening in a play, or a dark week during the filming of a movie . . . and I'd say, 'I'm so scared, I think I'm going to fail, I don't know how to do this . . .

[But] you can't continue to challenge yourself and take these huge risks and expect there to be some safety net underneath—there's not. So if you go out there, that's the risk; you fall and pick yourself back up again, or you fly . . . I realized that those dark nights, those dark moments are part of it; just as much a part of it as that feeling of exhilaration when you're flying.

And part of that risk—where the actor may fail or fly—is the possibility of self-exposure. Revealed and illuminated by light, film actors, in all their human imperfection and glory, offer themselves up to the gaze of the audience. The courage and fearlessness of actors is that they are willing to explore and use their most intimate experiences to build a character. Lindsay Crouse speaks of the auto-portraiture that is acting:

"It's amazing how people will avoid using themselves in art, because we instinctively know that everything we do is a self-portrait. Acting is the art of self-revelation. We want to avoid that knowledge like the plague because of all the ambivalence we have about ourselves. We are not good enough, we are not good-looking enough, we're not whatever enough, and if what we are doing is a self-portrait, everybody is going to see us. Oh my God, what will happen then? Technique is there to enable us to step forward and shine and remove all that fear, remove the tension, the self-consciousness, the defenses, all the reasons we say we can't step out. But what a great example we set when we do."

The actors and directors represented in this book, almost without exception, claim that the objective of their work is the disclosure of some element of human truth. The actor stands as a great example in his forthright mission to tell the truth, no matter how painful, humiliating, or self-revealing. To find the truth of their character, to fully inhabit and disclose their world, actors ground themselves in a specific reality based on the circumstances of the script. In *Figures of Light*, actors discuss their own unique amalgamation of research, analysis, rehearsal, and intuition used to construct the physical and psychological universe of a character. For many of the actors the next step is—as Christine Lahti says—to "put it all in there, and then forget about it and play off the other person." The flexible and spontaneous relationships that develop among actors—the moment-to-moment behavior of interaction—further the dimension of truthfulness in performance. A creative tension exists between the control of technique and the immediate rush of the moment, which is essential to acting for film. As Henry Jaglom puts it, "When actors are really not prepared for the moment, but they've actually been prepared by their years of training to allow that moment to fully happen, those are the most exciting film moments."

If acting was merely a faithful reproduction of human life, it would hold no interest for us. But actors and directors—like all artists—are pioneers; they seek to challenge the convention, complacency, and smallness of our daily lives. Part of the function of art, and drama in particular, is to transport us, to take us away from our quotidian existence, whether, as Mary Steenburgen says, "through enlightenment, or just by laughing your head off at something that's ridiculous and silly." Acting is the living embodiment of the grander themes of drama; the actor expresses the depths and heights, the darkness and light that comprise the essence of the human spirit. I look to Lindsay Crouse again to articulate the power of acting:

> Most people spend their lives—and I'm including myself—taking an average. In other words, 'Well, I'd really like to, but this is all I can do. If only I could save my mother, or, if only I hadn't done that.' We're filled with wishes. And actors are meant to get out there and take themselves to the edge of the edge of the edge. To go as far as they can, not to take an average . . . Because everybody needs to be told that they can shoot for that dream . . . that's what all our stories are about. That's what all our myths are for. To take us to the next level, to say life can be better. You can bust through the thing you never thought you could. You can change tomorrow what you thought you couldn't today.

Crouse's remarks evoke another theme that circulates through *Figures of Light*. The actor and director play the role of the storyteller in our society. The stories they tell—the struggle between good and evil; the quest for romance, adventure, or other forms of fulfillment; the movement from innocence to experience—incorporate classical motifs that underlie the narratives of our civilization. Stories are transfigured by the power of collective understanding into myth—and the meaning of myth has universal connotations. Myth is born of a common need; it subtends the significant motivations, fears, and desires of a particular culture. The universal meaning of myth endows it with powers that are magical in their potency and resonance. And film actors, particularly those who are movie stars, are participants in these dramas of universal meaning. As such, actors serve as one of the primary bearers of myth in our culture. The actor's magical status is intimately bound up in his projection on the screen as a figure of light. Consider Richard Dreyfuss' observations on the subject:

> I think there's a clear difference between celluloid and video and the stage. Celluloid helps to create a mysterious feeling, a kind of semi-religious experience that you can't articulate. Each person who becomes a film star speaks to something in people's hearts. Whether it's Kevin Costner, or Robert De Niro, or Jimmy Cagney, people are fulfilled by something, they recognize something, they want to see it again. Not everyone can do it; a person can look exactly like Jimmy Cagney and not have it. A person can act exactly like Kevin, and not be Kevin. It's a chemical thing that is mysterious . . . stardom is a love affair. It's a friendship and a love affair between the audience and the performer, and you love someone for a reason. Why does a man fall in love with whomever he falls in love with? . . . Because it's mysterious, and it should be. Because there's something in his or her heart that is being fulfilled.

The film actor fulfills—through a mysterious power—the needs of his or her audience. This is a deeply rich and suggestive relationship on several levels. Acting for film is a communal process in which a transaction takes place between the performer and the spectator. The audience wishes for fulfillment, and the actor satisfies this collective desire. It is not unlike the emotional need for catharsis that is gratified by the ministrations of the shaman in ancient societies. The film actor, like the shaman, provides a service to the community that is healing in nature. Because fulfillment is, in a sense, a soothing of anxiety, a pacification of a need. And that healing is a marvelous and essential function of the actor. As Lindsay Crouse says, "Actors are leaders, taking people, as Joseph Campbell would say, 'into the forest of original experience.' They're going in themselves and coming back to recount what it was like, and we can witness them." It is the actor's task to go into the night of the soul and return intact, to show people that the journey can be made. It is a ritual healing through personal risk and testimony that is felt and experienced by the audience. Sitting in the darkness, watching the light of the screen, the audience makes intimate and profound contact with the actor. And it is a connection that is shared with thousands, if not millions, of other people, each viewing the same film. In that space of communal ritual lies one of the most potent effects of film—to make people feel less isolated, less alone. Film is a voyage in the dark, into the bright light of shared experience, and actors show us the way.

Glossary of Film and Theater Terms

Backstory   A story, usually concerning a character's past history, that explains a character's actions in the present. It may be written in the script or play, or it may be created by the actor or director to further understand a character's motivations.

Beat   The mini-objectives in a scene. A beat would start with an intention, action, or objective and end with its completion.

Blocking   The patterns created by actors or directors that indicate how actors will move around a set or a stage.

Close-up   Shooting an actor's face or an object from close proximity.

Continuity   Continuity is used in two different senses in this book. In the first sense, it means that events and actions must match each other from one shot to the next to give the illusion that they are happening continuously. In the second sense, films are usually not shot in the order in which they appear in the finished film. A director will sometimes try to shoot "in continuity" to help his or her actors with the development of their performance.

Coverage, to cover   Shooting a shot from different angles or using more film than is necessary in order to make sure that there are enough choices in the editing of the film and that each action is covered sufficiently.

Cross-cutting   Cutting between two or more different actions occurring in different locations. Cross-cutting may suggest that these actions are happening simultaneously.

Cue-track   A soundtrack that was originally recorded during the making of a film may be too noisy to use. This noisy track is used as a cue-track or guide-track for the actors to redo their lines postsynchronously through the process of looping.

Cut   When a piece of film is edited, the place where the film is severed is called a cut. Also used as in "cutting together" a film—the way the shots in a film are edited in their final version. An actor's work may be cut, or deleted, from a film. When a director says "cut" at the end of a take, the action stops.

Cut-away   A cut from a scene to either a shot of the same scene taken from another angle or to another action happening elsewhere.

Cutting point   An actor gestures or moves in a certain way in order to provide the film editor with a place to cut more easily.

Dailies (a.k.a. Rushes)   Shots from the day's or several days' shooting that may be screened for the director, technical crew, and actor to check the progress of their work.

Editor, editing   The person who oversees the cutting together, or editing, of a film.

Emotional memory   An actor's recreation of the specific feelings of a past event through the use of sensory stimuli. First used by Stanislavsky.

Focus puller   A technician whose job it is to change the focus of the camera's lens as the film is shot.

Frame   The smallest photographic unit on a strip of film. Also refers to the borders of the film composition.

Lighting grid   The pattern in which the lights are placed on the set to create specific compositions.

Line reading   The way in which a particular line is interpreted and read by an actor. An actor may ask for a line reading from a director.

Long-take   A shot of long temporal duration.

Looping   The technique whereby actors redo their dialogue for a film after the film has been shot. An actor will listen to the cue-track and rehearse the movement of their lips and the timing of the words so that the newly recorded dialogue will fit the existing film image.

Mark (hitting a)   Tape or chalk marks on the floor of a set that actors must walk to (or hit) during the course of a shot. This enables the cinematographer, director of photography, or director to create planned patterns of action that will be performed by the actor. Marks also serve to keep the actor in focus.

Master shot (a.k.a. Establishing shot)   A long or distant shot, usually used to establish spatial relationships among characters and their setting before the scene is broken into closer shots.

Master two-shot   A shot that establishes the spatial relationship between two characters before close-ups and/or over-the-shoulder shots are used to break up the scene into smaller units.

Medium shot   When the camera is at a medium distance from the action.

Method acting   A personal, interiorized style of acting in which actors may call upon their own experiences to develop their characterizations. Almost uniquely an American phenomenon, this style is closely associated with Lee Strasberg and The Actors Studio.

Moderator   One who conducts sessions at The Actors Studio.

Observer   One who may attend sessions at The Actors Studio, but is not a member.

Overlap   When actors speak dialogue simultaneously or without waiting for the other actor to finish their lines.

Over-the-shoulder shot   A shot filmed, literally, over the shoulder of one actor in order to focus on the other actor in a scene. Or, the cutting pattern may suggest that the shot was taken over the shoulder of an actor, when, in reality, only one actor was present.

Overdubbing   Building up a soundtrack after the film has been shot, using dialogue, sound effects, music, etc.

Postproduction   The period after the film has been shot during which the film is edited, music and sound effects are added, dialogue is looped, and all finishing touches are added to the film before it is released.

Post synchronization   The synchronization of sound and image after the film has been shot; also called dubbing.

Pre-casting   When a film is written for a particular actor or actors or when actors are part of a production package that pre-exists the making of a film. A director, producer, agent, or actor may be involved in this process.

Preproduction   The numerous tasks that must be undertaken before a film is made: casting, hiring of personnel, research, scouting for locations, and making adjustments to the script, among others.

Private moments   An exercise in which an actor performs an activity he or she would normally do when alone. It is meant to free the actor and to develop his skill of being "private in public," a term used by Stanislavsky.

Reaction shots   A shot that cuts away from a scene to show another actor's response.

Sense memory   The use of the physical senses to recreate a feeling or sensation.

Sessions   A workshop situation at The Actors Studio in which scenes from plays are performed by members and critiqued by the moderator and members in the audience.

Set-up   A specific scene is readied to be shot from a particular angle or angles for filming.

Song exercise   An exercise designed to liberate actors and enable them to achieve more varied expressiveness by changing their ordinary use of sound and words. Developed by Lee Strasberg.

Storyboard   A director's detailed shot-by-shot renderings of the action given in advance of shooting a particular scene.

Subtext   The meanings and motivations that lie beneath the lines of a play or script.

Super-objective   The main motivation, need, or desire underlying a character's actions in a play.

Take   A director shoots one or several takes of a shot; only one version appears in the finished film.

Tech rehearsal   The rehearsal, in theater, when the lighting, sound cues, costumes, and props are all used for the first time together.

Through-line (or through-action)   The main theme or ideas that run through a script or a play. A character's through-line, or principal objectives and motivations, derives from the main through-line of the written material.

Two-shot   A shot with two actors in the frame.

Walk-on   A small part for an actor consisting of either a few lines of dialogue or no dialogue.

Films: Synopses and Credits

The Adventures of Buckaroo Banzai (1984)
Direction: W. D. Richter.
Cast: Peter Weller (Buckaroo Banzai), John Lithgow (Dr. Emilio Lizardo/Lord John Whorfin), Ellen Barkin (Penny Priddy), Christopher Lloyd (John Bigboote).

A science-fiction comedy in which Buckaroo Banzai, a neurosurgeon, test-driver, and rock musician, uses an oscillation overthruster to crash through the eighth dimension. Lithgow has dual roles as a demented scientist and as the leader of a colony of aliens.

Alice (1990)
Direction: Woody Allen.
Cast: Joe Mantegna (Joe), Mia Farrow (Alice), William Hurt (Doug), Keye Luke (Dr. Yang), Judy Davis (Vicki).

A bored, unhappy New York matron, Farrow, seeks a cure for her ailments from a Chinese herbalist. The doctor's concoctions enable her to experience life in magical new ways. Joe Mantegna plays a musician to whom Farrow is attracted, but who is still entangled with ex-wife, Davis.

At Play in the Fields of the Lord (1991)
Direction: Hector Babenco.
Cast: Tom Berenger (Lewis Moon), John Lithgow (Leslie Huben), Aidan Quinn (Martin Quarrier).

A group of American missionaries (led by Quinn and Lithgow) set out to civilize the Indians in Brazil's rainforest, with disastrous consequences.

Avalon (1990)
Direction: Barry Levinson.
Cast: Aidan Quinn (Jules Kaye), Elizabeth Perkins (Ann Kaye), Armin Mueller-Stahl (Sam Krichinsky), Joan Plowright (Eva Krichinsky).

Five decades in the life of a Baltimore immigrant clan are depicted, reflecting the growing dissolution of the American family. Quinn plays the upwardly-mobile son of an old-world father, whose efforts to start a discount department store end disastrously.

Baby Doll (1956)
Direction: Elia Kazan.
Cast: Karl Malden (Archie), Carroll Baker (Baby Doll), Eli Wallach (Silva Vacarro), Mildred Dunnock (Aunt Rose Comfort).

Written by Tennessee Williams, *Baby Doll* is the story of the oafish owner (Malden) of a decrepit country cotton gin, who has an unconsummated marriage with the eponymous heroine (Baker). Eli Wallach is an outsider who sets out to find out who burned down his cotton gin by seducing the willing Baby Doll.

Benny and Joon (1993)
Direction: Jeremy Chechik.
Cast: Benny (Aidan Quinn), Joon (Mary Stuart Masterson), Sam (Johnny Depp).

Masterson plays a mentally ill young woman—a passionate painter and pyromaniac—who lives with her overprotective brother, Quinn. Depp, a bizarre man who dresses like Buster Keaton, enters their closed world and falls in love with Masterson.

Bobby Deerfield (1977)
Direction: Sydney Pollack.
Cast: Al Pacino (Bobby), Marthe Keller (Lillian), Anny Duperey (Lydia).

Pacino is a top-flight race car driver who falls in love with a terminally ill woman. She teaches him to live without the fear that cripples him emotionally.

The Cemetery Club (1993)
Direction: Bill Duke.
Cast: Ellen Burstyn (Esther Moskowitz), Olympia Dukakis (Doris Silverman), Diane Ladd (Lucille Rubin), Danny Aiello (Ben Katz).

One by one, three women friends lose their husbands. When one of them, Burstyn, begins dating Aiello, her shocked friends try to destroy the relationship.

City of Hope (1991)
Direction: John Sayles.
Cast: Vincent Spano (Nick), Tony Lo Bianco (Joe), Joe Morton (Wynn), Angela Bassett (Reesha), John Sayles (Carl).

Nearly three dozen featured players inhabit fictional Hudson City, New Jersey. They share the typical problems of urban America, from political corruption to homelessness to ethnic tensions.

Cliffhanger (1993)
Director: Renny Harlin.
Cast: Sylvester Stallone (Gabe Walker), John Lithgow (Qualen), Michael Rooker (Hal Tucker), Janine Turner (Jessie Deighan).

A mountain rescuer (Stallone) loses his nerve after a fatal incident. He regains his mettle when he foils a big-time caper led by ultrabaddie Lithgow. A thriller set on the highest peaks of the Dolomite Mountains.

Daniel (1983)
Direction: Sidney Lumet.
Cast: Timothy Hutton (Daniel), Mandy Patinkin (Paul Isaacson), Lindsay Crouse (Rochelle Isaacson), Amanda Plummer (Susan).

Based on the story of Ethel and Julius Rosenberg, as seen through their grown-up children's eyes. Adapted from E. L. Doctorow's novel. Crouse plays the doomed mother.

Deep Cover (1992)
Direction: Bill Duke.
Cast: Larry Fishburne (John Q. Hull), Jeff Goldlum (David Jason).

A police officer (Fishburne) goes undercover as a cocaine dealer and becomes enamoured of the corrupt lifestyle.

Eating (1990)
Direction: Henry Jaglom.
Cast: Gwen Welles (Sophie), Mary Crosby (Kate), Frances Bergen (Mrs. Williams), Nelly Alard (Martine), Lisa Richards (Helene).

A group of women gather to celebrate milestone birthdays for their friends. A French documentary filmmaker films interviews with the celebrants about their attitudes toward eating and life.

The Executioner's Song (1982)
Direction: Lawrence Schiller.
Cast: Tommy Lee Jones (Gary Gilmore), Rosanna Arquette (Nicole Baker), Christine Lahti (Brenda Nicol), Steven Keats (Larry Samuels), Eli Wallach (Vern Damico).

Based on Norman Mailer's account of the life and death of multiple murderer Gary Gilmore. Filmed on location in Utah, this made-for-television movie touches on Gilmore's obsessions with his own death and his past and future lives, and his "soulmate," Nicole.

Five Easy Pieces (1970)
Direction: Bob Rafelson.
Cast: Jack Nicholson (Bobby Dupee), Karen Black (Rayette Dipesto), Susan Anspach (Catherine Van Ost), Lois Smith (Patty Dupee).

A young man (Nicholson) from an eccentric and genteel family of classical musicians lives with a country-music-loving waitress (Black), and works on an oil rig. A conflict is created when the vulgar Black shows up at his family's home, where he is indulging in an affair with his brother's fiancée.

The Gambler (1974)
Direction: Karel Reisz.
Cast: James Caan (Axel), Paul Sorvino (Hips), Lauren Hutton (Billie).

A New York English professor's compulsive gambling sends him on a downward path.

The Godfather, Part III (1990)
Direction: Francis Ford Coppola.
Cast: Al Pacino (Michael Corleone), Diane Keaton (Kay Adams), Andy Garcia (Vincent Mancini), Joey Zasa (Joe Mantegna), Eli Wallach (Don Altobello).

The Godfather saga continues as patriarch Al Pacino strives for legitimacy and power in a scheme that involves the Vatican. Joe Mantegna is a stylish and dangerous hood who has taken over the criminal interests of the Corleone family. Eli Wallach is an outwardly servile but inwardly scheming old don.

Goin' South (1978)
Direction: Jack Nicholson.
Cast: Jack Nicholson (Henry Moon), Mary Steenburgen (Julia Tate), Christopher Lloyd (Towfield), John Belushi (Hector).

Nicholson is a scruffy Texas outlaw saved from the gallows by a decree that gives a criminal his freedom if a woman with property marries him. Steenburgen is the woman who saves him and eventually falls in love with him.

The Good, the Bad, and the Ugly (1968)
Direction: Sergio Leone.
Cast: Clint Eastwood (Joe), Eli Wallach (Tuco), Lee Van Cleef (Setenza).

In the West during the Civil War, the 3 characters are anxious to get hold of a hidden $200,000. Wallach plays a nefarious Mexican bandido.

Havana (1990)
Director: Sydney Pollack.
Cast: Robert Redford (Jack Weil), Lena Olin (Bobby Duran), Alan Arkin (Joe Volpi).

Redford, a hapless gambler, meets and falls in love with the idealistic Olin, whose husband, a revolutionary leader, has disappeared and is presumed dead. Their uneasy relationship is played against the background of the final days of Batista's Cuba.

Homicide (1991)
Direction: David Mamet.
Cast: Joe Mantegna (Bobby Gold), William H. Macy (Tim Sullivan), Naltalija Nogulich (Chava).

A tough cop (Mantegna) investigates the murder of an elderly Jewish woman. He gradually becomes aware of an anti-Semitic conspiracy and begins to seriously reassess his own attitudes about his religion.

Housekeeping (1987)
Director: Bill Forsyth.
Cast: Christine Lahti (Sylvie), Sara Walker (Ruth), Andrea Burchill (Lucille).

An eccentric aunt comes to take care of 2 little girls when the grandmother who has raised them dies. Christine Lahti plays a woman who has little concern for the amenities or social graces of bourgeois life, alienating one of her charges and engaging the other with her bizarre lifestyle.

House of Games (1987)
Direction: David Mamet.
Cast: Lindsay Crouse (Dr. Margaret Ford), Joe Mantegna (Mike), J. T. Walsh (businessman).

Crouse plays a psychiatrist and author of a book, *Driven*, a study of obsession. In a misguided attempt to help a patient, she becomes involved with a group of dangerous conmen.

Isadora (1968)
Direction: Karel Reisz.
Cast: Vanessa Redgrave (Isadora Duncan), James Fox (Gordon Craig), Jason Robards (Paris Singer).

A biography of celebrated interpretive dancer Isadora Duncan. The film, told in flashback, chronicles the flamboyant Duncan's career from dance-hall girl to her tempestous, creative years in Europe and Russia.

JFK (1991)
Direction: Oliver Stone.
Cast: Kevin Costner (Jim Garrison), Sissy Spacek (Liz Garrison), Gary Oldman (Lee Harvey Oswald), Tommy Lee Jones (Clay Shaw).

The film asserts that the Kennedy assassination was a conspiracy of right-wing zealots, rather than the work of a lone gunman. *JFK* is the story of New Orleans District Attorney Jim Garrison's investigation and prosecution of the conspirators. Tommy Lee Jones plays a flamboyant gay fanatic under indictment.

King of Marvin Gardens (1972)
Direction: Bob Rafelson.
Cast: Jack Nicholson (David Staebler), Bruce Dern (Jason Staebler), Ellen Burstyn (Sally).

Dern is a dreamer with a wild scheme to buy an island in the Pacific, while, in reality, he fronts for the mob in Atlantic City. Burstyn is his wife, agitated both by Dern's attentions to his stepdaughter and by her own fear of aging. Nicholson is the more restrained brother, a late-night FM radio personality with a philosophical streak.

The Landlord (1970)
Direction: Hal Ashby.
Cast: Beau Bridges (Elgar Enders), Diana Sands (Fanny), Lee Grant (Mrs. Enders), Pearl Bailey (Marge).

A rich white boy shocks his family when he asserts his independence by buying an apartment house in a black neighborhood. Lee Grant plays his upper-crust mother.

Leaving Normal (1992)
Direction: Ed Zwick.
Cast: Christine Lahti (Darly), Meg Tilly (Marianne), Lenny Von Dohlen (Harry).

A hard-boiled cocktail waitress (Lahti) teams up with a mousy, abused wife (Tilly) on a trek to Alaska. The unlikely duo become close friends after revealing intimate secrets to one another.

Lonesome Dove (1989)
Direction: Simon Wincer.
Cast: Robert Duvall (Augustus McCrae), Tommy Lee Jones (Woodrow F. Call), Diane Lane (Lorena), Robert Urich (Jake Spoon).

An 8-hour made-for-television movie about 2 ex-Texas Rangers, Duvall and Jones, who lead a group of cowboys and a herd of cattle from Texas to Montana. Based on Larry McMurtry's novel, *Lonesome Dove* centers on the friendship of the 2 men, the search for lost love, and the hardships of the old West.

Melvin and Howard (1980)
Direction: Jonathan Demme.
Cast: Paul LeMat (Melvin Dummar), Mary Steenburgen (Lynda Dummar), Jason Robards (Howard Hughes).

The film chronicles the story of good samaritan Melvin Dummar, who picks up an injured Howard Hughes in the desert. Mary Steenburgen is Dummar's unsatisfied wife, Lynda, who divorces and remarries him and finds short-lived happiness when she wins the jackpot on a TV game show.

The Misfits (1961)

Direction: John Huston.

Cast: Clark Gable (Gay Langland), Marilyn Monroe (Roslyn Taber), Montgomery Clift (Perce Howland), Eli Wallach (Guido).

Two cowboys (Gable and Clift) and a mechanic (Wallach) meet in Reno, Nevada, before taking off for the hills to capture wild mustangs. Monroe is a new divorcee who accompanies them on their journey and arouses various emotions in all 3 of the men.

Once Around (1991)

Direction: Lasse Halstrom.

Cast: Richard Dreyfuss (Sam Sharp), Holly Hunter (Renata Bella), Danny Aiello (Joe Bella), Gena Rowlands (Marilyn Bella).

A noisy, obnoxious, and wealthy businessman (Dreyfuss) marries the over-protected, desperate-to-be-married daughter (Hunter) of a close-knit Italian family, much to their chagrin.

Passion Fish (1992)

Direction: John Sayles.

Cast: Mary McDonnell (May-Alice), Alfre Woodard (Chantelle), Angela Bassett (Dawn/Rhonda), David Strathairn (Rennie).

A soap opera star (McDonnell) paralyzed in an accident becomes embittered and angry, firing or scaring away nurses who attempt to treat her. Enter Woodard as a tough nurse with her own dark secrets, who helps McDonnell come to terms with her situation.

Places in the Heart (1984)

Direction: Robert Benton.

Cast: Sally Field (Edna Spalding), Lindsay Crouse (Margaret Lomax), Ed Harris (Wayne Lomax), Amy Madigan (Viola Kelsey), John Malkovich (Mr. Will), Danny Glover (Moze).

A widowed farm woman (Sally Field) and her children battle against nature and an insensitive business establishment to grow a successful cotton crop. Crouse plays a hairdresser, the sister of Field, who must cope with the infidelity of her husband, played by Ed Harris.

The Postman Always Rings Twice (1981)

Direction: Bob Rafelson.

Cast: Jack Nicholson (Frank Chambers), Jessica Lange (Cora Papadakis), John Colicos (Nick Papadakis).

David Mamet's screenplay of James M. Cain's novel about down-and-out lovers Nicholson and Lange. They are irresistibly drawn to each other and plot to murder her much older husband.

A Rage in Harlem (1991)
Direction: Bill Duke.
Cast: Forest Whitaker (Jackson), Gregory Hines (Goldy), Robin Givens (Imabelle), Zakes Mokae (Big Kathy).

In the 1950s, a beautiful woman (Givens) hijacks a trunk of gold during a robbery in the deep South. She seeks sanctuary in Harlem, where she meets with unworldly funeral parlor employee Forest Whitaker.

Raising Cain (1992)
Direction: Brian De Palma.
Cast: John Lithgow (Carter/Cain/Dr. Nix/Josh/Margo), Lolita Davidovitch (Jenny), Steven Bauer (Jack), Frances Sternhagen (Dr. Waldheim).

Lithgow is a man scarred by ruthless psychological experiments conducted by his own father. He plays five roles, including that of his father, a little boy, and a woman, in this tale about multiple personalities and murder.

Rambling Rose (1991)
Direction: Martha Coolidge.
Cast: Laura Dern (Rose), Robert Duvall (Daddy), Diane Ladd (Mother), Lukas Hass (Willcox Hillyer).

A young girl with a troubled past is sent to live with a kindly family as their housekeeper. Set in the Depression, the film depicts the family's struggle to deal with the wayward, sexually eager Rose (Dern). Diane Ladd plays the mystical mother lost in the "fourth dimension" (as her husband says), who's writing her master's thesis for Columbia University.

Reckless (1984)
Direction: James Foley.
Cast: Aidan Quinn (Johnny Rourke), Daryl Hannah (Tracey Prescott), Kenneth McMillan (John Rourke, Sr.).

Quinn plays a defiant, working-class teenager and romantic outcast who wants more out of life than a dead-end job in his factory town. He hooks up with well-bred cheerleader Hannah to escape a dreary future.

Rosencrantz and Guildenstern Are Dead (1991)
Direction: Tom Stoppard.
Cast: Gary Oldman (Rosencrantz), Tim Roth (Guildenstern), Richard Dreyfuss (The Player).

A version of Stoppard's 1968 hit play, which features the events of *Hamlet* as seen through the eyes of 2 peripheral characters. Dreyfuss is the leader of a band of itinerant actors, and also a well-spoken con artist.

Runaway Train (1985)
Direction: Andri Konchalovsky.
Cast: Jon Voight (Oscar Mannheim/Manny), Eric Roberts (Buck), Rebecca De Mornay (Sara), John P. Ryan (Rankin).

Two convicts, Voight and Roberts, escape from a maximum-security prison in the wilds of Alaska. They board a train, whose conductor falls victim to a heart attack. The train careens out of control, trapping the prisoners and challenging them to find a means of escape.

Running on Empty (1988)
Direction: Sidney Lumet.
Cast: Christine Lahti (Annie Pope), Judd Hirsch (Arthur Pope), River Phoenix (Danny Pope), Martha Plimpton (Lorna Phillips).

Lahti and Hirsch play 2 leftist radicals who have been living underground since the early 1970s, when they bombed a university laboratory and wounded a janitor. With the help of network activists, they move around the country with their young sons, taking low-level jobs and changing identities every few months. Lahti must come to terms with her son's (River Phoenix) need to live his own life.

Star 80 (1983)
Direction: Bob Fosse.
Cast: Mariel Hemingway (Dorothy Stratten), Eric Roberts (Paul Snider), Cliff Robertson (Hugh Hefner).

Based on the story of Dorothy Stratten, *Playboy*'s 1980 Playmate of the Year, and her small-time hustler husband, Paul Snider. Snider deteriorates as Stratten becomes more successful; the film ends in a bizarre murder-suicide.

Straight Time (1978)
Direction: Ulu Grosbard.
Cast: Dustin Hoffman (Max Dembo), Theresa Russell (Jenny Mercer), Harry Dean Stanton (Jerry Schue), Gary Busey (Willy Darin).

Study of an ex-con (Hoffman) who struggles to live by the constraints of the "straight" world. Frustrated by his lack of success, he and several friends pull a heist, which goes disastrously wrong.

Sweet Dreams (1985)
Direction: Karel Reisz.
Cast: Jessica Lange (Patsy Cline), Ed Harris (Charlie Dick), Ann Wedgeworth (Hilda Hensley).

Chronicles the life of legendary country singer Patsy Cline.

Swing Shift (1984)
Direction: Jonathan Demme.
Cast: Goldie Hawn (Kay), Kurt Russell (Lucky), Christine Lahti (Hazel), Ed Harris (Jack).

A woman's husband goes off to fight in World War II. The wife (Goldie Hawn) gets a job in an aircraft factory and begins an affair with a fellow worker. Christine Lahti is her hard-bitten neighbor, also an aspiring singer.

Tell Me a Riddle (1980)
Direction: Lee Grant.
Cast: Melvyn Douglas (David), Lila Kedrova (Eva), Brooke Adams (Jeannie).

An elderly couple reaffirm their relationship when they must come to terms with the wife's terminal illness. Based on Tillie Olsen's novella.

Tracks (1977)
Direction: Henry Jaglom.
Cast: Dennis Hopper (Sergeant), Taryn Power (Stephanie), Dean Stockwell (Mark), Michael Emil (Emile), Zack Norman (Gene).

Hopper plays a paranoid Vietnam vet accompanying a fallen friend's body across the United States by train.

True Confessions (1981)
Direction: Ulu Grosbard.
Cast: Robert De Niro (Des Spellacy), Robert Duvall (Tom Spellacy),
Charles Durning (Jack Amsterdam).

A version of John Gregory Dunne's novel about 2 brothers, one an
up-and-coming monsignor of the Catholic Church (De Niro), the other a
Los Angeles detective (Duvall) of questionable background. The film is set
in Los Angeles of the late 1940s, where it begins with the grisly murder of
a "party girl." The investigation comes to involve corruption in the upper
echelons of the church.

Twilight Zone-The Movie (1983)
(The movie consists of a prologue and four segments. Segment 4,
directed by George Miller, stars John Lithgow as Valentine.)

John Lithgow is a reluctant air passenger traveling during an intense
storm. He believes a gremlin is destroying one of the plane's engines, and
his hysteria mounts uncontrollably.

The Verdict (1982)
Direction: Sidney Lumet.
Cast: Paul Newman (Frank Galvin), Charlotte Rampling (Laura Fis-
cher), Jack Warden (Mickey Morrissey), James Mason (Ed Concannon),
Lindsay Crouse (Kaitlin Costello Price).

A washed-up, alcoholic lawyer (Newman) takes a heroic stand against
corruption in a church-owned hospital. Lindsay Crouse, as a nurse,
provides crucial evidence that helps Newman win the case, and thus
redeem himself.

Who'll Stop the Rain? (1978)
Direction: Karel Reisz.
Cast: Nick Nolte (Ray Hicks), Tuesday Weld (Marge Converse),
Michael Moriarty (John Converse), Ray Sharkey (Smitty), Richard Masur
(Danskin).

The film starts in Vietnam, where a reporter (Moriarty) makes a deal to
send heroin to the United States. Nolte is the ex-Marine who smuggles the
drug and then must deal with crooked F.B.I. men when the deal goes
awry. Based on Robert Stone's novel *The Dog Soldiers*.

Wild at Heart (1990)

Direction: David Lynch.

Cast: Nicolas Cage (Sailor Ripley), Laura Dern (Lula Fortune), Diane Ladd (Marietta Fortune), Willem Dafoe (Bobby Peru).

After completing his sentence for manslaughter, Cage is released from prison and begins an odyssey through the underbelly of the South with his girlfriend, Dern. Diane Ladd is Dern's former beauty queen mother, who disapproves of her relationship to Cage and will stop at nothing to end it.

The World according to Garp (1982)

Direction: George Roy Hill.

Cast: Robin Williams (T. S. Garp), Glenn Close (Jenny Fields), Mary Beth Hurt (Helen Holm), John Lithgow (Roberta Muldoon).

A picaresque journey through the life of a writer, who must deal with incarnations of feminism around him. John Lithgow is the transsexual Roberta Muldoon, a former football player, who befriends Garp.

Index